Tobacco Regulation, Economics, and Public Health, Volume III

Samuel C. Hampsher-Monk ·
James E. Prieger · Sudhanshu Patwardhan

Tobacco Regulation, Economics, and Public Health, Volume III

Clearing the Air on E-Cigarettes and Harm Reduction

palgrave
macmillan

Samuel C. Hampsher-Monk
Santa Clarita, CA, USA

Sudhanshu Patwardhan
Chilworth, UK

James E. Prieger
School of Public Policy
Pepperdine University
Malibu, CA, USA

ISBN 978-3-031-47095-0 ISBN 978-3-031-47096-7 (eBook)
https://doi.org/10.1007/978-3-031-47096-7

This Palgrave Macmillan imprint is published by the registered company Springer Nature Switzerland AG
The registered company address is: Gewerbestrasse 11, 6330 Cham, Switzerland

Paper in this product is recyclable.

Funding Disclosure

This book was funded with a grant from the Foundation for a Smoke-Free World, an independent, U.S. nonprofit 501(c)(3) grantmaking organization with the purpose of improving public health by ending combustible tobacco use. Through September 2023, the Foundation received charitable gifts from PMI Global Services Inc. ("PMI"). Independent from PMI since its founding in 2017, the Foundation operates in a manner that ensures its independence from PMI and any commercial entity. The contents, selection, and presentation of facts, as well as any opinions expressed herein are the sole responsibility of the authors and under no circumstances shall be regarded as reflecting the positions of the Foundation for a Smoke-Free World, Inc.

We enjoyed complete editorial discretion throughout the conception, design, research, writing, and publishing of this book. None of the Foundation's staff reviewed any portion of the manuscript prior to its publication.

Samuel C. Hampsher-Monk
James E. Prieger
Sudhanshu Patwardhan

In grateful memory of Mark Kleiman.

For Amanda, Melanie, Pooja, Seth, Kaia, Jenna, Alex, Grant, Kabir, Saachi, and a billion people around the world still using combustible tobacco.

Foreword

The regulation of e-cigarettes shows the wisdom of economist Thomas Sowell's observation: "There are no solutions. There are only tradeoffs."[1] The e-cigarette is an innovation that is disrupting tobacco markets. Given that tobacco use is estimated to cause over 8 million deaths each year across the world, why isn't tobacco market disruption the solution to a major public health problem?

E-cigarettes contain nicotine, the chemical that makes tobacco addictive. However, contrary to a misperception common among the general public and even among some healthcare professionals, nicotine is not the chemical in tobacco smoke that causes cancer or the other serious health consequences of smoking. E-cigarettes are disrupting tobacco markets because they contain nicotine, but the nicotine content is also the source of health tradeoffs between smokers and vapers. Smokers can benefit by using e-cigarettes to cut down or quit using combustible cigarettes, but other groups can be harmed by e-cigarettes. Never-smokers who start vaping e-cigarettes can become addicted, although even there one must recognize that some, perhaps many, of them would have become addicted to cigarettes in the absence of e-cigarettes. Smokers of combustible cigarettes may maintain their nicotine addiction by vaping e-cigarettes

[1] Thomas, S. A Conflict of Visions: Ideological Origins of Political Struggles. William Morrow & Co,1986.

in addition to smoking, instead of quitting entirely. There also might be adverse health consequences to vaping other than nicotine addiction.

Economists and public health professionals tend to view the tradeoffs created by e-cigarettes differently. Economists recognize that people make tradeoffs every day between their health and their consumption of goods and enjoyment of activities that they value. Almost none of us is as healthy as we could be, because personal health is not our only goal in life. The economic approach is to conduct cost-benefit analysis (or other formal approaches from the field of welfare economics, as the authors discuss in Vol. III, Chapter 2) of e-cigarette regulations to judge whether the consequences of reduced smoking are more valuable than the consequences of increased vaping. In other policy contexts, many public health professionals *do* recognize tradeoffs. For example, many support policies that reduce the harms associated with injection drug use, such as needle exchange programs and clean injection sites. But among public health professionals, tobacco harm reduction remains controversial; the authors discuss the extent of the polarization and examine the reasons for it in Vol. II, Chapter 3. In a recent editorial in the *American Journal of Public Health*, 15 past Presidents of the Society of Nicotine and Tobacco Research concluded that "vaping can benefit public health, given substantial evidence supporting the potential of vaping to reduce smoking's toll."[2] However, in the same issue, other public health professionals argued that regulating e-cigarettes involves "an intergenerational tradeoff" between helping older smokers addicted to nicotine versus "uncertain health risks for younger individuals."[3] Evidence on the health risks of using e-cigarettes, real and imagined, is reviewed in Vol II, Chapter 1.

[2] Balfour, D.J.K., Benowitz, N.L., Colby, S.M., Hatsukami, D.K., Lando, H.A., Leischow, S.J., Lerman, C., Mermelstein, R.J., Niaura, R., Perkins, K.A., Pomerleau, O.F., Rigotti, N.A., Swan, G.E., Warner, K.E., West, R. Balancing Consideration of the Risks and Benefits of E-Cigarettes [published correction appears in Am J Public Health. 2022 Apr;112(4):e6]. Am J Public Health. 2021;111(9):1661–1672. https://doi.org/10.2105/AJPH.2021.306416

[3] Samet, J.M., Barrington-Trimis, J. E-Cigarettes and Harm Reduction: An Artificial Controversy Instead of Evidence and a Well-Framed Decision Context. Am J Public Health. 2021;111(9):1572–1574. https://doi.org/10.2105/AJPH.2021.306457

To shed light on the controversial regulatory tradeoffs, it is interesting to imagine an alternative, or counter-factual, history of e-cigarette regulation in the U.S. Soon after e-cigarettes began to be sold in the U.S. markets, in 2009 the FDA denied their import on the grounds that e-cigarettes were an unapproved medical device that delivered nicotine to treat the withdrawal symptoms of nicotine addiction. The FDA lost the legal battle; the courts ruled that e-cigarettes could not be regulated as medical devices unless they were marketed with a therapeutic purpose. Because of this ruling and the 2009 Tobacco Control Act's restrictions on tobacco product health claims, e-cigarette manufacturers avoided making claims about cessation or any health benefits in their advertising. It is interesting to consider how different this could have been. In an alternative history, regulators and manufacturers could have made different strategic choices. Vol. II, Chapter 2 of this book reviews evidence that e-cigarettes are effective smoking cessation aids. Vol. II, Chapter 1 reviews evidence that vaping e-cigarettes is much less harmful than smoking combustible cigarettes. Could the manufacturers have made the case to the FDA to regulate e-cigarettes as an approved over-the-counter medical device for smoking cessation, and/or as a modified risk tobacco product for smokers to switch to? Could they still? In the real world, e-cigarette manufacturers frequently relied on what economists call "image advertising" that associated their products with attractive settings and attractive young people. In a counter-factual world, e-cigarette manufacturers might instead have used advertising mainly to inform the large market of millions of established smokers about how e-cigarettes could help smokers quit and reduce risks to their health. In essence, if they had been allowed to do so, the e-cigarette manufacturers would have run a large and continuing anti-smoking campaign without taking a dollar from public funding available for tobacco control efforts.[4] At the same time, the content and targeting of the e-cigarette advertisements might have avoided appealing to young people. E-cigarettes would have seemed more like a medical product that treats a health problem faced by older people than a cool new product for the young. Compared to the actual history of

[4] Research on smoking cessation pharmaceutical product advertising illustrates the potential gains (Rosemary Avery, R., Donald Kenkel, D., Dean Lillard, D., and Alan Mathios, A. Private Profits and Public Health: Does Advertising of Smoking Cessation Products Encourage Smokers to Quit? J Polit Econ. 2007;115, 447–481. https://doi.org/10.1086/520065).

e-cigarette regulation, this optimistic alternative history shows how regulation could have helped adult smokers while avoiding the tradeoff of increased youth vaping.

The issues raised by e-cigarette regulation are complex, including interactions between health and regulatory science, economics, policy, law, and marketing. The many interdisciplinary questions surrounding e-cigarettes and their impact on public health and consumer behavior are all explored in this text. As such, this book is a valuable resource for policy-makers and others wrestling with the tradeoffs involved in e-cigarette regulation in the real world. The polarized debate about e-cigarettes puts regulators and social scientists in a difficult position. It is easy to conclude that the health consequences of vaping are uncertain, but that does not answer the harder questions about how to regulate e-cigarettes. The health consequences of smoking are well documented and large. Regulating or banning e-cigarettes on the precautionary principle that they might cause harm (discussed in Vol. II, Chapter 3) ignores the harms of smoking that could be prevented if smokers switch to vaping. Based on their review of the scientific literature, the authors conclude that "the available evidence is more than sufficient to inform the development of optimal regulations….in the interests of the whole public." In particular, the authors explore in Vol. III, Chapter 2 how regulation could help adult smokers while mitigating the possible harms resulting from increases in youth vaping. Even readers who disagree about the best solutions to tobacco control and e-cigarette regulation will agree that this book provides a careful review of the evidence and thoughtful analysis of the policy tradeoffs.

Donald Kenkel, Ph.D.
Brooks School of Public Policy
Cornell University
Ithaca, USA

The original version of the book has been revised. A correction to this book can be found at https://doi.org/10.1007/978-3-031-47096-7_5

Acknowledgments

A book such as this one is, by necessity, a collective enterprise. A great many individuals helped formulate the ideas presented herein, define the scope, develop the structure, provide source material, and enhance the analysis. Friends and colleagues have read drafts and provided welcome criticism and suggestions, all of which improved the text immeasurably. The authors are indebted to the following individuals in particular. This is by no means an exhaustive list. To anyone we have omitted to thank; our sincerest apologies. The oversight is ours alone. We also own the opinions and any errors in the text; none of those should be ascribed to those we thank below.

First, thanks are due to Foundation for a Smoke-Free World, Inc. ("FSFW"), a U.S. non-profit 501(c)(3) private foundation which funded the production of this book with a grant. FSFW allowed us complete editorial discretion from inception to publication. The contents, selection and presentation of facts, as well as any opinions expressed herein, are ours alone.

Particular thanks are also due to the staff at Palgrave Springer; Bronwyn Geyer, Wyndham Hacket Pain, Geetha Chockalingam, Susan Westendorf, Matthew Savin, and Meera Seth, for your interest in the topic, and especially for your patience with us while we fit the pieces together.

We owe a special debt of gratitude to Prof. Don Kenkel for writing the foreword; a difficult task at the best of times, made harder by the burden of competing priorities; teaching, publishing, public speaking engagements, and international travel.

This book would not have been possible without Lowry Heussler's humor, wisdom, dedication, and countless hours reading and re-reading drafts, providing comments and suggestions, all of which helped make the book before you what it is. Thanks also to Eliza Hunt, who balances appropriate skepticism with cautious optimism; your clarity of vision and perspective have improved the text immeasurably. Thanks to Lucy Evans and Rachel Ashton for providing editorial and referencing support on the science and public health sections. Special thanks to Sarah Cooney on publication planning.

We benefited greatly from in-depth discussions with Annie Kleykamp, Sally Satel, and Marewa Glover that helped refine the focus of this book. And thank you to Ian Irvine and David Sweanor, not only for your thoughtful insights and suggestions, but also for your example. It is not always easy to participate in the debate about tobacco control and harm reduction with grace and poise, and there are many who would do well to learn from your example.

We also owe a debt of gratitude to the many scholars and researchers who, whether they agree with our analysis or not, have helped build the knowledge base, providing much-needed rigor and analysis, often in the face of considerable pressures to the contrary. In this regard special thanks is due to Clive Bates, for convening academics, authors, practitioners, regulators, and other stakeholders and creating a "safe space" in which rigorous and analytical discussion of the nuances of the emerging literature on Harm Reduction can take place, including occasional, but always respectful, disagreement. This book, indeed the development of the discourse, would not be possible without the thoughtful analyses and careful writing, much cited herein, of a great many individuals to whom we owe a considerable debt of gratitude. Our citation of published work should not be construed as the cited authors' endorsement of our thesis (nor our theirs), explicit or implicit. Nonetheless, our respectful thanks are warranted.

We also thank Elise Rasmussen, Gerry Stimson, Paddy Costall, Jessica Harding, Grzegorz Krol, and Dave MacKintosh for providing a platform at their global events for us to introduce the book's topic during the various stages of the book's evolution. Our special thanks go to Fiona Patten for putting a spotlight on the book at the Global Forum on Nicotine.

To Amanda Hampsher-Monk, Melanie Prieger, and Pooja Patwardhan, thanks (with apologies) for accommodating the late nights and working weekends necessary to complete this text, and for putting up with our borderline obsession with the issue, resulting in our annoying tendency to bring every conversation back to nicotine and tobacco.

Contents

List of Figures

CHAPTER 1

E-cigarette Regulations and Why They Fail

To reject one paradigm without simultaneously substituting another is to reject science itself.

—Thomas S. Kuhn, The Structure of Scientific Revolutions

1 The Recent History of E-cigarette Regulation

In their nascency, e-cigarettes were often not covered by many of the regulations applied to combustible tobacco products. However, in a relatively brief period, local, regional, national governments, under the influence of international bodies, developed and enshrined in law robust (though diverse) strategies to regulate the product category. Policymakers have pursued different strategies toward e-cigarettes and the regulatory environment is accordingly diverse, shaped and re-shaped by interactions between academic research, the innovating industry, lobbyists, litigation, civil society, media reporting, politics, and advocacy. These interactions continue to play out in a dynamic process of interacting feedback loops. Academic research informs (or misinforms) media reporting, which then influences public attitudes, knowledge, beliefs, and values toward e-cigarettes, which in turn shape consumer behavior. Public sentiment, consumer behavior, and research also inform regulatory decisions with, in turn, consequences for both the demand and supply-side behaviors. Such feedback loops create a sort of chicken-and-egg problem for regulators. Regulators look to researchers to report consumer behavior

S. C. Hampsher-Monk et al., *Tobacco Regulation, Economics, and Public Health, Volume III*, https://doi.org/10.1007/978-3-031-47096-7_1

patterns with the intention of having that evidence inform regulatory decisions. But regulatory decisions inform consumer patterns, as well as the study of them, and the reporting of those studies. The process of regulation therefore should, ideally, be an iterative one, with decisions informed by emerging evidence and responding to evolving behavior patterns. However, as this chapter discusses, course-correction is challenged by political factors and, perhaps, cognitive biases, as highlighted by the behavioral economics literature.

Understanding the interactions between these influences is therefore a vital component of understanding why public decisions regarding e-cigarettes are made and, in turn, the consequences (intended and otherwise) of those decisions. We start with a historical overview of recent developments in e-cigarette regulation.

1.1 *The Emergence of E-cigarette Regulation (2008–2012)*

Eager to demonstrate the value of their innovations, e-cigarette producers have often supported research investigating issues around safety and efficacy. As early as 2008, Health New Zealand reported the results of a study[1] funded by Ruyan,[2] which concluded that carcinogens and toxicants in the aerosol of Ruyan's e-cigarettes were below harmful levels. Health New Zealand rated the tested e-cigarettes as several orders of magnitude less dangerous than combustible cigarettes and a "very safe alternative to smoking." However, as discussed in Volume II, Chapter 3, the long history of tobacco industry misinformation has left the public, and the public health community in particular, deeply skeptical of any research funded by the industry.[3] Wanting to get ahead of what it perceived as industry misinformation, the WHO issued a press release in September 2008 stating that it did not consider e-cigarettes to be a legitimate smoking cessation aid.[4,5] The influence of the WHO's skepticism toward e-cigarettes can hardly be overstated. In the following year, Australia, Jordan, Hong Kong, Panama, Israel, Brazil, Canada, and Saudi Arabia banned e-cigarettes, often citing the WHO's concerns as justification. The U.S. Food and Drug Administration (FDA) categorized e-cigarettes as unapproved drug delivery devices in 2009 and directed customs authorities to bar shipments of electronic cigarettes from entering the U.S.[6] In response, two e-cigarette manufacturers sued the FDA, arguing that e-cigarettes were tobacco products, not medical devices, and therefore were outside the FDA's authority which, at that time, did not extend to tobacco. Before the suits were resolved, the U.S. enacted the Family Smoking Prevention and Tobacco Control Act (FSPTA) of 2009, giving the FDA the power to regulate tobacco products. The FSPTA thus paved the way for all subsequent federal e-cigarette regulation.

Despite their new remit, however, the FDA did not extend to e-cigarettes all of the restrictions applied to combustibles. Instead, trying to understand more about the novel e-vapor products, the FDA tested what were at the time leading e-cigarette brands—NJOY and Smoking Everywhere,[7] finding only trace amounts of tobacco-specific nitrosamines (TSNAs) in e-liquids at levels similar to those found in NRTs. Neither TSNAs nor diethylene glycol, another chemical of concern, were detected in the e-cigarettes' emissions. The study confirmed that the products contained nicotine and that some cartridges labeled as nicotine-free did, in fact, contain trace amounts of nicotine. A subsequent press release reporting these findings advised the public against the use of e-cigarettes,[8] but failed to mention that the level of carcinogens in the tested products was similar to those found in FDA-approved NRTs and therefore was unlikely to be injurious to human health. The statement also failed to emphasize that the harmful substances that were identified were found not in the e-vapor inhaled by the consumer but instead in the unprocessed e-liquid. In an op-ed in the *Washington Times*, the president of the American Council on Science and Health, Dr. Elizabeth Whelan, described the FDA's statements as "distorted, incomplete, and misleading" and a violation of "its long-cherished tradition of sticking to sound science as the basis for its policies." Whelan suggested that the statements were designed to scare Americans away from cigarette substitutes, and warned that they would give consumers the false impression that it would be safer to stick to combustible cigarettes.[9]

Despite the absence of federal restrictions, some states began to formulate their own e-cigarette restrictions. In September 2009 California passed SB-400, banning the sale of e-cigarettes statewide. Governor Schwarzenegger, however, vetoed the bill, arguing that, "if adults want to purchase and consume these products with an understanding of the associated health risks, they should be able to do so unless and until federal law changes the legal status of these tobacco products."[10] Adopting a more moderate approach, New Jersey included e-cigarettes in the state's smoke-free legislation.[11] Perhaps fearing that their e-commerce sites could fall foul of what could soon become a patchwork of state-level restrictions, Amazon prohibited the sale of e-cigarettes on its website in October 2009, and PayPal subsequently froze the accounts of U.S. e-cigarette vendors.

Across the Atlantic, however, the public health community in the U.K. was taking a different approach. Action on Smoking and Health (ASH), an influential anti-smoking organization set up by the Royal College of Physicians in the 1970s, endorsed a role for e-cigarettes in tobacco harm reduction in October 2009,[12] articulating that, while smoking cessation should remain a priority, for those that are unable or unwilling to quit, products that deliver nicotine without all the harmful components found in tobacco should be made available. The briefing stated that e-cigarettes were likely to be a safer alternative to smoking and could reduce second-hand smoke exposure. ASH noted three concerns. First, the relatively lower nicotine doses delivered by the e-cigarettes available at the time may not satisfy nicotine-dependent smokers. Second, available products were unregulated (other than as consumer products) and few manufacturers disclosed ingredients. Finally, there were, as yet, no clinical trials proving e-cigarettes' efficacy for smoking cessation. ASH therefore continued to recommend the use of nicotine replacement therapy, Champix, or Zyban (bupropion) for those trying to quit.

Some evidence for e-cigarettes' efficacy as a cessation support was forthcoming. In 2011, a study published in the *American Journal of Preventive Medicine* reported that about a third of e-cigarette users achieved smoking abstinence at six months, outperforming the background success rates by a factor of two or three.[13] According to another study published in the journal *Addiction* in 2011, 96% of survey respondents reported that e-cigarettes helped them to quit smoking, while 92% said that e-cigarettes helped them reduce smoking.[14] This and other early studies based on Internet surveys may be vulnerable to selection and reporting bias, but later that year the first clinical study was published in *BMC Public Health*. It provided more robust evidence: In a cohort of regular e-cigarette users experimenting with e-cigarettes for a period of 24 weeks, 23% quit and about a third of the subjects reduced cigarette smoking by at least 50%, leading the authors to conclude that e-cigarettes could substantially reduce cigarette consumption.[15] The emerging evidence fell on receptive ears in the halls of the British government. A 2011 report by the newly formed Behavioral Insights Team (BIT) operating under the Cabinet Office voiced optimism that e-cigarettes could be an effective substitute for combustible tobacco. The BIT noted that "it will be important to get the regulatory framework for these products right, to encourage new products.... If more alternative and safe nicotine products can be developed which are attractive enough to substitute people away from traditional cigarettes, they could have the potential to save tens of thousands of lives a year."[16]

Outside the U.K., however, that optimism was largely unmatched. Most regulators were deeply skeptical about the utility of e-cigarettes as a cessation aid and feared that framing them as such would expose the public to risks of unknown but perhaps considerable magnitude. In 2011, the FDA announced that it would regulate e-cigarettes as it does traditional tobacco products under the Food Drug and Cosmetics Act. This prevented e-cigarette companies from claiming that their products were, in any way, helpful for the purposes of smoking cessation; or even that they were less harmful than combustible tobacco. Such claims would prompt the FDA to treat the products as an unapproved medical device, presenting nearly insuperable regulatory burdens for most e-cigarette manufacturers which, at that point, were still small independent companies.

1.2 *Major Regulatory Changes in Europe and North America 2013–2016*

1.2.1 EU TPD

As with the FDA in the U.S., regulators in the EU were initially unsure how to classify e-cigarettes. In the absence of EU-level legislation on e-cigarettes, member states were free to adopt different approaches. However, in 2013, the EU rejected a ban on e-cigarettes and, like the FDA in the U.S., chose not to regulate e-cigarettes as medicines unless they made health-related claims or suggested that they could assist smoking cessation. Instead, like the FDA had done, the EU decided that many aspects of traditional tobacco control, namely health warnings, advertising restrictions, and age limits, along with novel rules on nicotine strength, should be applied to e-cigarettes.[17] These restrictions were finalized with the adoption of the Tobacco Products Directive (TPD) in May 2014, which was intended to "facilitate the smooth functioning of the internal market for tobacco and related products"[18] while ensuring a "high level of health protection, especially for young people."[19] Although the EU member states were supposed to implement the TPD in their national laws within 18 months, the final members did not do so until 2017.

The TPD imposed a maximum nicotine concentration of 20 mg/ml, volume limits for e-liquid vials (10 ml) and single-use cartridges (2 ml), and the requirement that e-liquids be sold in tamper-proof child-resistant containers. Certain substances were banned in e-liquids, including vitamins and any other additives implying a health benefit, caffeine or other actual or perceived stimulants, additives intended to produce colored vapor, and any substance that is carcinogenic, mutagenic, or toxic in non-combusted form. The TPD implemented a reporting standard for manufacturers, forcing them to disclose to national authorities the constituents in e-liquids. The TPD also mandated labeling requirements including external health warning labels, the inclusion of ingredient lists, and a statement of nicotine content as well as additional information inside the packaging on adverse effects, addictiveness, and toxicity. Promotional elements on e-cigarette packages were banned and advertising restrictions were adopted, subjecting e-cigarettes to the same standards as were applied to combustible tobacco. There were, however, notable omissions from the TPD: internet sales were not banned, flavors were not directly restricted, and no minimum taxes were established. Member states remained free to adopt their own policies surpassing the requirements of the TPD, including regulations on areas not covered by the Directive, so long as they remained compliant with the TPD and the FCTC. This led to important differences among national regulations, particularly with regard to taxation and restrictions on where e-cigarettes could be used in public.[20]

1.2.2 *FDA Deeming Rule*

Just as the TPD brought in more robust e-cigarette regulation in the EU, standardized (at least to some extent) across member states, the FDA's deeming regulations of May 2016 subjected U.S. states to federal restrictions: E-cigarettes could no longer be sold to anyone under the age of 18. Vendors would need to ask for photo ID, vending machine sales would be banned (except in age-gated venues), and the distribution of free samples would be prohibited. The new deeming regulations would also require all manufacturers, importers, and retailers of e-cigarettes to register and list products with the FDA and obtain regulatory authorization via a process known as a Premarket Tobacco Product Application (PMTA). As with combustibles, producers would now be required to place health warnings on product packages and advertisements and would be prevented from describing their products using terms such as "light," "low," or "mild."

Just as the TPD had been challenged in the EU,[21] the FDA's deeming rule faced legal challenges from advocacy groups and the e-cigarette industry.[22] The FDA also faced criticism from elected representatives. Ron Johnson, a Republican senator from Wisconsin serving as chairman of the Senate Homeland Security and Governmental Affairs Committee, wrote to FDA Commissioner Robert Califf arguing that the deeming rule would create undue burdens on small businesses and could lead to negative unintended health consequences.[23] Conversely, 17 Democratic senators wrote to Califf applauding the FDA for finalizing the deeming rule and calling for further restrictions on youth-friendly e-cigarette marketing and flavors.[24]

1.2.3 Canada TVPA

In Canada, the Tobacco and Vaping Products Act 2018 (TVPA) banned the sale of e-cigarettes to anyone under the age of 18, limited nicotine concentrations to 20 mg/ml, and imposed packaging and labeling requirements for e-liquids. The TVPA required nicotine concentration to be stated on the packaging in mg/ml along with a hazard symbol, a toxicity warning, and first aid statement. Child-proof containers are required for any e-liquid with a concentration of 0.1 mg/ml or more. The TVPA also prohibited the use of certain ingredients (including caffeine, coloring agents, probiotics, taurine, and vitamins) along with any marketing which suggested their use. Pre-approved health warning labels in both English and French must cover 35% of the packaging face and must be included in any advertisements. Advertising techniques that appeal to young people (including lifestyle advertising, testimonials, endorsements, and sponsorship) were also banned. Advertisements that discourage tobacco cessation or promote the resumed use of tobacco products were further prohibited. The TVPA also banned e-cigarette product display in non-age-gated venues, and required e-commerce sites to conduct age-verification before a visitor could view any products online. The TVPA required manufacturers to submit information about their products to the Minister of Health and forbade any claims of health benefits without the expressed authorization of Health Canada. While e-cigarette flavors were not banned, the TVPA allowed the federal government to ban them (which it later proposed to do in 2021). The legislation also prohibited marketing of certain flavor profiles that are attractive to young people, including confectionery, dessert, cannabis, soft drink, energy drink, etc.

1.3 Emphasizing Risks

1.3.1 Bans and Prohibitions

The regulatory frameworks adopted in the EU, U.S., and Canada may seem comprehensive, but elsewhere, more draconian measures were being taken against e-cigarettes. India, in 2019, passed the Prohibition of Electronic Cigarettes (Production, Manufacture, Import, Export, Transport, Sale, Distribution, Storage, and Advertisement) Act, 2019 (No. 42 of 2019) which, absenting inadequate enforcement, bans e-cigarettes nationwide. Similarly, in February 2020, Mexican President Andrés Manuel Lopez Obrador banned all vaping products, including zero-nicotine e-liquid and hardware sold without liquid. The ban was somewhat ironic given that his 2018 campaign had championed opposition to prohibition regarding the failed war on drugs and supported cannabis legalization.[25] Australia banned the import of nicotine vapor products without a doctor's prescription in June 2020.[26] Proposals to sanction violators with fines of up to $220,000 AUD (equal to roughly $150,000 USD at the time) were suspended following criticism that doing so would push Australians back to combustible cigarettes.[27] Australian Senator Mathew Canavan and MP George Christensen created a petition to overturn the ban, proposing instead that nicotine e-cigarettes be legalized and regulated. In January 2021, less than 90 days before the ban was due to go into effect, the government established the Select Committee on Tobacco Harm Reduction to investigate vaping and establishing clear e-cigarette laws.[28] However, in May 2023, Australia's Health Minister Mark Butler announced that it would ban "recreational vaping" by prohibiting the import of non-prescription products, including nicotine-free products. E-cigarettes now can be sold only in pharmacies and must be in "pharmaceutical-type" packaging. The new regulations also restrict flavors (to mint, menthol, or tobacco), colors, and other ingredients, and limit nicotine levels and quantities. Disposable "single-use" products would also be banned. Some of the announced changes were codified into regulations in late 2023, with staggered roll-out in 2024.[29]

1.3.2 WHO Reporting on E-cigarettes (2016)

The WHO's vocal skepticism of e-cigarettes' utility as a cessation aid and endorsements of stringent restrictions and bans on e-cigarettes provided a powerful catalyst for prohibitions. In August 2016, the WHO issued a report titled *Electronic Nicotine Delivery Systems and Electronic Non-Nicotine Delivery Systems (ENDS/ENNDS)*[30] in response to a request made by the 6th Conference of the Parties to the WHO Framework Convention on Tobacco Control. Ostensibly, the report aimed to survey the evidence on the health impact of e-cigarettes, their potential role in tobacco cessation and impact on tobacco control efforts, assess policy options, and consider the methods to measure the contents and emissions of these products. The report argued that ENDS are a threat to public health and called for member states to enact bans and prohibitions. The report was heavily criticized by the U.K. Center for Tobacco and Alcohol Studies (CTAS).[31] In particular, the CTAS criticized the WHO for focusing on risk while failing to acknowledge the potential for e-cigarettes to support harm reduction, which is explicitly included in the FCTC's definition of tobacco control.[32] CTAS argued that the WHO report failed to quantify and misrepresented the risks posed by e-cigarette use. Further criticism was directed against the WHO's failure to acknowledge that e-cigarette marketing (also heavily criticized in the report) could serve as anti-tobacco marketing, promoting an alternative to smoking that might lead to desirable behavioral change in a group that conventional stop-smoking interventions fail to reach. The WHO claimed that flavors appeal to teenagers, driving youth vaping. However, CTAS argued that the WHO's statements on this topic ignored the evidence that flavors are an integral part of the appeal of e-cigarettes to adults using the devices to quit or reduce tobacco use. Furthermore, CTAS claimed that the WHO had misrepresented the role of transnational tobacco companies in the e-cigarette market and failed to account for the desirable effect of disruption in the tobacco industry. According to CTAS, the interventions called for by the WHO could help the tobacco industry by inhibiting disruption and shaping the e-cigarette industry in ways which allow TTCs to profit: "Almost every policy listed in the WHO's paper could easily have the effect of protecting the incumbent cigarette trade, promoting smoking rather than vaping, and lead to increases in non-communicable diseases." The CTAS also called out the unjustified support for e-cigarette prohibition as a default regulatory option, which was not only out of proportion to the risks, but unjustified given the pervasive availability of cigarettes. "It is unethical to deny smokers much lower risk options than cigarettes, and there is no scientific support for ENDS prohibition as a public health intervention." The WHO report made no attempt to evaluate other policy options for efficacy or cost-effectiveness and made no reference to the tradeoffs and unintended consequences inherent in e-cigarette regulation. Those, as this chapter explores, are significant.

1.3.3 Concerns for Youth: E-cigarettes as a Gateway to Smoking

Skepticism toward e-cigarettes has often centered upon concerns for the well-being of young people. An FDA press release issued to coincide with the deeming rules adopted in 2016 describes the agency's priority: "As cigarette smoking among those under 18 has fallen, the use of other nicotine products, including e-cigarettes, has taken a drastic leap… Current e-cigarette use among high school students has skyrocketed from 1.5% in 2011 to 16% in 2015 (an over 900% increase)."[33] As discussed in previous chapters, concerns for youths use of e-cigarettes center around the belief that nicotine is addictive and therefore harmful even in the absence of combustion; that the long-term health consequences of e-cigarette use are unknown but potentially significant; and that vaping could serve as a gateway to smoking.[34] Although, as the WHO report noted, research had not established a causal link between youth vaping and subsequent smoking, that did not preclude the organization from using causal language when asserting that e-cigarette "use by minors who have never smoked at least doubles their chance of starting to smoke." However, as discussed in Volume II, Chapter 1, methodological flaws undermined the validity of the gateway hypothesis.

In addition to the discussion there, consider also the following. A 2017 article in the *Journal of Drug and Alcohol Dependence*[35] highlighted several shortcomings in studies purporting to demonstrate evidence for a gateway effect. In particular, many failed to control for other tobacco product use, paying insufficient attention to confounding variables. Youth who experiment with one risky behavior are more likely than the general population to engage in another risky behavior. Given this common liability, it doesn't necessarily follow that smoking is *caused* by e-cigarette use, even if the latter occurred first. Moreover, even if a gateway effect were evident in some groups, at the population level any "gateway" effect must be overwhelmed by opposing factors, since smoking rates continued to decline even as vaping rates increased.[36] CDC data published in 2018 reported that fewer than 14% of U.S. adults smoked in 2017—the lowest figures recorded since records began in 1965,[37] and the NYTS data for 2021 show that less than 2% of middle and high school students were current smokers in 2021—again the lowest levels ever recorded.[38] If vaping did lead to smoking on aggregate, smoking trends should eventually increase.[39] The fact that they have not, contradicts the "gateway hypothesis."

Further evidence refuting the "gateway hypothesis" came in May 2021, when an NIH-funded study using data from Monitoring the Future demonstrated that high school seniors who use e-cigarettes would likely have otherwise been smokers.[40] In New Zealand, research[41] suggested that the growth in demand for e-cigarettes among young people was contributing to a reduction in smoking prevalence, with the effects were concentrated among young people. With greater uptake among older people, e-cigarettes could "make a substantial contribution to reducing smoking." However, in the U.K., a 2020 YouGov poll[42] suggested that there were of 400,000 fewer e-cigarette users in the U.K., than 12 months prior—a fact which ASH (U.K.) blamed on misinformation surrounding vaping.[43]

A long-term decline in smoking rates has been a feature of many markets in which e-cigarettes are present. Data from the Canadian Tobacco Use Monitoring Survey, and the Canadian Alcohol Tobacco and Survey document a decline of almost 40% in the rates of smoking for all Canadians aged 15 and older between 2000 and 2017.[44] In the U.K., adult smoking declined by more than 25% from 2011 to 2017, with the largest greatest reductions occurring in 18–24-year-olds.[45] In the same year, the French public health agency announced that there were one million fewer daily smokers in 2017 than a year previously.[46] While these trends were welcomed, there was disagreement about the degree to which e-cigarettes were responsible and, in the U.S. and Canada at least, the rising rates of e-cigarette use among young people overshadowed the falling smoking rates. In the U.S., an estimated 5.3 million middle and high school students (27.5% [95% CI, 25.3%-29.7%] of high school students and 10.5% [95% CI, 9.4%-11.8%] of middle school students) reported current e-cigarette use in 2019.[47] In Canada, past-month vaping among Canadians aged 16–19 more than doubled, from 8.4% in 2017 to 17.8% in 2019, with frequent use (>20 use-days in the past 30 days) increasing by 55%.[48] However, while youth vaping rates in the U.S. and Canada were obviously significant, the "epidemic" in youth vaping was not matched elsewhere. In the U.K., in 2019, less than 2% of 11–17-year-olds were using e-cigarettes regularly.[49] Moreover, population surveys showed a consistent pattern: "Most e-cigarette experimentation does not turn into regular use, and levels of regular use in young people who have never smoked remain very low."[50]

That e-cigarettes were safer than combustible cigarettes was also increasingly evident, as reviewed in Volume II, Chapter 1. A 2017 study funded by Cancer Research U.K. and published in the *Annals of Internal Medicine* investigating the effects of "long-term" use reported that, compared with those using combustible tobacco, exclusive users of e-cigarettes and NRT users had significantly lower bio-markers for toxin exposure.[51] Emerging data also showed that e-cigarette users may be less nicotine-dependent than smokers using conventional cigarettes: Using data from the Population Assessment of Tobacco and Health (PATH) survey, research published in the journal *Preventative Medicine* reported that, compared to comparable smokers, "established, everyday exclusive e-cig users" reported taking longer to use the their product after waking. In addition, relative to e-cigarette users, cigarette smokers were significantly more likely to consider themselves addicted; smokers more frequently reported having strong cravings; finding it difficult to refrain from using their product in places where it was prohibited; and feeling the urgent need to use their product. These findings correspond with previous studies, suggesting that e-cigarettes indeed provide an off-ramp from smoking.[52,53,54,55]

1.3.4 Renewed Concerns About Youth Vaping

Data from the U.S. NYTS reported a year-on-year decline in youth vaping between 2019 and 2020.[56] Though it wasn't clear at the time whether this reduction resulted from the COVID-19 era restrictions, the following year's data from the NYTS reported a further reduction in both youth e-cigarette use and youth smoking.[57] There has, at other times too, been cause to hope that rates of vaping by youth were declining: NYTS data suggested, initially, that teen e-cigarette use peaked in 2015, when about 16% of high school students reported past 30-day current use, subsequently declining to around 11.5% in 2016 and 2017. However, in June 2018, Nancy Brown, CEO of the American Heart Foundation (AHA) issued a statement[58] advising that the pause in the decline in youth-vaping rates be viewed with caution. "Our greatest fear is that this may be a warning sign of a reversal, and in the coming years we may see a disturbing rise in the number of middle and high school students who smoke e-cigarettes (sic)."[59] Brown pointed to flavors as a key driver of youth vaping and called on the FDA to crackdown on "sloppy enforcement" of age restrictions and follow in the footsteps of the City of San Francisco, which in June 2018 voted to ban flavored tobacco products. Brown's comments proved prescient: Between 2017 and 2018, current e-cigarette use increased 78% among high-school students and 48% among middle-school students.[60] By then, 3.6 million middle and high school children in the U.S. were using e-cigarettes. In November 2018, FDA commissioner, Dr. Scott Gottlieb, described these levels as an "epidemic." There was, Gottlieb argued, an obvious cause: "More than two-thirds [of school-aged users] are using flavored e-cigarettes."

For years, U.S. e-cigarettes and e-liquids had been available in thousands of flavors, including fruit, candy, and various desserts.[61] Some of these flavors mimicked brands that were marketed to children, including gummy bears, twinkie bars, and breakfast cereal. Gottlieb's proposed solution was to ensure that flavored e-cigarette products (other than tobacco, mint, and menthol flavors or non-flavored products) could only be sold in age-restricted venues, and require e-commerce sites to implement more stringent age verification processes. Still, the FDA highlighted that mint, menthol, and tobacco flavors were not as popular with children and that these products "may be important to adult smokers seeking to transition away from cigarettes," not least because these flavors were available in combustible tobacco products. "I don't want to create a situation where the combustible products have features that make them more attractive than the non-combustible products."[62]

In March 2019, the FDA issued a new draft compliance policy, reversing the former decision to allow e-cigarette products that had not received pre-market review to remain on the market until August 2022. Under the new guidelines, manufacturers and retailers of flavored e-cigarette products would be subject to enforcement. Days later, U.S. drugstore retailer Rite Aid announced that it would discontinue sales of vaping products,[63] though combustible tobacco products would continue to be sold. That move put the company at odds with competitors CVS, which sold neither e-cigarettes nor combustible tobacco, and Walgreens, which sold both. Rite Aid's announcement also seemed juxtaposed to Gottlieb's qualification about not making combustibles more attractive than non-combustible products.

1.4 U.S. E-cigarette Regulation 2019–2023

Following the release of the FDA guidelines in 2019, two democrats, Rep. Frank Pallone Jr, New Jersey, and Rep. Donna Shalala, Florida, introduced a bill proposing to raise the minimum sales age for all tobacco products to 21 years old, ban all flavored tobacco and vapor products, including menthol cigarettes, and prohibit all online sales of vapor products.[64] Some U.S. municipalities were unwilling to wait for federal regulation: Aspen, Colorado banned the sale of all flavored tobacco and non-pharmaceutical nicotine products in June 2019. Days later, San Francisco's Board of Supervisors voted unanimously to ban the sale and distribution of e-cigarettes, becoming the first major U.S city to do so. On September 3rd, Michigan Governor Gretchen Whitmer used her executive authority to impose a six-month ban on the sale of flavored e-cigarettes.[65] However, a week after the ban took effect, Michigan judge Cynthia Stephens blocked the order, arguing that the ban could push adults to return to smoking more-harmful tobacco products. Others disagreed. On September 11, 2019, the Trump Administration announced that it intended "to clear the market" of flavored e-cigarettes in an attempt to tackle the "deeply concerning epidemic of youth e-cigarette use."[66] In September, Bloomberg Philanthropies announced that it would spend $160 million to support initiatives to ban flavored e-cigarettes at the local state and federal level, encourage the FDA toward greater oversight, and assist local agencies who might face litigation in response to flavor restrictions.[67]

In the U.S., calls to ban or restrict e-cigarettes accelerated with the onset of the COVID-19 pandemic. Rep. Raja Krishnamoorthi (D-IL), Chairman of the House Committee on Oversight and Reform Subcommittee on Economic and Consumer Policy, wrote to FDA commissioner Dr. Stephen Hahn in August 2020, calling on his agency to remove all e-cigarettes from the market[68] on the grounds that the co-occurrence of youth vaping with the COVID-19 pandemic created a much deadlier force and that demanded FDA action. Though similar findings have since been reported elsewhere,[69] Krishnamoorthi cited, as evidence, a single report based on an online survey suggesting that young e-cigarette users, dual users in particular, were more likely to self-report having been diagnosed with or experiencing symptoms of COVID-19.[70] The cited paper did not control for the number of COVID-19 tests taken, the age of respondents, or the frequency or duration of vaping, leading to widespread criticism.[71]

The proposed ban was never enacted, but further restrictions were forthcoming. That summer, the U.S. passed the Preventing Online Sales of E-Cigarettes to Children Act (S.1253), requiring package delivery service providers to verify the age of customers purchasing e-cigarette products upon delivery and requiring sellers to collect and remit state and local taxes. President Trump signed the act into law in December 2020, giving the USPS 120 days to cease delivery. However, in April 2021 the USPS delayed its ban, saying that it needed more time to implement the new rules. FedEx and UPS, for their part, announced that they would cease to deliver e-cigarettes (with or without nicotine) in January 2021.

In the U.S. at least, the topic of e-cigarette flavors has taken center-stage in the e-cigarette debate. In response to the perception that flavored e-cigarettes were driving youth vaping, the U.S. banned the sale of vaping cartridges and pods containing nicotine e-liquids flavored with anything other than tobacco and menthol in January 2021, and the FDA announced that it would enforce against companies violating the restrictions,[72] which it subsequently has done by sending warning letters to violators.[73] Open tank systems were exempt from these restrictions, on the basis that those products were less appealing to youth. Disposable devices were also exempt, and subsequent data on youth use documents a significant swing in demand to those products following the restriction.[74] In New York, Governor Andrew Cuomo announced in January 2020 that his state would ban all flavored vaping products, *including* menthol, as well as banning e-cigarette advertisements targeted to young audiences, e-liquids, and online, phone, and mail order sales. Cuomo's ban was, however, struck down by state Supreme Court Justice Catherine Cholakis, who sided with industry plaintiffs arguing that the ban violated the State's Constitution. However, New York's 2021 budget legislation included an e-cigarette flavor ban exempting only flavors for products that had received a PMTA approval. At the time of writing, no flavored e-cigarettes have received a PMTA authorization.

The logic of banning e-cigarette flavors was challenged by research published in the *Annals of the American Thoracic Society* in March 2020. Evidence showed that the flavor preferences of adult e-cigarette users, specifically a preference for sweet flavors, closely correspond with those of younger users, and suggesting that the federal ban on non-tobacco-flavored pod and pre-filled cartridge systems may have negative consequences for adults who use the products.[75] As will shortly be discussed, the negative unintended consequences of e-cigarette regulation are not limited to flavor bans. Research published in February 2020 also suggested that taxes on e-cigarette could also push consumers back to combustible tobacco.[76] Altria published data around the same time purporting to show that older ex-smokers were indeed returning to combustibles in response to misinformation about vaping.[77]

Nonetheless, calls for restrictions on e-cigarettes continued to gain pace. In September 2020, California Governor Gavin Newsom signed into law SB793, banning the retail sale of flavored tobacco products in the state. In response, the industry-funded California Coalition for Fairness obtained over a million signatures in support of a veto referendum, which was subsequently included on the November 2022 ballot, delaying the implementation of the bill. However, voters roundly supported the contested legislation, passing Proposition 31 with more than 63% of the vote.

January 2021 saw Colorado and Oregon implement a novel tax on vaping products. Colorado's levied, initially, 30% of the manufacturer's list price, but this was to increase gradually to 62%[78]; Oregon's e-cigarettes were taxed at 65% of wholesale.[79] The following month, Maryland's legislature overrode a gubernatorial veto of the state's tax bill, adding a 6% specific sales tax on tank systems (effectively doubling the states standard sales tax), and adding a 60% tax on e-liquids in containers smaller than 5 ml. In late 2021, the Biden administration's Build Back Better Act originally contained plans to tax e-cigarettes at the Federal level. Michael Pesko and other leading economists wrote to the U.S. Congress, advising them that doing so would increase the numbers of teen smokers in the U.S. by half a million; increase daily adult smokers by 2.5 million, reduce daily e-cigarette users by a similar number; and increase smoking among pregnant women.[80] This provision was dropped in the final version of the legislation.

Other municipalities were going further still. In July 2021, Brookline, MA banned the sale of tobacco products to anyone born in the twenty-first century, meaning that future adults would never be of legal age to purchase tobacco. Seven months earlier, West Hollywood, CA banned the sale of all non-tobacco-flavored tobacco and vapor products, preempting calls by House Democrats in March 2021 for the FDA to take all flavored e-cigarettes off the market.[81] In May 2021, Rep. Krishnamoorthi (D-IL) introduced a proposal to cap nicotine in e-liquids to

20 mg/ml, modeled on the limits adopted in the U.K., EU, and—later that year—Canada. The bill, tellingly titled the END ENDS (Ending Nicotine Dependence from Electronic Nicotine Delivery Systems) was designed to tackle what Krishnamoorthi characterized, predictably, as the "youth-vaping epidemic."

1.5 PMTA Results: A De Facto Flavor Ban?

In August 2021, the FDA issued the first Marketing Denial Orders to 55,000 flavored products from three applicants on the grounds that the applications failed to document sufficient evidence that their products benefited adult smokers sufficiently to override concerns for youth use.[82] In September of that year the FDA announced that it had "taken action on more than 6 million applications, including a Refuse to File order for 4.5 million products from a single producer, and 132 MDOs [marketing denial orders]."[83] Still, some of the best-known brands including Juul, Vuse, and NJOY awaited the FDA's response. The first authorization was awarded in October 2021 to R.J. Reynolds Vuse Solo.[84] Since then, a handful of other applicants have received marketing authorizations, notably, exclusively for non-flavored products.[85] However, litigation challenging MDOs has kept other products, including former market leader Juul, on the market. In particular, the FDA's refusal to grant PMTAs to any e-vapor product flavored with anything other than tobacco, has led to the criticism that the agency is trying to implement a de facto flavor ban.[86] In March 2023, the 5th circuit decided in favor of RJR Vapor Company in its appeal against an MDO issued by the FDA against the menthol-flavored Vuse-Vibe e-cigarette, arguing that the MDO's decision likely qualified as "arbitrary and capricious." In particular, in FDA ruling is a result, in part, of the Fatal Flaw memorandum, which de facto banned all non-tobacco-flavored e-cigarettes without adhering to the mandated notice-and-comment rulemaking procedures.[87] According to the court ruling, the FDA's "Fatal Flaw memo... 'bears all the hallmarks' of a substantive rule...the memo is binding on its face... has been applied in a way that indicates it is binding... it took away the FDA reviewers' former discretion to consider individual PMTAs solely on their merits ...[and]...it affected the rights of literally hundreds of thousands of applicants whose PMTAs were denied. This is not a close call." The FDA could yet appeal the 5th circuit ruling at the Supreme Court, but the ruling calls into question the "hundreds of thousands of applicants whose PMTAs were denied." The future of flavored e-cigarettes in the U.S. is far from settled.

1.6 The Laboratory of Policy-Differences

In many of the largest e-cigarette markets, e-cigarettes are regulated on a multi-lateral basis, with authority shared between federal, state or provincial, and municipal levels of government. Alongside the national and international restrictions imposed by the FDA in the U.S., the TPD in the EU, and the TVPA in Canada, states, countries, provinces, and individual cities and counties have adopted local e-cigarette restrictions that often predate and, in many cases, surpass the stringency of the policies latterly adopted by the overarching authority. As a result, in addition to the inter-jurisdictional differences in the details of e-cigarette regulations between these jurisdictions at the macro-level,[88] there are important intra-jurisdictional differences between localities too. Such differences allow localities to serve as policy laboratories, testing the efficacy, costs, and unintended consequences of policy-decisions, and providing inspiration and evidence to inform subsequent legislation elsewhere. Specifically, regulatory differences can offer important insights into how regulatory choices affect consumption patterns. In this regard, there are important differences between the frameworks adopted by Canada, the EU, and the U.S. For example, the TPA limited nicotine concentrations to 20 mg/ml in the EU, but in Canada, nicotine content regulations (until 2021) limited only concentrations above 66 mg/ml. The relative laxity of the Canadian restriction and the lack of a comparable restriction in the U.S. meant that the nicotine content of North American e-cigarettes has been much higher than in products used in the EU and the U.K. (which retained the TPD restrictions in its e-cigarette regulations upon leaving the EU in 2021). It has been suggested that higher nicotine levels may help explain why rates of youth use in North America have been consistently higher than those found in Europe.[89] Australia and New Zealand have also not reported the same levels of youth vaping that have alarmed many in North America,[90,91] though, at least in the case of Australia, a radically different policy agenda likely also contributes to differences in consumer behaviors across national boundaries.

Another key difference between these countries can be found in the restrictions on e-cigarette marketing and advertising. In Europe, the TPD explicitly banned e-cigarette promotion via digital and print media, and prohibited promotions, sponsorships, and cross-border advertising. Canada's TVPA likewise banned lifestyle advertising, testimonials, and sponsorship promotion as well as prohibiting advertisements which might reasonably appeal to youth. The TVPA also restricts e-cigarette products designed to appeal to youth and bans marketing strategies intended to appeal to young people including marketing "dessert" or "confectionary" flavors. However, the FDA's deeming rule was less restrictive, only banning e-cigarette producers from using "modified risk" messages that suggest that their products are less harmful than combustible cigarettes, and banning the use of false or misleading claims and from suggesting that a product is "approved" or "endorsed" by FDA. This left opportunities for U.S. e-cigarette producers to market products in ways that were illegal in other national contexts. In the U.S., e-cigarette advertising, often using celebrity endorsements, has been associated with increases in demand,[92] particularly among school-age consumers.[93] By 2017, ever use by 18–24-year-olds was 28% in the EU, 29% in Canada but it was 40% in the U.S.[94] Regulatory differences between these countries and differences in messaging around e-cigarettes may help explain the differences in consumption patterns between nations.

2 Contemporary Approaches to E-cigarette Regulation

As of July 2022, the Johns Hopkins Global Tobacco Control initiative identifies 109 countries that regulate or prohibit e-cigarettes. The nature and extent of these regulations vary widely between jurisdictions, and the regulatory landscape evolves quickly as regulators try to respond to the rapid pace of commercial innovation and, relatedly, shifting consumption patterns.

As discussed in Volume II, Chapter 3, perspectives regarding e-cigarettes are informed by disagreements about how the available data on e-cigarettes' safety and efficacy should be produced, reported, and interpreted; and philosophical differences about what the goal of regulation should be, which groups should be prioritized, what standards of evidence are necessary to inform policy, and how regulators should respond to imperfect information. The prevalence of misinformation and its effect on public perceptions of risk; and the legacy of the tobacco industry's attempts to mislead the public and their regulators also inform knowledge, beliefs, attitudes, and decisions both at the public and the regulatory level. Unfortunately, as Campus et al.[95] highlight, e-cigarette regulation is often over-simplified and presented as a binary option driven by two fundamentally opposing ideologies: the health protection camp and the harm reduction camp. This is a false binary. There are numerous different approaches to regulating e-cigarettes including, but not limited to, prohibitions, regulation on parity with combustibles, commercial regulation with restrictions on certain products and characteristics, medicalization, risk-proportionate regulation, and a *laissez faire* free-market approach, as explored in Volume III, Chapter 2.

2.1 Classification of E-cigarettes for the Purposes of Regulation

Confronted by an innovation such as e-cigarettes, one of regulators' first challenges is to classify it. E-cigarettes have been classified variously as commercial products, medical devices, drug delivery systems, tobacco products, and even as poisons. Classifying e-cigarettes using these pre-established categories allows regulators to apply to e-cigarettes an existing regulatory framework, saving them from "reinventing the wheel." Classifications are not set in stone; they can be revised (if necessarily, upon court-order[96]), but fitting e-cigarettes into a pre-existing regulatory model at least buys time for regulators to collect information about the products, their use, and resulting consequences which could then inform the development of more nuanced, and arguably more appropriate regulations. Regardless, classification decisions do inform subsequent regulations decisions which, in turn, influence the manner in which e-cigarettes are designed, manufactured, and marketed by industry; and understood, perceived of, and consumed by the public. Different classifications also lead to different levels of scrutiny and enforcement, both of which affect consumption patterns by informing consumer knowledge, beliefs, and attitudes in different ways. This is especially evident when classification limits the claims that manufacturers can make about the safety, utility, and efficacy of e-cigarettes for the purposes of adult smoking cessation. Often the characterization of e-cigarettes and other alternative nicotine products is informed by the characterization of conventional cigarettes. In countries where conventional cigarettes are considered a consumer good, e-cigarettes are often considered likewise.[97] This characterization does not necessarily exempt e-cigarettes from additional specific restrictions. For example, under Article 20 of the 2014 Tobacco Product Directive (2014/40/EU), the European Union established additional and specific rules for e-cigarettes. Thus, while classifications do inform regulation, the details of subsequent regulations are not dictated by classification alone.[98]

2.1.1 *Classifying E-cigarettes as Consumer Products*

Even classified simply as consumer products, general safety requirements apply. For example, the EU's General Product Safety Directive 2001/95/EC (GPSD) requires that consumer products be supervised by a national regulatory agency. Further, businesses must comply with safety standards, inform consumers of risks associated with the product, and ensure products are traceable to make possible a product recall in the event a product is found to be defective or otherwise harmful. The consumer product classification does not preclude more specific rules from being applied. For example, in the EU, rules governing electrical safety and compatibility contained in the Low Voltage Directive 2006/95/EC and the Electromagnetic Compatibility Directive 2004/108/EC, apply to electronic components of an e-cigarette. Commercial categorization may also provide restrictions on product composition, packaging, and instructions; interaction with other products; and warning labels. Additionally, testing methodologies may be regulated under the consumer product classification, and advertising regulations for consumer products may also restrict the claims that manufacturers can make about their products. False or unfounded claims may lead producers to be reported to the regulator (e.g., OFCOM or OFT in the U.K., FTC in the U.S.). Consumer product laws may also restrict manufacturers from making health/medical claims, which would trigger them to be considered a medical product by the regulator and regulated accordingly.

Applied to e-cigarettes, the consumer product categorization has several advantages: The opportunity to ensure at least minimum standards of safety/consumer protection, and flexibility, which could foster innovations that make these products more appealing to smokers, accelerating substitutions away from combustibles. By avoiding the more burdensome compliance barriers associated with the tobacco and medical product classifications (discussed shortly), this categorization may also foster greater market competition, ensuring that smaller firms can bring products to the marketplace, reducing the potential for large firms (including the tobacco industry) to monopolize the marketplace. One consequence of this competition relates to product prices. Greater competition may exert downward pressure on prices. Less-expensive e-cigarettes would increase the appeal of the product category relative to combustibles. Lower prices can therefore reasonably be expected to accelerate substitutions away from combustibles. However, lower prices also make those products more appealing to the general public, raising concerns for e-cigarette use among non-smokers and especially youth who are traditionally price-sensitive because they tend to lack full-time employment or work in entry-level jobs. The consumer product designation also means that e-cigarettes can be sold by non-specialist retailers increasing access (again with both positive and negative consequences for public health). One clear downside of the commercial categorization is that it forgoes an opportunity to enact more robust safety standards, and performance and quality checks including pre-market notification and post-market monitoring or surveillance.

2.1.2 *Classifying E-cigarettes as Tobacco Products*

The U.S. Tobacco Control Act (2009) categorized e-cigarettes as tobacco products, after which many countries followed suit. Tobacco products may be a subset of consumer good, but they are almost universally subject to specific restrictions. Classifying e-cigarettes as tobacco products allows regulators to leverage the existing tobacco control infrastructure to limit access to e-cigarettes. For this reason, this characterization tends to allow for regulations with greater stringency. Once again, that stringency brings both challenges and opportunities. The tobacco-product characterization provides an opportunity to utilize existing mandates and established infrastructure for pre-market review and post-market monitoring and surveillance. This designation also provides regulatory clarity, applying frameworks that are already in place, creating a shorthand for e-cigarettes to be restricted in all the ways that apply to tobacco (advertising, plain packaging, etc.). However, classification as a tobacco product creates a significant compliance burden for manufacturers, which likely favors larger firms, including tobacco manufacturers, who have the infrastructure and capital to support regulatory compliance. This may stifle innovation and, if increased regulatory compliance costs do increase market concentration, the result may be higher product prices. While that may serve as a deterrent against experimental use, it may also decrease the relative appeal of e-cigarettes in relation to combustibles, and impede substitutions away from the more risky products. This strategy may leave the cigarette producers "cornering the market," since those firms are better capitalized in relation to independents. A smaller number of firms may be less burdensome for the regulator. However, market power may also lead dominant firms to raise prices, reducing the relative appeal of e-cigarettes in relation to cigarettes. Moreover, by equating e-cigarettes with e-cigarettes, even semantically, the regulator gives the false impression that these products are of commensurate risk, and may sacrifice an opportunity to create advantages through taxes and other restrictions that might otherwise educate the consumer about the benefits of switching to safer alternatives, and create incentives for them to do so.

2.1.3 *Classifying E-cigarettes as Medical Devices*

A third option is to categorize e-cigarettes as medical devices, as the FDA previously tried to do, in an attempt to bring e-cigarettes under their purview before Congress extended that to include tobacco products in 2009. There is some logic to this categorization. In utility, at least, nicotine e-cigarettes may have more in common with NRTs than combustible cigarettes. NRTs are typically regulated as medicines (though they are often sold without prescription). By the same logic, e-cigarettes may, intuitively, fit this description. Consider, for example, that the EU defines a "medicinal product" as: (a) Any substance or combination of substances presented as having properties for treating or preventing disease in human beings; or (b) Any substance or combination of substances which may be used in, or administered to, human beings either with a view to restoring, correcting, or modifying physiological functions by exerting a pharmacological, immunological, or metabolic action; or to making a medical diagnosis (Directive 2001/83/EC). The U.K.'s medical and healthcare products regulatory agency (MHRA) has argued, as the FDA once did, that e-cigarettes may under certain circumstances qualify as medical products.[99] But, as Caponnetto et al.[100] note, many substances including alcohol and chocolate exert a pharmacological effect, but this does not make them medicines. Further, unlike NRTs there is no developed dosing paradigm for e-cigarettes which makes it difficult to categorize use as medicinal. "Take 500 mg of amoxicillin, three times a day with food for a week" constitutes specific medical advice. "Use e-cigarettes instead of smoking" falls somewhat short of that standard. Which specific products? How frequently? For how long? These are not rhetorical questions. While answers may be forthcoming, in their absence, the medical classification may be premature. Such was the conclusion of the German Supreme

Administrative Court, which ruled, in November 2014, that nicotine-containing liquids did not have a scientifically verified therapeutic utility as a cessation aid, and as such did not qualify as medicines.[101]

It is noteworthy, however, that many nations (including the U.K., U.S., and Australia) still provide a parallel pathway for manufacturers willing to shoulder the compliance costs to apply for medical designation for their products. In the U.S., for example, the Food and Drug Administration (FDA) does, in theory at least, provide a pathway for manufacturers to submit their products to the Center for Drug Evaluation and Research (CDER) for approval as medicinal products. If approved, this would allow them to make therapeutic claims comparing the relative safety of the product to combustible tobacco and advertise them as cessation aids. However, since applications via this pathway are private, it is not clear if any have chosen to do so, and certainly none has been approved at the time of writing. In the U.K., in November 2015, BAT's eVoke e-cigarette was granted marketing authorization as a medicinal product by the U.K.'s MHRA. However, BAT never commercialized the product; apparently the pace of commercial innovation and regulatory burdens impeding commercialization prompted BAT to re-evaluate the product's resonance with consumers.[102] In 2021, however, the MHRA issued a request for e-cigarette manufactures to submit applications for their products to be considered medical devices.[103] This presents an interesting case: If approved devices were made available on the National Health Service (NHS), this would make them available to the public, on a prescription basis for the cost of a prescription charge (currently £9.35—significantly less than a starter kit and 30-day supply of e-liquid). Many Britons, including recipients of tax credits, those over 60, expectant mothers, those who have given birth in the past 12 months, and those with medical exemption certificates are exempted from these charges. For this group the hypothetical e-cigarette would be free. This may increase uptake, both by reducing the cost and by assuaging concerns about the safety and efficacy of the devices. While commercial products would, presumably, remain available, they would have to compete with the medical product on price, to some degree, possibly exerting downward pressure on the parallel consumer market, making them still more attractive relative to combustibles. The U.K. government committed to giving away e-cigarette starter-kits to up to one in five smokers as part of the 2023 swap to stop campaign.[104] Note however, this does not change the status of e-cigarettes in the U.K. Klein et al.[105] note, the fact that there are no therapeutic e-cigarettes available suggest that manufacturers may not consider seeking medical authorization to be a valuable endeavor in the current regulatory environment, preferring instead to focus on commercial offerings and forgo the opportunity to communicate therapeutic messages to the public.

Like other classifications, the medical designation has both advantages and disadvantages. Classifying e-cigarettes as a medical product would require higher product safety standards, greater oversight over production and ingredients, and would establish a system for regulators to approve devices and monitor the effects of consumption post-market. A medical designation could also provide an opportunity for the issuing of point-of-sale advice, for example between a pharmacist and consumer which might help deter experimental use, and provide an opportunity to remind those utilizing e-cigarette for cessation purposes of the importance of completely substituting cigarettes for e-cigarettes and that frequency of use has been shown to be an important factor in determining cessation efficacy (see Volume II, Chapter 2). Medical designation would also allow manufacturers to advertise their products using scientifically verified claims to support messages encouraging substitution while warning against uptake by non-smokers. That could help address the misperception that e-cigarettes are comparable to combustible tobacco products, fostering greater public trust in the product category and removing an impediment to uptake among current smokers and, by extension, accelerating smoking cessation. However, the medical designation is, like the other categorizations, not without downsides: As discussed previously, NRTs have gained medical authorization, in part, because they have acceptably low abuse potential. This is a feature of the dose of nicotine delivered and the pace at which it is delivered. In contrast to NRTs, e-cigarettes deliver higher doses of nicotine and more quickly, raising their potential to confer or perpetuate nicotine dependence. By this standard, it is not clear that all of today's e-cigarettes would qualify as medicines, though of course some could be adapted for these purposes. Problematically, however, such adaptations may affect the efficacy and appeal of the hypothetical products in relation to contemporary options. Indeed, as discussed in Volume II, Chapter 2, the popular appeal of contemporary e-cigarettes is a key component of their utility as a smoking cessation aid. E-cigarettes are as popular as they are, at least in part, precisely because they are not considered medicines. Many smokers do not engage with medical cessation support because they don't see their nicotine use as a medical problem. On this basis there is a reason to suggest that the demand for e-cigarettes designated as medicines may be underwhelming. On the other hand, so long as commercial product remained available, it is difficult to imagine the introduction of a medical product *reducing* demand for e-cigarettes in aggregate. Moreover, given that many smokers cite safety concerns regarding e-cigarettes, or a lack of confidence that they will be useful as reasons for not switching,[106] the approval of a medical regulator may increase consumer confidence in the product category as a whole and encourage greater substitutions. Chapter 3 of this volume discusses this topic further.

The medical classification creates regulatory burdens for producers. Gaining approval for a product from a medical regulator is extremely time-consuming and expensive. This may seem of little import to the public, but the burden of compliance may have consequences for public health. Regulatory burdens favor larger firms, able to accommodate the costs of compliance, at the expense of smaller less well-capitalized firms. The beneficiaries are likely to be the largest and wealthiest firms and those with the most experience complying with regulation. Transnational tobacco companies are likely to be in that group; smaller independent e-cigarette companies are not. If the result is a market populated by safer regulation-compliant products, the fact that the available products are produced by tobacco companies may be acceptable to some, but the association with the tobacco industry is likely to perpetuate stigma, mistrust, and misinformation regarding the products.

Producers who can afford the costs of medical product authorization will try to recoup their costs. This, and the fact that there are likely relatively few such firms who will benefit from market power, will likely result in increased product prices, reducing the appeal of e-cigarettes relative to combustibles. Higher product prices may also incentivize illicit sales of non-compliant products on the black market. Moreover, in a less competitive market with high compliance costs, innovation may be stifled, reducing opportunity for product developments that could make future e-cigarettes more appealing to smokers or simply less risky, thereby reducing uptake and subsequent smoking cessation, and increasing e-cigarette specific risks (whatever those turn out to be), relative to the counterfactual. Finally, the medical categorization may result in sales being limited to pharmacies resulting in non-trivial access barriers.

Since the 1980s, nicotine use has increasingly been framed as a medical condition. The medicalization of nicotine dependence has been contested by the tobacco industry, smokers' advocacy groups and smokers themselves who reject the assertion that the choice to use tobacco qualifies as a disorder. The formal categorization of tobacco use as a disorder in the Diagnostic and Statistical Manual-V (DSM-V) also drew criticism as being supported by the psychopharmaceutical industry which has a vested interest in this categorization, standing to gain substantially from the sale of NRTs.[107] Criticisms of the medicalization of e-cigarettes have parallels with a central tenant of Conrad and Scheider's 1980 book *Deviance and Medicalization: from bad to sick*,[108] in which the authors argue that medicalization, specifically as pertains to addiction, results in the individualization of societal issues and the displacement of individual responsibility. Individualizing the societal problem of smoking also displaces the responsibility of tobacco companies in being held accountable for smoking consequences. The hypothesis that smoking harms may be specific to individuals genetically predisposed to addiction received massive funding from the tobacco industry as it floundered against mass anti-tobacco campaigns in the early 2000s.[109] This, like the argument that tobacco control disadvantages minorities and historically disadvantaged communities in which smoking often becomes concentrated, provides a powerful, if controversial, social justice argument against overly stringent regulation. As with the topic of illicit trade, critics tend to dismiss these arguments as industry talking points, but the fact that they are enunciated by the industry does not, in itself, mean the arguments are invalid, nor that they are false. The topic of medicalization is discussed further in Chapter 2 of this volume.

2.1.4 Classifying E-cigarettes as Poison

A fourth, smaller group of countries[110] classify nicotine-containing e-cigarettes as a poison or toxic chemical. Malaysia and Brunei Darussalam serve as two examples. According to the 1952 Malaysian Poisons Act, nicotine is a Class C poison that can only be procured and dispensed by licensed pharmacists and medical professionals. Penalties for trading or possessing non-medically prescribed nicotine include a fine up to RM5,000 (approximately US$1,100 in 2022 dollars). This classification amounts to a prohibition, denying the public of access to any of the benefits of regulated e-cigarettes classified in any other manner. Of course, prohibitions rarely eliminate use, rather they merely push demand underground (at least a portion of it); thereby increasing the risks for consumers of such products. Until recently, it was theoretically possible to be put in jail for possession of an e-cigarette according to Malaysian law, though the Minister of Health made a comment clarifying that individual possession would not result in jail time, though illegal sales could.[111] This categorization is especially problematic considering that none of the countries that have adopted it ban combustible cigarettes, which leaves the most harmful nicotine products widely available while eliminating access to legal safer alternatives.

2.2 Classification Challenges

Different stakeholder groups may be vocal advocates for a specific categorization, with particular policy approaches in mind. For example, producers, retailers, and trade associations might favor categorizing e-cigarettes as a consumer good, hoping that doing so would lead to regulations that favor market innovation and commercial opportunity. Legislators may be more inclined to regulate e-cigarettes as tobacco products to avoid the burden of generating a novel regulatory framework while allowing them sufficient oversight and the opportunity to implement taxes and other restrictions. Healthcare professionals may support the medicalization category if they are confident that it affords opportunities to maximize their patients' well-being while controlling access to communities among whom the uptake of e-cigarettes could introduce novel risks.

Categorization is, however, an imperfect lens through which to analyze e-cigarette regulations. Under the 2021 Therapeutic Goods (Standard for Nicotine Vaping Products) (TGO 110), Australia technically regulates nicotine e-cigarettes as unapproved therapeutic products, and the Australian Therapeutic Goods Administration (TGA) requires a physician-issued prescription to buy e-cigarettes. At the time of writing, e-cigarettes may be imported for personal use.[112] In practice, however, very few physicians are willing to issue prescriptions for unapproved products which makes e-cigarette largely unavailable to Australian smokers,[113] an outcome more readily associated with a prohibition. The further restrictions announced in May 2023 contribute to what has been framed as a de facto prohibition.[114]

Moreover, two countries with ostensibly similar categorizations may adopt very different policy approaches. For example, both Argentina and the U.S. categorize e-cigarettes as tobacco products; but in Argentina, the sale, advertisement, distribution, and importation of e-cigarettes are banned, whereas in the U.S. such activities are legal, albeit with regulatory restrictions. Relatedly, two countries with apparently similar e-cigarette regulations may adopt different categorizations. For example, both the U.K. and New Zealand ban e-cigarette advertising, mandate health warning labels, regulate ingredients and flavors, have minimum legal sale age restrictions (18 years of age in each case), and have enacted reporting/notification standards; but the U.K. considers e-cigarettes to be a consumer product, while New Zealand classifies e-cigarettes as a distinctive product class. Evidently, while categorization plays a role in guiding regulatory decisions, it does not dictate the approach adopted by the regulator (Fig. 1).

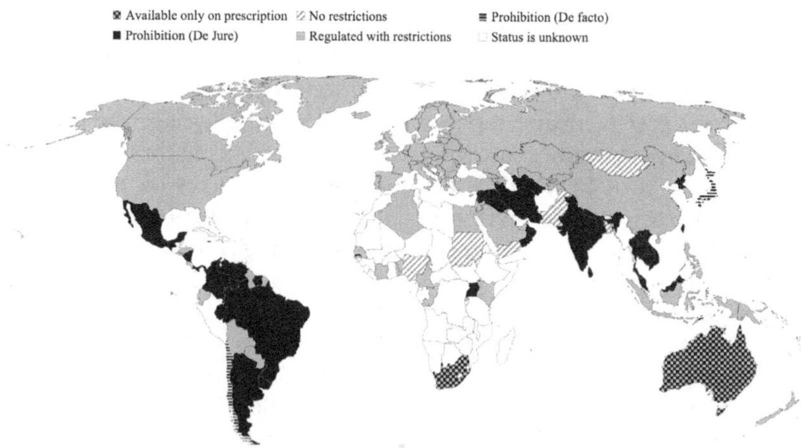

Fig. 1 Legal status of nicotine e-cigarettes around the world (*Note* The countries shaded green in the figure above include nations categorizing e-cigarettes as tobacco products, ENDSs, or commercial products. Such countries include a wide variety of regulations including but not limited to taxes, flavor and content restrictions, age limits, marketing restrictions, warning-label requirements, and child-proof packaging mandates. *Source* Author's interpretation of data provided by Johns Hopkins Institute for Global Tobacco Control https://globaltobaccocontrol.org/en/policy-scan/e-cigarettes/countries?country=263)

2.3 E-cigarette Policies

The following describes some of the different elements of e-cigarette regulations adopted around the world to curb their use. A brief discussion of the case for and against each intervention, and examples of the approach implemented or proposed in various jurisdictions is provided. Following that, the consequences of those regulations, both intended and unintended, are explored. That evidence base helps illuminate the options for e-cigarette regulation, and the attendant risks and opportunities, for those considering similar interventions elsewhere.

2.3.1 Taxation

The experience of the past several decades has shown that in many places around the world, the most effective weapon in the tobacco control arsenal is taxation.[115,116,117,118,119,120] Taxing a tobacco product raises its price, reducing consumer demand for the good.[121] Given the apparent success of taxing tobacco products, especially cigarettes, regulators wishing to reduce use of e-cigarettes find it both familiar and promising to turn to taxation. Accordingly, excise taxes on e-cigarettes have begun to spread in developed and less-developed countries alike.[122] As of May 2023, 30 U.S. states and the District of Columbia had adopted taxes on e-cigarettes.[123] Both the structure and level of these taxes vary. On the low end, Delaware, Kansas, Louisiana, North Carolina, and Wisconsin levy unit taxes of $0.05 per milliliter (ml) of e-liquid and New Hampshire levies an ad valorem tax of 8% of wholesale price for e-liquids containing nicotine for open (i.e., refillable with the user's choice of e-liquid) vaping systems. At the other end of the range, Kentucky taxes closed system cartridges (e.g., Juul pods) at a rate of $1.50 each, Minnesota levies an ad valorem tax of 95% of the wholesale price of nicotine-containing vaping products (except refillable devices themselves), and California, Colorado, Massachusetts, Vermont, and Washington, D.C. also have relatively high taxes working out to more than US$1.00 per ml.[124] There is no federal taxation of e-cigarettes in the U.S., although it has been proposed.[125] At least 47 other countries tax at least some types of e-cigarette devices or e-liquids.[126]

Excise taxes on tobacco products are an example of a so-called sin tax, a term applied most often to excises on alcohol and tobacco. Sin taxes generally apply to consumption of any culturally disfavored commodity thought to be driven by a loss of self-control or moral strength, or (to behavioral economists) any form of myopia. Sin taxes are often an easy sell to voters, especially (as in the case of nicotine-containing products in most developed countries) when the median voter does not consume any of the product in question.[127] From the point of view of politicians, taxing tobacco is unlikely to cost much in terms of lost campaign contributions from the tobacco lobby, which were always sporadic[128] and sometimes modest,[129] and have anyway dwindled as the industry has shrunk.[130] Furthermore, raising sin taxes appears not to affect a political candidate's support from voters to any significant degree, at least in the U.S. context (for which there is evidence).[131]

Proponents argue that taxation produces a quintet of desired outcomes by discouraging initiation (particularly by youth), encouraging users to quit, reducing the volume of use by users who do not quit completely, reducing externalities, and raising revenue for the state. The first three are various ways in which the demand reduction is expressed. How much demand for e-cigarettes drops in total when taxes are levied or raised on vaping products depends on the elasticity of demand, the standard economic measure of how sensitive demand for a good is to changes in its price. While there is a voluminous body of econometric evidence on the demand for cigarettes, with a consensus that the price elasticity is −0.4 (i.e., that a 1% increase in price reduces demand by 0.4%) or lower,[132,133,134,135,136] results for e-cigarette demand are much less certain. The bulk of the estimates of price elasticity of demand for e-cigarettes range from −0.8 to −2.3.[137] The great range of estimates reflects the rapidly changing mix of products and consumer attitudes toward them, as well as the varying statistical techniques used to produce the estimates. Regardless of the magnitude of elasticity, however, it is nearly always estimated to be negative to a statistically significant degree, implying that the demand curve for e-cigarettes indeed is downward sloping. Hence, higher prices, caused by taxation, will lower demand.

There is little evidence as yet on the relative importance of taxation on non-initiation, quitting, and reducing use in the overall price elasticity for e-cigarettes. For cigarettes, the conventional wisdom is that about half of demand reduction from higher prices comes from the extensive margin—non-initiation and cessation—while the other half comes from the intensive margin of reduced consumption by remaining smokers.[138,139] There is scant evidence yet for what the exact split for e-cigarettes might be, but it is not unreasonable to expect that it may be similar to the experience with cigarettes. Regardless, taxes that increase prices may be expected to impact both of these margins, if indeed taxation raises prices. Available evidence indicates that this is so, if not dollar for dollar. Non-economists are sometimes surprised to learn that only under certain, rather special, conditions is a dollar unit tax on a good expected to raise the price to the consumer by an equal amount. In general, the amount of pass-through of a tax to final prices is determined by the relative elasticities of supply and demand, the degree of market power or competition, pre-existing seller margins, and other factors.[140] In the case of e-cigarette taxes, the final pass-through to consumers is also magnified because most states in the U.S. and many other countries tax wholesale prices, which are then marked up by distributors and retailers. For the U.S., a US$1 wholesale tax has been estimated to increase the retail price by $0.90 to $1.33[141,142] and a 10% increase in the tax rate increases the retail price by about 5.3%.[143,144] In summary, while the tax pass-through rate and price elasticity of demand for e-cigarettes are not known with precision, there seems to be no question that taxing e-cigarettes indeed reduces their demand.

The externalities rationale for cigarette taxes is based primarily on the ill health effects of second-hand smoke and secondarily, in some cases, on the reduced burden to the state from the improved health of those who quit or reduce smoking. Taxation to reduce negative consequences to others from a consumer's choices, "Pigouvian taxes" in the parlance of public economics, can improve economic welfare in society by bringing the private and social costs of consumption into line with each other.[145] If valid in this application—and some estimates suggest that tobacco taxes are too high to be justified by appealing to the external costs imposed by second-hand smoke[146]—the externalities argument is much weaker for e-cigarettes (refer to the discussion on second-hand vapor in Volume II, Chapter 1) and would lead to much lower tax rates.[147,148,149]

The final desired outcome from taxing e-cigarettes is the revenue generated. Raising a tax rate on a good with inelastic demand (i.e., one for which a one-percent increase in price leads to less than a one-percent decrease in quantity demanded) increases the amount of tax revenue collected. Since demand for cigarettes is nearly always estimated to be inelastic, at least at the aggregate market level, the decision to raise taxes on traditional tobacco products is an easy one for many public health experts; consumption of cigarettes will fall and the government will raise more money. In addition to other uses for the tax revenue, tobacco control experts view taxation of tobacco products as particularly effective when the proceeds are spent on tobacco control measures such as media campaigns, telephone, texting, or online quitlines, and cessation services.[150,151] Such intentions increase support among the voting public for tobacco taxes, making them easier to implement.[152] However, this notion is sometimes more of a justification to make tobacco taxes more palatable to the public than an actual reason, since (at least in the U.S.) less than 3% of the revenue collected from state tobacco taxes and other tobacco-related sources is spent on tobacco prevention and cessation programs.[153] Even setting aside the issue of how the revenue is spent, demand for e-cigarettes is often estimated to be elastic, not inelastic (refer to the range of estimates mentioned above, most of which are above 1.0 in magnitude). Furthermore, often the elasticity of demand rises as the price of the good rises. So, while inelastic demand is not a necessary condition for increased tax rates to raise more revenue,[154] at some point it may be expected (and apparently much sooner with e-cigarettes than with cigarettes, given the existing differential in elasticities) that raising tax rates on e-cigarettes may begin to reduce the total tax revenue collected.

There are several arguments raised against sin taxes in general or taxes on e-cigarettes in particular. One traditional argument against such taxes is that they are regressive and therefore unfair.[155,156] Individuals with less income spend a larger proportion of it on consumption, and thus any sales or excise tax is regressive, but this is compounded in the case of tobacco. Both smoking and vaping are most common among lower-income households,[157] making sin taxes on cigarettes and e-cigarettes doubly regressive.[158,159,160] Already by 1990, individuals earning less than US$10,000 in the U.S. paid almost twice as much in cigarette taxes as people who made more than $50,000. Given how both excise taxes and the socioeconomic gap in smoking have risen since then, this differential is much greater today. In response to the charge that tobacco taxes make the social distribution of wealth more unequal, proponents of sin taxes argue that by encouraging smokers or vapers to quit they are better off by being freed from an expensive habit, saved from their myopic choices, and granted reduced expected costs to their health. Of course, the habit is so expensive only *because* of the taxation in most places; excise taxes on cigarettes in many jurisdictions routinely double retail prices or more. Taxes on e-cigarettes in Minnesota, with the highest wholesale tax rate, have been found to increase some prices for e-liquids sold online by 65%.[161]

Another argument against sin taxes is that they are discriminatory. While for a sales tax, the burden is the same for any two households spending the same amount for retail purchases, excise taxes redistribute wealth based on how consumers choose to maximize their self-perceived welfare.[162] Thus, the principle of horizontal equity for taxation is violated. Similar to this argument is the notion of tax exploitation: shifting the tax burden onto politically disfavored minority—in this case, users of e-cigarettes.[163] As with the regressively argument, those on the opposing side of the debate rely on paternalism to argue in response that consumers are instead both objectively better-off and subjectively happier if "nudged" toward better decisions.[164]

Finally, apart from the theoretical or philosophical arguments against sin taxes, inconvenient for advocates of this argument is the observation that e-cigarette taxes do not appear to reduce use by youth. Recall that tobacco taxes, whether on traditional or novel products, are often thought to be highly effective at discouraging initiation by youth, since they have less disposable income and are more price-sensitive.[165] However, data from the U.S. that exploits variation among state policies shows that little if any case can be made that excise taxes on e-cigarettes reduce the prevalence of current use by high school students.[166,167,168,169] Even for young adults in the 18–24 age group, the evidence is currently mixed at best.[170,171,172] Two other objections to taxing e-cigarettes, namely, that they can encourage substitution toward combustible cigarettes and illicit markets for e-cigarettes, will be addressed in Section D.2.d below.

2.3.2 *Restrictions on Flavors*

Flavors are a particularly contentious issue in e-cigarette regulation. There are thousands of e-cigarette flavors available.[173] Non-tobacco flavors, including mint, menthol, fruit, spices, candy, and desserts increase the appeal of e-cigarettes for both youth experimenters and adults using e-cigarettes to quit smoking.[174] Such flavors may increase tobacco-naïve consumers' willingness to try and use e-cigarettes and also appear to decrease the public's perceptions of the risk that e-cigarettes present.[175,176] The use of flavored e-cigarettes has been associated with greater levels of perceived dependence among youth.[177] As such, e-cigarette flavors have been widely criticized for driving youth vaping.[178,179,180] Undeniably, some flavor profiles and product descriptions are intended to appeal to young people specifically. Many e-cigarette flavors intentionally mimic food and drinks that are designed for children.

Additionally, the manner in which flavors are marketed also has relevance for their appeal. Consider, for example, some of the descriptors of products available at a vape shop in southern California: One brand of e-liquid describes itself as "Golden graham cracker dunked in a glass of cold milk"; another as "Green Apple O's," "a delicious Granny Smith apple flavor that finishes with a gummy candy taste. A delectable E-Liquid treat." Critics suggest that such flavor descriptors are designed to cater to an immature palate, prompting calls for broad flavor restrictions.

Proponents of flavor bans also point to the potential harms that may result from the use of specific flavorings,[181,182] but the toxicology of flavor constituents is complex. Manufacturers typically use ingredients that are designated GRAS (Generally Recognized As Safe) for ingestion, but that designation may not mean that these substances are "safe" for inhalation,[183] not least because the chemical constituents for flavorings can interact with each other, and with the other constituents of e-liquids both before and during the aerosolization process, producing chemicals with potentially significant toxicology.[184,185,186] While it is unclear whether inhalation of flavor constituents causes end-point harm in human populations, cell culture studies have documented that flavor constituents may be harmful to a range of cells[187,188,189] especially airway epithelial cells[190,191] which serve as the first contact point between inhaled aerosol and the body. Cell studies document that contact with some chemical flavorings decreases the viability of bronchial epithelial cells contributing to apoptosis (cell death) and that exposure to some e-liquid flavorings may inhibit phagocytic clearance[192,193]—the process by which the body recognizes and removes bacteria and other foreign material. However, other studies have reported that the flavorings present in e-cigarette aerosols are insufficient to cause endothelial disfunction.[194]

Heterogeneity in the chemical constituents of different e-liquids may contribute to the conflicting reports. Different manufacturers use different flavors and in different quantities to produce ostensibly similar flavor profiles,[195] precluding clarity on which flavor profiles are more or less risky than others and how harmful, if at all, they would be. The types of chemicals present, their concentration, and the complexity of the flavor profile all contribute to potential risk profile.[196] Importantly, evidence that *some* e-cigarette chemicals might plausibly cause harm does not support conclusion that *all* such products would do so. A recent risk assessment analysis of e-cigarettes for 14 chemicals based on the EU

Chemical Labeling and Packaging (CLP) regulatory framework identified a single flavoring chemical in the tested e-liquids present at levels qualifying as toxic on the basis of the EU regulatory framework. For the remainder, “the maximum reported concentrations were 71.6 to > 99.9% lower than those needed to classify them as toxic.”[197] This is just one study of 14 chemicals, and it goes without saying that there are many other chemicals in e-cigarette flavors that went untested. It could also be argued that the EU's CLP standards need to be updated. But the study clearly demonstrates, at least, that there is a degree of heterogeneity in the toxicity of e-cigarette flavorings. That heterogeneity undermines the rationale for a broad ban. There may be a justification for banning particular flavoring constituents if they were consistently linked to evidence of harm, but unless those ingredients were necessary to produce a particular flavor profile, it is not clear why the flavor profile, and not simply the constituent ingredient should be banned. If a chemical were necessary to produce a flavor profile that still wouldn't demonstrate that other flavors, especially all non-tobacco flavors were harmful. Even if non-tobacco flavors as a group were demonstrably riskier, it is not clear that the associated risks could not be sufficiently mitigated by restricting the use of chemicals beyond a threshold, rather than banning them outright. However, that prospect raises practical objections. Establishing appropriate thresholds for thousands of possible chemical constituents and considering the possible interactions between them would be arduous in the extreme.

While some flavors and the way they are marketed doubtlessly appeal to young non-smokers, flavors also appeal to adults.[198] Indiscriminate flavor bans could reduce smoker's willingness to use e-cigarettes to quit smoking.[199,200,201] This concern is supported by the observation that adults who initiate e-cigarette use with non-tobacco flavors are more likely to quit than those who use tobacco flavored e-cigarettes.[202] Among dual users, reductions in smoking frequency also appear more likely among users of flavored e-cigarettes.[203,204,205,206] A longitudinal analysis of data from England's Smoking Toolkit Study found that flavor preferences change over time as consumers transition from experimentation to regular use,[207] suggesting that the availability of diverse flavors may contribute to e-cigarettes' efficacy as a substitute, protecting specifically against relapse. Similarly, in the U.S., e-cigarette users of all age groups appear to have transitioned away from tobacco and mint/menthol flavors toward fruit and dessert flavors.[208] A 2018 study of more than 20 thousand adult current frequent e-cigarette users in the U.S. found that between 2011 and 2016, as the U.S. e-cigarette market evolved, preferences for tobacco and mint/menthol e-cigarettes declined, while preferences for non-tobacco flavors including fruit and dessert have increased.[209] According to the research findings, the inclination toward non-tobacco flavors among e-cigarette users who never smoked, dual users, and switchers was comparable. The authors inferred that if more adults were to adopt e-cigarettes with non-tobacco flavors, it could potentially discourage former smokers from resuming their smoking habits and prevent non-smoking individuals from initiating cigarette use.

Plausibly, some flavor profiles may help facilitate substitutions among current smokers by offering an ostensibly familiar flavor profile to the tobacco products they are familiar with (tobacco and mint/menthol), while different flavor profiles may then help them prevent relapse once their tastes change. Given the public health case for moving smokers away from combustible tobacco, the preference for, and availability of, non-tobacco e-cigarette flavors would appear to contribute to that transition. Further work may help interrogate the different flavor preferences of different consumers, and how those change over time. The literature on e-cigarette flavors and their resulting utility could be improved: Controlling for smoking history would allow researchers to differentiate the different flavor preferences between smokers and non-smokers, or between adults and youth. Standardizing flavor profiles would help cross-study comparisons.[210,211] In particular, the tendency to aggregate flavors into only two groups, "tobacco flavors" and all "other flavors," creates a duality that is significantly less helpful than a distinction between discrete flavors would be. Given the heterogeneity of chemical constituents of e-cigarette flavor profiles, it is somewhat arbitrary, from a toxicological perspective, to regulate specific flavor profiles; much more so for groups of flavors.

Flavor bans have been adopted by several nation, including Finland (2016), Estonia (2019), Denmark (2020), Hungary, (2020), the Netherlands (2021, but taking effect in 2024), Ukraine (2021), Lithuania (2022), and China (2022).[212] In the U.S., the FDA banned flavored e-cigarette pods from the market in January 2020 but exempted disposables and e-liquids leaving flavors broadly available. In response, demand for exempt flavored products increased.[213] The agency has since denied PMTAs to any e-vapor product flavored with anything other than tobacco, leading to the criticism that the agency was trying to implement a de facto flavor ban.[214]

The future of e-cigarette flavors also remains contested elsewhere: In June 2021, Health Canada signaled its intention to ban almost all flavored e-cigarettes other than tobacco, mint, and menthol flavors.[215] However, subsequent Departmental Plans issued by the agency made no mention of a flavor ban and whether it is still under consideration is unknown. Regardless, under existing Canadian federal law, it is illegal to promote or label e-cigarettes with flavor profiles including confectionary, dessert, cannabis, soft drink, and energy drink flavors for e-cigarettes, or to advertise vaping products' flavors that appeal to youth.[216] As of August 2021, New Zealand prohibits the sale of e-cigarettes in flavors other than tobacco, mint, and menthol from being sold other than by specialist vape retailers, echoing a policy adopted in 2020 by the Canadian province of Ontario. In the U.S. and Canada, sub-national flavor restrictions have also been imposed. For example, in Canada, provincial e-cigarette flavor bans have been adopted by Nova Scotia (2020), Prince Edward Island (2021), New Brunswick (2021), the Northwest Territories (2022), Quebec (2023), and Nunavut (2023). In addition, non-tobacco flavors may only be sold in age-gated venues in British Columbia, Ontario and Saskatchewan. And in the U.S. non-tobacco flavors are banned in Massachusetts (2019), New Jersey (2020), New York (2020), Rhode Island (2020), and the District of Columbia (2022). In November 2022, voters in California passed Proposition 31, a referendum on SB-793 which banned the sale of flavored tobacco products, including e-cigarettes, in stores statewide. While the law did not apply to online purchases, the pre-existing Preventing All Cigarette Trafficking (PACT Act) 2021 prohibits the shipping of e-cigarettes by the U.S. Postal Service, and prevents the delivery of e-cigarettes across state lines. Consumers in California may purchase on a store's website and then collect the order from the store in-person. Utah also prevents the sale of non-tobacco flavors to age-gated specialty vape shops. In addition, Chicago, Los Angeles, San Diego, Sacramento, Oakland and San Jose, and Boulder are among hundreds of cities and counties to have flavor bans on the books.

2.3.3 *Restrictions on Nicotine Content*

For those concerned by nicotine dependence per se, capping the amount of nicotine in e-cigarettes might seem like a logical method of curbing the transition from experimental use to frequent current use, thereby contributing to a reduction in in youth vaping. However, more severe nicotine dependence has been reported among dual- and poly-users,[217] leading to fears that nicotine limits might lead to compensatory increases in smoking among dual users,[218] which would increase their risk of smoking-related harms in the short term, and might make it harder to subsequently quit smoking. On the other hand, if high nicotine potency e-cigarettes did exacerbate nicotine addiction, then even those who used e-cigarettes to successfully quit smoking might face difficulties weaning themselves off e-cigarettes, raising fears that e-cigarettes could perpetuate nicotine addiction.

The value of capping nicotine in e-cigarettes is lent weight by the evidence that jurisdictions that have enacted restrictions on the nicotine potency of regulated e-cigarettes tend to exhibit lower rates of youth use than markets in which nicotine restrictions have been yet to be enacted, or those in which restrictions have been enacted relatively recently.[219] Nicotine limits of 20 mg/ml have been adopted for e-cigarettes sold in the EU (2016), U.K. (2017), and Canada (2021). Saudi Arabia[220] and Israel[221] also cap nicotine to 20 mg/ml, and New Zealand limits the strength of free-base nicotine to that level and the strength of nicotine salt to 50 mg/ml. Notably, the restrictions are absent in the U.S. and nicotine salt solutions are widely available at 5.5% by volume—approximately two and a half times the levels in European, British, and Canadian products. A 2015 study of e-liquids in the U.S., Poland, and South Korea,[222] found that Korean e-liquid nicotine concentrations ran as high as 150.3 mg/ml (15%); almost seven times the limit in the EU, U.K., and Canada. However, while higher rates of nicotine may accelerate the transition from experimental to regular use, the ability of e-cigarettes to deliver satisfying levels of nicotine in a less risky format is precisely what makes them a popular substitute and effective cessation aid. E-cigarette usage helps decrease and eliminate smoking even if the user's nicotine dependence remains (though that too may decrease following complete substitution).[223]

According to the latest Cochrane review, the evidence on e-cigarettes efficacy for smoking cessation is more compelling for products with nicotine than without it.[224] Limiting the nicotine concentration of e-liquids, at least to a point, could make e-cigarettes less effective cessation aids, prompting fewer current smokers to quit, and perhaps nudging some who have quit using higher-strength nicotine e-cigarettes to relapse back to combustibles if the regulatory-compliant products were no longer capable of satisfying their need for nicotine. Consumer satisfaction may be subjective, but it has objective importance for public health. Current smokers who have tried e-cigarettes but continue smoking often cite a lack of satisfaction with the products as a primary reason for discontinuing use.[225] That dissatisfaction with lower nicotine strength products can lead to continued smoking supports the suggestion that limiting nicotine concentration may have harms as well as benefits. E-cigarette use and sales data from the EU,[226] the U.K.,[227] and Canada,[228] suggest that e-cigarettes remain popular, even with lower levels of nicotine. However, that less potent e-cigarettes are satisfying for some does not mean they will be satisfying for all. Different consumers also require different levels of nicotine to satisfy their cravings. Limiting the nicotine content of e-cigarettes could undermine the utility of the product category for the very people who need them most.

Another plausible, though perverse, demand-side response to nicotine limits may be an increase in the frequency with which consumers use limit-compliant products. Compensatory behavior could, logically, increase consumers' exposure to the other constituents of e-cigarette aerosols, though it is not clear whether this would be sufficient to increase health risks for such consumers. In response to Canada's nicotine limit enacted in July 2021, volume sales of some consumables (e-liquids, not devices) increased, suggesting that some consumers were compensating for the lower levels of nicotine by consuming more.[229] The logic of the nicotine limit is further challenged by the fact that nicotine content may only be a rough proxy for the amount of nicotine consumed by a user; behavioral characteristics including the type of product used, device settings, frequency of use, and puffing topography also inform the amount of nicotine absorbed by the user. Moreover, supply-side adaptations should be expected, many of which could also have health-related consequences: larger wick sizes and more powerful devices could deliver similarly satisfying levels of nicotine with less-potent e-liquids. But device power, and specifically the temperature of the heating element has been shown to inform the chemical constituents of e-cigarette aerosols with toxicological relevance.[230] Once again, it is not clear that relative to using smaller quantities of e-liquid with higher nicotine content, larger volumes with a lower nicotine content would indeed be less risky, and some evidence that it would be more so: by one estimate, carbonyl emissions increase by between 25% and 150% when the lower-concentration liquid are used.[231]

2.3.4 *Restrictions on Marketing and Advertising*

While the evidence on the efficacy of tobacco advertising bans is mixed,[232] the advertising of cigarettes on television, radio, websites, billboards, public transportation, and other outdoor venues is banned in many countries. Commensurate bans on advertising of e-cigarettes have been less commonplace. In response to rapidly increasing use, particularly among youth, robust restrictions on e-cigarette marketing have been called for. Klein et al.[233] describe e-cigarette marketing as including advertising, promotion, and sponsorship. E-cigarette marketing may be restricted at both the point-of-sale or more generally applied to online and print media, broadcast (television and radio), and outdoor advertising (billboards). The WHO's European regional office has signaled its intent to adopt a comprehensive ban on all e-cigarette advertising, promotion, and sponsorship by 2025.[234] To date, however, different national regulators have restricted different facets of e-cigarette advertising and to different degrees. The U.S. has no federal restrictions on e-cigarette advertisements,[235] whereas New Zealand permits product display and information in vape stores and e-commerce sites.[236] In Canada, the TVPA restricts the advertising and promotion of vaping products that appeal to youth.[237] Some Canadian provinces and U.S. states have enacted additional restrictions though in many cases exemptions are made for vape stores or age-gated venues selling tobacco products. Costa Rica and Ecuador do likewise.[238] Meanwhile, in the U.K. and EU, e-cigarettes are subject to the same marketing restrictions as combustible cigarettes: direct tobacco advertising on national television and radio, in local magazines and newspapers and on billboards is banned.

Somewhat unsurprisingly, exposure to e-cigarette advertisements appears to be higher in countries with fewer restrictions compared with countries that have more restrictions.[239] But, once again, there are both advantages and disadvantages to consider: On the one hand, e-cigarette marketing may stimulate experimental use by non-smokers and youth. In Canada for example, new federal legislation liberalized the marketing environment for e-cigarettes in 2018. As a result, the percent of Canadian youth (aged 16–19) exposed to e-cigarette advertising doubled from 2017 to 2019. Hammond et al.[240] report, somewhat unsurprisingly, that general exposure to marketing was more prevalent in provinces with fewer regulatory restrictions. Youth who reported noticing marketing often or very often were more likely to report vaping in the past month, the past week, and more than 20 times in the past month. (Of course, causality, if there is any, could be in the reverse direction.) The association between e-cigarette advertisements and youth use has been documented elsewhere,[241,242] and e-cigarette marketing has targeted youth specifically, and used "lifestyle themes" to do so.[243] On the other hand, e-cigarette marketing could increase awareness and uptake of e-cigarettes for the purposes of smoking cessation, or dispel misinformation that impedes the uptake of e-cigarettes by smokers.[244] According to one U.S. study,[245] television e-cigarette advertisements are associated with increased smoking cessation, mostly due to more successful (as opposed to more frequent) quit attempts. Another U.S. study reports that, among young adult cigarette smokers aged 18–34, exposure to e-cigarette advertising was positively associated with both subsequent e-cigarette use, and e-cigarette use specifically for the purposes of quitting.[246]

Under their designation as consumer tobacco products, e-cigarette manufacturers are often explicitly prohibited from making therapeutic claims about their products. That helps protect against fraudulent claims, but it also prevents manufacturers from making truthful claims which the public in general, and smokers in particular, would benefit from exposure to. It could be argued that if e-cigarette manufacturers wanted to make evidence-based claims about the therapeutic value of their products, they could do so by applying to have their products authorized as medical devices by their respective regulators. That remains technically an option in many countries, including the U.S.,[247] and Australia,[248] and the U.K.[249] However, the regulatory burdens are significant, and to date, no commercially available e-cigarette has gained medical approval. But whether switch messages have value in public health terms, and whether it is possible, or commercially viable for manufacturers to gain medical authorization for their products are different questions. Predicating the legality of substitution marketing themes on the larger issue of medical authorization leads to the somewhat perverse conclusion that by nature of a restriction intending to prevent manufacturers from making false claims, they are unable to make claims that may be true either.

2.3.5 *Minimum Legal Sale Age Laws*

Evidence suggests that smoking is almost always initiated before the age of 21, and often before the age of 18.[250] Those who initiate smoking in adolescence tend to smoke more frequently, for longer and experience greater difficulty quitting.[251,252,253,254] Minimum legal sale age (MLSA) laws are generally considered to have been effective at reducing youth smoking, enforcement issues withstanding.[255] If patterns of e-cigarette use are similar, age restrictions could help prevent the uptake of e-cigarette use before it becomes established.[256,257,258,259] Dave et al. explain that it is anticipated that prohibiting the legal sale of e-cigarettes to children will raise the cost of getting the product indirectly. Additional markups may be applied by those buying e-cigarettes for younger friends, thus the limitation may further impede social distribution.[260]

As of 2022, 57 countries have national age restrictions for e-cigarettes, with several enabling subnational authorities to impose local regulations.[261] In the U.K., like cigarettes, e-cigarettes may not be sold to anyone below the age of 18. In the U.S., the minimum legal sale age of e-cigarettes is 21. In most other countries (including Canada and the EU), the minimum legal sale age for e-cigarette purchases is 18, though in Jordan, South Korea, and Turkey it is 19 and it is 21 years in Kuwait, Niue, Honduras, the Philippines, and Palau.[262]

Few serious commentators, including manufacturers, argue that children should have access to e-cigarettes. As such, the question is not whether such restrictions are appropriate but at what age should they be set. The suggestion that nicotine could harm developing brains[263] supports the case for higher-age restrictions: Human brains continue developing until the mid-20s so if nicotine is harmful to brain development, it may be appropriate to set the MLSA higher than 18. Because those in their final year of secondary school are often 18 years of age before graduating, setting a legal sale age limit at 18 often means that legally purchased e-cigarettes can end up in the hands of minors.[264] This provides further rationale for an age restriction that prevents people of school-aged from obtaining e-cigarettes. However, there are moral objections to limiting e-cigarettes to adults aged 21 and older based on the view that the restriction violates the liberty of 18 to 20 year-olds who are, in the U.S., have reached the legal age of majority. According to this argument, those who are viewed as adults under the law should not be restricted from accessing legal products that are available to other adults. Those objections have been refuted[265] but there are, perhaps, more compelling arguments for allowing 18–20 years-olds access to e-cigarettes. Despite the widely adopted, if imperfectly enforced, age restrictions, some minors and younger adults (18–20) still smoke. Setting the age limit for e-cigarettes lower than the limit for more harmful combustibles could prevent the uptake of smoking by some of those in this age range. By presenting 18 to 20 year-olds with a less risky alternative, MLSAs set lower for e-cigarettes than combustibles might persuade young people who are tempted to experiment to do so with a safer product, or provide an incentive for those who already do to switch to a safer alternative.[266]

2.3.6 Public-Use Bans

Smoke-free laws originated with a desire to protect the health of bystanders, but by de-normalizing smoking and making smoking less convenient, smoke-free laws may also encourage cessation. Concerns that e-cigarette aerosol could harm bystanders and that public displays of vaping could renormalize smoking[267] have prompted calls for e-cigarettes to be included in smoke-free legislation. The WHO's Seventh Conference of the Parties (COP7) recommended prohibiting the use of e-cigarettes where combustible cigarette smoking is banned,[268] as has the European Network for Smoking and Tobacco Prevention.[269] This intervention has been widely adopted: By 2017, vaping was banned in enclosed public spaces such as bars restaurants and workplaces in at least 25 countries,[270] and according to the *Global Tobacco Control* policy scan, 53 countries[271] now prohibit or restrict the use of e-cigarettes in public places. In addition, as of March 2021, 23 U.S. states[272] and hundreds of U.S. municipalities have also banned vaping in smoke-free areas.[273]

However, unlike combustible tobacco smoke, it is not clear that e-cigarette aerosol poses a significant risk of harm to bystanders (Volume II, Chapter 1 explored the evidence on this topic). Given that harm to bystanders was the central justification of smoke-free laws, if e-cigarettes pose little or perhaps just less harm to bystanders than is posed by cigarette smoke, then the inclusion of vaping in smoke-free laws lacks the same basis as smoke-free laws. Second, if vaping were excluded from the smoke-free laws, the performance of an alternative behavior might contribute to the denormalization of smoking.[274] If restrictions on public vaping were somehow less stringent than those applied to smoking, those who are impacted by the ban might be tempted to switch to vaping instead. Conversely, if vaping were treated, falsely, as though it were of commensurate risk, as would be implied by the inclusion of e-cigarettes in smoke-free laws, that might dissuade some smokers from trying e-cigarettes which could reduce their subsequent chances of quitting. Placing e-cigarette users in proximity to smokers would also expose e-cigarette users to second-hand smoke and could tempt them to relapse.

2.3.7 Other Restrictions

Taxes, flavor restrictions, nicotine caps, marketing restrictions, MLSA limits, and vape-free laws are the mainstays of e-cigarette regulation, but there are other components of the regulatory environment. According to the *Global Tobacco Control* policy scan, forty-two nations require pre-marketing notification and additional reporting requirements, such as annual reporting on e-cigarette sales. The use of sales discounts as a marketing strategy has also been banned in many places including the U.S.[275] and the EU.[276] Many jurisdictions, including the U.S.,[277] ban distributions of free samples, a widely used marketing ploy in the early days of both cigarettes and e-cigarettes. In addition, vending machine sales are banned in several countries including Belgium, the U.K., France, Finland, Norway, Hungary, and the Netherlands.[278] Many countries including the U.S., U.K., EU, and Canada require e-cigarettes to carry health warning labels. The precise wording differs among jurisdictions, but warning labels typically advise the consumer that the contents contain nicotine and that nicotine is addictive. Product restrictions also limit the quantity of e-liquid that may be sold in a single unit. For example, in the EU, the TPD capped e-cigarette pods at 2 ml and containers at 10 ml. Many countries also require childproof packaging; the EU again serves as an example, requiring e-cigarettes to only be sold in child-resistant and tamper-proof containers, protected against breakage and leakage and have a mechanism that ensures filling without leakage.[279] Additives, other than nicotine and flavoring also receive regulatory scrutiny. Canada bans amino acids, caffeine, coloring agents, essential fatty acids, glucuronolactone, probiotics, taurine, vitamins, and mineral nutrients,[280] while the EU TPD, prohibits additives (including vitamins, coloring, caffeine, taurine, and other stimulants) and further requires that ingredients (other than nicotine) not pose a risk to human health in heated or unheated form.[281] Likewise, Canada and the Philippines, prohibit the use of ingredients, other than nicotine, which pose a risk to human health, and France and Iceland prohibit additives that facilitate inhalation; including substances that have local anesthetic effects that might permit the user to inhale more deeply.[282] Some jurisdictions, including some U.S. states (Arkansas, Georgia, Maine, New York, Oregon, South Dakota, and Vermont) restrict online e-cigarette purchases, ostensibly to facilitate age-gating of sales. California takes a different approach, banning in-person purchases of flavored e-cigarettes as of December 2022. Under the PACT Act, U.S. federal law also prohibits interstate shipments of nicotine e-cigarettes and mailing e-cigarettes via the USPS. Finally, local ordinances, zoning laws, and licensing requirements can also serve to limit where e-cigarettes can be sold.

3 Evaluating E-cigarette Regulation

3.1 *Efficacy*

If the goal of e-cigarette regulation is to reduce demand for e-cigarettes, then there is good evidence that many of the policies described above do aid that endeavor. Whether that should be the goal is a different question.

3.1.1 *Do Taxes Reduce E-cigarette Use?*

Corroborating the economic theory underpinning their status as economic substitutes for combustible tobacco, e-cigarette taxes have been found to reduce demand for e-cigarettes. In the U.S., between 2010 and the middle of 2019, ten U.S. states and two large counties adopted e-cigarette taxes. Abouk and colleagues[283] examined data from the Monitoring the Future and Youth Risk Behavior Surveillance System surveys to explore the impact of ENDS taxes on youth tobacco use. They report that e-cigarette taxes reduce youth ENDS consumption: “a $1.00 increase in the standardized tax, (about twice the observed standard deviation in the tax), reduces the likelihood of currently using ENDS by 1.9 percentage points. Frequent and adolescent users appear to be especially susceptible to reducing e-cigarette use in response to taxation.” The authors estimated ENDS tax elasticities of −0.06 to −0.21.

Other studies concur, although the magnitude of the response varies between studies and across populations. Cotti et al.[284] use scanner data collected at the point of sale for e-cigarette transactions between 2013 and 2019 to show that a US$1.00 increase in e-cigarette taxes reduces e-cigarette sales by 919 fluid ml and increases cigarette sales by 4,863 packs for every 100,000 adult residents. Using data from 2011 to 2018 taken from the Behavioral Risk Factor Surveillance Survey and the National Health Interview Survey, Pesko et al.[285] also find that adult e-cigarette users respond to e-cigarette taxes by reducing consumption: “A $1.00 increase in tax per fluid ml of vaping liquid reduces the probability of current vaping by 0.5 ppts ($p < 0.10$) or 15.3%; [reduces] the probability of daily vaping by 0.2 ppts ($p > 0.10$) or 14.2%; [and reduces] the probability of dual use by 0.4 ppts ($p < 0.10$), or 24.4%.” Friedman and

Pesko[286] also report that ENDS taxes yield "statistically significant reductions in daily ENDS use and ... marginally non-significant reductions in recent ENDS use ($P = 0.07$)." Pesko and Warman[287] use quasi-experimental methods to compare variations in price and taxes with survey data reporting current use of e-cigarettes and cigarettes. Data are obtained for over 94,000 students in grades 6 through 12 from the National Youth Tobacco Survey (NYTS) collected between 2011 and 2015. The authors find that a $1 increase in e-cigarette cartridge prices prompts school students to smoke on average 4.6 extra cigarettes per month. Unsurprisingly, the effect is concentrated among established smokers, who consume an additional 3 packs.

E-cigarette taxes may have other important effects. Abouk et al.[288] report that such taxes increase news coverage regarding e-cigarettes and increase public perceptions that e-cigarettes are risky, both of which could reduce e-cigarette use as a second-order effect.

3.1.2 Do Flavor Restrictions Reduce E-cigarette Use?

There is also evidence that flavor bans reduce the demand for e-cigarettes, in line with the evidence that the use of flavors is associated with greater duration and frequency of e-cigarette use.[289] However, the impact on the prevalence of use appears to be relatively small. Yang et al.[290] used a convenience sample of 247 San Francisco residents surveyed both before and after the city enacted a comprehensive flavor ban, finding that "the prevalence of flavored e-cigarettes decreased from 57% and 56% to 45% and 48% for 18–24 years and 25–34 years old, respectively." Romm et al.'s 2022 mixed-methods analysis of U.S. young adult e-cigarette users' responses to flavored e-cigarette sales restrictions[291] found that the enacted restrictions prompted fewer than one in ten (8.4%) of respondents to decrease use. Exploring the effects of flavor restrictions adopted in Massachusetts, Rhode Island, New York, and Washington D.C., Ali et al.'s[292] difference-in-differences analysis of e-cigarette retail data reports that flavor restrictions were associated with reductions of between 25% and 31% in total e-cigarette unit sales compared with total sales in states without restrictions. However, the authors note compensatory increases in tobacco-flavored e-cigarettes and admit that the study ignores online and vape-shop sales, which disregard the law and continue to sell flavored products. It should also be noted that reductions of jurisdiction-specific flavored e-cigarette sales in response to flavor restrictions do not necessarily equate to reductions in consumption. As research by the Tax Foundation shows, cross-border trade can significantly offset any intra-jurisdictional demand reduction prompted by a state flavor ban. For example, following Massachusetts' comprehensive flavor ban in 2020, year-on-year cigarette sales declined by 24% statewide, but surrounding states saw sales increase and the New England region as a whole only declined by about 1%—in line with the national average.[293]

3.1.3 Do Nicotine Limits Reduce E-cigarette Use?

There is surprisingly little data on consumer's ex-post responses to the adopted nicotine limits for e-cigarettes and e-liquids. As previously noted, the sales and consumption data for states where nicotine bans have been enacted suggests that e-cigarettes remain popular even in the presence of such restrictions. Of course, that popularity is not incompatible with the notion that there will be some users who find lower-strength nicotine to be dissatisfying and therefore continue smoking. In the short term, point-of-sales data, such as provided by Nielsen, might help researchers conduct trends analyses. If the introduction of the limit followed a sizable shift in demand, that may be attributed to the limit (though of course other factors would need to be controlled for). There are, however, several problems with this strategy: first, the scanner data for e-cigarettes does not capture specialist vape stores and e-commerce sales, both of which are a significant portion of the national market. A drop in sales from grocery and convenience stores may not, therefore, be indicative of a reduction in *use*, only a shift toward other sources not captured by the data. Another factor limiting the use of sales data to interrogate the consequences of nicotine limits is that compensatory behavior may confound any reduction in demand caused by unsatisfied consumers abandoning the product category and returning to cigarettes. More comprehensive sales data, perhaps used in combination with consumer survey data may be able to help researchers understand consumer responses to nicotine limits.

3.1.4 Do Marketing Restrictions Reduce E-cigarette Use?

Exposure to e-cigarette advertisements appears to increase vaping, although there is no strong causal evidence yet in the literature. Ali et al.,[294] for example, report that "Exposure to one additional e-cigarette advertisement on TV was associated with a 0.18, 0.13 and 0.03 percentage point increase, respectively, in awareness, ever use and current use of e-cigarettes among all adults ($P < 0.05$)." Camenga et al.[295] used a longitudinal cohort analysis of U.S. adolescents to examine whether exposure to advertisements in social networking sites (Facebook, Twitter, YouTube, Pinterest/Google Plus), traditional media (television/radio, magazines, billboards), or retail stores (convenience stores, mall kiosks, tobacco shops) was associated with additional e-cigarette use between baseline (fall 2013) and follow-up (spring 2014). The authors report that exposure to Facebook advertising was strongly associated with the uptake of e-cigarette use, however only a small portion of the study population reported exposure to such marketing, and the evidence for other marketing strategies affecting e-cigarette uptake was less compelling.

There is additional evidence that e-cigarette marketing makes young people perceive e-cigarettes more favorably. Duke et al.[296] report that 13 to 17 year-old never-e-cigarette-users who were exposed to televised e-cigarette advertisements were more likely to perceive e-cigarettes as "cooler, more fun, healthier, and more enjoyable. Youth who thought the ads were more effective were more likely to have a positive attitude toward e-cigarettes and greater intention to try e-cigarettes in the future." A randomized controlled trial by Farrelly et al.[297] found that 13 to 17 year-old never-e-cigarette-users randomized to a treatment group exposed to 4 e-cigarette TV commercials were significantly more likely to try an e-cigarette soon (1.54, $p = 0.001$). Those in the treatment group were also more likely to agree that e-cigarettes could be used in contexts where smoking is banned (1.71, $p < 0.001$); could be used without affecting bystanders (OR = 1.83, $p < 0.001$); are a safer alternative to cigarettes (OR = 1.19, $p = 0.01$). Similar findings have been reported by Villanti et al.,[298] this time measuring the impact of brief exposure to four e-cigarette print advertisements on perceptions, intention, and subsequent use of e-cigarettes, and cigarettes in U.S. young adults: Never-e-cigarette-users randomized to advertising exposure exhibited greater curiosity to try an e-cigarette (AOR = 1.63, 95% CI = 1.18, 2.26) and greater likelihood of e-cigarette actually trying them (AOR = 2.85; 95% CI = 1.07, 7.61).

There is also evidence that the adoption of marketing restrictions is associated with decreased e-cigarette use. Exploring the effects of federal and provincial regulation on e-cigarette use among Canadian youth, Hammond et al.[299] found that while e-cigarette consumption increased over the study time frame (2017–2019), rates of youth e-cigarette use were lower in provinces with comprehensive marketing restrictions. The authors note that their findings are in line with both experimental[300,301] and prospective cohort studies,[302,303] suggesting a causal effect of e-cigarette advertising on youth and young-adult e-cigarette use.

3.1.5 Do Minimum Legal Sale Age Restrictions Reduce E-cigarette Use?

There is also evidence that the adoption of minimum legal sale age restrictions discourage demand for e-cigarettes among youth.[304] However, the increases in youth-vaping during much of the period in which e-cigarettes have been available—even during which MLSAs have been in effect—suggest that enforcement remains a challenge, and that social sources may provide a means of bypassing them. It may also be difficult to disentangle the causal effect of MLSAs from other contemporaneously enacted policies. Abouk and Adams[305] report suggestive evidence that the adoption of retail sales bans to minors in the U.S. decreased e-cigarette use among 12th graders, but not 8th or 10th graders. In Canada, Nguyen[306] reports that provincial age restrictions slowed, but did not reverse, the increase in youth e-cigarette use relative to provinces without restrictions. Provincial MLSAs were also associated with greater risk perception among youths in provinces with a ban on e-cigarette sales to minors. Those subject to age restrictions, not surprisingly, had greater difficulty obtaining e-cigarettes, though social distribution, again, challenged the efficacy of the age-restrictions adopted. Perhaps, with improved enforcement, minors' access to e-cigarettes could be more effectively restricted without sacrificing adult smoking cessation.

3.1.6 Do Public-Use Restrictions Reduce E-cigarette Use?

In its 2018 report, the U.S. National Academy of Science Engineering and Medicine calls for e-cigarettes to be included in smoke-free laws. The report argues that extending smoke-free laws to e-cigarettes would protect against the introduction of airborne toxicants into enclosed public spaces. Among the advantages noted by the report, banning e-cigarette use in enclosed spaces would help protect non-users, simplify implementation and enforcement, discourage e-cigarette use, and protect, norms against smoking in public.

The evidence on whether such restrictions have reduced e-cigarette use is mixed. Reporting on BRFSS data from the 2016–2017 survey, Du et al.[307] observe lower odds ratios for current e-cigarette use among adults living in states prohibiting the use of e-cigarettes in indoor workplaces, restaurants, and bars (0.90; 95% CI, 0.83–0.98). The authors adjust for demographic, socioeconomic, and lifestyle factors, including conventional cigarette use. Examining the effect of the implementation of state-level "e-cigarette-inclusive smoke-free (ESF) policies" on youth e-cigarette use using the Youth Risk Behavior Survey (YRBS) surveys (2017 and 2019), Choi et al.[308] report that the prevalence of ever and past 30-day youth e-cigarette use decreased during 2017–2019 in ESF states and increased in states without such measures. However, among frequent users the presence of ESF policies was not sufficient to reduce e-cigarette use, though the increase in frequent use did slow in states combining ESF and tobacco 21 restrictions. According to Azagba et al.,[309] respondents to the Tobacco Use Supplement to the Current Population Survey (2018) living in households with vaping restrictions were less likely to use e-cigarettes. Those subject to workplace restrictions also exhibited lower environmental exposure to e-cigarette aerosol. However, while smoke-free workplace laws have been associated with lower levels of smoking,[310] work-place restrictions on e-cigarette use were not associated with reduced prevalence of vaping in this study.[311]

Not all studies on this topic have found that state-level public-use restrictions succeed in reducing e-cigarette use, at least for all groups. In a stratified analysis of data from the 2016 Behavioral Risk Factor Surveillance System, Lee et al.[312] report an association between state aerosol-free policies and lower odds of e-cigarette use only in adults aged 25–59, and not among younger adults (aged 18–24). A longitudinal retrospective study by Yang et al.[313] implementing a quasi-experimental design used a nationally representative sample of Population Assessment of Tobacco and Health (PATH) (2013–2018) to examine the association between the implementation of statewide aerosol-free policies and e-cigarette-use behaviors. The authors compared the three measures of e-cigarette use: past 30-day e-cigarette abstinence, number of use days, and past-12-month-use frequency, before and after the implementation of restrictions. Their results not only indicate that e-cigarette-use behaviors were not significantly different between states with public-use restrictions and those without, but also that, in states where public-use restrictions were adopted, there were not significantly significant changes in consumption following implementation.

3.2 *Opportunity Costs and Unintended Consequences*

3.2.1 *Heterogeneous Responses*

The restrictions discussed are all well-intended to reduce the harms that might follow from e-cigarette use, especially by non-smoking people, youth in particular. Some of these policies evidently do decrease the demand of e-cigarettes. Where there is less evidence for that effect, advocates of such restrictions may still point to the value of risk-communication, which might lead to secondary effects on behavior such as reduced odds of subsequent uptake. Those ultimate effects may be temporally removed and not readily visible in the national or regional prevalence data. The contemporaneous adoption of other restrictions makes it difficult to disentangle the causal effects of one policy from another. So, the absence of evidence certainly does not demonstrate that such policies are ineffective at reducing youth vaping.

However, to the extent that these policies do, or will yet, reduce youth vaping, that comes at a cost. Both economic theory and consumer testimony[314,315,316,317] suggest that consumer responses to e-cigarette restrictions will be mixed: Reductions in demand are one response to e-cigarette restrictions but that does not necessarily equate to a reduction in nicotine product use as might be hoped. Demand is often taken as a proxy for consumption, but in the context of e-cigarettes, the cross-elasticity of demand between combustible tobacco and non-combustible alternatives[318] suggests that any gains realized via reduced demand for e-cigarettes will increase demand for substitutes. In other words, while e-cigarette restrictions may suppress vaping in the population, they may also increase smoking.

Consumer testimony provides the first clue that e-cigarette users might switch, or switch back, to combustibles in response to e-cigarette restrictions. Most surveys inquiring about consumers' responses to prospective or hypothetical bans have taken place in the U.S., and the literature focuses in particular on flavors, which is perhaps unsurprising given the FDA's emphasis on that topic. Buckell et al.'s 2018 discrete choice experiment,[319] which surveyed 2,031 adult smokers and recent quitters, reports that a comprehensive flavor ban affecting both e-cigarettes and cigarettes would decrease the demand for e-cigarettes by almost 8% but increase the demand for cigarettes by 2.7%.

A similar study by Freitas-Lemos and colleagues[320] explored the hypothetical purchasing patterns of exclusive cigarette smokers, exclusive e-cigarette users, and frequent dual users in an experimental tobacco marketplace under three conditions: no ban, vaping ban, and flavored vaping ban. All groups exhibited a tendency to respond to restrictions by purchasing from the illicit market, but e-cigarette users were especially likely to choose the illicit option and were more resistant to financial penalties for doing so.

Gravely et al.[321] also report that a significant portion of adult e-cigarette users in the U.S., Canada, and the U.K. would respond to a hypothetical flavor restriction by flouting the restriction: 28.3% of those surveyed reported that they would "find a way to get their banned flavor(s)" and 28.8% said would continue vaping an available flavor. Alarmingly, 17.1% reported that they would stop vaping and smoke instead, and only 12.9% said that they would stop vaping and not smoke. Posner et al.[322] also report that significant proportions of e-cigarette users would respond to flavor limits and sales bans by switching to combustible cigarettes: approximately one in three would switch to cigarettes if e-cigarettes were restricted to tobacco flavors and approximately 39% would do so in response to a complete vape product sales restriction.

Pacek et al.'s[323] survey of 240 young adult users of both e-cigarettes and combustible cigarettes reports that, in response to restrictions on e-cigarette nicotine content, marketing, devices and flavors, dual users were especially likely to quit or reduce e-cigarette use and increase or maintain smoking.

Consumer testimony may not be 100% reliable, not least because consumers' intended responses may only be a rough indication of what their actual responses will be. This is particularly relevant regarding those who suggest their response will include a quitting attempt. *Ex ante*, the suggestion that any e-cigarette users would quit entirely might be an encouraging response for those concerned by the possible harms that vaping may lead to. But the data on smoking cessation suggests that the overwhelming majority of quit attempts ends in failure (see Volume I, Chapter 2). For those who do not quit, or do not try, other options are available: regulation-compliant e-cigarettes, perhaps in conjunction with after-market modifications, illicit e-vapor products, other alternative nicotine products (if available) and combustibles. The degree to which these different responses are net harmful, beneficial, or neutral to public health deserves consideration. That such unintended consequences occur is not mere theory, but is supported by empirical studies. The next sections review the evidence.

3.2.2 *Unintended Consequences of E-cigarette Restrictions: Increased Smoking*

Of all these unintended responses, increased smoking is perhaps the most harmful from a public health perspective. This has been observed in response to taxes,[324,325,326,327] flavor bans,[328,329,330] and minimum legal sale age restrictions.[331,332,333]

Increased Smoking in Response to E-cigarette Taxes

While the taxation of e-cigarettes reduces e-cigarette use among youth, it should be of great concern that cross-tax effects working to increase smoking have also been observed. Abouk and colleagues'[334] 2022 analysis of data from large national U.S. surveys, (including the Monitoring the Future and the Youth Risk Behavior Surveillance System) collected between 2010 and mid-2019, reported that "about 2%" of adolescents are changing their e-cigarette use in response to taxation, but more than two-thirds of the effected group (68%) also switched to cigarettes. Similar responses are evident in the YRBSS data: Almost one in four (23%) of teens who respond to higher e-cigarette taxes with reduced vaping, are substituting toward regular cigarette use.

These are not isolated findings. Cotti et al.[335] use point-of-sale data to interrogate the relationship between e-vapor sales and combustible cigarette sales. They report that "a $1.00 increase in e-cigarette taxes, per 100,000 adult residents, is anticipated to increase cigarette sales by 4863 packs." Using an estimated substitution rate between e-cigarette pods and cigarette packs, the authors suggest that for every one e-cigarette pod eliminated due to an e-cigarette tax, approximately 1.9 packs of cigarettes are sold instead. It should be noted that it is not clear from this analysis which groups would consume the additional cigarettes: Increases in cigarette consumption among dual users already smoking might have less public health harm than if the additional cigarette consumption in response to a ban were found among those who were previously only used e-cigarettes. Pesko et al.[336] report that a federal tax of $1.65 per milliliter of vaping liquid would increase the adult smoking prevalence by approximately 1 percentage point, adding roughly 2.5 million extra adult daily smokers compared with the counterfactual. Similarly, Saffer et al.[337] investigate the effects of Minnesota's 2010 e-cigarette tax of 35% (subsequently raised to 95% in 2013) and find that, in the decade following implementation, 32,400 adult smokers did not quit who would have done so in the absence of the tax. The authors use the state-level estimates to project that, an equivalent tax implemented on a federal basis would deter about 1.8 million smokers from quitting over a ten-year period. If that hypothetical e-cigarette tax were brought in line with combustible cigarette taxes, as many as 2.75 million smokers would be deterred from quitting.

Much of the literature investigating the perverse response to e-cigarette taxes focuses on youth. For example, Pesko and Warman[338] examine contemporaneous and intertemporal effects of e-cigarette and cigarette price and tax changes by comparing Nielsen Retail Scanner data with survey data on current use of e-cigarettes and cigarettes among school students grades 6 to 12 taken from the National Youth Tobacco Survey (NYTS) for years 2011 to 2015. The authors suggest that, among teenagers, raising the price of e-cigarette cartridges by $1 increases subsequent cigarette use by 2.9 pp. Friedman and Pesko[339] report a similar effect among young adults. Using an observational study of data from the Current Population Survey's 2010–2019 Tobacco Use Supplements, the authors find that a $1 increase in e-cigarette taxes led to both significant reductions in young adults' daily vaping[340] and increases in recent smoking.[341] The noted increase largely reflects greater dual use.[342]

Alongside youth and young adults, e-cigarette taxes have also been found to increase pre-pregnancy and prenatal smoking. Abouk et al.[343] examined the effect of e-cigarette taxes (the mean of which was valued at US$1.13) on pre-pregnancy and prenatal smoking among mothers conceiving between 2013 and 2019. Using fixed effects regressions, the authors demonstrated that a $1.00 increase in e-cigarette tax leads to a 1.8 pp reduction in pre-pregnancy e-cigarette use, but increases pre-pregnancy smoking by 0.5 ppts and prenatal smoking by 0.4 ppts.

As discussed earlier, the majority of U.S. states have adopted an ENDS tax.[344] Such taxes could potentially prove net-harmful to public health if reducing e-cigarette use is accompanied by increases in combustible tobacco use. Indeed, given that current research on the relative risk-gap between combustible tobacco and e-cigarettes, even small increases in smoking may be sufficient outweigh the advantages associated with the reduction in vaping. The harm from these taxes is also compounded if the additional smokers they create are also less likely to use e-cigarettes in the future to quit smoking. Abouk et al.[345] found that taxes on e-cigarettes negatively affected youth's perceptions of the health risks from using e-cigarettes.

Increased Smoking in Response to Flavor Restrictions

E-cigarette taxes are not the only restriction that leads to increased smoking. The literature also reports that flavor restrictions and bans have a similar effect. The 2019 U.S. flavor ban (applied to pod systems) prompted, according to one study, 14% of adult e-cigarette users to return to smoking.[346] Abigail Friedman's difference-in-differences analysis[347] of students in San Francisco reports that the ban was associated with more than twice the odds of recent smoking among underage high school students relative to other districts.[348] Friedman's conclusions are in accordance with Yang et al.'s survey[349] of adult tobacco product users in response to the San Francisco ban, which reports low levels of compliance (65% of e-cigarette flavor users continued to use flavored products after the ban) and increased smoking in the 18–24 age group, along with, predictably, increased use of ban-compliant e-cigarettes. These results have been challenged[350] on the basis that the timeline for YRBSS data collection was inappropriate to accurately measure responses to the intervention and that in neighboring Oakland, a similar ban preempted both lower vaping *without* increased smoking rates among youth. Regardless, other research has documented evidence for similar responses to flavor restrictions. Posner et al.'s survey of young adult (18–34) e-cigarette users in Atlanta, Boston, Minneapolis, Oklahoma City, San Diego, and Seattle[351] reports that if restricted to tobacco flavors, 33.2% would likely smoke instead. This figure would go up to about 39% in response to complete vape product sales restrictions. Xu and colleagues[352] used difference-in-differences and generalized synthetic control methods to estimate the impacts of emergency e-cigarette bans and flavor restrictions on cigarette sales by comparing treatment locales (Massachusetts, Washington, and Rhode Island) with control states. The authors find that the full ban on e-cigarettes in Massachusetts was associated with an increase in overall cigarette sales of between 3.4% and 8.8%. The flavor bans in Washington and Rhode Island resulted in increases in cigarette sales of between 3.6% and 8.7%, and 0.9% and 5.7%, respectively. The rise in cigarette sales in Massachusetts in response to the EVALI-prompted ban has also been noted by Liber et al.[353] and by Katchmar et al.,[354] who note e-cigarette taxes did not significantly reduce e-cigarette purchases. Instead, in response to the ban, consumers sourced e-cigarettes from out of state.

Increased Smoking in Response to Minimum Legal Sale Age Restrictions

Minimum legal sale age restrictions for e-cigarettes have also been documented to increase smoking among youth. Dave et al.[355] use difference-in-differences models and individual-level data from the national and state Youth Risk Behavior Surveillance System from 2005 to 2015 to investigate the effect of MLSA laws in the U.S. The authors report that a 30% decrease in youth e-cigarette use resulting from MLSAs comes at the expense of a 7% relative increase in youth smoking and an 18% relative increase in regular or heavy cigarettes smoking by youth.[356] Again, this is not an isolated report. Friedman's 2015 regression analysis[357] examines the causal impact of e-cigarette access on conventional cigarette use by adolescents (12 to 17 year-olds) and reports that MLSAs yield a 0.9 percentage point increase in recent smoking in this age group, relative to states without such bans. The effect is statistically significant and large: counteracting 70% of the downward pre-trend in youth-smoking for a given two-year period. These results are in accord with Pesko et al.'s 2016 study[358] of data from the Youth Risk Behavior Surveillance System (2007–2013), which finds causal evidence that ENDS age purchasing restrictions increased adolescent regular cigarette use by 0.8 percentage points.

As Abouk et al.[359] found with taxation, Pesko and Currie[360] found that the unintended increase in smoking in response to MLSA could increase smoking prior to and during pregnancies. Reviewing birth data from 2010 to 2016 in 32 states, the authors find that MLSAs were associated with a 0.6 pp increase in prenatal smoking in a given trimester. The impact of ENDS MLSAs appeared to affect pre-pregnancy smokers more significantly than non-smokers, indicating that the laws did not have a substantial influence on those who did not smoke prior to pregnancy. This suggests that the rise in prenatal smoking rates associated with ENDS MLSAs may be due to a decrease in quitting cigarette smoking rather than an increase in starting smoking.

Not all studies have reported that greater smoking follows MLSAs. Abouk and Adams,[361] for example, found contemporaneous decreases in youth vaping and youth smoking following the enactment of MLSAs among 8th, 10th, and 12th graders in their analysis of Monitoring the Future surveys from 2007 to 2014. It is possible that methodological differences, specifically Abouk and Adams' narrower focus on specific age groups, may explain why their finding differs from others.

The notion that young people barred from their first-order preference would increase their use of previously restricted products of second-order preference may be counter-intuitive. A possible explanation lies not only in the economic literature confirming that the two products are substitutes, but in the observation that, while technically restricted to over 21s, combustible tobacco may be more readily available to youth than age-gated e-cigarettes due to differences in social distribution for each product.[362]

Increased Smoking in Response to E-cigarette Marketing Restrictions

Marketing restrictions on e-cigarettes may also increase smoking harms by inadvertently inhibiting substitutions.[363] While, as discussed, e-cigarette marketing can increase young consumers' willingness to try e-cigarettes, marketing may also serve as a public health tool, informing smokers about the existence of an alternative behavior. Tuchman's[364] model of demand for cigarettes suggests that e-cigarette marketing stimulates demand for e-cigarettes and reduces demand for combustibles. Tuchman concludes that the demand for traditional cigarettes could rise in the absence of e-cigarette promotion, indicating that a ban on e-cigarette advertising would have unforeseen consequences. The suggestion that e-cigarette marketing encourages smoking cessation is corroborated by Dave et al.,[365] who provide evidence confirming that e-cigarette advertising encourages adult smokers to quit. The authors' results suggest that a ban on television advertising of e-cigarettes would have deterred approximately 3% of those who quit smoking in the recent past from doing so. Absenting regulatory and public scrutiny, e-cigarette advertisements on U.S. televisions might have reached parity with TV advertising of NRTs. The authors suggest that, had that occurred, the proportion of recent quitters could have increased by roughly 10%.[366]

E-cigarette marketing could also have second-order effects, informing public perceptions of e-cigarettes both regarding their harms and their benefits. Majeed et al.[367] report that relative to 2012 the odds of U.S. adults believing that e-cigarettes were equally or more harmful than combustible cigarettes doubled in 2014,[368] and tripled in 2015.[369] To what extent that regrettable shift could be resolved by appropriately themed e-cigarette marketing remains to be seen. Still, this evidence shows that e-cigarette restrictions which succeed in reducing e-cigarette use may have the unintended consequence of simultaneously increasing smoking. For similar reasons, public health campaigns designed to prevent youth e-cigarette use may also discourage substitutions, reducing smoking cessation among adults.[370,371]

If demand for e-cigarettes falls as a result of a policy, but smoking increases because those who have recently quit return to combustibles; never-smoking e-cigarette users find themselves unable to access their preferred product; new-comers to nicotine initiate with combustible cigarettes instead of e-cigarettes; or the pace at which adult smokers switch to e-cigarettes and stop or reduce smoking slows, any public health gains realized by the reduction in demand for e-cigarettes will be undermined by harms associated with those responses. Considering that e-cigarettes are unlikely to represent more than 5% of the risk of cigarette smoking,[372] it could take only a small fraction of e-cigarette users to respond in this way to overwhelm the benefit of reduced vaping in a larger group.[373]

3.2.3 *Unintended Consequences of E-cigarette Restrictions: DIY and After-Market Modifications*

In addition to increased smoking, consumer responses to e-cigarette regulations within the broader e-cigarette category could have other unintended consequences.

The heterogeneity in the e-cigarette market challenges the efficacy of restrictions intended to curb use. Different categories of products (pod systems, refillable tank systems, disposables, etc.) may be variously affected by regulation. Consumers of one subset of e-cigarette products may respond to restrictions not by abandoning the major product category (as regulators might hope) but by simply switching to another sub-group less affected by the regulation. For example, in response to the FDA's ban on flavored pods, sales of flavored disposables (exempt from the restriction) rose.[374] In some cases, the public health risks associated with such responses may be relatively neutral, likely less beneficial than quitting vaping outright, but preferable to switching to combustibles. For example, in responding to a ban on non-tobacco flavors, e-cigarette users may simply switch to compliant flavor profiles. But responses of this type are not necessarily without costs: For example, in response to a nicotine limit, consumers might be expected to consume more e-liquid to compensate, thus increasing their exposure to any dose-dependent risks associated with the other constituents of e-liquid.[375,376,377,378] High-dose nicotine is an important feature of e-cigarettes used for smoking cessation. Nicotine-dependent smokers need higher doses of nicotine, especially in the early stages of quitting.[379] Low doses may be insufficient for satisfying nicotine-dependent smokers and limits could therefore reduce switching.[380]

For another example, consider a hypothetical ban on all e-cigarette flavors, or a broad nicotine limit affecting all e-cigarette devices regardless of form: Users of closed tank systems would be unable to game this type of regulation (assuming closed systems are not modifiable), but the same is not true for users of open tank systems. Pure nicotine and other food-grade flavorants might be added to regulatory-compliant e-liquids after-market. That is not inconsequential. While accidents with prepared e-liquids do occur,[381] the severity of such events is limited, at least to some extent, by the fact that the nicotine in commercial e-liquids is diluted. If, as a response to regulation, consumers switched to do-it-yourself (DIY) e-liquids and after-market modification, the use of concentrated nicotine could increase the frequency and severity of accidents related to e-liquids.

Even when prepared with due care and precautions, DIY e-liquids may pose additional health risks. El Hellani et al. analyzed the emissions of harmful substances from various DIY e-liquid aerosols, discovering that when DIY additives were added to unflavored, menthol-flavored, or tobacco-flavored e-liquids, the level of toxicant emissions increased to levels that are similar to those found in commercially flavored e-liquids.[382] But certain modifications resulted in considerably higher emissions of ROS, carbonyl, and phenol for the same concentration of additives. According to the authors, the findings indicate that DIY additives can have an impact on the toxicant emissions from e-cigarettes, and policy-makers should take this into account when regulating commercially available flavored e-liquids. Cox et al.[383] have also reported that DIY preparations could be more economical than commercially available options and allow the producer to attain a higher nicotine content than might otherwise be available. Cox and colleagues' analysis of DIY e-liquid preparations also confirms the several potentially harmful chemicals and respiratory irritants, including cinnamaldehyde, benzaldehyde, and acetoin.

Whether DIY preparations are necessarily more dangerous than commercial products remains to be seen. But if regulators do perceive that controlling flavors, nicotine content, and e-liquid constituents is valuable, then the implementation of policies that increase the use of DIY preparations by consumers motivated to obtain flavor or aroma profiles, nicotine levels, or a price point that would not be possible using commercial products,[384] could be counter-productive. Moreover, a culture of such behavior could see the addition of other adulterants, including those that are broadly restricted in regulated markets (stimulants for example); that could both pose direct health risks when vaped and might have undesirable second-order effects, contributing to experimental and youth use.

3.2.4 *Unintended Consequences of E-cigarette Restrictions: Illicit E-vapor*

Yet another complication results from market restrictions: they can create illicit markets for alternatives. Illicit markets thrive in response not only to outright prohibitions but also in response to taxes. The economic theory is simple and ineluctable: illicit products are economic substitutes for licit products, and thus when the price of the legal product rises demand for the illicit substitute perforce must rise. The salient questions are then, 'to what degree such substitution occurs', 'which aspects of regulation can mitigate this tendency', and 'what can be done to combat illicit trade.' Despite protestations to the contrary from some in the tobacco control community,[385] price-increasing regulation—mainly taxation—is known to lead to tax avoidance, tax evasion, and other forms of illicit trade.[386,387,388,389,390] Similarly, the removal of desirable product features from the regulated market, or regulations that exclude a group of consumers (for example those aged 18 to 21 years old) from the legal market may also serve as an implicit ban, stimulating illicit trade in response.[391] The illicit trade in tobacco products (ITTP) results in several harms: lost tax revenues, reductions in smoking cessation[392], increases in sales to minors,[393] health risks associated with the use of unregulated (and sometimes counterfeit) products,[394,395] and increased crime associated with smuggling.[396] Illicit trade is already a problem around the world. For combustibles, the illicit market is estimated to be 8–21% of the total in the U.S.[397] Economic theory suggests that a similar response may follow restrictions on e-cigarettes. Indeed, while in 2012 e-cigarettes represented a negligible fraction of tobacco product seizures, by 2019 e-cigarettes represented more than 7%.[398] The growth in illicit e-cigarette sales may reflect the changing preferences of nicotine product users, but it could also be a response to the increased regulation and taxation of the product category.

The emerging literature on illicit e-cigarette markets suggests that prohibitions would shift some demand to illicit markets with greater sales to youth.[399] Rich Marianos, a retired federal law enforcement officer with the U.S. Bureau of Alcohol, Tobacco, Firearms and Explosives raised this concern in response to the city and state-level flavor restrictions in Massachusetts: "If this bill [H 4089/S 2357] passes and we bring in prohibition, we're going to bring crime into the city... We're going to replace store owners and manufacturers with people selling out of backpacks, people selling out of cars, and worst of all, people selling directly to the children we're trying to protect."[400]

While illicit e-vapor might be a new phenomenon, the mechanism is well established: Tobacco products are frequently purchased in bulk in jurisdictions where they are taxed less heavily and shipped into jurisdictions with higher taxes, and sold under the counter or on the streets for profit. Enforcement against ITTP takes time and resources away from other law enforcement priorities, including illicit drug markets. The annual report of Massachusetts' Multi-Agency Illegal Tobacco Task Force (2022)[401] documents the rise in illicit trade in e-vapor products in the U.S. In 2021, state law enforcement and the Department of Revenue made 106,775 seizures of e-cigarettes. The report suggests that the rise in confiscation of menthol cigarettes and flavored e-cigarettes, along with the decline in revenue for tobacco and other related items, is possibly indicative of a surge in smuggling of such products across borders. As noted in the report, neighboring states saw increases in tobacco revenue following Massachusetts restrictions. The report brings attention to instances of illegal activity involving e-cigarettes, such as the arrest of a man in New Hampshire in June 2021, charged in relation to a large-scale organization that was distributing untaxed tobacco and e-cigarettes and engaging in marijuana trafficking. Following the execution of search warrants in various facilities across multiple states, law enforcement officials confiscated, among other items, 250 cases of unlawful e-cigarettes.

In addition to challenging law enforcement and eroding tax revenues, illicit e-cigarette sales endanger public health. Illicit vapor products are unlikely to be as safe as regulated ones, and likely to be much less so. As evidence, recall that the episodes of EVALI appear to be associated specifically with illicit THC products[402] and were accordingly less common in states with legal cannabis.[403] The absence of regulatory oversight denies illicit product users the quality control and product oversight afforded by regulation. Furthermore, consumers buying deceptive counterfeit e-cigarettes are likely to encounter false or misleading claims regarding health, a lack of any health warnings, an incorrect listing of ingredients, nicotine in products claimed to be nicotine-free, and other misstatements of nicotine concentration in the e-liquid.[404,405] Illicit sales also deny opportunities for age-gating; illicit vendors already operate outside of the law and thus, unlike licensed retailers, have no additional motive to limit sales to youth. Because illicit markets under-cut regulated markets on price to gain customers, the relatively lower cost of illicit products may appeal especially to price-sensitive groups including youth. Accordingly, it is well documented that illicit tobacco markets are associated with increased youth smoking.[406]

Of course, if the illicit market operates not in parallel with a regulated one (as in the case with tobacco), but against the backdrop of an enforced prohibition (as in heroin), illicit market prices may be considerably higher than analogous commercial ones. E-cigarette bans appear to be ineffective at eliminating consumption. In 2019 the Indian Ordinance and Act prohibited both nicotine and nicotine-free e-cigarette throughout India. However, Amalia et al.[407] report that almost one in five (18.6%) of retailers surveyed in Bengaluru, Chandigarh, Dehradun, Delhi, Indore, Kolkata, Ludhiana, Raipur, and Ranchi was non-compliant. In Kolkata more than 8 out of 10 (83.9%) retailers were non-compliant. E-commerce also undermines the efficacy of India's restriction. In another study Amalia et al.[408] found that more than a third of websites surveyed would deliver to an address in New Delhi, demonstrating further evidence of non-compliance. The authors report a widespread lack of age verification methods, and the absence of safety warnings. The use of promotional strategies, including price discounts, and unsubstantiated health claims appears to be commonplace.

Australia's Therapeutic Goods Administration has acknowledged that the country's de facto prohibition has failed to prevent e-cigarette use by young Australians, or to provide access to adult smokers.[409] E-cigarette use has increased in Australia, despite the restrictions aimed broadly to reduce it. In New South Wales (NSW), Australia's most populous state, 32.7% of 16 to 24 year-olds had ever used an e-cigarette in 2021.[410] Meanwhile, broad skepticism toward e-cigarettes among Australian physicians means that fewer than 1% are listed as nicotine prescribers.[411] Even though the possession of nicotine without a prescription carries a A$45,000 penalty and risks a prison sentence of up to two years[412] less than one-in-ten e-cigarette users has a prescription, and it is estimated that as few as 2% of Australian e-cigarette users purchase nicotine from pharmacies on a prescription basis.[413] That demand gap is met by a thriving black market[414] in which untested and improperly labeled products are sold with only minimal enforcement. The results of this failed policy include a substantial increase in youth vaping, forgone tax revenues and the criminalization of otherwise law-abiding citizens.[415] Dessaix et al.[416] report e-cigarettes are being illegally imported and sold at Australian retail outlets, including both brick-and-mortar stores and e-commerce sites, and by individuals exploiting social media channels. Importers were not, at least to date, required to demonstrate that imported nicotine-free e-cigarettes are indeed nicotine-free, and packaging is non-standardized. This means that consignments that are labeled as not containing nicotine are subject only to random laboratory testing by the Therapeutic Goods Administration. Cancer Council Australia describes the levels of sales to minors in Australia as "rampant."[417]

Evidently e-cigarette restrictions can and do lead to unintended consequences, as consumers respond to bans and restrictions of various kinds by switching to other substitutes; combustible and non-combustible, legal and otherwise. Different consumer groups will respond differently to regulations and the resulting disparities may serve as further unintended consequences. For example, adverse responses to regulation might be concentrated in price-sensitive consumers (including young and lower SES groups) who may be more affected by policies that make e-cigarettes more expensive (or more difficult) to obtain. For example, in responding to a ban or a tax on disposables, wealthier e-cigarette users may have fewer reservations about investing in a tank system. That would allow them, to some extent, to subvert the intended benefit of the ban. But for others, the up-front costs may preclude this response. Combustibles, widely available, require no comparable start-up cost to begin using, and may prove an attractive alternative to price-sensitive groups. Such a disparity, while hypothetical, would likely perpetuate smoking by facilitating a resurgence of smoking among would-be e-cigarette users, and possibly exacerbate the concentration of smoking harms among socioeconomically disadvantaged communities.

Similar concerns have been noted by, among others, the ACLU who, in a 2020 letter to Frank Pallone, Chairman, House Committee on Energy and Commerce claimed that the complete ban on flavors stipulated in the Reversing the Youth Tobacco Epidemic Act of 2019 (H.R. 2339) would result in an unfair impact on individuals and communities of color. Additionally, the letter pointed out that the ban would lead to the imposition of criminal penalties, giving precedence to criminalization rather than public health and harm reduction. The letter also warned that this ban could lead to unconstitutional policing and other adverse encounters with local law enforcement. California's flavor ban SB 793, faced opposition on similar grounds. The Orange County Coalition of Police and Sheriffs wrote to State Senator Jerry Hill and the State Assembly Health Committee on July 9th[418] arguing that the flavor ban would boost the illicit trade in tobacco in the state which already accounts for 45% of all cigarettes consumed in California, leading the state to lose more than US$1.85 billion in tax revenues and undermining tobacco regulation. Prohibiting flavored tobacco items, such as menthol cigarettes, in California, would not put an end to their availability. Instead, it would lead to the growth of criminal enterprises catering to the demand and evading taxes, disregarding age verification, and flouting any other legal requirements or restrictions, much like what happens with tax hikes. SB793 ultimately survived a referendum in the November 2022 ballot.

Problematically, many of these unintended consequences may not be readily visible in the data. First, as mentioned, consumer responses may be heterogeneous; if so a reduction in demand that might be in effect in one sub-population might be confounded by an opposing effect in another. Relatedly, because the population of smokers is much greater than the population of e-cigarette users, a shift in demand toward combustibles that is significant in public health terms may still not be immediately obvious, especially against the backdrop of declining prevalence. Moreover, the volume of illicit demand is hard to quantify at the best of times; empirical evidence of increased illicit activity in response to e-cigarette regulations may not be forthcoming. Further, because such e-cigarette regulations affect the future decisions of current smokers (not only those who have recently quit, or are currently in the process of doing so; but also those who might do so in the future) the ultimate effects of any e-cigarette regulation may take time to occur. Analyses of the short-term sales or survey data following e-cigarette interventions may fail to capture these ultimate effects. However, the difficulties in detecting such unintended consequences do not mean they should be dismissed. As the empirical evidence describes in this chapter shows, such responses are real and can be expected to follow future e-cigarette restrictions.

4 Why Do We Have Sub-optimal E-cigarette Policies?

There are other factors that help explain the adoption of apparently flawed e-cigarette policies.

4.1 Risk Aversion and Other Regulatory Biases

Behavioral economics examines how decision-making can be adversely affected by the presence of cognitive biases. In the presence of such biases, decisions are characterized by bounded rationality at best, leading to systematic errors in decision-making. Results from behavioral economic studies are increasingly cited in support of regulatory interventions, both in general[419] and specifically for tobacco policy,[420,421,422] to correct for cognitive bias. However, cognitive biases may also affect regulators.[423] While the behavioral economic literature concerning regulatory failure often focuses on regulation in general, or specific areas of regulation such as financial markets,[424] or drug regulation,[425] several of the biases discussed may also influence regulatory decisions regarding e-cigarettes.

Decision-makers are often informed by prior experience or knowledge of historical events. Rationally, however, the value of such "priors" for the purposes of informing decision-making in the present hinges on how accurately the historical context (or the decision-makers understanding of it) reflects current conditions. Cooper[426] suggests that regulators may use heuristics—mental short-cuts—to inform long-term policy decisions. Crucially, however, if future risk and benefits differ from those implied by the heuristic on either the intensive or extensive margin, that may bias decision-making. This is known as availability bias.[427] Relatedly, the hindsight bias inclines us to perceive past events as more predictable of future events than they may actually be. In the context of regulatory decision-making, that may lead to the perpetuation of sub-optimal strategies.[428] To illustrate, consider that NRTs and pharmacotherapies have helped smokers quit; however, that they have helped some does not suggest that those who they have *not* helped will benefit in the future. In fact, that today's smokers have not been persuaded to quit with the traditional interventions suggests that they will be *less* likely to do so than the smokers of the past (as discussed in Volume I, Chapter 2).

For another example, consider that the greatest heuristic short-cut of all regarding e-cigarettes is to view them as a redux of the experience with smoking. Government officials allowed the tobacco industry to set the narrative and promote cigarettes with no substantive intervention for decades,[429] to the great detriment of public health. Cognizant of this failure to protect the public in the past, public health officials may be primed toward excessive caution toward e-cigarettes.

Furthermore, regulators may be unduly optimistic regarding the likely success of their adopted regulatory strategy.[430] Choi and Pritchard[431] suggest that overconfidence of regulators may lead to errors and regulatory overreach. This failing, of course, is not peculiar to regulators. In general, experts of all types "tend to be overly optimistic in assessing their own decision-making ability." As Griffin and Tversky observe pithily, experts are "often wrong but rarely in doubt."[432] To illustrate, consider that tobacco taxation has been an effective strategy with which to curb demand. Regulators may therefore assume that the story is equally as simple for e-cigarettes: impose a tax, watch demand go down; what could go wrong? However, as discussed in this chapter, the cross-substitutability of demand between e-cigarettes and cigarettes (a dynamic that was historically absent) creates a large unintended consequence that seriously diminishes or reverses the sign of the net health improvements attending high levels of e-cigarette taxation.

Regulators may also exhibit confirmation bias, which is the tendency for information to be interpreted so as to confirm preexisting beliefs or hypotheses, while disregarding or downplaying contradictory evidence.[433] Thus, the observation that nicotine products *cause* end-point health risks (true, in the case of combustible cigarettes) may lead regulators to be quick to jump from evidence that e-cigarettes contain some potentially harmful substances to the conclusion that there will be significant health risks from their use. Similarly, confirmation bias may explain why so many regulators and some public researchers are quick to treat correlation (from observational studies) as causation when it comes to vaping and damage to health. A severely flawed study purporting to show that using e-cigarettes causes heart attacks, eventually retracted by the publishing journal due to failure to account for the fact that many of the heart attacks occurred before the first use of e-cigarettes,[434] is still cited.[435] Predisposition to believe such health impacts exist can lead to an overly cautious approach by decision-makers reluctant to update their priors in the fact of contrary evidence.

Confirmation bias may be especially influential when decision-makers are, in their agencies and via media reporting, consistently exposed to a one-sided perspective. Repeated exposure to messages emphasizing risks (youth nicotine addiction, for example) may lead decision-makers to ignore potential benefits (supporting smoking cessation), eroding critical thinking on the inherent tradeoffs between the two. This is referred to as the "availability cascade."[436] Confirmation bias may also result from a "framing effect": Ostensibly subtle variations in the framing of similar information can lead to large differences in judgment based on those framings, as evident in the historical differences between the public health communities' approach to e-cigarettes in the U.S. and the U.K.[437]

There are also practical and structural reasons why cognitive biases may persist in the agencies responsible for regulatory decisions. As Choi and Pritchard explain, developing a new regulatory strategy requires in-depth analysis of complex phenomena and is therefore costly.[438] Such costs may deter creative thinking and consideration of agency budgets and staffing may lead decision-makers to "double down" on strategies that have been secured financial and human resources in the past. Thus, Choi and Pritchard suggest that "cognitive biases may encourage regulators to equate self-interest and the public interest," given that regulatory action increases the prestige and power of the regulatory agency, and by extension the individual regulator, self-interest may bias the regulator toward intervention.[439] Perceived interests may lead to groupthink, in which individuals operating within an institution are implicitly discouraged from considering other points of view or from questioning their agencies' established perspective. Although individual agency staff may hold divergent opinions, members of a group typically defer to the consensus, reducing the range of hypotheses that an organization considers when faced with a problem.[440]

Cooper further recognizes that a separate class of cognitive errors may bias decision-makers toward the status quo. The experimental literature reports an "endowment effect" (also known as loss aversion), in which subjects require more compensation to part with an existing benefit than they would be willing to pay to gain it de novo.[441] Again, this may bias regulators in favor of the "tried and tested" strategy, leading them to disregard the possibility that other approaches may be better, or even worthy of consideration.

The separation of disciplinary expertise into silos may reinforce the some of the biases discussed.[442] Individually, technical training often develops specialists with deep, but not necessarily broad, subject-matter expertise. Organizational hiring practices may also narrow the range of expertise available to regulatory decision-makers, leading potentially valuable contributions from other bodies of knowledge to be overlooked. This may explain why the base of evidence from economists using quasi-experimental methods showing that higher taxes or stricter regulation of e-cigarettes increases the prevalence of smoking has had a difficult time gaining traction in the public health and regulatory communities. These agencies are typically staffed largely with experts from disciplines used to thinking of RCTs as the only valid method to ascertain causal effects, but over the past several decades empirical microeconomists have developed convincing methodologies to achieve the same using observational data. Officials trained in medicine or public health may have learned simplistic hierarchies of evidence (which typically have RCTs at the top, followed by cohort studies, other observational studies, and finally expert opinion), leading them to simultaneously distrust economic studies using population data while not understanding the methodological strength of a well-designed quasi-experimental study.[443]

Whereas the biases of other institutional decision-makers, corporations for example, may be corrected over time with feedback from the market, a lack of competition enjoyed by regulatory agencies suggests that regulators' biases may go unchallenged. Cooper argues that "regulatory outputs have no necessary relationship to consumer welfare." Even if funding, for example, were tied more closely to outcomes in the population, "time lags and measurement problems make it difficult to link clear regulatory failures to specific regulators, especially given their relatively short tenures."[444] Regulatory agencies and their managers will likely continue to receive funding so long as the agencies produce quantifiable results that are valuable to the elected representatives to whom they are accountable. Political expediency, however, may be a poor proxy for consumer welfare. Even where competition exists between agencies, for example in law enforcement, this does not safeguard welfare since competition for scarce resources may lead to activities that maximize the appearance of action (arrests, for example) in lieu of genuine progress (reduced crime).[445] Finally, interest group theory and public choice theory suggests that to the extent that regulators *do* engage in a market, albeit one without competition, for they are the monopoly supplier, that market is for regulatory favors and the demand side of the market is composed of all parties interested in the outcome of regulation, not just consumers or proponents of social welfare.[446,447] None of these considerations lead to confidence in the view of the regulator as a disinterested maximizer of social benefit.

Another consideration that may affect regulators' decisions relates to the tension between action and inaction. (Whether this is a "bias" or a principled stand depends on whether a utilitarian or deontological view is adopted.) The literature on moral philosophy uses the famous thought experiment of the "trolley problem"[448] to investigate moral choices.[449] Reductively, at least, the consequentialist thinker tends to justify actions that harm few to save many on the grounds that the ends justify the means. Conversely, many deontological ethical frameworks proscribe action in this scenario, holding that it is always wrong to cause harm. However, for most people, the ratios of lives lost by choice to those lost by inaction are important. Surveys of respondents presented with various iterations of the trolley experiment suggest that many people would endorse, or at least permit, killing one to save 100, but respondents are evenly split on whether it would be justifiable to kill one to save five.[450] This dichotomy seems to challenge both the consequentialist (utilitarian) and deontological perspectives; the former holds that it is always right to maximize the number of people alive after the dust settles, and the latter holds that the ends never justify the means. The dichotomous perspective, intuitive to many, has been referred to as threshold deontology.[451] The threshold deontological perspective holds that the objection to causing harm may be over-ridden only if the ratio of harm to benefit is sufficiently large. There is no consensus on what the acceptable margin of harm to benefit is, but applications of risk-aversion in real-world decision-making suggest that it is non-trivial.

In 1993, Lenert et al.[452] observed that practicing physicians weighing risk and benefits in relation to treatment options typically view morbidity and mortality associated with an existing disease as a more acceptable outcome than similar outcomes resulting from treatment (known as iatrogenesis in the medical literature). On average, between four and five additional lives had to be saved by a new treatment of the disease, relative to existing treatment, for each additional death caused by the new treatment itself. In other words, physicians, on average, give more weight to harms that they cause, even when in pursuit of treatment, than those they allow to happen. It is interesting to consider how different stakeholders may apply different weights: patients, for example often give lower weighting to iatrogenic outcomes.[453,454] Perhaps this is unsurprising. For the physician, the psychological burden of harm caused by positive action may be greater than that caused by harms that, reasonably, would have transpired in their absence. For the patient, it may be easier to live with the consequences of iatrogenic harms knowing that they and their physicians "explored all the options." But it is noteworthy that the considerations of the decision-maker and those affected are different. Might such a disparity apply in the case of e-cigarette regulation? It is possible, even likely. Like patients, smokers may want to explore all the options, and like physicians, regulators may be reluctant to be responsible for decisions which could introduce new harms. In regulatory regimes that require a physician's prescription to obtain e-cigarettes, such as in Australia, the anti-iatrogenic bias of the regulator and the physician will compound.

4.2 *Misinformation and the Power of Emotion*

One reason why sub-optimal e-cigarette regulations prevail is their resonance with the general public, owing to their intuitive appeal. Passionately articulated arguments grounded in emotionally charged rhetoric are often more powerful than more nuanced analyses of empirical evidence. Concerns about the well-being of young people are particularly powerful: we owe a greater duty of care to children who are still learning to make good decisions for themselves than we do to adults. Perhaps that is one reason why those skeptical about e-cigarettes focus on the risks that e-cigarettes pose to youth, rather than non-smoking adults. But that intuition goes against the legislative mandates of public health regulators, none of which are instructed by law to focus on the health of children and young people regardless of consequences to older citizens. Of course, the apparent ambiguities in the evidence base, and the prevalence of misinformation regarding e-cigarettes (recall that the majority of the public—and, indeed, the majority of physicians and other medical professionals—still think that nicotine is the cause of smoking-related disease) may also contribute to the tendency for rhetoric to win over rationality.

Moreover, regulatory agencies are accountable to elected officials, themselves responsible to the voting public. Fighting to implement policies that will win them support at the ballot box, representatives may be especially responsive to hot-button topics—those which arouse a strong emotional response among their constituents. Since regulators are at least indirectly accountable to the public, these public values exert a powerful influence on decision-making, even if the premises of those values are contradicted by the data. More plainly: what is *believed* often matters more than what is *known*. And, of course, while regulators should balance the interests of the whole public (in which the interests of particular stakeholder groups may be at odds), other stakeholders need not be so balanced. For parents worried about the risks posed by e-cigarettes to young people, the fact that e-cigarettes may cause greater benefits than risks by helping adult smokers quit matters little. As a result, sentiment may inform policy at the expense of science and a rational policy calculus.

4.3 Short-Termism

Another factor contributing to sub-optimal policies is short-termism. Faced with immediate and pressing concerns, government officials may prioritize short-term wins, discounting longer-term consequences precisely because the consequences are, in perception or reality, temporally remote. The rapidly increasing rates of e-cigarette use among young non-smokers is, for many, a pressing and immediate concern, and reversing that trend would be seen as a public health victory. If that short-term victory comes at the cost of a future reduction in smoking cessation, that cost may be largely ignored by regulators precisely because it is remote. Furthermore, society has lived with the consequences of smoking for generations. Those costs are known but are, to some extent, discounted by those who see smoking as an issue of the past, or at least a long-standing, incalcitrant problem. As such those costs are, rhetorically, less easily laid at the feet of those who are now in a position to reduce them, than are the consequences of vaping—which is viewed as a novel concern. Youth vaping is a pressing public health concern, but it is incorrect to assume that it is of greater concern than smoking.

Just as people who smoke may discount the long-term harms of smoking in favor of the short-term benefits, perceived or otherwise; regulators too may discount the future costs associated with e-cigarette restrictions in favor of the political capital gained from being seen to "do something(!)" in the short term. The public may also prioritize short-term goals at the expense of future costs. With only a handful of exceptions, the passage of new policies gets significantly more media coverage than the latent unintended consequences of poor regulatory decisions of the past. In many cases policies can expire, be phased out or be revoked with little or no public scrutiny while the media focuses on the day's latest crisis. That environment may encourage policy decision-makers to worry less about doing something that might turn out to be wrong, than about not being seen to take decisive action. According to

Cooper,[455] regulators may focus excessively on short-run considerations, pursuing interventions with measurable increases that are associated with their decisions, in lieu of strategies which may be optimal in the long term, but which may not "pay off" until after the regulator's tenure.

Thus, positive action, even if it turns out to be the wrong action, may garner more political support than inaction which has positive consequences.

Once again, political priorities may exacerbate this short-termism. Elected officials, ever mindful of securing their next term in office, may be tempted to prioritize policies with immediate effects that will deliver support at the ballot. Even if there is evidence to suggest that those policies have long-term consequences (which may be hidden, or merely theoretical—at least initially), those may be discounted: after all, those championing the short-term intervention will likely have moved on by the time the costs of those policies come to light. All of this creates a sense of urgency, but caution may be the better part of valor. Agency chiefs and philanthropies may also suffer from this blinkered approach, for similar reasons.

4.4 Inability or Unwillingness to Correct Course

Further contributing to the challenges of short-termism, psychologists have noted a tendency for individuals to only acknowledge the errors in our judgment when we are forced to confront the results. So too with regulators; flaws in the *ex-ante* analysis that lead to unintended consequences may only become apparent when the evidence for unintended consequences becomes too great to ignore. But even then, policy-makers may be slow to course-correct due to lengthy bureaucratic procedures, lack of prioritization and—perhaps most prominently—the political cost of admitting error. Thus, Choi and Pritchard argue, legislated policy and regulation often takes on a "life of its own" and even ill-conceived regulation become difficult to replace.[456] In response to the evidence that their e-cigarette tax was driving a return to smoking,[457] the Minnesota legislature has neither revoked nor reduced the tax, nor apparently even discussed doing so. Likewise, Massachusetts' ban on e-cigarette flavors stands despite the evidence that it is driving illicit sales, and San Francisco has not revisited its ban on e-cigarettes despite evidence that it was pushing young consumers to combustibles.[458]

If policy-makers are slow to correct their course in response to evidence of unintended consequences, the unseen opportunity costs—for which the evidence is seen as being merely theoretical—are likely to be still less consequential. There is no small measure of inconsistency here. As discussed in Volume II, Chapter 3, those appealing to the precautionary principle to voice concerns about the mere possibility that e-cigarettes will expose the public to novel risks need to acknowledge that acting to mitigate or prevent those risks can bring about other harms too. The harms resulting from unintended consequences of policy decisions, including the forgone benefits, tradeoff against the intended benefit, and it is plausible that in some cases the resulting harms overwhelm the intended benefits. One important silver lining resulting from the emergence of these unintended consequences is that they contribute to the evidence basis available to future regulators. Whether future regulators will be eager to learn from the negative experiences of earlier adopters remains to be seen, but there is little evidence of it yet.

4.5 Policy Sharing

In the haste to prevent potential public health harms, policy sharing often seems like a smart approach. But the preference for evidence-based practices often means that first-movers' policy choices are replicated purely on the basis that they have been tried before. Unless serious consideration is given to the efficacy of the initial intervention, the full consequences of the intervention have been measured, and any unintended consequences can be positively demonstrated to be overwhelmed by the intended benefits, then policy sharing risks replicating failure.

Rather than adopt the approach of another jurisdiction, regulators may choose instead to apply to e-cigarettes the same restrictions as they themselves applied to another product. By classifying e-cigarettes as tobacco, medicines or drug delivery devices, poisons, or commercial products, regulators can deploy various "tried and tested" policy frameworks without having to reinvent the wheel. But e-cigarettes do not necessarily fit perfectly into any of these frameworks, and though this approach is an expedient means of creating a regulatory framework for the novel products, it forgoes an opportunity to craft policies better tailored to the unique risks and benefits these products present.

4.6 *A False Dichotomy: Insufficient Understanding of the Options*

Both skeptics and advocates of e-cigarettes confidently pronounce that the evidence supports their policy position. Endorsements of tougher restrictions to protect youth or more lenient regulation to assist smokers have often lacked detailed suggestions for policies that might advance those goals. Given that the market for e-cigarettes is still relatively immature, with commercial offerings and consumption patterns evolving rapidly, it may be perceived that there is insufficient data with which to develop a comprehensive list of policy alternatives, still less to adjudicate between options. Furthermore, facing financial and organizational constraints, many agencies—especially those of localities and even less affluent countries facing more pressing public health challenges—may have few resources available to develop the evidence base to inform decisions.

There are certainly external agencies and organizations who could help with this effort, but often the most qualified candidates have a stake in the policy outcome. Many public health charities rely on funding sources that could be threatened by the perception that they are supporting a product that drives addiction, so public health agencies tend to be extremely cautious in voicing anything approaching optimism toward tobacco harm reduction. Manufacturers would be only too willing to help develop this evidence, but the legacy of tobacco-funded pseudo-science used to commit health fraud and deny the truth about how dangerous and addictive cigarettes has had lasting effects, one of which is that many public health journals will not publish studies from researchers with ties to industry. E-cigarettes are neither wholly good nor wholly bad, but the net benefit from them depends in no small part on the regulatory environment. It is therefore imperative that regulators consider carefully the options available to them and use the available evidence, incomplete as it may be, to adjudicate between them. An inadequate understanding of the options impedes the generation of optimal strategy.

4.7 *Reputational Risks and Challenges*

Regulatory agencies have a legal obligation to act on their mandate and can face legal action for failing to do so. For example, in 2018 the FDA was sued by Campaign for Tobacco-Free Kids, American Cancer

Society Cancer Action Network, American Heart Association, American Lung Association, Truth Initiative, American Academy of Pediatrics, Democracy Forward, and several pediatricians after the FDA extended the deadline for e-cigarette manufactures to apply PMTA until 2021. At the time the decision was made, the regulator had argued that the extension would allow the agency more time to explore how to make e-cigarettes less toxic, appealing, and addictive while giving the industry more time to develop thorough and accurate applications. The plaintiffs argued that the extension was "arbitrary and capricious and not the product of reasoned decision-making," and that, by delaying, the FDA had abdicated the responsibilities it was granted in 2009 under the Tobacco Control Act.

When faced with lawsuits from entities widely seen as having the public's interests at heart, the mere threat of reputational damage, regardless of the outcome, may be sufficient to coerce hasty decisions. Of course, the FDA has also faced suits from the tobacco industry. However, in those cases, the risk of reputational damage for the regulator is insignificant, and in fact the litigation may almost be taken as a point of pride, given most of the public's attitude toward the parties bringing suit. As a result of this disparity, decisions made under threat of legal action tend to be one-sided. This does not conflict with the interest group theory mentioned above, but instead shows that industry is not the interest group that won favors from the regulator. Reputational risk gives a reason why the interest groups motivated by the precautionary principle appear to have much more sway with the regulator.

4.8 A Lack of High-Profile Champions

Finally, given how controversial the topic of e-cigarettes is, any elected official prepared to publicly champion harm reduction risks the ire of the voting public. Even if agency chiefs and elected officials may be, in private, cautiously optimistic about the role of e-cigarettes in reducing smoking harms, few are prepared to risk their reputations much less their careers with a vocal public endorsement. Public Health England serves as an unusual exception. Well after its original finding that e-cigarettes have fewer than 5% of the health risk of smoking, PHE was disbanded during the COVID-19 pandemic. Today, the Office for Health Improvement and Disparities (OHID) in the Department of Health and Social Care now has responsibility for smoking-related aspects of public health, and it has not made any pronouncements that would appear to contradict

PHE's stance. Since OHID enjoys less independence than PHE did[459] its future actions on the subject may be more subject to political influence. However, the U.K. government commissioned an independent report in 2022 that strongly endorsed e-cigarettes "as an effective tool to help people to quit smoking tobacco."[460]

In contrast, those advocating more stringent controls have powerful figureheads in the form of the WHO, the Campaign for Tobacco-Free Kids, the American Heart Association, the American Lung Association, etc. Such organizations, typically well-viewed by the public, can exert enormous pressure on regulators, lobbying in public for regulation that they see as benefiting their cause. But while these organizations enjoy broad public support, the mechanisms by which they are accountable to the public for their policy positions are less clear, or indeed absent altogether. Meanwhile, it is often taken as writ that anything not directly detrimental to the commercial interests of the tobacco industry is antithetical to the public's interests. That view is certainly understandable, but in the case of e-cigarettes and other less risky substitutes for ubiquitous and harmful combustibles, it needs interrogating. If e-cigarettes can help move people who smoke, away from the primary cause of harm (combustible tobacco), then such products have important utility for public health, regardless of which firm profits from their sale.

Much then depends on the degree to which regulations can balance the apparent tradeoffs between helping adult smokers switch to safer alternatives and reducing the mechanisms by which those products appeal to young non-smokers. Are these propositions antithetical? Can tradeoffs be mitigated? How can e-cigarette regulations be optimized? Volume III, Chapter 2 seeks to approach these questions.

Notes

1. Laugesen, M. Safety Report on the Ruyan® E-cigarette Cartridge and Inhaled Aerosol, Health New Zealand Ltd. 2008, available at: https://casaa.org/wp-content/uploads/10-30-08-RuyanCartridgeReport30-Oct-08.pdf.
2. According to its own promotional materials, the Chinese company known as Ruyan Group (Holdings) Limited (now known as Dragonite International Limited) was the first manufacturer of an e-cigarette device in 2003. In 2013, Imperial

Tobacco purchased Dragonite's electronic cigarette division. See Volume 1 Chapter 3. for further details on the Ruyan Group.

3. Carroll, D.M., Denlinger-Apte, R.L., Dermody, S.S., King, J.L., Mercincavage, M., Pacek, L.R., Smith, T.T., Tripp, H.L., White, C.M. Polarization Within the Field of Tobacco and Nicotine Science and Its Potential Impact on Trainees. Nicotine Tob Res. 2021 Jan 7;23(1):36–39. https://doi.org/10.1093/ntr/ntaa148.
4. WHO. Marketers of Electronic Cigarettes Should Halt Unproved Therapy Claims, World Health Organisation, pressrelease, 2008, available at: https://www.who.int/news/item/19-09-2008-marketers-of-electronic-cigarettes-should-halt-unproved-therapy-claims.
5. The WHO admitted that further testing might show that the devices could be useful means toward that end.
6. CASAA. (n.d.). Historical Timeline of Vaping and Cigarettes, Consumer Advocates for Smoke-free Alternatives Association, webpage, available at: https://casaa.org/education/vaping/historical-timeline-of-electronic-cigarettes/.
7. U.S. Food and Drug Administration. (2009, July 22). *Evaluation of E-cigarettes*, Center for Drug Evaluation and Research through the Office of Compliance, available at: https://casaa.org/wp-content/uploads/Evalution-of-electronic-cigarettes.pdf.
8. U.S. Food and Drug Administration (2009, July 22). *FDA and Public Health Experts Warn About Electronic Cigarettes*, Press release. http://web.archive.org/web/20091002165557/http://www.fda.gov/NewsEvents/Newsroom/PressAnnouncements/ucm173222.htm.
9. *Washington Times*. FDA Smoke Screen on E-cigarettes. *Washington Times*, 2009, available at: https://www.washingtontimes.com/news/2009/aug/06/fda-smoke-screen-on-e-cigarettes/.
10. Office of the Governor of California. Letter California State Senate: Senate Bill 400, Office of the Governor of California, 2009, available at: http://leginfo.ca.gov/pub/09-10/bill/sen/sb_0351-0400/sb_400_vt_20091012.html.
11. New Jersey State Legislature. (2010). New Jersey Smokefree Air Act A4227/A4228/S3053/S3054 (amended 2006 NJ Smoke-free Air Act).

12. ASH. What are electronic cigarettes? Action on Smoking and Health UK, 2009, available at: https://www.casaa.org/wp-content/uploads/ASH_715-October-2009.pdf.
13. Siegel, M.B., Tanwar, K.L., Wood, K.S. Electronic Cigarettes as a Smoking-Cessation: Tool Results from an Online Survey. Am J Prev Med. 2011 Apr;40(4):472–475. https://doi.org/10.1016/j.amepre.2010.12.006.
14. Etter, J.F., Bullen, C. Electronic Cigarette: Users Profile, Utilization, Satisfaction and Perceived Efficacy. Addiction. 2011;106:2017–2028. https://doi.org/10.1111/j.1360-0443.2011.03505.x.
15. Polosa, R., Caponnetto, P., Morjaria, J.B. et al. Effect of an Electronic Nicotine Delivery Device (E-cigarette) on Smoking Reduction and Cessation: A Prospective 6-Month Pilot Study. BMC Public Health. 2011;11:786. https://doi.org/10.1186/1471-2458-11-786.
16. Cabinet Office Behavioural Insights Team (2011, September). Annual Update 2010–11. https://casaa.org/wp-content/uploads/Behaviour-Change-Insight-Team-Annual-Update_acc.pdf.
17. "Tobacco: Larger Warnings, Flavours Banned, E-cigarettes Regulated," European Parliament News, Press release, 2013, available at: https://www.europarl.europa.eu/news/en/press-room/20131004IPR21539/tobacco-larger-warnings-flavours-banned-e-cigarettes-regulated.
18. 'Smooth' from the government's point of view, presumably not from industry's.
19. Directive 2014/40/EU. The approximation of the laws, regulations and administrative provisions of the Member States concerning the manufacture, presentation and sale of tobacco and related products and repealing Directive 2001/37/EC, Official Journal, L 127, 29.4.2014, pp. 1–38.
20. Prieger, J., Kleiman, M.A., Kulick, J., Aziani, A., Levi, M., Hampsher, S., Manning, C., Hahn, R. (2019, June 15). The Impact of E-Cigarette Regulation on the Illicit Trade in Tobacco Products in the European Union. http://dx.doi.org/10.2139/ssrn.3435177.
21. Court of Justice of the European Union. Judgment of the Court (Second Chamber) of 4 May 2016: Pillbox

38 (UK) Limited, Trading as Totally Wicked v Secretary of State for Health. ECLI:EU:C:2016:324, 2016, available at: https://eur-lex.europa.eu/legal-content/HR/TXT/?uri=ECLI:ECLI:EU:C:2016:324_1.
22. CASAA. (n.d.). Nicotine Complaint, Consumer Advocates for Smoke-Free Alternatives Association, webpage, available at: https://casaa.org/wp-content/uploads/Nicopure-Complaint.pdf.
23. Johnson, R. Letter to FDA Commissioner Califf, Office of the Chairman of the Senate Homeland Security Committee, 2016, available at: https://www.hsgac.senate.gov/wp-content/uploads/imo/media/doc/2016-07-15%20RHJ%20to%20Califf%20(FDA)%20re%20e-cigarette%20regulation%20-%20follow%20up.pdf.
24. Murray, P., et al. Letter to Secretary of Health and Human Services and FDA Commissioner, U.S. Senate, 2016, available at: https://www.help.senate.gov/imo/media/doc/051116%20HHS%20FDA%20Tobacco%20Deeming%20Letter.pdf.
25. "Mexico Bans Import of All Vaping Products, Cites WHO Guidance." Vaping360. https://vaping360.com/vape-news/88831/mexico-bans-import-of-all-vaping-products-cites-who-guidance/. Accessed 10 May 2023.
26. "Move to Ban Vapers Importing Liquid Nicotine." ABC News, June 23, 2020. www.abc.net.au. https://www.abc.net.au/news/2020-06-24/liquid-nicotine-import-ban-proposal-shocks-industry/12383876.
27. "Will the July 1 Vaping Ban Push People Back to Cigarettes?" Triple j, June 23, 2020. https://www.abc.net.au/triplej/programs/hack/will-the-july-1-vaping-ban-push-people-back-to-cigarettes/12385698.
28. Rgabi., C. (2021, January 26). "Vaping In Australia Continues as Government Scraps Proposed Ban on Nicotine E-cig Imports." Vaping Post. https://www.vapingpost.com/2021/01/26/vaping-in-australia-continues-as-government-scraps-proposed-ban-on-nicotine-e-cig-imports/.
29. Davey, M. Australia's New Vaping Import Ban: What We Do and Don't Know so Far. *The Guardian*, 2022, available at: https://www.theguardian.com/society/2023/may/03/australia-vaping-ban-import-vape-vapes-crackdown-what-we-know-and-dont-know-so-far. For the first stage of the regulations,

see: Department of Health and Aged Care, Therapeutic Goods Administration. "New Regulation of Vapes Starting January 2024" [press release]. Dec. 15, 2023. Australian Government. https://www.tga.gov.au/news/media-releases/new-regulation-vapes-starting-january-2024.

30. Conference of the Parties to the WHO Framework Convention on Tobacco Control (August 2016). Electronic Nicotine Delivery Systems and Electronic Non-Nicotine Delivery Systems (ENDS/ENNDS). WHO Framework Conventional on Tobacco Control, FCTC/COP/7/11. https://fctc.who.int/publications/m/item/fctc-cop-7-11-electronic-nicotine-delivery-systems-and-electronic-non-nicotine-delivery-systems-(ends-ennds).
31. Britton, J., et al. Commentary on WHO Report on Electronic Nicotine Delivery Systems And Electronic Non-Nicotine Delivery Systems, UK Centre for Tobacco and Alcohol Studies, 2016, available at: https://www.clivebates.com/documents/WHO/ENreport.pdf.
32. HO Framework Convention on Tobacco Control & World Health Organization. (2003). WHO Framework Convention on Tobacco Control. World Health Organization. https://apps.who.int/iris/handle/10665/42811.
33. FDA. "FDA Takes Significant Steps to Protect Americans from Dangers of Tobacco through New Regulation." Office of the Commissioner, 2016, available at: https://www.fda.gov/news-events/press-announcements/fda-takes-significant-steps-protect-americans-dangers-tobacco-through-new-regulation.
34. Hair, E.C., Barton, A.A., Perks, S.N., Kreslake, J., Xiao, H., Pitzer, L., Leventhal, A.M., Vallone, D.M. Association Between E-cigarette Use and Future Combustible cigarette Use: Evidence from a Prospective Cohort of yoUth and Young Adults, 2017–2019. Addict Behav. 2021 Jan;112:106593. https://doi.org/10.1016/j.addbeh.2020.106593.
35. Kozlowski, L.T., Warner, K.E. Adolescents and E-Cigarettes: Objects of Concern May Appear Larger Than They Are, Drug and Alcohol Dependence. 2017;174:209–214. https://doi.org/10.1016/j.drugalcdep.2017.01.001.
36. Balfour, D.J.K., Benowitz, N.L., Colby, S.M., Hatsukami, D.K., Lando, H.A., Leischow, S.J., Lerman, C., Mermelstein, R.J., Niaura, R., Perkins, K.A., Pomerleau, O.F., Rigotti, N.A., Swan,

G.E., Warner, K.E., West, R. Balancing Consideration of the Risks and Benefits of E-Cigarettes. Am J Public Health. 2021 Sep;111(9):1661–1672. https://doi.org/10.2105/AJPH.2021.306416.
37. Cigarette Smoking Among U.S. Adults Lowest Ever Recorded: 14% in 2017 | CDC Online Newsroom | CDC. 11 Apr. 2019. https://www.cdc.gov/media/releases/2018/p1108-cigarette-smoking-adults.html.
38. Gentzke, A.S., Wang, T.W., Cornelius, M. et al. Tobacco product use and associated factors among middle and high school students—National Youth Tobacco Survey, United States, 2021. MMWR Surveill Summ. 2022; 71(No. SS-5):1–29.
39. Balfour, D.J.K., Benowitz, N.L., Colby, S.M., Hatsukami, D.K., Lando, H.A., Leischow, S.J., Lerman, C., Mermelstein, R.J., Niaura, R., Perkins, K.A., Pomerleau, O.F., Rigotti, N.A., Swan, G.E., Warner, K.E., West, R. Balancing Consideration of the Risks and Benefits of E-Cigarettes. Am J Public Health. 2021 Sep;111(9):1661–1672. https://doi.org/10.2105/AJPH.2021.306416.
40. Sokol, N.A., Feldman, J.M. High School Seniors Who Used E-Cigarettes May Have Otherwise Been Cigarette Smokers: Evidence From Monitoring the Future (United States, 2009–2018). Nicotine Tob Res. 2021 Oct 7;23(11):1958–1961. https://doi.org/10.1093/ntr/ntab102.
41. Edwards, R. et al. (2020). Patterns of Use of Vaping Products among Smokers: Findings from the 2016–2018 International Tobacco Control (ITC) New Zealand Surveys. *International Journal of Environmental Research and Public Health*. https://doi.org/10.3390/ijerph17186629.
42. Lay, K. Decline of Vaping Raises Smoking Fears. *The Times*, 2020, available at: https://www.thetimes.co.uk/article/decline-of-vaping-raises-smoking-fears-hv6trdr56.
43. Scully, E. (2020, October 15). "Vape Use Falls in Britain by 400,000 in 12 Months." *Mail Online*. https://www.dailymail.co.uk/news/article-8841759/Vape-use-falls-400-000-12-months-amid-fears-unfounded-health-worries-scaring-people-off.html.

44. Current Smoking Prevalence | Tobacco Use in Canada. https://uwaterloo.ca/tobacco-use-canada/adult-tobacco-use/smoking-canada/current-smoking-prevalence. Accessed 10 May 2023.
45. Kozlowski, L.T. Pack Size, Reported Cigarette Smoking Rates, and Public Health. Am J Public Health. 1986 Nov;76(11):1337–1338. https://doi.org/10.2105/AJPH.76.11.1337.
46. Tabagisme en France: 1 million de fumeurs quotidiens en moins. https://www.santepubliquefrance.fr/liste-des-actualites/tabagisme-en-france-1-million-de-fumeurs-quotidiens-en-moins.
47. Cullen, K.A., Gentzke, A.S., Sawdey, M.D., Chang, J.T., Anic, G.M., Wang, T.W., Creamer, M.R., Jamal, A., Ambrose, B.K., King, B.A. E-cigarette Use Among Youth in the United States. JAMA. 2019 Dec 3;322(21):2095–2103. https://doi.org/10.1001/jama.2019.18387.
48. Hammond, D., Rynard, V.L., Reid, J.L. Changes in Prevalence of Vaping Among Youths in the United States, Canada, and England from 2017 to 2019. JAMA Pediatr. 2020;174(8):797–800. https://doi.org/10.1001/jamapediatrics.2020.0901.
49. AHS UK. Use of E-cigarettes (Vapes) Among Young People in Great Britain. Figure 2. Level of use of e-cigarettes, GB youth (11–17), 2014–2022, 2022, available at https://ash.org.uk/uploads/Use-of-e-cigarettes-among-young-people-in-Great-Britain-2022.pdf?v=1661866458.
50. Bauld, L., MacKintosh, A.M., Eastwood, B., Ford, A., Moore, G., Dockrell, M., Arnott, D., Cheeseman, H., McNeill, A. Young People's Use of E-cigarettes Across the United Kingdom: Findings from Five Surveys 2015–2017. Int J Environ Res Public Health. 2017 Aug 29;14(9):973. https://doi.org/10.3390/ijerph14090973.
51. Shahab, L., Goniewicz, M.L., Blount, B.C., Brown, J., McNeill, A., Alwis, K.U., Feng, J., Wang, L., West, R. Nicotine, Carcinogen, and Toxin Exposure in Long-Term E-cigarette and Nicotine Replacement Therapy Users: A Cross-sectional Study. Ann Intern Med. 2017 Mar 21;166(6):390–400. https://doi.org/10.7326/M16-1107.
52. Etter, J.F., Eissenberg, T. Dependence Levels in Users of Electronic Cigarettes, Nicotine Gums and Tobacco Cigarettes. Drug Alcohol Depend. 2015;147:68–75.

53. Farsalinos, K.E., Romagna, G., Tsiapras, D., Kyrzopoulos, S., Voudris, V. Evaluating Nicotine Levels Selection and Patterns of Electronic Cigarette Use in a Group of "Vapers" Who Had Achieved Complete Substitution of Smoking. Subst. Abus. 2013;7:139–146.
54. Foulds, J., Veldheer, S., Yingst, J., Hrabovsky, S., Wilson, S.J., Nichols, T.T., et al. Development of a Questionnaire for Assessing Dependence on Electronic Cigarettes Among a Large Sample of Ex-smoking E-cigarette Users. Nicotine Tob Res. 2015;17(2):186–192.
55. Rostron, B.L., Schroeder, M.J., Ambrose, B.K. Dependence Symptoms and Cessation Intentions Among US Adult Daily Cigarette, Cigar, and E-cigarette Users, 2012–2013. BMC Public Health. 2016;16(1):814.
56. Gentzke, A.S., Wang, T.W., Jamal, A., Park-Lee, E., Ren, C., Cullen, K.A., Neff, L. Tobacco Product Use Among Middle and High School Students—United States, 2020. MMWR Morb Mortal Wkly Rep. 2020 Dec 18;69(50):1881–1888. https://doi.org/10.15585/mmwr.mm6950a1.
57. CDC. (n.d.). National Youth Tobacco Surveys, Centers for Disease Control and Prevention Statistics, available at: https://www.cdc.gov/tobacco/data_statistics/surveys/nyts/index.htm.
58. American Heart Association. (2018). "Stall in E-cigarette Use Among Youth, Reflected in CDC Survey, Worrisome, Says American Heart Association." American Heart Association. https://newsroom.heart.org/news/stall-in-e-cigarette-use-among-youth-reflected-in-cdc-survey-worrisome-says-american-heart-association.
59. The verb "to smoke" is inappropriate in the context of e-cigarette use since there is no combustion.
60. FDA. (2018). "Results from 2018 National Youth Tobacco Survey Show Dramatic Increase in E-Cigarette Use Among Youth Over Past Year." FDA. https://www.fda.gov/news-events/press-announcements/results-2018-national-youth-tobacco-survey-show-dramatic-increase-e-cigarette-use-among-youth-over.
61. Hsu, G., Sun, J.Y., Zhu, S.H. Evolution of Electronic Cigarette Brands from 2013–2014 to 2016–2017: Analysis of Brand Websites. J Med Internet Res. 2018;20(3):e80.

62. FDA. (2018). "Statement from FDA Commissioner Scott Gottlieb, M.D., on Proposed New Steps to Protect Youth by Preventing Access to Flavored Tobacco Products and Banning Menthol in Cigarettes." Office of the Commissioner FDA. https://www.fda.gov/news-events/press-announcements/statement-fda-commissioner-scott-gottlieb-md-proposed-new-steps-protect-youth-preventing-access.
63. Weixel, N. (April 12, 2019). "Rite Aid Will No Longer Sell E-Cigarettes." The Hill. https://thehill.com/policy/healthcare/438678-rite-aid-will-stop-selling-e-cigarettes/.
64. "Bill Seeks to Ban Online Sales of E-Cigarettes, Raise Age to Buy Tobacco to 21." AJMC, April 17, 2019. https://www.ajmc.com/view/bill-seeks-to-ban-online-sales-of-ecigarettes-raise-age-to-buy-tobacco-to-21.
65. LaVito, A. (September 4, 2019). "Michigan Becomes First State to Ban Sales of Flavored E-Cigarettes." CNBC. https://www.cnbc.com/2019/09/04/michigan-bans-sales-of-flavored-e-cigarettes-restricts-vaping-marketing.html.
66. FDA. Trump Administration Combating Epidemic of Youth E-Cigarette Use with Plan to Clear Market of Unauthorized, Non-Tobacco-Flavored E-Cigarette Products, Office of the Commissioner, 2019, available at: https://www.fda.gov/news-events/press-announcements/trump-administration-combating-epidemic-youth-e-cigarette-use-plan-clear-market-unauthorized-non.
67. McGinley, L. (September 10, 2019). "Bloomberg to Spend $160 Million to Ban Flavored E-Cigarettes." *Washington Post*. www.washingtonpost.com. https://www.washingtonpost.com/health/bloomberg-to-spend-160-million-to-ban-flavored-e-cigarettes/2019/09/09/5abc1e5c-d33c-11e9-9343-40db57cf6abd_story.html.
68. Krishnamoorthi, R. Letter to the Commissioner Food and Drug Administration Regarding Vaping and COVID-19, U.S. Congress, 2020, available at: http://cdn.cnn.com/cnn/2020/images/08/11/2020.08.11.rk.to.fda.re.vaping.and.coronavirus.pdf.
69. Li, D., Croft, D.P., Ossip, D.J., Xie, Z. The Association Between Statewide Vaping Prevalence and COVID-19. Prev Med

Rep. 2020 Dec;20:101254. https://doi.org/10.1016/j.pmedr.2020.101254.

70. Gaiha, S.M., Cheng, J., Halpern-Felsher, B. (August 11, 2020). Association Between Youth Smoking, Electronic Cigarette Use and Coronavirus Disease 2019. J Adolesc Health. www.sciencedirect.com/science/article/abs/pii/S1054139X20303992.
71. Redmond, H. (August 17, 2020). "Anti-Vaping Forces Again Leverage COVID to Seek Prohibition." Filter. https://filtermag.org/vaping-coronavirus-prohibition/.
72. Office of the Commissioner. (March 24, 2020). "FDA Finalizes Enforcement Policy on Unauthorized Flavored Cartridge-Based e-Cigarettes That Appeal to Children, Including Fruit and Mint." FDA. https://www.fda.gov/news-events/press-announcements/fda-finalizes-enforcement-policy-unauthorized-flavored-cartridge-based-e-cigarettes-appeal-children.
73. Office of the Commissioner. (July 21, 2020). "FDA Notifies Companies, Including Puff Bar, to Remove Flavored Disposable E-Cigarettes and Youth-Appealing E-Liquids from Market for Not Having Required Authorization." FDA. https://www.fda.gov/news-events/press-announcements/fda-notifies-companies-including-puff-bar-remove-flavored-disposable-e-cigarettes-and-youth.
74. "FTC Report Highlights Dramatic Surge in Sale of Flavored Disposable E-Cigarettes and Menthol E-cigarette Cartridges." Federal Trade Commission, August 30, 2022. https://www.ftc.gov/news-events/news/press-releases/2022/08/ftc-report-highlights-dramatic-surge-sale-flavored-disposable-e-cigarettes-menthol-e-cigarette.
75. Du, P., Bascom, R., Fan, T., Sinharoy, A., Yingst, J., Mondal, P., Foulds, J. Changes in Flavor Preference in a Cohort of Long-Term Electronic Cigarette Users. Ann Am Thorac Soc. 2020 May;17(5):573–581. https://doi.org/10.1513/AnnalsATS.201906-472OC.
76. Cotti, C., Courtemanche, C., Maclean, J.C., Nesson, E., Pesko, M.F., Tefft, N.W. The Effects of E-cigarette Taxes on e-cigarette Prices and Tobacco Product Sales: Evidence from Retail Panel Data. J Health Econ. 2022 Dec;86:102676. https://doi.org/10.1016/j.jhealeco.2022.102676.

77. McGrady, M. (2020). "Anti-Vaping Activism Driving Smokers Back to Cigarettes, Data Show." InsideSources, May 20, 2020. https://insidesources.com/anti-vaping-activism-driving-smokers-back-to-cigarettes-data-show/.
78. Nicotine Products Tax | Colorado General Assembly. https://leg.colorado.gov/agencies/legislative-council-staff/nicotine-products-tax#:~:text=The%20nicotine%20tax%20is%2030,on%20state%20revenue%20and%20spending.
79. Oregon Department of Revenue: Tobacco Products Tax and Licensing: Businesses: State of Oregon. https://www.oregon.gov/dor/programs/businesses/Pages/tobacco-overview.aspx#:~:text=Inhalant%20delivery%20systems%20are%20taxed,delivery%20systems%20to%20Oregon%20retail.
80. Pesko, M. et al. Open Letter to Congress Regarding NIH-Funded Research. CASAA, 2021, available at: https://casaa.org/wp-content/uploads/Pesko-Congress_ecigtax_11.8.2021-Build-Back-Better-2021.pdf.
81. Lonas, L. (March 23, 2021). "Democrats Urge FDA to Clear Market of All Flavored E-Cigarettes." The Hill. https://thehill.com/policy/healthcare/544583-lawmakers-urge-fda-to-clear-market-of-all-flavored-e-cigarettes/.
82. Office of the Commissioner. "FDA Denies Marketing Applications for About 55,000 Flavored E-cigarette Products for Failing to Provide Evidence They Appropriately Protect Public Health." FDA, August 26, 2021. https://www.fda.gov/news-events/press-announcements/fda-denies-marketing-applications-about-55000-flavored-e-cigarette-products-failing-provide-evidence.
83. Office of the Commissioner. "FDA Makes Significant Progress in Science-Based Public Health Application Review, Taking Action on Over 90% of More Than 6.5 Million 'Deemed' New Tobacco Products Submitted." FDA, September 20, 2021. https://www.fda.gov/news-events/press-announcements/fda-makes-significant-progress-science-based-public-health-application-review-taking-action-over-90.
84. Office of the Commissioner. "FDA Permits Marketing of E-cigarette Products, Marking First Authorization of Its Kind by the Agency." FDA, October 18, 2021. https://www.fda.gov/news-events/press-announcements/fda-permits-marketing-e-cigarette-products-marking-first-authorization-its-kind-agency.

85. Products, Center for Tobacco. "Premarket Tobacco Product Marketing Granted Orders." FDA, April 2023. www.fda.gov. https://www.fda.gov/tobacco-products/premarket-tobacco-product-applications/premarket-tobacco-product-marketing-granted-orders.
86. "FDA Signals It Won't Authorize Flavored E-Liquid PMTAs." Vaping360. https://vaping360.com/vape-news/110937/fda-signals-it-wont-authorize-flavored-e-liquid-pmtas/.
87. United States Court of Appeals for the Fifth Circuit (2023), R.J. Reynolds Vapor Company; RJR Vapor Company, L.L.C.; Avail Vapor Texas, L.L.C.; Mississippi Petroleum Marketers and Convenience Stores Association, Petitioners, Versus Food & Drug Administration; Robert Califf, in his official capacity as Commissioner of the United States Food & Drug Administration; United States Department of Health and Human Services; Xavier Becerra, in his official capacity as Secretary of the United States Department of Health and Human Services, United States Court of Appeals for the Fifth Circuit. Available at: https://www.ca5.uscourts.gov/opinions/pub/23/23-60037-CV0.pdf.
88. Snell, L.M., Nicksic, N., Panteli, D., Burke, S., Eissenberg, T., Fattore, G., Gauci, C., Koprivnikar, H., Murauskiene, L., Reinap, M., Barnes, A.J. Emerging Electronic Cigarette Policies in European Member States, Canada, and the United States. Health Policy. 2021 Apr;125(4):425–435. https://doi.org/10.1016/j.healthpol.2021.02.003.
89. Hammond, D., Reid, J.L., Rynard, V.L., Fong, G.T., Cummings, K.M., McNeill, A., et al. Prevalence of Vaping and Smoking Among Adolescents in Canada, England, and the United States: Repeat National Cross Sectional Surveys. BMJ. 2019;365:l2219 https://doi.org/10.1136/bmj.l2219.
90. ASH—Action for Smokefree 2025. ASH Year 10 Snapshot Survey. https://www.ash.org.nz/ash_year_10.
91. Guerin, N., White, V. (2020). ASSAD 2017 Statistics & Trends: Australian Secondary Students' Use of Tobacco, Alcohol, Over-the-counter Drugs, and Illicit Substances. 2nd ed. Cancer Council Victoria. https://www.health.gov.au/sites/default/files/documents/2020/07/secondary-school-students-use-of-tobacco-alcohol-and-other-drugs-in-2017.pdf.

92. King, B.A, Alam, S., Promoff, G., Arrazola, R., Dube, S.R. Awareness and Ever Use of Electronic Cigarettes Among U.S. Adults, 2010–2011. Nicotine Tob Res. 2013;15(9):1623–1627.
93. Centers for Disease Control and Prevention. Tobacco Use Among Middle and High School Students—United States, 2011–2015. Morbidity and Mortality Weekly Report 2016;65(14):361–367.
94. Morgan Snell, L., Nicksic, N., Panteli, D., Burke, S., Eissenberg, T., Fattore, G., Gauci, C., Koprivnikar, H., Murauskiene, L., Reinap, M., Barnes, A.J., Emerging Electronic Cigarette Policies in European Member States, Canada, and the United States. Health Policy. 2021;125(4):425–435. https://doi.org/10.1016/j.healthpol.2021.02.003.
95. Campus, B. Fafard, P., St. Pierre, J., Hoffman, S.J. Comparing the Regulation and Incentivization of E-cigarettes Across 97 Countries. Soc Sci Med. 2021;291:114187. https://doi.org/10.1016/j.socscimed.2021.114187.
96. "Germany: Federal Court of Justice Classifies Liquids for E-Cigarettes as Tobacco Products." Library of Congress, Washington, D.C. 20540 USA. https://www.loc.gov/item/global-legal-monitor/2016-02-23/germany-federal-court-of-justice-classifies-liquids-for-e-cigarettes-as-tobacco-products/. Accessed 10 May 2023.
97. Country Laws Regulating E-Cigarettes | Global Tobacco Control. https://www.globaltobaccocontrol.org/en/policy-scan/e-cigarettes. Accessed 10 May 2023.
98. Caponnetto, P., Saitta, D., Sweanor, D., Polosa, R. What to Consider When Regulating Electronic Cigarettes: Pros, Cons and Unintended Consequences. Int J Drug Policy. 2015 Jun;26(6):554–559. https://doi.org/10.1016/j.drugpo.2015.03.001.
99. Guidance for Licensing Electronic Cigarettes and Other Inhaled Nicotine-Containing Products as Medicines." Government of the United Kingdom. October 29, 2021. https://www.gov.uk/guidance/licensing-procedure-for-electronic-cigarettes-as-medicines.
100. Caponnetto, P., Saitta, D., Sweanor, D., Polosa, R. What to Consider When Regulating Electronic Cigarettes: Pros, Cons and Unintended Consequences. Int J Drug Policy. 2015 Jun;26(6):554–559. https://doi.org/10.1016/j.drugpo.2015.03.001.

101. "Germany: Federal Court of Justice Classifies Liquids for E-cigarettes as Tobacco Products." Library of Congress, Washington, D.C. 20540 USA. https://www.loc.gov/item/global-legal-monitor/2016-02-23/germany-federal-court-of-justice-classifies-liquids-for-e-cigarettes-as-tobacco-products/. Accessed 10 May 2023.
102. Tobacco Reporter. "Fun in, Harm Out." Tobacco Reporter. February 1, 2016, 2016, available at: https://tobaccoreporter.com/2016/02/01/fun-in-harm-out/.
103. "Guidance for Licensing Electronic Cigarettes and Other Inhaled Nicotine-Containing Products as Medicines." GOV.UK, October 29. 2021. https://www.gov.uk/guidance/licensing-procedure-for-electronic-cigarettes-as-medicines.
104. Dept. Health and Social Care. Smokers Urged to Swap Cigarettes for Vapes in World First Scheme, Press release, 2023, available at: https://www.gov.uk/government/news/smokers-urged-to-swap-cigarettes-for-vapes-in-world-first-scheme.
105. Klein, D.E., Chaiton, M., Kundu, A., et al. A Literature Review on International E-cigarette Regulatory Policies. Curr Addict Rep. 2020;7:509–519. https://doi.org/10.1007/s40429-020-00332-w.
106. ASH UK. Use of E-cigarettes (Vapes) Among Adults in Great Britain. Reasons Why Smokers Haven't Tried or Have Stopped Using E-cigarettes, 2022, available at: https://ash.org.uk/uploads/Use-of-e-cigarettes-vapes-among-adults-in-Great-Britain-2022.pdf?v=1661865959.
107. Hirshbein, L.D. Politics, Profit, and Psychiatric Diagnosis: A Case Study of Tobacco Use Disorder. Am J Public Health. 2014 Nov;104(11):2076–2084. https://doi.org/10.2105/AJPH.2014.302125.
108. Conrad, P., Schneider, J.W. *Deviance and Medicalization, From Badness to Sickness*. Temple University Press, 1980.
109. Gundle, K.R., Dingel, M.J., Koenig, B.A. To Prove This Is the Industry's Best Hope': Big Tobacco's Support of Research on the Genetics of Nicotine Addiction. Addiction. 2010 Jun;105(6):974–983. https://doi.org/10.1111/j.1360-0443.2010.02940.x.
110. At the time of writing, Belgium, Australia, Brunei, and Malaysia consider nicotine-containing e-cigarettes as dangerous substances.

111. Zainuddin, A. "Khairy: Teens Won't Be Jailed For Individual Possession of Cigarettes, Vape." CodeBlue, July 8, 2022. https://codeblue.galencentre.org/2022/07/08/khairy-teens-wont-be-jailed-for-individual-possession-of-cigarettes-vape/.
112. Australian Government, Department of Health and Aged Care, Therapeutic Goods Administration. Nicotine vaping products hub, 2022, available at: https://www.tga.gov.au/products/medicines/prescription-medicines/nicotine-vaping-products-hub.
113. Mendelson, C. *Stop Smoking Start Vaping: The Healthy Truth About Vaping*. Aurora House, 2021.
114. Davey, M. "Australia to Ban Non-Prescription Vapes in Biggest Smoking Reforms in a Decade." *The Guardian*, May 1, 2023. https://www.theguardian.com/australia-news/2023/may/01/australia-to-ban-non-prescription-vapes-in-biggest-smoking-reforms-in-a-decade.
115. Chaloupka, F.J., Yurekli, A., Fong, G.T. Tobacco Taxes as a Tobacco Control Strategy. Tob Control. 2012;21(2):172–180.
116. Levy, D., de Almeida, L.M., Szklo, A. The Brazil SimSmoke Policy Simulation Model: The Effect of Strong Tobacco Control Policies on Smoking Prevalence and Smoking-Attributable Deaths in a Middle Income Nation. PLoS Medicine. 2012;9(11);e1001336.
117. Levy, D.T., Nikolayev, L., Mumford, E. Recent Trends in Smoking and the Role of Public Policies: Results from the SimSmoke Tobacco Control Policy Simulation Model. Addiction. 2005;100(10):1526–1536.
118. Levy, D.T., Boyle, R.G., Abrams DB. The Role of Public Policies in Reducing Smoking: The Minnesota SimSmoke Tobacco Policy Model. Am J Prev Med. 2012;43(5):S179–S186.
119. Levy, D., Rodríguez-Buño, R.L., Hu, T.W., Moran, A.E. The Potential Effects of Tobacco Control in China: Projections from the China SimSmoke Simulation Model. BMJ. 2014:348.
120. Levy, D.T., Blackman, K., Currie, L.M., Mons, U. Germany SimSmoke: The Effect of Tobacco Control Policies on Future Smoking Prevalence and Smoking-Attributable Deaths in Germany. Nicotine & Tobacco Research: Official Journal of the Society for Research on Nicotine and Tobacco. 2013;15(2):465–473. https://doi.org/10.1093/ntr/nts158.

121. For an overview of the rationale behind tobacco taxes, see Prieger, J.E. (2021). Smoke or Vapor? Regulation of Tobacco and Vaping. In Hoffer A, Nesbit T (Eds.), *Regulation and Economic Opportunity: Blueprints for Reform* (Ch. 18). The Center for Growth & Opportunity at Utah State University.
122. The taxes discussed here are excise taxes that are specific to e-cigarette products. In most markets, sales of e-cigarettes are also subject to general sales taxes, a VAT, or import duties even in the absence of an excise tax.
123. Thompson, J. (2023). Vape & E-Cig Tax by State. IGEN. https://igentax.com/vape-tax-state/.
124. Abouk, R., Courtemanche, C., Dave, D., Feng, B., Friedman, A.S., Maclean, J.C., Safford, S, et al. Intended and Unintended Effects of E-cigarette Taxes on Youth Tobacco Use. J Health Econ. 2023;87:102720.
125. Durbin, R.J. 2021. "Text - S.1314 - 117th Congress (2021–2022): Tobacco Tax Equity Act of 2021." Legislation. 2021/2022. April 22, 2021. https://www.congress.gov/bill/117thcongress/senate-bill/1314/text.
126. McDonald, J. (2024). Vaping Taxes in the United States and Around the World. Vaping360.com. https://vaping360.com/learn/tax-rates-on-vaping-products/#vape-taxes-around-the-world.
127. Hunter, W.J., Nelson, M.A. Excise Taxation and the Theory of Tax Exploitation, 45 Pub. Fin. 268, 269 (1990).
128. Wright, J. Campaign Contributions and Congressional Voting on Tobacco Policy, 1980–2000. Business and Politics. 2004;6(3):1–26.
129. The tobacco industry makes sizable political contributions in aggregate, but the amounts offered to individual politicians do not appear to be largely relative to other sources. In the 2019–2020 election cycle, tobacco political action committees (PACs) donated $1.36 million to candidates for federal office (cite: Campaign for Tobacco Free Kids (2021). Tobacco Company Political Action Committee (PAC) Contributions to Federal Candidates by Election Cycle, PAC, and Party, 2005–2020. https://www.tobaccofreekids.org/assets/content/what_we_do/federal_issues/campaign_contributions/Tob_Co_PAC_Donations_2005-2020_SUMMARY_TABLES.pdf), which constituted only 0.3% of total campaign funding from all PACs (see: Federal Election Commission (April 2, 2021). Statistical Summary of

24-Month Campaign Activity of the 2019–2020 Election Cycle, Press release. https://www.fec.gov/updates/statistical-summary-24-month-campaign-activity-2019-2020-election-cycle). The tobacco industry would have to contribute more than 50 times as much money just to make it into the top 20 in the list of political contributions by industry (see: Which Industries Are Giving the Most Money to PACS, Parties and Candidates? OpenSecrets.org. https://www.opensecrets.org/elections-overview/industries). The average contribution to politicians accepting money from tobacco PACs was about $19,000 for an eight-year period in the 1990s (which would be about $35,000 in 2022), [cite: Luke, DA, & Krauss, M. (2004). Where there's smoke there's money: tobacco industry campaign contributions and U.S. Congressional voting. Am J Prev Med. 27(5), 363–372] which is less than two days of contributions raised by the typical senator (see: Ratliff, Amisa [October 20, 2022]. The Congressional Fundraising Treadmill: Six Numbers to Know from New Campaign Finance Filings, July – September 2022. Issueone.org. https://issueone.org/articles/the-congressional-fundraising-treadmill-six-numbers-to-know-from-new-campaign-finance-filings-july-september-2022).

130. From 2005 to 2020, Contributions to Candidates for federal office in the U.S. from tobacco company political action committees declined by over 40%. See Campaign for Tobacco Free Kids (2021). Tobacco Company Political Action Committee (PAC) Contributions to Federal Candidates by Election Cycle, PAC, and Party, 2005–2020.
131. Stults, B.G., Winters, R.F. (2005). *The Political Economy of Taxes and the Vote*. Unpublished Manuscript. https://citeseerx.ist.psu.edu/document?repid=rep1&type=pdf&doi=31a9e34a55c894e359aae542c2d218043feeaa1f.
132. Chaloupka, F.J., Warner, K.E. The Economics of Smoking. Handbook of Health Economics. 2000;1:1539–1627.
133. DeCicca, P., Kenkel, D. Synthesizing Econometric Evidence: The Case of Demand Elasticity Estimates. Risk Analysis. 2015;35(6):1073–1085. https://doi.org/10.1111/risa.12363.
134. IARC Working Group on the Effectiveness of Tax and Price Policies for Tobacco Control, & International Agency for Research on Cancer. (2011). *Effectiveness of Tax and Price Policies for Tobacco*

Control (Ser. IARC Handbooks of Cancer Prevention, v. 14). International Agency for Research on Cancer.

135. Andrews, R.L., Franke, G.R. The Determinants of Cigarette Consumption: A Meta-Analysis. J Public Policy & Mark. 1991;10(1):81–100. https://doi.org/10.1177/074391569101000107.
136. Gallet, C.A., List, J.A. Cigarette Demand: A Meta-Analysis of Elasticities. Health Econ. 2003;12(10):821–835. https://doi.org/10.1002/hec.765.
137. Prieger, J.E. Optimal Taxation of Cigarettes and E-cigarettes: Principles for Taxing Reduced-Harm Tobacco Products. Forum Health Econ Policy. 2023;26(2):41–64. https://doi.org/10.1515/fhep-2022-0025.
138. IARC Working Group on the Effectiveness of Tax and Price Policies for Tobacco Control, & International Agency for Research on Cancer. (2011). *Effectiveness of tax and price policies for tobacco control* (Ser. IARC Handbooks of Cancer Prevention, v. 14). International Agency for Research on Cancer.
139. DeCicca, P., Kenkel, D. Synthesizing Econometric Evidence: The Case of Demand Elasticity Estimates. Risk Analysis. 2015;35(6):1073–1085. https://doi.org/10.1111/risa.12363.
140. Auerbach, A.J. The Theory of Excess Burden and Optimal Taxation. In Auerbach, AJ. Feldstein M. (Eds.), *Handbook of public economics*, Vol. 1. Elsevier, 1985.
141. Saffer, H., Dench, D., Grossman, M., Dave, D. E-cigarettes and Adult Smoking: Evidence from Minnesota. J Risk Uncertainty. 2020;60:207–228.
142. Cotti, C., Courtemanche, C., Maclean, J.C., Nesson, E., Pesko, M.F., Tefft, N.W. The Effects of E-cigarette Taxes on e-cigarette Prices and Tobacco Product Sales: Evidence from Retail Panel Data. J Health Econ. 2022;86:102676.
143. Allcott, H., Rafkin, C. Optimal Regulation of E-cigarettes: Theory and Evidence. Am Econ J: Econ Policy. 2022;14(4):1–50.
144. Allcott and Rafkin estimate an approximate elasticity (defined in their case as $\partial \ln(p)/\partial \ln(t+1)$, where p is the retail price of e-cigarettes and t is the tax rate in percent) of 0.54. Given the non-standard denominator, this expression is a bit larger than a true elasticity by a factor of $r + 1/r$. For example, for a 50% ad valorem tax rate (which would be middle-of-the-pack in the data

they used), the estimate of 0.54 converts to an elasticity of prices with respect to tax rate of 0.53.

145. Pigou, A.C. *The Economics of Welfare*. Macmillan, 1920.
146. One study found that the Pigouvian tax (i.e., a tax meant to reflect external costs from environmental tobacco smoke) would have been US$0.27 per pack in the 1990s (cite: Viscusi, W.K. Cigarette Taxation and the Social Consequences of Smoking. Tax Policy and the Economy. 1995;9:51–101), which was about half the actual federal + state excise tax rate faced by the average consumer in the U.S. at the time (see Fig. 2 of Prieger (2021)[158] and note that the trend line for the population-weighted federal and state tax rate is the highest one in the graph, though mislabeled). That tax rate, inflation adjusted, would be only $0.53 today, when the average consumer in the U.S. faces cigarette taxes of about $3 per pack.
147. For discussion of the fiscal externalities argument for taxing unhealthy products (see Browning, E.K. The Myth of Fiscal Externalities. Public Finance Review. 1999 Jan;27(1):3–18; Manning, W.G. et al. The Taxes of Sin: Do Smokers and Drinkers Pay Their Way? JAMA 1989;261(11):1604–1609, https://doi.org/10.1001/jama.1989.03420110080028; Prieger, J.E. (2021). Smoke or Vapor? Regulation of Tobacco and Vaping. In A. Hoffer & T. Nesbit (Eds.), *Regulation and Economic Opportunity: Blueprints for Reform*. The Center for Growth and Opportunity, Utah State University).
148. Prieger, J.E., Optimal Taxation of Cigarettes and E–cigarettes: Principles for Taxing Reduced-Harm Tobacco Products. Forum Health Econ Policy. 2023;26(2):41–64. https://doi.org/10.1515/fhep-2022-0025.
149. Gruber, J., Köszegi, B. *A Modern Economic View of Tobacco Taxation*. Paris, France: International Union Against Tuberculosis and Lung Disease. 2008.
150. Chaloupka, F.J., Yurekli, A., Fong, G.T. Tobacco Taxes as a Tobacco Control Strategy. Tob Control. 2012;21(2):172–180.
151. Hamilton, W.L., Biener, L., Rodger, C.N. Who Supports Tobacco Excise Taxes? Factors Associated with Towns' and Individuals' Support in Massachusetts. J Public Health Manag Pract. 2005;11(4):333–340.

152. Lum, K.L, Barnes, R.L, Glantz, S.A. Enacting Tobacco Taxes by Direct Popular Vote in the United States: Lessons from 20 Years of Experience. Tob Control. 2009;18(5):377–386.
153. Campaign for Tobacco-Free Kids, *A State-by-State Look at the 1998 Tobacco Settlement 21 Years Later*, 2020. https://www.tobaccofreekids.org/what-we-do/us/statereport.
154. As with tax pass-through, the relationship between the elasticity of demand and whether tax revenue rises from a tax hike depends on many factors, including the elasticity of supply (or marginal cost, in the case of a non-competitive industry), pre-existing taxes, and the markups set by suppliers. In the simple case of competitive supply at constant marginal cost, raising the unit tax rate will increase tax revenue if and only if the absolute value of the elasticity of demand is less than the ratio of the tax-inclusive retail price to the producer price. Since the latter ratio is greater than one, being in the inelastic portion of the demand curve is a sufficient but not necessary condition for revenue to rise; demand in the elastic (but not too elastic) region also yields that result.
155. Chaloupka, F.J., Yurekli, A., Fong, G.T. Tobacco Taxes as a Tobacco Control Strategy. Tob Control. 2012;21(2):172–180.
156. Reiter, J.B. Citizens or Sinners the Economic and Political Inequity of Sin Taxes on Tobacco and Alcohol Products. Colum J L Soc Probl. 1996;29(3):443–468.
157. Perhaps contrary to common perception, use of e-cigarettes is more than twice as likely for an individual in a household earning less than US$5,000 a year than for one in a household earning $150,000 or more (see: Prieger, J.E. Optimal Taxation of Cigarettes and E-cigarettes: Principles for Taxing Reduced-Harm Tobacco Products. Forum Health Econ Policy. 2023;26(2):41–64. https://doi.org/10.1515/fhep-2022-0025].
158. Prieger, J.E. (2021). Smoke or Vapor? Regulation of Tobacco and Vaping. In A Hoffer, T Nesbit (Eds.), *Regulation and Economic Opportunity: Blueprints for Reform*. The Center for Growth and Opportunity, Utah State University.
159. Prieger, J.E. Optimal Taxation of Cigarettes and E-cigarettes: Principles for Taxing Reduced-Harm Tobacco Products. Forum Health Econ Policy. 2023;26(2):41–64. https://doi.org/10.1515/fhep-2022-0025.

160. Farrelly, M.C., et al. Response by Adults to Increases in Cigarette Prices by Sociodemographic Characteristics. South Econ J. 2001;68(1):156–165. https://doi.org/10.2307/1061518.
161. Ma, S., Jiang, S., Ling, M., Lu, B., Chen, J., Shang, C. Excise Taxes and Pricing Activities of E-liquid Products Sold in Online Vape Shops. Tobacco Control. 2022.
162. Reiter, J.B. Citizens or Sinners the Economic and Political Inequity of Sin Taxes on Tobacco and Alcohol Products. Columbia J Law Soc Probl. 1996;29(3):443–468.
163. Hunter, W.J., Nelson, M.A. Excise Taxation and the Theory of Tax Exploitation, 45 Pub. Fin. 1990;268: 269.
164. Gruber, J.H., Mullainathan, S. Do Cigarette Taxes Make Smokers Happier. BE J Econ Anal Policy. 2005;5(1).
165. Chaloupka, F.J., Cummings, K.M., Morley, C.P., Horan, J.K. Tax, Price and Cigarette Smoking: Evidence from the Tobacco Documents and Implications for Tobacco Company Marketing Strategies. Tobacco Control. 2002;11(suppl 1):i62–i72.
166. While two of the studies cited report that taxes on e-cigarettes are associated with lower prevalence of current use of e-cigarettes, the estimates are insignificant by the usual criterion of a 5% level hypothesis test.
167. Choi, K., Omole, T., Wills, T., Merianos, A.L. E-cigarette-Inclusive Smoke-Free Policies, Excise Taxes, Tobacco 21 and Changes in Youth E-cigarette Use: 2017–2019. Tob Control. 2022;31(6):758–761.
168. Abouk, R., Courtemanche, C., Dave, D., Feng, B., Friedman, A.S., Maclean, J.C., Safford, S., et al. Intended and Unintended Effects of E-cigarette Taxes on Youth Tobacco Use. J Health Econ. 2023;87:102720. https://doi.org/10.1016/j.jhealeco.2022.102720.
169. Anderson, D.M., Matsuzawa, K., Sabia, J.J. Cigarette Taxes and Teen Marijuana Use. Natl Tax J. 2020;73(2):475–510. https://doi.org/10.17310/ntj.2020.2.06.
170. One of the two studies available finds no significant impact on current use of e-cigarettes but does find a significant effect on daily use. The other finds no significant impact of taxes on current use.

171. Jun, J., Kim, J.K. Do State Regulations on E-cigarettes Have Impacts on the E-cigarette Prevalence? Tob Control. 2021;30:221–226.
172. Friedman, A.S., Pesko, M.F. Young Adult Responses to Taxes on Cigarettes and Electronic Nicotine Delivery Systems. Addiction. 2022;117(12):3121–3128.
173. Zhu, S.H. Four Hundred and Sixty Brands of E-cigarettes and Counting: Implications for Product Regulation. Tob Control. 2014;23(Suppl 3):iii3–iii9.
174. Audrain-McGovern, J., Strasser, A.A., Wileyto, E.P. The Impact of Flavoring on the Rewarding and Reinforcing Value of E-cigarettes with Nicotine Among Young Adult Smokers. Drug Alcohol Depend. 2016;166:263–367. https://doi.org/10.1016/j.drugalcdep.2016.06.030.
175. Meernik, C., Baker, H.M., Kowitt, S.D. Impact of Non-menthol Flavours in E-cigarettes on Perceptions and Use: An Updated Systematic Review. BMJ Open. 2019;9(10). https://www.doi.org/10.1136/bmjopen-2019-031598.
176. Ford, A. Adolescents' Responses to the Promotion and Flavouring of E-cigarettes. Int J Public Health. 2015:1–10.
177. Morean, M.E., Butler, E.R., Bold, K.W., Kong, G., Camenga, D.R., et al. Correction: Preferring More E-cigarette Flavors Is Associated with E-cigarette Use Frequency Among Adolescents But Not Adults. PLoS ONE. 2018;13(9):e0204349. https://doi.org/10.1371/journal.pone.0204349.
178. Harrell, M.B., Weaver, S.R., Loukas, A., Creamer, M., Marti, C.N., Jackson, C.D., Heath, J.W., Nayak, P., Perry, C.L., Pechacek, T.F., Eriksen, M.P. Flavored E-cigarette Use: Characterizing Youth, Young Adult, and Adult Users. Prev Med Rep. 2016 Nov 11;5:33–40. https://doi.org/10.1016/j.pmedr.2016.11.001.
179. American Academy of Pediatrics. E-cigarettes. https://www.aap.org/en-us/advocacy-and-policy/aap-health-initiatives/Richmond-Center/Pages/Electronic-Nicotine-Delivery-Systems.aspx. Accessed 6 August 2019.
180. Berry, K.M., Fetterman, J.L., Benjamin, E.J., et al. Association of Electronic Cigarette Use with Subsequent Initiation of Tobacco Cigarettes in US Youths. JAMA Netw Open. 2019;2(2):e187794. https://doi.org/10.1001/jamanetworkopen.2018.7794.

181. Muthumalage, T., Lamb, T., Friedman, M.R. et al. E-cigarette Flavored Pods Induce Inflammation, Epithelial Barrier Dysfunction, and DNA Damage in Lung Epithelial Cells and Monocytes. Sci Rep. 2019;9:19035. https://doi.org/10.1038/s41598-019-51643-6.
182. Lee, W., Ong, S., Zhou, Y., et al. Modeling Cardiovascular Risks of E-Cigarettes with Human-Induced Pluripotent Stem Cell–Derived Endothelial Cells. J Am Coll Cardiol. 2019 Jun, 73 (21) 2722–2737.
183. Ween, M.P., Moshensky, A., Thredgold, L., Bastian, N.A., Hamon, R., Badiei, A., Nguyen, P.T., Herewane, K., Jersmann, H., Bojanowski, C.M., Shin, J., Reynolds, P.N., Crotty, Alexander, L.E, Hodge, S.J. E-cigarettes and Health Risks: More to the Flavor Than Just the Name. Am J Physiol Lung Cell Mol Physiol. 2021 Apr 1;320(4):L600-L614. https://doi.org/10.1152/ajplung.00370.2020.
184. Erythropel, H.C., Jabba, S.V., DeWinter, T.M., Mendizabal, M., Anastas, P.T., Jordt, S.E., Zimmerman, J.B. Formation of Flavorant–Propylene Glycol Adducts with Novel Toxicological Properties in Chemically Unstable E-cigarette Liquids. Nicotine Tob Res. 2019 Sept;21(9):1248–1258. https://doi.org/10.1093/ntr/nty192.
185. Erythropel, H.C., Jabba, S.V., DeWinter, T.M., Mendizabal, M., Anastas, P.T., Jordt, S.E., Zimmerman, J.B. Formation of Flavorant–Propylene Glycol Adducts with Novel Toxicological Properties in Chemically Unstable E-cigarette Liquids. Nicotine Tob Res. 2019;21:1248–1258. https://doi.org/10.1093/ntr/nty192.
186. Jabba, S.V., Diaz, A.N., Erythropel, H.C., Zimmerman, J.B., Jordt, S.E. Chemical Adducts of Reactive Flavor Aldehydes Formed in E-cigarette Liquids Are Cytotoxic and Inhibit Mitochondrial Function in Respiratory Epithelial Cells. Nicotine Tob Res. 2020;22:S25–S34. https://doi.org/10.1093/ntr/ntaa185.
187. Ween, M., Ahern, J., Carroll, A., Hodge, G., Pizzutto, S., Jersmann, H., Reynolds, P., Hodge, S. A Small Volume Technique to Examine and Compare Alveolar Macrophage Phagocytosis of Apoptotic Cells and Non Typeable Haemophilus Influenzae (NTHi). J Immunol Methods. 2016;429: 7–14. https://doi.org/10.1016/j.jim.2015.12.004.

188. Ward, A.M., Yaman, R., Ebbert, J.O. Electronic Nicotine Delivery System Design and Aerosol Toxicants: A Systematic Review. PLoS ONE 2020;15:e0234189.
189. Behar, R.Z., Wang, Y., Talbot, P. Comparing the Cytotoxicity of Electronic Cigarette Fluids, Aerosols and Solvents. Tob Control. 2018;27:325–333.
190. Schweitzer, K.S., Chen, S.X., Law, S., Van Demark, M., Poirier, C., Justice, M.J., Hubbard, W.C., Kim, E.S., Lai, X., Wang, M., Kranz, W.D., Carroll, C.J., Ray, B.D., Bittman, R., Goodpaster, J., Petrache, I. Endothelial Disruptive Pro-inflammatory Effects of Nicotine and E-cigarette Vapor Exposures. Am J Physiol Lung Cell Mol Physiol. 2015;309:L175–L187. https://doi.org/10.1152/ajplung.00411.2014.
191. Scheffler, S., Dieken, H., Krischenowski, O., Forster, C., Branscheid, D., Aufderheide, M. Evaluation of E-cigarette Liquid Vapor and Mainstream Cigarette Smoke After Direct Exposure of Primary Human Bronchial Epithelial Cells. Int J Environ Res Public Health. 2015;12:3915–3925. https://doi.org/10.3390/ijerph120403915.
192. Ween, M.P., Hamon, R., Macowan, M.G., Thredgold, L., Reynolds, P.R., Hodge, S.J. Effects of E-cigarette E-liquid Components on Bronchial Epithelial Cells: Demonstration of Dysfunctional Efferocytosis. Respirology. 2020;25:620–628. https://doi.org/10.1111/resp.13696.
193. Ween, M.P., Whittall, J.J., Hamon, R., Reynolds, P.N., Hodge, S.J. Phagocytosis and Inflammation: Exploring the Effects of the Components of E-cigarette Vapor on Macrophages. Physiol Rep. 2017;5:e13370. https://doi.org/10.14814/phy2.13370.
194. Wölkart, G., Kollau, A., Stessel, H., Russwurm, M., Koesling, D., Schrammel, A., et al. Effects of Flavoring Compounds Used in Electronic Cigarette Refill Liquids on Endothelial and Vascular Function. PLoS ONE. 2019;14(9):e0222152. https://doi.org/10.1371/journal.pone.0222152.
195. Ween, M.P., Moshensky, A., Thredgold, L., Bastian, N.A., Hamon, R., Badiei, A., Nguyen, P.T., Herewane, K., Jersmann, H., Bojanowski, C.M., Shin, J., Reynolds, P.N., Crotty, Alexander, L.E., Hodge, S.J. E-cigarettes and Health Risks: More to the Flavor Than Just the Name. Am J Physiol Lung Cell

Mol Physiol. 2021 Apr 1;320(4):L600–L614. https://doi.org/10.1152/ajplung.00370.2020.
196. Ween, M.P., Moshensky, A., Thredgold, L., Bastian, N.A., Hamon, R., Badiei, A., Nguyen, P.T., Herewane, K., Jersmann, H., Bojanowski, C.M., Shin, J., Reynolds, P.N., Crotty, Alexander, L.E., Hodge, S.J. E-cigarettes and Health Risks: More to the Flavor Than Just the Name. Am J Physiol Lung Cell Mol Physiol. 2021 Apr 1;320(4):L600–L614. https://doi.org/10.1152/ajplung.00370.2020.
197. Farsalinos, K., Lagoumintzis, G. Toxicity Classification of E-cigarette Flavouring Compounds Based on European Union Regulation: Analysis of Findings from a Recent Study. Harm Reduct J. 2019;16:48. https://doi.org/10.1186/s12954-019-0318-2.
198. Audrain-McGovern, J., Strasser, A.A., Wileyto, E.P. The Impact of Flavoring on the Rewarding and Reinforcing Value of E-Cigarettes with Nicotine Among Young Adult Smokers. Drug Alcohol Depend. 2016;166:263–367. https://doi.org/10.1016/j.drugalcdep.2016.06.030.
199. Russell, C., McKeganey, N., Dickson, T., Nides, M. Changing Patterns of First E-cigarette Flavor Used and Current Flavors Used by 20,836 Adult Frequent E-cigarette Users in the USA. Harm Reduct J. 2018;15(1):33. https://doi.org/10.1186/s12954-018-0238-6.
200. Friedman, A.S., Xu, S. Associations of Flavored E-Cigarette Uptake with Subsequent Smoking Initiation and Cessation. JAMA Netw Open. 2020;3(6):e203826. https://doi.org/10.1001/jamanetworkopen.2020.3826.
201. Li, L., Borland, R., Cummings, K.M., et al. How Does the Use of Flavored Nicotine Vaping Products Relate to Progression Towards Quitting Smoking? Findings from the 2016 and 2018 ITC 4CV Surveys. Nicotine Tob Res. 2021;ntab033; e-pub ahead of print February 25, 2021. https://doi.org/10.1093/ntr/ntab033.
202. Friedman, A.S., Xu, S. Associations of Flavored E-Cigarette Uptake with Subsequent Smoking Initiation and Cessation. JAMA Netw Open. 2020;3(6):e203826. https://doi.org/10.1001/jamanetworkopen.2020.3826.

203. Glasser, A.M., Vojjala, M., Cantrell, J., et al. Patterns of E-Cigarette Use and Subsequent Cigarette Smoking Cessation Over Two Years (2013/2014 to 2015/2016) in the Population Assessment of Tobacco and Health (PATH) Study. Nicotine Tob Res. 2021;23(4):669–677. https://doi.org/10.1093/ntr/ntaa182.
204. Friedman, A.S., Xu, S. Associations of Flavored E-Cigarette Uptake with Subsequent Smoking Initiation and Cessation. JAMA Netw Open. 2020;3(6):e203826. https://doi.org/10.1001/jamanetworkopen.2020.3826.
205. Farsalinos, K., Romagna, G., Tsiapras, D. et al. Impact of Flavour Variability on Electronic Cigarette Use Experience: an Internet Survey. Int J Environ Res Public Health. 2013;10:7272–7282. https://doi.org/10.3390/ijerph10127272.
206. Etter, J.F. Electronic Cigarettes: A Survey of Users. BMC Public Health. 2010;10. https://doi.org/10.1186/1471-2458-10-231.
207. Gentry, S.V., Ward, E., Dawkins, L., et al. Reported Patterns of Vaping to Support Long-Term Abstinence from Smoking: A Cross-Sectional Survey of a Convenience Sample of Vapers. Harm Reduct J. 2020;17:70. https://doi.org/10.1186/s12954-020-00418-8.
208. Du, P., Bascom, R., Fan, T., Sinharoy, A., Yingst, J., Mondal, P., Foulds, J. Changes in Flavor Preference in a Cohort of Long-Term Electronic Cigarette Users. Ann Am Thorac Soc. 2020 May;17(5):573–581. https://doi.org/10.1513/AnnalsATS.201906-472OC.
209. Russell, C., McKeganey, N., Dickson, T., Nides, M. Changing Patterns of First E-Cigarette Flavor Used and Current Flavors Used by 20,836 Adult Frequent E-cigarette Users in the USA. Harm Reduct J. 2018;15(1):33. https://doi.org/10.1186/s12954-018-0238-6.
210. Krüsemann, E.J.Z., Boesveldt, S., de Graaf, K., Talhout, R. An E-Liquid Flavor Wheel: A Shared Vocabulary Based on Systematically Reviewing E-Liquid Flavor Classifications in Literature. Nicotine Tob Res. 2019 Sep 19;21(10):1310–1319. https://doi.org/10.1093/ntr/nty101.
211. Krüsemann, E.J.Z., Havermans, A., Pennings, J.L.A., de Graaf, K., Boesveldt, S., Talhout, R. Comprehensive Overview of Common E-liquid Ingredients and How They Can Be Used

to Predict an E-liquid's Flavour Category. Tob Control. 2021 Mar;30(2):185–191. https://doi.org/10.1136/tobaccocontrol-2019-055447.
212. Physicians for a Smoke Free Canada. E-cigarette Flavour Restrictions. Physicians for a Smoke Free, 2021, available at: https://smoke-free.ca/SUAP/2021/e-cigarette-flavour%20restrictions.pdf.
213. Boakye, E., Dzaye, O., Erhabor, J., et al. Impact of the Food and Drug Administration Enforcement Policy on Flavored E-cigarettes on the Online Popularity of Disposable E-cigarettes: Analyses of Google Search Query Data. BMC Public Health. 2022;22:1937. https://doi.org/10.1186/s12889-022-14367-3.
214. "FDA Signals It Won't Authorize Flavored E-Liquid PMTAs." Vaping360. https://vaping360.com/vape-news/110937/fda-signals-it-wont-authorize-flavored-e-liquid-pmtas/. Accessed 10 May 2023.
215. Health Canada. Consultation: Proposed Vaping Products' Flavour Regulations and Order. June 18, 2021. https://www.canada.ca/en/health-canada/programs/consultation-proposed-vaping-product-flavour-regulations-order.html.
216. Health Canada. Vaping Product Regulation [Internet]. Aem, 2020, available at: https://www.canada.ca/en/health-canada/services/smoking-tobacco/vaping/product-safety-regulation.html.
217. Azagba, S., Shan, L., Latham, K. Adolescent Dual Use Classification and Its Association with Nicotine Dependence and Quit Intentions. J Adolesc Health. 2019 Aug;65(2):195–201. https://doi.org/10.1016/j.jadohealth.2019.04.009.
218. Ali, M., Gray, T.R., Martinez, D.J., Curry, L.E., Horn, K.A. Risk Profiles of Youth Single, Dual, and Poly Tobacco Users. Nicotine Tob Res. 2016;18:1614–1621. https://doi.org/10.1093/ntr/ntw028.
219. Hammond, D., Rynard, V.L., Reid, J.L. Changes in Prevalence of Vaping Among Youths in the United States, Canada, and England from 2017 to 2019. JAMA Pediatr. 2020;174(8):797–800. https://doi.org/10.1001/jamapediatrics.2020.0901.
220. Saudi Food and Drug Authority. Controls and Requirements for Electronic Smoking Devices Version No. 1. Kingdom of Saudi

Arabia, 2019, available at: https://d3vqfzrrx1ccvd.cloudfront.net/uploads/legislation/Saudi%20Arabia/Saudi-Arabia-SFDA-E-Cig-Requirements.pdf.

221. Ministry of Health. (n.d.). Law on Restriction on Advertising and Marketing of Tobacco and Smoking Products (5743) 1983, State of Israel. Available at: https://d3vqfzrrx1ccvd.cloudfront.net/uploads/legislation/Israel/Israel-APS-Law.pdf.
222. Goniewicz, M.L., Gupta, R., Lee, Y.H., Reinhardt, S., Kim, S., Kim, B., et al. Nicotine Levels in Electronic Cigarette Refill Solutions: A Comparative Analysis of Products from the US, Korea, and Poland. Int J Drug Policy. 2015 Jun;26(6):583–588.
223. Yingst, J., Wang, X., Lopez, A.A., Breland, A., Soule, E., Barnes, A., Cohen, J., Underwood, M., Crabtree, M., Foulds, J.; Randomized Control Trial Methods Workgroup of the Center for the Study of Tobacco Products. Changes in Nicotine Dependence Among Smokers Using Electronic Cigarettes to Reduce Cigarette Smoking in a Randomized Controlled Trial. Nicotine Tob Res. 2022 Jun 25:ntac153. https://doi.org/10.1093/ntr/ntac153.
224. Hartmann-Boyce, J., Lindson, N., Butler, A.R., McRobbie, H., Bullen, C., Begh, R., Theodoulou, A., Notley, C., Rigotti, N.A., Turner, T., Fanshawe, T.R., Hajek, P. Electronic cigarettes for smoking cessation. Cochrane Database of Systematic Reviews 2022, Issue 11. Art. No.: CD010216. https://doi.org/10.1002/14651858.CD010216.pub7.
225. Yong, H.H., Borland, R., Cummings, K.M., Gravely, S., Thrasher, J.F., McNeill, A., Hitchman, S., Greenhalgh, E., Thompson, M.E., Fong, G.T. Reasons for Regular Vaping and for Its Discontinuation Among Smokers and Recent Ex-Smokers: Findings from the 2016 ITC Four Country Smoking and Vaping Survey. Addiction. 2019 Oct;114 Suppl 1(Suppl 1):35–48. https://doi.org/10.1111/add.14593.
226. Kapan, A., Stefanac, S., Sandner, I., Haider, S., Grabovac, I., Dorner, T.E. Use of Electronic Cigarettes in European Populations: A Narrative Review. Int J Environ Res Public Health. 2020 Mar 17;17(6):1971. https://doi.org/10.3390/ijerph17061971.
227. Dept. Health & Social Care Nicotine Vaping in England: 2022 Evidence Update. Available at: https://www.gov.uk/government/publications/nicotine-vaping-in-england-2022-evidence-update.

228. Statistics Canada. (2021). Canadian Tobacco and Nicotine Survey. https://www150.statcan.gc.ca/n1/daily-quotidien/220505/dq220505c-eng.htm.
229. Irvine, I., Hampsher, S. (April 15, 2022). Early Indications of Consumer Responses to Canada's Nicotine Limits on E-Cigarettes. BOTEC Analysis for the Foundation for a Smoke-Free World. Available at SSRN: https://ssrn.com/abstract=4179648.
230. Irvine, I. "Concentration of Nicotine in Vaping Products Regulations: A Commentary from an Economics Perspective," SSRN Scholarly Paper (Rochester, NY: Social Science Research Network, March 1, 2021). https://doi.org/10.2139/ssrn.3798634.
231. Kosmider, L. et al. Daily Exposure to Formaldehyde and Acetaldehyde and Potential Health Risk Associated with Use of High and Low Nicotine E-Liquid Concentrations. Nature—Scientific Reports. 2020 Apr 16;10(1):6546. https://doi.org/10.1038/s41598-020-63292-1.
232. Capella, M., Taylor, C.R., Webster, C. The Effect of Cigarette Advertising Bans on Consumption: A Meta-Analysis. J Advertising. 2008;37(2):7–18. https://doi.org/10.2753/JOA0091-3367370201.
233. Klein, D.E., Chaiton, M., Kundu, A., et al. A Literature Review on International E-cigarette Regulatory Policies. Curr Addict Rep. 2020;7:509–519. https://doi.org/10.1007/s40429-020-00332-w.
234. World Health Organization Regional Office for Europe. EUR/RC65/10 Roadmap of actions to strengthen implementation of the WHO Framework Convention on Tobacco Control in the European Region 2015–2025: Making Tobacco a Thing of the Past [Internet]. Available at: http://www.euro.who.int/__data/assets/pdf_file/0011/282962/65wd10e_Tobacco_150475.pdf?ua=1. Guidelines for WHO European Region for reducing tobacco use prevalence.
235. Klein, D.E., Chaiton, M., Kundu, A., et al. A Literature Review on International E-cigarette Regulatory Policies. Curr Addict Rep. 2020;7:509–519. https://doi.org/10.1007/s40429-020-00332-w.

236. New Zealand Legislation. Smoke-Free Environments and Regulated Products (Vaping) Amendment Bill 222-1 (2020), Government Bill Explanatory Note. [Internet]. New Zealand Legislation. Available at: http://legislation.govt.nz/bill/government/2020/0222/latest/d1393751e2.html.
237. Health Canada. Vaping Product Regulation [Internet]. Aem, 2020, available at: https://www.canada.ca/en/health-canada/services/smoking-tobacco/vaping/product-safety-regulation.html.
238. Klein, D.E., Chaiton, M., Kundu, A., et al. A Literature Review on International E-cigarette Regulatory Policies. Curr Addict Rep. 2020;7:509–519. https://doi.org/10.1007/s40429-020-00332-w.
239. Cho, Y.J., Thrasher, J.F., Reid, J.L., Hitchman, S., Hammond, D. Youth Self-Reported Exposure to and Perceptions of Vaping Advertisements: Findings from the 2017 International Tobacco Control Youth Tobacco and Vaping Survey. Preventive Medicine. 2019;126:105775. https://doi.org/10.1016/j.ypmed.2019.105775.
240. Hammond, D., Reid, J.L., Burkhalter, R., Rynard, V.L. E-cigarette Marketing Regulations and Youth Vaping: Cross-Sectional Surveys, 2017–2019. Pediatrics. 2020 Jul;146(1):e20194020. https://doi.org/10.1542/peds.2019-4020.
241. Do, V.V., Nyman, A.L., Kim, Y., Emery, S.L., Weaver, S.R., Huang, J. Association between E-Cigarette Advertising Exposure and Use of E-Cigarettes among a Cohort of U.S. Youth and Young Adults. Int J Environ Res Public Health. 2022 Oct 3;19(19):12640. https://doi.org/10.3390/ijerph191912640.
242. Reinhold, B., Fischbein, R., Bhamidipalli, S.S., Bryant, J., Kenne, D.R. Associations of Attitudes Towards Electronic Cigarettes with Advertisement Exposure and Social Determinants: a Cross Sectional Study. Tobacco Induced Diseases. 2017 Feb;15:13. https://doi.org/10.1186/s12971-017-0118-y.
243. Padon, A.A., Maloney, E.K., Cappella, J.N. Youth-Targeted E-cigarette Marketing in the US. Tob Regul Sci. 2017 Jan;3(1):95–101. https://doi.org/10.18001/TRS.3.1.9.
244. Britton, J. et al. Commentary on WHO Report on Electronic Nicotine Delivery Systems And Electronic Non-Nicotine

Delivery Systems, UK Centre for Tobacco and Alcohol Studies, 2016, available at: https://www.clivebates.com/documents/WHO/ENreport.pdf.
245. Dave, D., Dench, D., Grossman, M., Kenkel, D.S., Saffer, H. Does E-cigarette Advertising Encourage Adult Smokers to Quit? J Health Econ. 2019 Dec;68:102227. https://doi.org/10.1016/j.jhealeco.2019.102227.
246. Chen-Sankey, J., Lopez, M., Elhabashy, M., Broun, A. How the Other Half Sees It: E-cigarette Advertising Exposure and Subsequent E-cigarette Use Among U.S. Young Adult Cigarette Smokers. Nicotine Tob Res. 2022 Jul 8:ntac169. https://doi.org/10.1093/ntr/ntac169.
247. US Food and Drug Administration. (2020). Vaporizers, E-cigarettes, and other electronic nicotine delivery systems (ENDS) [Internet]. FDA; Available at: https://www.fda.gov/tobacco-products/products-ingredients-components/vaporizers-e-cigarettes-and-other-electronic-nicotine-delivery-systems-ends.
248. Australian Government Department of Health. About e-cigarettes [Internet]. [cited May 11, 2020]. Available at: https://www.health.gov.au/health-topics/smoking-and-tobacco/about-smoking-and-tobacco/about-e-cigarettes.
249. "Guidance for Licensing Electronic Cigarettes and Other Inhaled Nicotine-Containing Products as Medicines." Government of the United Kingdom, October 29, 2021. https://www.gov.uk/guidance/licensing-procedure-for-electronic-cigarettes-as-medicines.
250. US Department of Health and Human Services. The Health Consequences of Smoking—50 Years of Progress: a Report of the Surgeon General, 2014, available at: http://www.surgeongeneral.gov/library/reports/50-years-of-progress.
251. Institute of Medicine. Public Health Implications of Raising the Minimum Age of Legal Access to Tobacco Products, 2015, available at: http://www.nationalacademies.org/hmd/Reports/2015/TobaccoMinimumAgeReport.aspx.
252. Everett, S.A., Warren, C.W., Sharp, D., Kann, L., Husten, C.G., Crossett, L.S. Initiation of Cigarette Smoking and Subsequent Smoking Behavior Among U.S. High School Students. Prev Med. 1999;29(5):327–333.

253. Breslau, N., Peterson, E.L. Smoking Cessation in Young Adults: Age at Initiation of Cigarette Smoking and Other Suspected Influences. Am J Public Health. 1996;86(2):214–220.
254. Dierker, L., Swendsen, J., Rose, J., He, J., Merikangas, K. Tobacco Etiology Research Network (TERN) Transitions to Regular Smoking and Nicotine Dependence in the Adolescent National Comorbidity Survey (NCS-A). Ann Behav Med. 2012;43(3):394–401.
255. Agaku, I.T., Nkosi, L., Agaku, Q.D., Gwar, J., Tsafa, T. A Rapid Evaluation of the US Federal Tobacco 21 (T21) Law and Lessons From Statewide T21 Policies: Findings From Population-Level Surveys. Prev Chronic Dis. 2022;19:210430. http://dx.doi.org/10.5888/pcd19.210430.
256. Yörük, CE., Yörük, B.K. Do Minimum Legal Tobacco Purchase Age Laws Work? *Contemporary Economic Policy* See also DiFranza, J.R., Savageau, J.A., Fletcher, K.E. Enforcement of Underage Sales Laws as a Predictor of Daily Smoking Among Adolescents: A National Study. BMC Public Health. 2009 Apr 17;9:107.
257. Beard, E., Brown, J., Jackson„ S. et al. Long-Term Evaluation of the Rise in Legal Age-of-Sale of Cigarettes from 16 to 18 in England: A Trend Analysis. BMC Med. 2020;18:85. https://doi.org/10.1186/s12916-020-01541-w.
258. Millett, C., Lee, J.T., Gibbons, D.C., et al. Increasing the Age for the Legal Purchase of Tobacco in England: Impacts on Socio-Economic Disparities in Youth Smoking. Thorax. 2011;66:862–865.
259. Kim, S.C.J., Martinez, J.E., Liu, Y., Friedman, T.C. (2021). US Tobacco 21 Is Paving the Way for a Tobacco Endgame. Tobacco Use Insights. https://doi.org/10.1177_1179173X211050396.
260. Dave, D., Feng, B., Pesko, M.F. The Effects of E-cigarette Minimum Legal Sale Age Laws on Youth Substance Use. Health Econ. 2019 Mar;28:419–436. https://doi.org/10.1002/hec.3854.
261. Minimum Age | Global Tobacco Control. https://globaltobaccocontrol.org/en/policy-scan/e-cigarettes/minimum-age. Accessed 10 May 2023.

262. Minimum Age | Global Tobacco Control. https://globaltobaccocontrol.org/en/policy-scan/e-cigarettes/minimum-age. Accessed 10 May 2023.
263. U.S. Department of Health and Human Services. E-cigarette use among youth and young adults. A report of the Surgeon General. Atlanta, GA: U.S. Department of Health and Human Services, Centers for Disease Control and Prevention, National Center for Chronic Disease Prevention and Health Pro-motion, Office on Smoking and Health; 2016.
264. Institute of Medicine (IOM). (2015). *Public Health Implications of Raising the Minimum Age of Legal Access to Tobacco Products*. Washington, D.C.: The National Academies Press.
265. Morain, S.R., Malek, J. Minimum Age of Sale for Tobacco Products and Electronic Cigarettes: Ethical Acceptability of US "Tobacco 21 Laws." Am J Public Health. 2017 Sep;107(9):1401–1405. https://doi.org/10.2105/AJPH.2017.303900.
266. Pesko, M.F. Combustible Tobacco Age-of-Sale Laws: An Opportunity? Addiction. 2022;117:514–516. https://doi.org/10.1111/add.15685.
267. For a discussion of how performative vaping behavior could interact with smoking denormalizations, see Lucherini M, Rooke C, Amos A. E-cigarettes, Vaping and Performativity in the Context of Tobacco Denormalization. Sociol Health Illn. 2018 Jul;40(6):1037–1052. https://doi.org/10.1111/1467-9566.12741. Epub 2018 Apr 17. PMID: 29664119; PMCID: PMC6055866.
268. Electronic Nicotine Delivery Systems and Electronic Non-Nicotine Delivery Systems (ENDS/ENNDS). Geneva: World Health Organization. Available at: http://www.who.int/fctc/cop/cop7/FCTC_COP_7_11_EN.pdf?ua=1.
269. European Network for Smoking and Tobacco Prevention. ENSP Calls for European Response to Electronic Cigarettes Rising Epidemic—European Network. Available at: http://ensp.network/ensp-calls-for-european-response-to-electronic-cigarettes-rising-epidemic/ [Ref list].
270. Kennedy, R.D., Awopegba, A., De León, E., Cohen, J.E. Global Approaches to Regulating Electronic Cigarettes. Tob Control.

2017 Jul;26(4):440–445. https://doi.org/10.1136/tobaccocontrol-2016-053179.

271. Excluding those where the use of e-cigarettes is banned.
272. American Non-Smokers Rights Foundation. (2021). "States and Municipalities with Laws Regulating Use of Electronic Cigarettes." April 1, 2021. https://no-smoke.org/wpcontent/uploads/pdf/ecigaretteslaws.pdf.
273. Bhalerao, A., Sivandzade, F., Archie, S.R., Cucullo, L. Public Health Policies on E-cigarettes. Curr Cardiol Rep. 2019;21(10):111. https://doi.org/10.1007/s11886-019-1204-y.
274. Mckeganey, N. Visible Vaping: E-cigarettes and the Further De-normalization of Smoking. Int Archives AddictiRes Med. 2016;2. https://doi.org/10.23937/2474-3631/1510023.
275. US Food and Drug Administration. Selling tobacco products in retail stores. [Internet]. FDA; 2020 [cited April 29, 2020]. Available at: https://www.fda.gov/tobacco-products/retail-sales-tobacco-products/selling-tobacco-products-retail-stores.
276. Council of the European Union, European Parliament. Directive 2014/40/EU of the European Parliament and of the Council of 3 April 2014 on the approximation of the laws, regulations and administrative provisions of the member states concerning the manufacture, presentation and sale of tobacco and related products and repealing Directive 2001/37/EC. Off J Eur Union. 2014;L127:1–38.
277. US Food and Drug Administration. Selling Tobacco Products in Retail Stores. [Internet]. FDA; 2020 [cited April 29, 2020]; Available at: https://www.fda.gov/tobacco-products/retail-sales-tobacco-products/selling-tobacco-products-retail-stores.
278. Caruana, D. "Belgium Will Ban Tobacco Vending Machines in Places of Entertainment." Vaping Post, November 10, 2022. https://www.vapingpost.com/2022/11/10/belgium-will-ban-tobacco-vending-machines-in-places-of-entertainment/.
279. Council of the European Union, European Parliament. Directive 2014/40/EU of the European Parliament and of the Council of 3 April 2014 on the approximation of the laws, regulations and administrative provisions of the member states concerning the manufacture, presentation and sale of tobacco and related

products and repealing Directive 2001/37/EC. Off J Eur Union. 2014;L127:1–38.
280. Health Canada. Vaping Product Regulation [Internet]. Aem, 2020, available at: https://www.canada.ca/en/health-canada/services/smoking-tobacco/vaping/product-safety-regulation.html.
281. Council of the European Union, European Parliament. Directive 2014/40/EU of the European Parliament and of the Council of 3 April 2014 on the approximation of the laws, regulations and administrative provisions of the member states concerning the manufacture, presentation and sale of tobacco and related products and repealing Directive 2001/37/EC. Off J Eur Union. 2014;L127:1–38.
282. Klein, D.E., Chaiton, M., Kundu, A., et al. A Literature Review on International E-cigarette Regulatory Policies. Curr Addict Rep. 2020;7:509–519. https://doi.org/10.1007/s40429-020-00332-w.
283. Abouk, R., Courtemanche, C., Dave, D., Feng, B., Friedman, A.S., Maclean, J.C., Safford, S., et al. Intended and Unintended Effects of E-cigarette Taxes on Youth Tobacco Use. J Health Econ. 2023;87:102720.
284. Cotti, C., Courtemanche, C., Maclean, J.C., Nesson, E., Pesko, M.F., Tefft, N.W. The Effects of E-cigarette Taxes on e-cigarette Prices and Tobacco Product Sales: Evidence from Retail Panel Data. J Health Econ. 2022 Dec;86:102676.
285. Pesko, M.F., Courtemanche, C.J., Maclean, J.C. The Effects of Traditional Cigarette and E-cigarette Taxes on Adult Tobacco Product Use. J Uncertain. 2020;60(3):229–258.
286. Friedman, A.S., Pesko, M.F. Young Adult Responses to Taxes on Cigarettes and Electronic Nicotine Delivery Systems. Addiction. 2022;117(12):3121–3128. 10.1111/add.16002 July, add.16002.
287. Pesko, M.F., Warman, C. Re-exploring the Early Relationship Between Teenage Cigarette and E-cigarette Use Using Price and Tax Changes. Health Econ. 2022;31:137–153. https://doi.org/10.1002/hec.4439.
288. Abouk, R., Adams, S., Feng, B.O., Maclean, J.C., Pesko, M.F. (2022). The Effect of E-cigarette Taxes on Pre-pregnancy and

Prenatal Smoking. NBER Work Pap Ser No. 26126. https://doi.org/10.3386/w26126.

289. Leventhal, A.M., Goldenson, N.I., Cho, J., et al. Flavored E-cigarette Use and Progression of Vaping in Adolescents. Pediatrics. 2019;144(5):e20190789. https://doi.org/10.1542/peds.2019-0789.
290. Yang, Y., Lindblom, E.N., Salloum, R.G., Ward, K.D. The Impact of a Comprehensive Tobacco Product Flavor Ban in San Francisco Among Young Adults. Addict Behav Rep. 11 (2020).
291. Romm, K.F., Henriksen, L., Huang, J., Le, D., Clausen, M., Duan, Z., Fuss, C., Bennett, B., Berg, C.J. Impact of Existing And Potential E-cigarette Flavor Restrictions on E-cigarette Use Among Young Adult E-cigarette Users in 6 US Metropolitan Areas. Prev Med Rep. 2022 Jul 9;28:101901. https://doi.org/10.1016/j.pmedr.2022.101901.
292. Ali, F.R.M., Vallone, D., Seaman, E.L., et al. Evaluation of Statewide Restrictions on Flavored e-Cigarette Sales in the US From 2014 to 2020. JAMA Netw Open. 2022;5(2):e2147813. https://doi.org/10.1001/jamanetworkopen.2021.47813.
293. Boesen, U. Massachusetts Flavored Tobacco Ban: No Impact on New England Sales, Tax Foundation, 2022, available at: https://taxfoundation.org/massachusetts-flavored-tobacco-ban-sales-jama-study/.
294. Ali, F.R.M., Dave, D.M., Colman, G.J., Wang, X., Saffer, H., Marynak, K.L., Dench, D., Grossman, M. Association of E-cigarette Advertising with E-cigarette and Cigarette Use Among us Adults. Addiction. 2021;116:1212–1223. https://doi.org/10.1111/add.15281.
295. Camenga, D., Gutierrez, K.M., Kong, G., Cavallo, D., Simon, P., Krishnan-Sarin, S. E-cigarette Advertising Exposure in E-cigarette Naïve Adolescents and Subsequent E-cigarette Use: A Longitudinal Cohort Study. Addict Behav. 2018;81:78–83.
296. Duke, J.C., Allen, J.A., Eggers, M.E., Nonnemaker, J., Farrelly, M.C. Exploring Differences in Youth Perceptions of the Effectiveness of Electronic Cigarette Television Advertisements. Nicotine Tob Res. 2016;18(5):1382–1386.
297. Farrelly, M.C., Duke, J.C., Crankshaw, E.C., et al. A Randomized Trial of the Effect of E-cigarette TV Advertisements on Intentions to Use E-cigarettes. Am J Prev Med. 2015;49(5):686–693.

298. Villanti, A.C., Rath, J.M., Williams, V.F., et al. Impact of Exposure to Electronic Cigarette Advertising on Susceptibility and Trial of Electronic Cigarettes and Cigarettes in US Young Adults: A Randomized Controlled Trial. Nicotine Tob Res. 2016;18(5):1331–1339.
299. Hammond, D., Reid, J.L., Burkhalter, R., Rynard, V.L. E-cigarette Marketing Regulations and Youth Vaping: Cross-Sectional Surveys, 2017–2019. Pediatrics. 2020 Jul;146(1):e20194020. https://doi.org/10.1542/peds.2019-4020.
300. Camenga, D., Gutierrez, K.M., Kong, G., Cavallo, D., Simon, P., Krishnan-Sarin, S. E-cigarette Advertising Exposure in E-cigarette Naïve Adolescents and Subsequent E-cigarette Use: A Longitudinal Cohort Study. Addict Behav. 2018;81:78–83.
301. Duke, J.C., Allen, J.A., Eggers, M.E., Nonnemaker, J., Farrelly, M.C. Exploring Differences in Youth Perceptions of the Effectiveness of Electronic Cigarette Television Advertisements. Nicotine Tob Res. 2016;18(5):1382–1386.
302. Farrelly, M.C., Duke, J.C., Crankshaw, E.C., et al. A Randomized Trial of the Effect of E-cigarette TV Advertisements on Intentions to Use E-cigarettes. Am J Prev Med. 2015;49(5):686–693.
303. Villanti, A.C., Rath, J.M., Williams, V.F., et al. Impact of Exposure to Electronic Cigarette Advertising on Susceptibility and Trial of Electronic Cigarettes and Cigarettes in US Young Adults: A Randomized Controlled Trial. Nicotine Tob Res. 2016;18(5):1331–1339.
304. Wang, T.W., Gentzke, A., Sharapova, S., Cullen, K.A., Ambrose, B.K., Jamal, J. Tobacco Product Use Among Middle and High School Students—United States, 2011–2017, 2018, available at: https://www.cdc.gov/mmwr/volumes/67/wr/mm6722a3.htm.
305. Abouk, R., Adams, S. Bans on Electronic Cigarette Sales to Minors and Smoking Among High School Students. J Health Econ. 2017;54:17–24.
306. Nguyen, H.V. Association of Canada's Provincial Bans on Electronic Cigarette Sales to Minors with Electronic Cigarette Use Among Youths. JAMA Pediatr. 2020;174(1) (2020):e193912. https://doi.org/10.1001/jamapediatrics.2019.3912–e193912.

307. Du, Y., Liu, B., Xu, G., Rong, S., Sun, Y., Wu, Y., Snetselaar, L.G., Wallace, R.B., Bao, W. Association of Electronic Cigarette Regulations With Electronic Cigarette Use Among Adults in the United States. JAMA Netw Open. 2020 Jan 3;3(1):e1920255. https://doi.org/10.1001/jamanetworkopen.2019.20255.
308. Choi, K., Omole, T., Wills, T., et al. E-cigarette-Inclusive Smoke-Free Policies, Excise Taxes, Tobacco 21 and Changes in Youth E-cigarette Use: 2017–2019. Tob Control. 2022(31):758-761.
309. Azagba, S., Shan, L., Manzione, L. Associations of Home and Workplace Vaping Restrictions with E-cigarette Use Among U.S. Adults. Prev Med. 2020 Oct;139:106196. https://doi.org/10.1016/j.ypmed.2020.106196.
310. Shields, M. Smoking-Prevalence, Bans and Exposure to Second-Hand Smoke, Health Rep. 2007;18(3):67-85.
311. Azagba, S., Shan, L., Manzione, L. Associations of Home and Workplace Vaping Restrictions with E-cigarette Use Among U.S. Adults. Prev Med. 2020 Oct;139:106196. https://doi.org/10.1016/j.ypmed.2020.106196.
312. Lee, B., Lin, H.C., Seo, D.C. Inclusion of Electronic Nicotine Delivery Systems in Indoor Smoke-Free Air Policies and Associated Vaping Behavior. Addict Behav. 2019(98):106061. https://doi.org/10.1016/j.addbeh.2019.106061.
313. Yang, M., Russell, A.M., Lin, H. Association Between Inclusion of E-Cigarettes in Statewide Comprehensive Smoke-Free Indoor Air Laws and Vaping Behaviors: Results from a Longitudinal Population Study. Substance Use & Misuse, 2022(57):806–814.
314. Soule, E.K., Mayne, S., Snipes, W., Thomas, L., Guy, M.C., Breland, A., Fagan, P. Electronic Cigarette Users' Reactions and Responses to a Hypothetical Ban of Flavoured Electronic Cigarette Liquids. Tob Control. 2022 Nov;31(Suppl 3):s197-s205. https://doi.org/10.1136/tc-2022-057454.
315. Posner, H., Romm, K.F., Henriksen, L., Bernat, D., Berg, C.J. Reactions to Sales Restrictions on Flavored Vape Products or All Vape Products Among Young Adults in the United States. Nicotine Tob Res. 2022 Feb 14;24(3):333–341. https://doi.org/10.1093/ntr/ntab154.
316. Gravely, S., Smith, D.M., Liber, A.C., Cummings, K.M., East, K.A., Hammond, D., Hyland, A., O'Connor, R.J., Kasza, K.A., Quah, A.C.K., Loewen, R., Martin, N., Meng, G., Ouimet, J.,

Thompson, M.E., Boudreau, C., McNeill, A., Sweanor, D.T., Fong, G.T. Responses to Potential Nicotine Vaping Product Flavor Restrictions Among Regular Vapers Using Non-Tobacco Flavors: Findings from the 2020 ITC Smoking and Vaping Survey in Canada, England and the United States. Addict Behav. 2022 Feb;125:107152. https://doi.org/10.1016/j.addbeh.2021.107152.

317. Cadham, C.J., Liber, A.C., Sánchez-Romero, L.M., et al. The Actual and Anticipated Effects of Restrictions on Flavoured Electronic Nicotine Delivery Systems: A Scoping Review. BMC Public Health. 2022;22:2128. https://doi.org/10.1186/s12889-022-14440-x.
318. Huang, J., Gwarnicki, C., Xu, X., Caraballo, R.S., Wada, R., Chaloupka, F.J. A Comprehensive Examination of Own- and Cross-Price Elasticities of Tobacco and Nicotine Replacement Products in the U.S. Prev Med. 2018 Dec;117:107–114. https://doi.org/10.1016/j.ypmed.2018.04.024.
319. Buckell, J., Marti, J., Sindelar, J.L. Should Flavours Be Banned in Cigarettes and E-cigarettes? Evidence on Adult Smokers and Recent Quitters from a Discrete Choice Experiment. Tob Control. 2018.
320. Freitas-Lemos, R., Stein, J.S., Tegge, A.N., Kaplan, B.A., Heckman, B.W., Cummings, K.M., et al. The Illegal Experimental Tobacco Marketplace I: Effects of VapingProduct Bans. Nicotine Tob Res. 2021;4.
321. Gravely, S., Smith, D.M., Liber, A.C., Cummings, K.M., East, K.A., Hammond, D., et al. Responses to Potential Nicotine Vaping Product Flavor Restrictions Among Regular Vapers Using Non-Tobacco Flavors: Findings from the 2020 ITC Smoking and Vaping Survey in Canada, England and the United States. Addict Behav. 2022;125:107152.
322. Posner, H., Romm, K.F., Henriksen, L., Bernat, D., Berg, C.J. Reactions to Sales Restrictions on Flavored Vape Products or All Vape Products Among Young Adults in the United States. Nicotine Tob Res. 2022 Feb 14;24(3):333–341.
323. Pacek, L.R., Rass, O., Sweitzer, M.M., Oliver, J.A., McClernon, F.J. Young Adult Dual Combusted Cigarette and E-cigarette Users' Anticipated Responses to Hypothetical E-cigarette Market

Restrictions. Substance Use & Misuse. 2019. https://doi.org/10.1080/10826084.2019.1626435.

324. Pesko, M.F., Warman, C. Re-exploring the Early Relationship Between Teenage Cigarette and E-cigarette Use Using Price and Tax Changes. Health Econ. 2022;31:137–153.
325. Abouk, R., Courtemanche, C., Dave, D., Feng, B., Friedman, A.S., Maclean, J.C., Safford, S., et al. Intended and Unintended Effects of E-cigarette Taxes on Youth Tobacco Use. J Health Econ. 2023;87:102720.
326. Friedman, A.S., Pesko, M.F. Young Adult Responses to Taxes on Cigarettes and Electronic Nicotine Delivery Systems. Addiction. 2022;117(12):3121–3128.
327. Pesko, M.F., Courtemanche, C.J., Catherine, M.J. The Effects of Traditional Cigarette and E-cigarette Tax Rates on Adult Tobacco Product Use. J Risk Uncertain. 2020;60:229–258.
328. Li, D., Ossip, D.J., Bansal-Travers, M., Xie, Z. Impact of the FDA Flavour Enforcement Policy on Flavoured Electronic Cigarette Use Behaviour Changes. Tob Control. 2022;31(Suppl 3):s176–s83.
329. Friedman, A.S. A Difference-in-Differences Analysis of Youth Smoking and a Ban on Sales of Flavored Tobacco Products in San Francisco, California. JAMA Pediatr. 2021 Aug 1;175(8):863–865. https://doi.org/10.1001/jamapediatrics.2021.0922. Erratum in: JAMA Pediatr. 2022 Sep 1;176(9):948.
330. Yang, Y., Lindblom, E.N., Salloum, R.G., Ward, K.D. The Impact of a Comprehensive Tobacco Product Flavor Ban in San Francisco Among Young Adults. Addict Behav Reports. 2020;11:100273. https://doi.org/10.1016/j.abrep.2020.100273.
331. Friedman, A.S. How Does Electronic Cigarette Access Affect Adolescent Smoking? J Health Econ. 2015;44:300–308.
332. Dave, D., Feng, B., Pesko, M.F. The Effects of E-cigarette Minimum Legal Sale Age Laws on Youth Substance Use. Health Econ. 2019;28:419–436.
333. Pesko, M.F., Hughes, J.M., Faisal, F.S. The Influence of Electronic Cigarette Age Purchasing Restrictions on Adolescent Tobacco and Marijuana Use. Prev Med. 2016;87:207–212.
334. Abouk, R., Courtemanche, C., Dave, D., Feng, B., Friedman, A.S., Maclean, J.C., Safford, S., et al. Intended and Unintended

Effects of E-cigarette Taxes on Youth Tobacco Use. J Health Econ. 2023;87:102720.

335. Cotti, C., Courtemanche, C., Maclean, J.C., Nesson, E., Pesko, M.F., Tefft, N.W. The Effects of E-cigarette Taxes on e-cigarette Prices and Tobacco Product Sales: Evidence from Retail Panel Data. J Health Econ. 2022 Dec;86:102676.
336. Pesko, M.F., Courtemanche, C.J., Maclean, J.C. The Effects of Traditional Cigarette and E-cigarette Taxes on Adult Tobacco Product Use. J Uncertain. 2020;60(3):229–258.
337. Saffer, H., Dench, D., Grossman, M., Dave, D. E-cigarettes and Adult Smoking: Evidence from Minnesota. Journal of Risk and Uncertainty. 2020;60:207–228. https://doi.org/10.1007/s11166-020-09326-5.
338. Pesko, M.F., Warman, C. Re-exploring the Early Relationship Between Teenage Cigarette and E-cigarette Use Using Price and Tax Changes. Health Econ. 2022;31:137–153.
339. Friedman, A.S., Pesko, M.F. Young Adult Responses to Taxes on Cigarettes and Electronic Nicotine Delivery Systems. Addiction. 2022;117(12):3121–3128. https://doi.org/10.1111/add.16002 July, add.16002.
340. $\beta\hat{}\beta = -0.025$; 95% CI, −0.037, −0.014.
341. $\beta\hat{}\beta = 0.037$; 95% CI, 0.013, 0.061.
342. $\beta\hat{}\beta = 2.078$; 95% CI, 0.890, 4.852; $P = 0.09$.
343. Abouk, R., Adams, S., Feng, B.O., Maclean, J.C., Pesko, M.F. (2022). The Effect of E-cigarette Taxes on Pre-pregnancy and Prenatal Smoking. NBER Work Pap Ser No. 26126. 10.3386/w26126.
344. Public Health Law Center. (2022). "E-cigarette Tax: States & Territories with Laws Taxing E-cigarettes." Saint Paul, Minnesota: Mitchell Hamline School of Law. https://www.publichealthlawcenter.org/sites/default/files/inline-files/States-with-Laws-Taxing-ECigarettes-March15-2022.pdf.
345. Abouk, R., Courtemanche, C., Dave, D., Feng, B., Friedman, A.S., Maclean, J.C., Safford, S., et al. Intended and Unintended Effects of E-cigarette Taxes on Youth Tobacco Use. J Health Econ. 2023;87:102720.
346. Li, D., Ossip, D.J., Bansal-Travers, M., Xie, Z. Impact of the FDA Flavour Enforcement Policy on Flavoured Electronic Cigarette

Use Behaviour Changes. Tob Control. 2022;31(Suppl 3):s176–s83.

347. Friedman, A.S. A Difference-in-Differences Analysis of Youth Smoking and a Ban on Sales of Flavored Tobacco Products in San Francisco, California. JAMA Pediatr. 2021 Aug 1;175(8):863–865. https://doi.org/10.1001/jamapediatrics.2021.0922. Erratum in: JAMA Pediatr. 2022 Sep 1;176(9):948.
348. AOR, 2.24 (95% CI, 1.42 – 3.53); $P = 0.001$.
349. Yang, Y., Lindblom, E.N., Salloum, R.G., Ward, K.D. The Impact of a Comprehensive Tobacco Product Flavor Ban in San Francisco Among Young Adults. Addict Behav Reports. 2020;11:100273. https://doi.org/10.1016/j.abrep.2020.100273.
350. Liu, J., Hartman, L., Tan, A.S.L., et al. Youth Tobacco Use Before and After Flavoured Tobacco Sales Restrictions in Oakland, California and San Francisco, California. Tob Control. Published Online First: 17 March 2022. https://doi.org/10.1136/tobaccocontrol-2021-057135.
351. Posner, H., Romm, K.F., Henriksen, L., Bernat, D., Berg, C.J. Reactions to Sales Restrictions on Flavored Vape Products or All Vape Products Among Young Adults in the United States. Nicotine Tob Res. 2022 Feb 14;24(3):333–341; ntab154, https://doi.org/10.1093/ntr/ntab154.
352. Xu, Y., Jiang, L., Prakash, S., Chen, T. The Impact of Banning Electronic Nicotine Delivery Systems on Combustible Cigarette Sales: Evidence from US State-Level Policies. Value Health. 2022;25:1352–1359.
353. Liber, A.C., Cahn, Z., Diaz, M.C., Donovan, E., Vallone, D., Schillo, B. The EVALI Outbreak and Tobacco Sales in the USA, 2014–2020: Tobacco Control 2021. tobaccocontrol-2021-056807.
354. Katchmar, A., Gunawan, A., Siegel, M. Effect of Massachusetts House Bill No. 4196 on Electronic Cigarette Use: A Mixed-methods Study. Harm Reduct J. 2021;18(1):50.
355. Dave, D., Feng, B., Pesko, M.F. The Effects of E-cigarette Minimum Legal Sale Age Laws on Youth Substance Use. Health Econ. 2019 Mar;28:419–436. https://doi.org/10.1002/hec.3854.
356. Dave, D., Feng, B., Pesko, M.F. The Effects of E-cigarette Minimum Legal Sale Age Laws on Youth Substance Use. Health

Econ. 2019 Mar;28:419–436. https://doi.org/10.1002/hec.3854.
357. Friedman, A.S. How Does Electronic Cigarette Access Affect Adolescent Smoking? J Health Econ. 2015;44:300–308. https://doi.org/10.1016/j.jhealeco.2015.10.003.
358. Pesko, M.F., Hughes, J.M., Faisal, F.S. The Influence of Electronic Cigarette Age Purchasing Restrictions on Adolescent Tobacco and Marijuana Use. Prev Med. 2016 June;87:207–212. https://doi.org/10.1016/j.ypmed.2016.02.0.
359. Abouk, R., Adams, S., Feng, B.O., Maclean, J.C., Pesko, M.F. (2022). The Effect of E-cigarette Taxes on Pre-pregnancy and Prenatal Smoking. NBER Work Pap Ser No. 26126. https://doi.org/10.3386/w26126.
360. Pesko, M.F., Currie, J.M. E-cigarette Minimum Legal Sale Age Laws and Traditional Cigarette Use Among Rural Pregnant Teenagers. J Health Econ. 2019 July;66:71–90. https://doi.org/10.1016/j.jhealeco.2019.05.003.
361. Abouk, R., Adams, S. Bans on Electronic Cigarette Sales to Minors and Smoking Among High School Students. J Health Econ. 2017;54:17–24. https://doi.org/10.1016/j.jhealeco.2017.03.003.
362. Dave, D., Feng, B., Pesko, M.F. The Effects of E-cigarette Minimum Legal Sale Age Laws on Youth Substance Use. Health Econ. 2019 Mar;28:419–436. https://doi.org/10.1002/hec.3854.
363. Mendelsohn, C., Wodak, A., Hall, W. How Should Nicotine Vaping Be Regulated in Australia? Drug Alcohol Rev. 2023. https://doi.org/10.1111/dar.13663.
364. Tuchman, A. (2019). Advertising and Demand for Addictive Goods: The Effects of E-cigarette Advertising. Market Sci. 2019 Nov-Dec;38(6):913–1084, ii.
365. Dave, D., Dench, D., Grossman, M., Kenkel, D.S., Saffer, H. Does E-cigarette Advertising Encourage Adult Smokers to Quit? J Health Econ. 2019 Dec;68:102227. https://doi.org/10.1016/j.jhealeco.2019.102227.
366. In contrast to TV advertising, print advertising of e-cigarettes was not found to be associated with a reduction in smoking, nor with increased vaping among youth. Perhaps print advertising is simply ineffective.

367. Majeed, B.A., Weaver, S.R., Gregory, K.R., Whitney, C.F., Pechacek, S.P., Eriksen, T.F., Michael, P. Changing Perceptions of Harm of E-Cigarettes Among U.S. Adults, 2011–2015. Am J Prev Med. 2017;52(3):331–338.
368. 95% CI = 1.64, 2.41.
369. 95% CI = 2.60, 3.81.
370. Sawyer, L.E., Brandon, T.H. Unintended Consequences: Testing the Effects of Adolescent-Targeted Anti-Vaping Media Upon Adult Smokers. Nicotine Tob Res. 2022.
371. Wackowski, O.A., Hammond, D., O'Connor, R.J., Strasser, A.A., Delnevo, C.D. Smokers' and E-cigarette Users' Perceptions About E-cigarette Warning Statements. Int J Environ Res Public Health. 2016;13:655.
372. McNeill, A., Brose, L.S., Calder, R., Hitchman, S.C., Hajek, P., McRobbie, H. E-cigarettes: An Evidence Update a Report Commissioned by Public Health England, 2015, available at: https://assets.publishing.service.gov.uk/government/uploads/system/uploads/attachment_data/file/733022/Ecigarettes_an_evidence_update_A_report_commissioned_by_Public_Health_England_FINAL.pdf.
373. Dave, D., Feng, B., Pesko, M.F. The Effects of E-cigarette Minimum Legal Sale Age Laws on Youth Substance Use. Health Econ. 2019 Mar;28:419–436. https://doi.org/10.1002/hec.3854.
374. Mendelsohn, C., Wodak, A., Hall, W. How Should Nicotine Vaping Be Regulated in Australia? Drug Alcohol Rev. 2023. https://doi.org/10.1111/dar.13663.
375. Kosmider, L., Kimber, C.F., Kurek, J., Corcoran, O., Dawkins, L.E. Compensatory Puffing with Lower Nicotine Concentration E-Liquids Increases Carbonyl Exposure in E-cigarette Aerosols. Nicotine Tob Res. 2018;20:998–1003.
376. Dawkins, L., Cox, S., Goniewicz, M., McRobbie, H., Kimber, C., Doig, M., et al. "Real-World' Compensatory Behaviour with Low Nicotine Concentration E-liquid: Subjective Effects and Nicotine, Acrolein and Formaldehyde Exposure. Addiction. 2018;113:1874–1882.

377. Talih, S., Salman, R., El-Hage, R., Karam, E., Karaoghlanian, N., El- Hellani, A., et al. Might Limiting Liquid Nicotine Concentration Result in More Toxic Electronic Cigarette Aerosols? Tob Control. 2021;30:348–350.
378. Kimber, C., Zaidell, L., Hunter, S., Cox, S., Notley, C., Dawkins, L. Comparing the Effects of the EU- Versus the US-JUUL Pod in a Sample of UK Smokers: Nicotine Absorption, Satisfaction and Other Nicotine-Related Subjective Effects. Nicotine Tob Res. 2022.
379. Mendelsohn, C., Wodak, A., Hall, W. How Should Nicotine Vaping Be Regulated in Australia? Drug Alcohol Rev. 2023. https://doi.org/10.1111/dar.13663.
380. Goldenson, N.I., Ding, Y., Prakash, S., Hatcher, C., Augustson, E.M., Shiffman, S. Differences in Switching Away from Smoking Among Adult Smokers Using JUUL Products in Regions with Different Maximum Nicotine Concentrations: North America and the United Kingdom. Nicotine Tob Res. 2021;23:1821–1830.
381. National Academies of Sciences, Engineering, and Medicine. *Public Health Consequences of E-Cigarettes*. Washington, D.C.: The National Academies Press, 2018. https://doi.org/10.17226/24952.
382. El-Hellani, A., Soule, E. K., Daoud, M., Salman, R., El Hage, R., Ardati, O., … & Shihadeh, A. Assessing Toxicant Emissions from E-Liquids with DIY Additives Used in Response to a Potential Flavour Ban in E-Cigarettes. Tob Control. 2022;31(Suppl 3):s245–s248.
383. Cox, S., Leigh, N.J., Vanderbush, T.S., Choo, E., Goniewicz, M.J., Dawkins, L. An Exploration into "Do-It-Yourself" (DIY) E-liquid Mixing: Users' Motivations, Practices and Product Laboratory Analysis. Addict Behav Reports. 2019;9:100151. https://doi.org/10.1016/j.abrep.2018.100151.
384. Balewska, A., Raciborski, F. "Do-It-Yourself" (DIY) E-liquid Mixing: Users' Motivations and Awareness of Associated Dangers—Analysis of Social Media and Online Content. J Health Inequalities. 2021;7(1):32–39. https://doi.org/10.5114/jhi.2021.107954.
385. Since tobacco companies have used the existence of illicit markets to argue against raising tobacco taxes, many in the tobacco

control community instinctively reject the argument. The position against the obvious economic logic rests on the weak empirical observation that (in cross-sectional data and controlling for no other factors), often countries with higher taxes on tobacco (e.g., the U.K.) have smaller illicit markets than other countries with lower taxes (e.g., Latvia). As anyone familiar with both the notion of substitutes and the concept of *ceteris paribus* would expect, however, this negative correlation between taxes and illicit markets switches sign after controlling for observed and unobserved differences among countries (providing a clear example of Simpson's Paradox) (see: Prieger JE, Kulick J. Cigarette Taxes and Illicit Trade in Europe. Economic Inquiry. 2018;56:1706-1723. https://doi.org/10.1111/ecin.12564). Secondarily, proponents of high tobacco taxes argue that even if taxation stimulates some illicit trade, other factors such as corruption are more important causes (see: Joossens L, Chaloupka FJ, Merriman D, Yurekli A. (2000). Issues in the Smuggling of Tobacco Products. In Jha P, Chaloupka F (Eds.), *Tobacco Control Policies in Developing Countries* [pp. 393–406]. Oxford: Oxford University Press).

386. Bate, R., Kallen, C., Mathur, A. *The Perverse Effect of Sin Taxes: The Rise of Illicit White Cigarettes*. American Enterprise Institute, 2017. http://www.jstor.org/stable/resrep24594.
387. Prieger, J.E., Kulick, J. Cigarette Taxes and Illicit Trade in Europe. Economic Inquiry. 2018;56:1706–1723. https://doi.org/10.1111/ecin.12564.
388. Prieger, J.E., Kulick, J. Tax Evasion and Illicit Cigarettes in California: Part IV— Smokers' Behavioral and Market Responses to a Tax Increase. Law & Society: Public Law—Tax eJournal. 2019. https://papers.ssrn.com/sol3/papers.cfm?abstract_id=3322095.
389. DeCicca, P., Kenkel, D., Liu, F. Excise Tax Avoidance: the Case of State Cigarette Taxes. J Health Econ. 2013 Dec;32(6):1130–1141. https://doi.org/10.1016/j.jhealeco.2013.08.005.
390. LaFaive, M. Prohibition by Price: Cigarette Taxes and Unintended Consequences (January 3, 2018). Excerpt from Adam J. Hoffer and Todd Nesbit, eds. (2018). *For Your Own Good: Taxes, Paternalism, and Fiscal Discrimination in the Twenty-First Century*. Arlington, VA: Mercatus Center at George Mason

University. Available at SSRN: https://ssrn.com/abstract=3173841.

Chiou, L., Muehlegger, E.J. Crossing the Line: The Effect of Cross-Border Cigarette Sales on State Excise Tax Revenues. BE J Econ Analysis & Policy. 2008;8:1 Article 48.

Coats, R.M. A Note on Estimating Cross-Border Effects of State Cigarette Taxes. Natl Tax J. 1995:573.

DeCicca, P., Kenkel, D., Liu, F. Excise Tax Avoidance: the Case of State Cigarette Taxes. J Health Econ. 2013 Dec;32(6):1130-1141.

Galbraith, J.W., Kaiserman, M. Taxation, Smuggling and Demand for Cigarettes in Canada: Evidence from Time-Series Data. J Health Econ. 1997;16(3):287–301.

Goel, R.K. Cigarette Smuggling: Price vs. Nonprice Incentives. Appl Econ Lett. 2008;15(8): 587–592.

Lovenheim, M.F. How Far to the Border? The Extent and Impact of Cross-Border Casual Cigarette Smuggling. Natl Tax J. 2008;61(1):7–33.

Saba, R.R., Beard, T.R., Ekelund, R.B., Ressler, R. The Demand for Cigarette Smuggling. Econ Inquiry. 1995;33(2):189–202.

Stehr, M. Cigarette Tax Avoidance and Evasion. J Health Econ. 2005;24(2):277–297.

Thursby, J.G., Thursby, M.C. Interstate Cigarette Bootlegging: Extent, Revenue, Losses, and Effects of Federal Intervention. Natl Tax J. 2000;53(1):59–77.

391. Kleiman, M., Prieger, J.E., Kulick, J. Illicit Trade as a Countervailing Effect: What the FDA Would Have to Know to Evaluate Tobacco Regulations. J Drug Policy Analysis. 2016;9(1):1–30. https://doi.org/10.1515/jdpa-2015-0016.
392. Goodchild, M., Paul, J., Iglesias, R., et al. Potential Impact of Eliminating Illicit Trade in Cigarettes: A Demand-Side Perspective. Tobacco Control. Published Online First: 3 November 2020. https://doi.org/10.1136/tobaccocontrol-2020-055980.
393. Aitken, C.K., Fry, T.R., Farrell, L., Pellegrini, B. Smokers of Illicit Tobacco Report Significantly Worse Health Than Other Smokers. Nicotine Tob Res. 2009 Aug;11(8):996–1001. https://doi.org/10.1093/ntr/ntp102.

394. Center for Regulatory Effectiveness. (July 2011). *The Countervaling Effects of Counterfeit Cigarettes*. Retrieved from www.ojp.gov: https://www.ojp.gov/sites/g/files/xyckuh241/files/media/document/sabappendixicounterfeitcig062012.pdf.
395. Stephens, W.E., Calder, A., Newton, J. Source and Health Implications of High Toxic Metal Concentrations in Illicit Tobacco Products. Environ Sci Technol. 2005 Jan 15;39(2):479–88. https://doi.org/10.1021/es049038s.
396. U.S. Bureau of Alcohol, Tobacco, Firearms, and Explosives (ATF). (2018, May). Fact Sheet—Tobacco Enforcement. Retrieved June 18, 2021, from https://www.atf.gov/resource-center/fact-sheet/fact-sheet-tobacco-enforcement.
397. National Research Council. (2015). *Understanding the U.S. Illicit Tobacco Market: Characteristics, Policy Context, and Lessons from International Experiences*, ed. Peter Reuter and Malay Majmundar. Washington, D.C.: The National Academies Press. https://doi.org/10.17226/19016.
398. Paraje, G., Stoklosa, M. Blecher EIllicit Trade in Tobacco Products: Recent Trends and Coming Challenges. Tob Control. 2022;31:257–262.
399. Freitas-Lemos, R., Stein, J.S., Tegge, A.N., Kaplan, B.A., Heckman, B.W., McNeill, A., et al. Illegal Experimental Tobacco Marketplace II: Effects of Vaping Product Bans—Findings from the 2020 International Tobacco Control Project. Tob Control. 2022;31(Suppl 3):s214–s222.
400. "Flavor Ban Will Feed Illegal Tobacco Sales, Stores Say." WWLP, November 4, 2019. https://www.wwlp.com/news/state-politics/flavor-ban-will-feed-illegal-tobacco-sales-stores-say/.
401. Commonwealth of Massachusetts. Annual Report of Multi-Agency Illegal Tobacco Task Force, Commonwealth of Massachusetts, 2022, available at: https://www.mass.gov/doc/task-force-fy22-annual-report/download.
402. Cirulis, M.M., Callahan, S.J., Aberegg, S.K. Marijuana Legislation and Electronic Cigarette– or Vaping–Associated Lung Injury: A Historical Perspective. JAMA Netw Open. 2020;3(4):e202238. https://doi.org/10.1001/jamanetworkopen.2020.2238.
403. Wing, C., Bradford, A.C., Carroll, A.E., Hollingsworth A. Association of State Marijuana Legalization Policies for Medical and Recreational Use with Vaping-Associated Lung Disease. JAMA

Netw Open. 2020;3(4):e202187. https://doi.org/10.1001/jamanetworkopen.2020.2187.

404. Zhu, S., Sun, J.Y., Bonnevie, E., et al. "Four Hundred and Sixty Brands of E-cigarettes and Counting: Implications for Product Regulation" Tob Control. 2014;23: 3–9.
405. Calabro, K.S., Khalil, G.E., Chen, M., et al. Pilot Study to Inform Young Adults About the Risks of Electronic Cigarettes Through Text Messaging. Addict Behav Reports. 2019;10:100224.
406. Kleiman, M., Prieger, J.E., Kulick, J. Illicit Trade as a Countervailing Effect: What the FDA Would Have to Know to Evaluate Tobacco Regulations. J Drug Policy Analysis. 2016;9(1):1–30. https://doi.org/10.1515/jdpa-2015-0016.
407. Amalia, B., Kapoor, S., Sharma, R., Singh, R.J. E-cigarette Retailer Storefront Availability Following a Nationwide Prohibition of E-cigarettes in India: A Multicentric Compliance Assessment. Tob Prev Cessat. 2020;9:1–11.
408. Amalia, B., Kapoor, S., Sharma, R., Fu, M., Fernández, E., Rana, J.S. Online Sales Compliance with the Electronic Cigarettes Ban in India: A Content Analysis. Int J Public Health. 2020;65(8):1497–505.
409. Therapeutic Goods Administration. Potential Reforms to the Regulation of Nicotine Vaping Products. Consultation Paper 2022. Available at: https://consultations.tga.gov.au/medicines regulation-division/proposed-reforms-to-the-regulation-of-nicotine-vap/.
410. New South Wales Ministry of Health. NSW Population Health Survey [Internet]. Sydney: Government of New South Wales, 2022. http://www.healthstats.nsw.gov.au/.
411. Therapeutic Goods Administration. Authorised Prescribers of Unapproved Nicotine Vaping Products. 2022. Available at: https://www.tga.gov.au/resources/resource/guidance/authorised-prescribers-unapproved-nicotine-vaping-products.
412. Morandin, P. Is Vaping Illegal in Australia? 2022, available at: https://www.criminaldefencelawyers.com.au/blog/is-vaping-illegal-in-australia/?utm_source=Mondaq&utm_medium=syndication&utm_campaign=LinkedIn-integration.
413. Australian Association of Convenience Stores. Nicotine Vaping Product Usages and Change. 2022. Available at: https://colinmendelsohn.com.au/wp-content/uploads/2022/10/AACS-CMA Research-Attachment.pdf.

414. ABC News. Street Sales, Online Dealers and Convenience Stores: Inside the Thriving Black Market for Nicotine Vapes, 2022, available at: https://www.abc.net.au/news/2022-06-27/inside-the-thriving-black-market-for-nicotine-vapes/101176544.
415. Mendelsohn, C., Wodak, A., Hall, W. How Should Nicotine Vaping Be Regulated in Australia? Drug Alcohol Rev. 2023. https://doi.org/10.1111/dar.13663.
416. Dessaix, A., Jardine, E., Freeman, B., et al. Undermining Australian Controls on Electronic Nicotine Delivery Systems: Illicit Imports and Illegal Sales. Tob Control. 2022;31:689–690.
417. Cancer Council Australia. Parents Right to Worry About E-cigarettes and Kids, Says Cancer Council, 2020. Available at: https://www.cancer.org.au/media-releases/2020/parents-right-to-worry-about-e-cigarettes-and-kids-says-cancer-council.
418. Orange County Coalition of Police and Sheriffs. Letter to Honorable State Senator Jerry Hill on SB793. Orange County Coalition of Police and Sheriffs, 2020, available at: https://tobacco.ucsf.edu/sites/g/files/tkssra4661/f/wysiwyg/OC%20Cops%20Opposition%20Letter%20to%20SB793_.pdf.
419. Sunstein, C., Thaler, R. (2009). *Nudge*. Penguin.
420. Cherukupalli, R. A Behavioral Economics Perspective on Tobacco Taxation. Am J Public Health. 2010;100(4):609–615.
421. Gruber, J., Koszegi, B. A Modern Economic View of Tobacco Taxation. International Union Against Tuberculosis and Lung Disease, 2008. https://untobaccocontrol.org/taxation/e-library/wp-content/uploads/2020/06/A-modern-economic-view-of-tobacco-taxation.pdf.
422. Farhi, E., Gabaix, X. Optimal Taxation with Behavioral Agents. Am Econ Rev. 2020;110(1):298–336.
423. Eichler, H.G., Bloechl-Daum, B., Brasseur, D., Breckenridge, A., Leufkens, H., Raine, J., Salmonson, T., Schneider, C.K., Rasi, G. The Risks of Risk Aversion in Drug Regulation. Nat Rev Drug Discov. 2013 Dec;12(12):907–16. https://doi.org/10.1038/nrd4129.
424. Choi, S.J., Pritchard, A.C. *Behavioral Economics and the SEC*. UC Berkeley: Berkeley Law, 2003, available at: https://escholarship.org/uc/item/4tf7r9tz.
425. Eichler, H.G., Bloechl-Daum, B., Brasseur, D., Breckenridge, A., Leufkens, H., Raine, J., Salmonson, T., Schneider, C.K.,

Rasi, G. The Risks of Risk Aversion in Drug Regulation. Nat Rev Drug Discov. 2013 Dec;12(12):907–16. https://doi.org/10.1038/nrd4129.

426. Cooper, J. Behavioral Economics and Biased Regulators MERCATUS ON POLICY, 2013, available at: https://www.mercatus.org/research/policy-briefs/behavioral-economics-and-biased-regulators.
427. Kuran, T., Sunstein., C.R. Availability Cascades and Risk Regulation. Stanford Law Review. 1999;51(4).
428. Cooper, J. Behavioral Economics and Biased Regulators MERCATUS ON POLICY, 2013, available at: https://www.mercatus.org/research/policy-briefs/behavioral-economics-and-biased-regulators.
429. Of course, tobacco was taxed during this time, but not at levels designed to discourage use.
430. Cooper, J. Behavioral Economics and Biased Regulators MERCATUS ON POLICY, 2013, available at: https://www.mercatus.org/research/policy-briefs/behavioral-economics-and-biased-regulators.
431. Choi, S.J., Pritchard, A.C. *Behavioral Economics and the SEC*. UC Berkeley: Berkeley Law, 2003, available at: https://escholarship.org/uc/item/4tf7r9tz.
432. Griffin, D., Tversky, A. The Weighing Evidence and the Determinants of Confidence, 24 COGNITIVE PSYCHOL.
433. Cooper, J. Behavioral Economics and Biased Regulators MERCATUS ON POLICY, 2013, available at: https://www.mercatus.org/research/policy-briefs/behavioral-economics-and-biased-regulators.
434. Bhatta, D.N., Glantz, S.A. Electronic Cigarette Use and Myocardial Infarction Among Adults in the US Population Assessment of Tobacco and Health. J Am Heart Assoc. 2019;8(12):e012317.
435. The article was retracted in February 2020. Some papers in the academic literature were still citing it in 2022 as if the findings were valid. There are even more instances of consumer-facing messaging from NGOs stating or implying that a causal link between vaping and heart attacks has been found. Some of the latter instances were likely posted when the original study came out and before the retraction, regardless, they remain available to consumers searching for health information today.

436. Kuran, T. "Availability Cascades and Risk Regulation" (University of Chicago Public Law & Legal Theory Working Paper No. 181, 2007).
437. Fairchild, A.L., Bayer, R., Lee, J.S. The E-Cigarette Debate: What Counts as Evidence? Am J Public Health. 2019 Jul;109(7):1000–1006. https://doi.org/10.2105/AJPH.2019.305107.
438. Choi, S.J., Pritchard, A.C. *Behavioral Economics and the SEC*. UC Berkeley: Berkeley Law, 2003, available at: https://escholarship.org/uc/item/4tf7r9tz.
439. Choi, S.J., Pritchard, A.C. *Behavioral Economics and the SEC*. UC Berkeley: Berkeley Law, 2003, available at: https://escholarship.org/uc/item/4tf7r9tz.
440. Choi, S.J., Pritchard, A.C. *Behavioral Economics and the SEC*. UC Berkeley: Berkeley Law, 2003, available at: https://escholarship.org/uc/item/4tf7r9tz.
441. Plott, C.R., Zeiler, K. The Willingness to Pay–Willingness to Accept Gap, the 'Endowment Effect,' Subject Misconceptions, and Experimental Procedures for Eliciting Valuations. Am Econ Rev. 2005;95(3).
442. Choi, S.J., Pritchard, A.C. *Behavioral Economics and the SEC*. UC Berkeley: Berkeley Law. 2003, available at: https://escholarship.org/uc/item/4tf7r9tz.
443. To be fair, most cohort studies in medicine and public health do *not* rise to the standards of causality demanded within the field of economics. Also to be fair, experts trained in public health typically were not exposed to quasi-experimental methods from econometrics unless their degree was recent.
444. Cooper, J. Behavioral Economics and Biased Regulators MERCATUS ON POLICY, 2013, available at: https://www.mercatus.org/research/policy-briefs/behavioral-economics-and-biased-regulators.
445. Cooper, J. Behavioral Economics and Biased Regulators MERCATUS ON POLICY, 2013, available at: https://www.mercatus.org/research/policy-briefs/behavioral-economics-and-biased-regulators.
446. Peltzman, S. Toward a More General Theory of Regulation. J L & Econ. 1976;19(2):211–240.

447. Buchanan, J.M., Tollison, R.D., Tullock, G. (Eds.). *Toward a Theory of the Rent-Seeking Society*. Texas A & M University Press, 1980.
448. Foot, P. "The Problem of Abortion and the Doctrine of the Double Effect." In Virtues and Vices (Basil Blackwell, Oxford), 1978.
449. Readers whose last exposure to the formal study of ethics was a long time ago in university may benefit from a description of the thought experiment. Imagine a runaway trolley that is on course to hit and likely kill $x > 1$ people. An observer can choose to divert the trolley to another track; this will save the x individuals but will kill one (other) person. The dilemma is whether to act to kill one life to save x other lives.
450. Ryazanov, A., Wang, S.T., Rickless, S.C., McKenzie, C.R.M., Nelkin, D.K. Sensitivity to Shifts in Probability of Harm and Benefit in Moral Dilemmas. Cognition, 209, 2021.
451. Moore, M. *Placing Blame: A Theory of the Criminal Law*. Oxford University Press, 1997.
452. Lenert, L.A., Markowitz, D.R. Blaschke, T.F. Primum Non Nocere? Valuing of the Risk of Drug Toxicity in Therapeutic Decision Making. Clin Pharmacol Ther. 1993;53:285–291.
453. McNeil, B.J., Pauker, S.G., Sox, H.C. Tversky Jr., A. On the Elicitation of Preferences for Alternative Therapies. N Engl J Med. 1982;306:1259–1262.
454. Johnson, F.R., et al. Are Gastroenterologists Less Tolerant of Treatment Risks Than Patients? Benefit–Risk Preferences in Crohn's Disease Management. J Manag Care Pharm. 2010;16:616–628.
455. Cooper, J. Behavioral Economics and Biased Regulators MERCATUS ON POLICY, 2013, available at: https://www.mercatus.org/research/policy-briefs/behavioral-economics-and-biased-regulators.
456. Choi, S.J., Pritchard, A.C. *Behavioral Economics and the SEC*. UC Berkeley: Berkeley Law, 2003, available at: https://escholarship.org/uc/item/4tf7r9tz.
457. Saffer, H., Dench, D., Grossman, M., Dave, D. E-cigarettes and Adult Smoking: Evidence from Minnesota. J Risk and Uncertainty. 2020;60:207–228.

458. For the evidence regarding Massachusetts, refer to Sect. 3.2.4 in this chapter; for the evidence regarding San Francisco, refer to Sect. 3.2.2.2.
459. Hunter, D.J., Littlejohns, P., Weale, A. Reforming the Public Health System in England. The Lancet Public Health. 2022;7(9):e797–e800.
460. Khan, J. (2022). The Khan Review: Making Smoking Obsolete: Independent Review into Smokefree 2030 Policies. GOV.UK. https://assets.publishing.service.gov.uk/government/uploads/system/uploads/attachment_data/file/1081366/khan-review-making-smoking-obsolete.pdf.

CHAPTER 2

Toward Optimal E-cigarette Policy

> We must not focus our efforts so narrowly on preventing tobacco use by youth that we send the message to smokers that we have abandoned them—that their action is their own fault and we don't care about them.
> —C. Everett Koop - Former Surgeon General[1]

What does optimal policy toward e-cigarettes and other tobacco products look like? To discuss optimization, be it of an engineering design, a personal investment plan, or a public policy, implies the existence of a well-articulated goal. In a formal approach to optimization, this overarching goal must be quantifiable and reducible to a single dimension. The restriction to a single final, optimized value does not mean that multiple factors cannot be considered. When there are competing desired outcomes involved, they are assigned importance weights or otherwise combined to arrive at a multivariable objective function that yields a scalar output. In crafting policy regarding e-cigarettes, competing goals emerge: first, encouraging smokers to switch away from cigarettes toward e-cigarettes and, second, discouraging adoption of either by youth. Once a goal is set, it almost always becomes apparent that the optimal approach will not maximize benefits accruing to one group *and* minimize harms caused for another, for that is inherently impossible. Instead, the optimal approach will be the option that delivers the greatest *net combination* of benefits and harms, as valued in the objective function. The optimal policy generally will not—indeed, cannot—maximize all benefits simultaneously nor fully minimize all possible harms.

S. C. Hampsher-Monk et al., *Tobacco Regulation, Economics, and Public Health, Volume III*, https://doi.org/10.1007/978-3-031-47096-7_2

Once the objective is formalized, mathematical tools can give insight into the tradeoffs between competing components of the objective and how to best attain the overarching goal. However, determining the optimal balance among competing objectives in economics or policy analysis is never purely a mathematical problem. As discussed in Chapter 1 of this volume, various interest groups place different values on different outcomes. Society, the median voter, politicians, regulators, or other experts must determine how to aggregate competing goals into a single objective function. Therefore, this chapter deals with more than a formal mathematical approach to optimization.

Describing policy-making this way assumes that a purely social point of view is guiding the development of the policy framework. However, policy-makers are real people, never merely conduits for the implementation of social preferences (the fictional "benevolent dictators" assumed to guide the economy in many an economics study).[2,3] Risk aversion might lead decision-makers to prefer risk avoidance over the securing of uncertain but expected net benefits, if the personal or institutional consequences of failure loom larger in their personal decisions than a social perspective would call for (as discussed in the previous chapter).[4] Any cognitive bias trotted out to justify governmental intervention in consumer affairs, whether short-termism, overconfidence, or confirmation bias, likely applies to regulators as well, as discussed in the previous chapter (Sect. 4).[5] Failure on the part of "behavioral bureaucrats" to advance decisions in service of the objective function is especially likely when policy-making is in response to strong populist (and often ill-informed) pressure,[6] as is the case with issues surrounding youth vaping. Similarly, for every claimed market failure there is at least one example of governmental failure.[7,8] Optimizing regulation therefore requires a clear eye, attention to both scientific evidence and the possibility of other agendas being in play, and a large dose of humility.

This chapter sets out the elements necessary to understand what the best policy toward e-cigarettes might entail. The exact social welfare function to be optimized is not prescribed for two reasons. The state of our knowledge about key parameters of such a function—the exact relative harms from e-cigarettes and their true causal effects on cessation from and initiation of smoking—is incomplete and evolving rapidly. Furthermore, while we can suggest that certain non-welfarist aspects such as a concern for equity be present in the objective function, the relative weight of such components should come from a deliberative and participatory political process, not by fiat from the present authors. Nevertheless, we point out the important tradeoffs inherent in the policy question, discuss which policy levers are available to regulators, and draw tentative conclusions about what optimal policy might look like.

In the first section below, the main different regulatory approaches to e-cigarettes are reviewed: implementation of product standards, the use of taxes and regulations to prevent or discourage e-cigarette use, and instituting regulatory differentials to encourage harm reduction by switching away from smoking. In Sect. 2, basic principles for e-cigarette regulation are laid out: regulation should not create net harm, an appropriate treatment of probabilistic evidence should guide decisions, policy-making must account for external influences on e-cigarette use and the latter's influence on other risky activities, and regulators should prioritize the overall public benefit when balancing risks and benefits. The key tradeoff between promoting e-cigarettes for cessation for current smokers versus not encouraging non-smokers to take up vaping is set forth in Sect. 3. Several models of the impact of e-cigarettes on the health or welfare of the population have already been introduced in the literature, and these are reviewed in Sect. 4. Section 5 discusses optimal regulation and a general approach is outlined. Section 6 discusses the opportunities to fine-tune the approach at the policy level, with insights from the literature, and further considerations are discussed in Sect. 7. The penultimate section argues that good regulation of e-cigarettes complements rather than hinders the proper goal of tobacco control, namely accelerating the reduction in smoking. The final section lays out thoughts on how to turn the theoretical discussion into practical policy.

1 What Can Regulators Do?

Before delving into the details of the most effective approaches to regulating e-cigarettes, it is useful to consider the broad goals that policymakers could adopt and the policy instruments available to achieve these goals. Three key goals for e-cigarette regulation could be to use standards for consumer products to protect users, to discourage use, or to facilitate use.[9]

1.1 Implement Product Standards

If a regulator is ambivalent about the balance of benefits and costs associated with e-cigarette use at the population level, or perhaps wants to wait until more evidence becomes available on these topics, a relatively impartial interim approach would be to enact consumer product standards regulating the production, manufacturing, and retail of e-cigarettes. Consumer product liability as a means of disciplining manufacturers has already been discussed in Volume II, Chapter 1, as have industry-led standards. The standards in question here would be in addition to product liability law, tort remedies, and voluntary efforts toward product stewardship.

One class of standards pertains to the provision of information. Standard examples include mandating labels listing all ingredients or the concentration of nicotine in e-liquids. The European Parliament, the FDA, and various other national authorities require data on the constituents of e-cigarettes and various compounds in emissions, including types, quantities, and origins. In the U.S., the FDA's Premarket Tobacco Product Applications (PMTA) authorization process demands that manufacturers demonstrate their e-cigarette products would be "appropriate for the protection of the public health" by, for example, encouraging existing cigarette smokers to switch while not encouraging use by non-smokers or youth.[10] Other regulations involve prohibiting certain types of information or claims. For example, in the EU manufacturers of e-cigarettes are disallowed from claiming that their product boosts energy, health, or even that e-cigarettes present reduced health risks compared to smoking.[11]

Product safety regulations could include maximum allowable levels of natural or unavoidable defects in e-cigarettes. For food items, such defects are under the oversight of national regulatory agencies such as the U.K.'s Department for Environment, Food and Rural Affairs (DEFRA) and Food Standards Agency,[12] or the U.S. FDA.[13] In the U.S., the Consumer Product Safety Commission does the same for certain other regulated products. In the case of e-cigarettes, the FDA can enforce any regulations it imposes through its PMTA process. Such regulations are intended to secure, to some extent, consumer confidence in the product.[14] Possible advantages of this approach include advancing (or at least not limiting) individual choice and ensuring that minimum safety standards are met, while limiting opportunities for the illicit market to fill with riskier products the vacuum in demand left by more coercive demand-reduction strategies. However, it is not clear that this approach is as neutral as it might appear. Safeguarding consumer trust can contribute to demand. That is, if consumers factor perceived risks into their personal decision-making, then reducing the riskiness of a product could encourage its demand. This is a variant of the Peltzman effect,[15] in which adding safety attributes to a product can perversely alter the consumer's behavior toward more dangerous use of the product.[16]

1.2 Implement Taxes and Rules to Prevent or Discourage Use

If the regulator is convinced by the evidence that e-cigarettes are, or might be, net harmful, then interventions that prevent or at least discourage use might be called for. Taxes can reduce demand[17] and other regulations can limit access or otherwise reduce the appeal of products.[18] Such policies might be facilitated by adopting a classification for e-cigarettes that mirrors that of combustible tobacco. Under such a framework, e-cigarettes could be required to comply with many or all of the general, often long-standing, tobacco restrictions—taxes, minimum legal sale ages, marketing and advertising restrictions, public-use bans, cautionary warning labels and health warnings, etc.

To take just one example, note that for decades regulation of tobacco products in most countries has involved requirements for textual (or more recently, graphical) hazard warnings on packages of cigarettes and other tobacco products. Such regulation is typically quite detailed, specifying the size of the warnings relative to the total surface area of packaging, required fonts and text size, and the content of the warnings themselves, whether textual or graphical.[19] It is worth noting that the health warnings go beyond the provision of information to rational consumers. At least part of the goal, particularly with graphical warnings, is to evoke what psychologists call "negative affect" in tobacco users, such as fear, anxiety, guilt, and disgust.[20,21,22] Regulators could require similar warnings for e-cigarettes, treating the two products with regulatory parity, if deemed warranted.[23]

Other regulation to reduce the attractiveness of the product could involve banning certain constituents on grounds other than direct health harm. Current regulation of e-cigarette products involves, in various countries, banning certain additives (candy and fruit flavorings in Finland, any flavors at all in Hungary, taurine, caffeine, vitamins, colorants, or any carcinogenic, mutagenic, or teratogenic substance in the EU, etc.) and restrictions on container sizes (as in the EU and U.K.) or nicotine concentration of e-liquids (as in the EU, U.K., and Canada). Such regulations do not involve product safety directly in the traditional sense but instead attempt to diminish the appeal of e-cigarettes, primarily to youth. Banning candy flavorings, for example, is usually intended to lower consumption by youth per se rather than to prevent any known direct harm from such additives.

Product bans and blanket prohibitions on use are the most stringent regulatory approach to e-cigarettes, often motivated by the precautionary principle (see discussion of risk in Volume II, Chapter 3).

Various aspects of the market for e-cigarettes (manufacture, importation, distribution, sale, or even use) might be prohibited by national, state, or municipal governments. It is noteworthy that restrictions, if onerous enough, may function as de facto prohibitions by imposing a cost on access that consumers are unwilling to pay, even if the products remain, technically, available. In this manner, taxation and other restrictions on desirable features may have similar effects as prohibitions.[24] A related example is the case of Australia, which recently required that e-cigarette only be sold in pharmacies with a doctor's prescription. This federal law in addition to similar existing state-level laws already in place for years.[25,26] At least in the first years of the state laws, virtually no physicians were willing to prescribe e-cigarettes as cessation aids and no e-cigarettes were approved by the pharmaceutical regulator as official smoking cessation aids, and so the laws effectively quashed the legal market for e-cigarettes in the country[27] (resulting in a lacuna the illicit market was happy to fill).[28] Such actions may be motivated by a desire to eliminate risk, but historical precedents suggest that eliminating use is fraught. Indeed, as the previous chapter explored, prohibitions and bans on e-cigarettes do not eliminate the use but push at least some portion of demand elsewhere, including back to smoking[29] - a theme to which we return in this chapter.

1.3 *Use Regulatory Differentials to Facilitate or Encourage Use*

A final approach uses regulation to create differentials between e-cigarettes and combustibles to encourage substitutions from riskier to less risky products. This should not be confused with a doctrine of *laissez faire*; a risk proportionate policy approach to e-cigarettes does not require that regulation is absent or even minimal. Instead, regulation can be designed so that products with lower health risks are regulated with less stringency than more risky products. The creation of regulatory differentials may be achieved in any of the traditional tobacco control policies: taxes on e-cigarettes may be lower than those applied to combustibles, marketing restrictions could be less stringent, public-use restrictions could, where feasible, distinguish between combustibles and e-cigarettes, and warning labels could be stronger for cigarettes than e-cigarettes (as they would have to be if evidence-based regulation is the law).

Of course, risk-proportionate regulation is open to the important criticism that many of the regulatory features that make e-cigarettes attractive to current adult smokers will also increase the appeal to non-smokers in general and young people in particular. Regulators balance concerns about the consequences of youth experimentation and uptake of e-cigarettes by never-smokers with the opportunity that e-cigarettes provide current smokers to reduce smoking-related risks. The U.K.'s "swap to stop" e-cigarette giveaways will be accompanied by a so-called crackdown on illicit e-cigarette sales with £3 million (US$3.7 million) in new funding dedicated to creating an "illicit vapes enforcement squad" to enforce existing regulations, tackle illicit sales, and bolster age-gating efforts. The challenge of confronting tradeoffs does not negate the value of risk-proportionate regulation. Other ways in which risk-proportionate regulation could simultaneously encourage substitutions away from combustibles among adult smokers, while deterring uptake by youth and non-smokers, are discussed in Sect. 6.

The different approaches to e-cigarette regulation outlined above may be incorporated into a single regulatory framework in practice. In Argentina, for instance, the sale of e-cigarettes is prohibited but their usage is subject to further tobacco control legislation, which includes restrictions on public use in places where smoking is banned. As a result, the regulations in Argentina encompass aspects of both a prohibitionist approach and an approach that treats e-cigarettes at parity with tobacco products. Mixed approaches are common. In the U.K., nicotine concentrations above 20 mg/ml are banned (prohibition), health warnings are mandated as per traditional cigarettes (parity), and e-cigarettes are taxed less stringently than cigarettes (risk proportionality). Mixed approaches are also evident to varying degrees in e-cigarette regulation in Canada, the U.S., and the EU.

2 First Principles of E-cigarette Regulation

Certain principles should undergird regulation regarding e-cigarettes. There are many particular specific policies that can be considered and debated, but the following first principles should undergird the regulation and guide the policy choices: regulation should not create net harm, informed and nuanced policy-making is possible even in the face of uncertainties, regulation is only one of many interconnected social, economic, and legal aspects that affect consumption, and public health should serve the entire public.

2.1 "First, Do No Harm," and Define Harm Broadly

Advocates of both the precautionary principle and tobacco harm reduction focus on harm, although they disagree about what constitutes harm and the best ways of responding to the risk of harm. The imperative to "first, do no harm" associated with the precautionary principle and the risk-aversion inherent in its application seems ostensibly unproblematic. However, regulations indeed *do* harm when they take steps that inadvertently prevent an otherwise beneficial outcome. Harm is created both through realized effects (seen) and opportunity costs (unseen). For example, restrictive e-cigarette policies designed to reduce young non-smokers' demand for e-cigarettes also discourage adult smokers from switching, introducing significant harm: reduced smoking cessation. As discussed in the previous chapter, it is problematic for policy analysts considering regulatory strategy that such unintended consequences may be far-off in time and uncertain, at least when the initial regulation is implemented. Recall, however, that the precautionary principle puts the onus of responsibility on those advocating a potentially risky activity to demonstrate that a reasonable standard of safety has been achieved. To be consistent, therefore, the responsibility for identifying potentially harmful unintended consequences of regulatory decisions should lie with the proponents of the initial intervention.

An intervention may also "do" harm by failing to prevent its occurrence, if that harm were foreseeable or could reasonably be expected to result from inaction. That could be justification for regulatory restrictions on harmful additives in e-liquids, but also *against* e-cigarette taxes and restrictions. The adoption of taxes and usage restrictions that were intended to protect against youth vaping also had the unintended consequence of increasing youth smoking (as will be discussed in Sect. 6 below). While that unintended consequence does not necessarily completely undermine the primary objective of safeguarding the health and well-being of non-smokers and youth, it is crucial to acknowledge that alternative policies may be more effective in achieving the desired outcomes. Harms from unintended consequences do not necessarily dictate the outcome of policy decisions: to do so, they would have to outweigh the intended benefits. But cost–benefit analyses should certainly include these harms in line with the evidence base for them. Again, if the mere possibility of harm is sufficient under the precautionary principle for e-cigarette skeptics to call for regulation, then the same standard should be applied to the possibility of unintended consequences resulting from regulatory action.

While there is broad disagreement about what counts as harm—e.g., is addiction to nicotine in the absence of medical risk a harm?—we should at least acknowledge that there *are* different kinds of harm. In the public health literature on tobacco, there is, unsurprisingly, a strong tendency to focus narrowly on health outcomes. But an individual's well-being is also influenced by psychological, economic, and social factors. Advocates for harm reduction highlight these additional vectors of harm, but they are often ignored by prohibitionist advocates. For example, proponents of tobacco harm reduction (THR) view the stigmatization of smokers as a harm in itself, and many consider the regressive nature of tobacco taxes to be an additional harm. Prohibitionists, however, argue that the disproportionate imposition of those harms on the remaining pockets of smokers serves as additional quitting incentives and hope that they will lead such smokers to quit, in which case the ends will justify the means (thus, reframing what others see as a harm to be a benefit). But, in the context of non-combustible nicotine products, that perspective is somewhat ironic and inconsistent. If those products do not cause long-term medical harms, and there is no good evidence yet that they do, then the harms eluded have to be something else, whether psychological, economic, or social. Either these things count as harms or they do not, but it cannot be both ways. A consistent definition of harm would include psychological, economic, and social harms along with medical harms. By that standard, THR advocates are right to claim that tobacco control imposes harms on those who continue to smoke, and e-cigarette skeptics are likely right to claim that the nicotine dependence generated by the uptake of e-cigarettes by non-smokers constitutes harm even in the absence of medical risks.

The immediate problem with this inclusive definition of "harm" is that it is far from clear how different categories of harm should be considered in relation to each other. How much stigma is worth avoiding a given medical risk? What economic costs justify the avoidance of smoking-related diseases? Regulation tends to apply fixed rules to all people, but the answers are likely highly personal. Given asymmetric information, consumers may be the best equipped to make decisions regarding risky products. THR advocates suggest that individuals should be provided with options and accurate health-related information with which to decide for themselves. But regulators appeal to behavioral and market failure rationales for intervention, since consumers may be irrational and in any event the consequences of individual decisions may impose public costs (externalities). To that end, informed by the broader definition of harms, and the best data on the extent and severity of those harms, regulators may want to use regulation to provide additional incentives to tip the scale in favor of the least harmful option for nicotine users. This theme is developed in Sect. 6 below.

2.2 Epistemic Probabilism

As discussed in Volume II, Chapter 2, while there is an increasingly robust evidence base on which to judge the safety and efficacy of e-cigarettes, there is considerable disagreement regarding its interpretation. E-cigarettes are less risky than combustible cigarettes and substitution to e-cigarettes reduces health risk significantly. But there are plausible pathways by which e-cigarettes may harm users, especially in the long term, even if those harms have not manifested yet. Interpretations of that incomplete evidence base often deploy rhetoric, using figures of speech and various illogical forms of argumentation (including appeals to reason, character or emotion) to convince the public. But such interpretations tend to devolve into subjective value judgments, appealing to risk-aversion in the absence of absolute evidence for e-cigarettes safety. That is profoundly unscientific, both because absolute certainty is an impossible scientific standard and because it ignores the mass of available evidence. While there may be a role for rhetoric in the communication of scientific data, rhetoric should not be employed to suborn the testimony of the empirical evidence. Of course, future outcomes are unobservable and the ultimate risks of e-cigarettes remain unknown. But this does not mean that rhetoric should determine the course of regulation action today.

Epistemic probabilism frames claims about knowledge as universally probabilistic; certainty is always both elusive and illusive. The best we can do is to assign probabilities to outcomes based on the currently available evidence. No consumer product can ever be proven to be absolutely safe, but we can infer that, beyond a reasonable doubt, one product is safer than another. The strength of those claims (and indeed all knowledge claims) must be judged on the basis of the available evidence, imperfect as it inevitably is. While epistemic probabilism is a philosophical notion, it finds strong echoes in modern statistical and economic analysis. Economics and decision science use probabilities to model and analyze human behavior under uncertainty, assigning prior probabilities to different outcomes based on available data. (Or, instead, assuming that the subjective probabilities of various outcomes are updated by the individual decision-makers as data become available.) These probabilities can be updated continually as new information becomes available, allowing computation of *ex-post* probabilities of different outcomes and make progressively more accurate predictions about future events. These predictions can inform decision-making in a wide range of areas, and accordingly, the idea of Bayesian updating of probabilities has applications in many areas including finance, consumer behavior, policy analysis, and health economics.

This empirical approach has several advantages, not least of which is that it allows researchers to handle complex and uncertain data and integrate information from a wide range of sources. However robust the methodologies applied, this approach is imperfect. Knowledge claims are never absolute. But it is the best approach we have. The probabilistic approach is applied in other areas of regulatory science, including medical testing. For example, statements such as "approximately 480,000 Americans die each year as a result of smoking,"[30] or "the use of standard-dose varenicline in a quitting attempt roughly doubles the odds of success compared to a placebo"[31] are "true" only in a probabilistic sense. It is not at all clear why a different investigative standard should apply to the harms and benefits of e-cigarettes. Certainly, more and better studies will always have value, not least since contextual differences between populations will lead different groups of consumers to respond differently to different influences. But that does not mean that the available evidence can be ignored on the premise that it has failed to provide absolute certainty.

2.3 E-cigarette Use Does Not Occur in a Vacuum

Another "first principle" is the recognition that e-cigarette use, like smoking, is influenced by a range of important influences. Regulatory decisions, the availability of substitutes, and public knowledge, beliefs, and attitudes feature prominently on this list. Regulation and laws not only shape human behavior, they can also shape public perception of the subject goods and activities. Public knowledge can be improved or degraded by official messaging concerning risks and benefits. Differential treatment of products exposing users to different potential for harm can signal important information to consumers. All of these interdependencies should be considered when crafting regulation toward tobacco products.

2.4 Public Health Should Serve the Whole Public

A final principium is objectivity. Different groups of consumers have different priorities: it is natural and healthy for stakeholders in a vibrant democracy to advocate different solutions reflecting their personal interests. But it is the job of politicians at a high level and regulators in detail to adjudicate between these interests, balancing priorities based on the information available. That does not mean any group of stakeholders should be disregarded, but it might mean that no group gets everything it wants. In balancing the risks and benefits available, the nature, extent, and severity of the risks and harms associated with any given response should be considered. Options that lead to total benefits that outweigh any harms are desirable, although thorny questions of how to aggregate individual measures of welfare to the social level remain. A course of action judged to be best may result in the introduction of some novel risk elements or the forgoing of other known benefits. While policy-makers should search for ways to avoid novel costs and forgone benefits, those efforts should not be to the detriment of pursuing the greatest public benefit.

3 The Dual Imperatives and the Centrality of Tradeoffs

Returning, then, to the topic of public benefit, two distinct imperatives emerge from this discussion:

1. Leverage e-cigarettes' capacity to facilitate smoking cessation among those who demonstrably cannot or will not quit with other means.
2. Take steps to mitigate the uptake of e-cigarettes by non-smokers, especially young non-smokers.

A naïve search for optimality would look for policies that do both to the utmost degree. No such policy exists. The preferences of smokers overlap considerably with the preferences of non-smokers; thus, increasing e-cigarettes' acceptability, access, appeal, and affordability in an attempt to maximize substitutions by smokers would also stimulate demand for e-cigarette among non-smokers. Whatever an optimal approach leads to, it cannot both maximize benefits to the first group *and* minimize harms to the second; that is impossible. Economists and engineers are familiar with the notion that optimality always involves tradeoffs. A consumer can increase her subjective sense of well-being by drinking a latte in the morning, but doing so leaves less disposable income for alternative purchases that she might also enjoy. A car can be designed to be very enjoyable to drive for thrill-seeking consumers, or to be very safe in a crash, or to be highly fuel-efficient, but pushing the design toward any one of these goals requires at least partial regress away from the others, at least at the frontier of best design. Policy-makers typically also understand that tradeoffs among competing objectives exist, although in many cases regulators (and certainly politicians) shy away from overt public discussion of tradeoffs. (It is easier to promise guns *and* butter than to discuss what the social marginal rate of substitution between the two should be.) Instead, optimal regulation, however defined, necessarily involves tradeoffs. The optimal approach will be the option that delivers the best balance. Thus, for the purposes of this chapter, "optimality" refers to the greatest total social benefit *net of* harms and other costs. An optimal policy will not maximize all benefits simultaneously nor fully minimize all possible harms.

Encouraging substitutions to e-cigarettes from combustible tobacco could be achieved in a number of ways. Risk proportionate regulation, i.e., the differential imposition of policy restrictions on products in accordance with their extant risks, could encourage substitutions down the risk continuum, both by creating incentives and by dispelling the false beliefs that currently hinder more people from substitution toward lower-risk products. Less stringent tax conditions relative to combustibles could create a price differential encouraging substitutions toward less risky products, even if the health benefits were less important to the end-user. Encouraging competition and discouraging the concentration of market power among producers could also keep product prices down, increasing the appeal of the product category relative to combustible products. For consumers who are highly motivated by health risks, substitutions could be further encouraged by improved public communication of the relative risks and the benefits of switching. Marketing and advertising restrictions and warning label rules could be designed for these purposes. Avoiding sales restrictions on mail and in-store purchases, eschewing volume limits, or even mandating that outlets selling combustible products also offer safer alternatives would all increase the public's access to these products. E-cigarettes' appeal could be increased by permitting levels of nicotine that closely replicate the pharmacokinetic experience of smoking, aiding up-take by smokers and guarding against relapse, and by permitting flavors that make e-cigarettes a more enjoyable way of consuming nicotine than inhaling tobacco smoke. All of these options are discussed below in Sect. 6.

But, as noted above, attractive features of e-cigarettes may also appeal to non-smokers, a group for whom the uptake of vaping represents a net increase in risks (if the vaping did not replace smoking in the counterfactual, that is). Conversely, restricting access to e-cigarettes, reducing their appeal by banning flavors, limiting nicotine, and levying taxes on e-cigarettes may greatly reduce uptake and use by non-smokers. However, such efforts will also inhibit substitutions by adult smokers and may encourage those who have already quit smoking with the assistance of e-cigarette back to more dangerous combustibles, or perhaps illicit e-vapor products. There are, as Thomas Sowell pithily summarizes most of economics, "There are no solutions, only trade-offs."[32]

The existence of second-order imperatives complicates things considerably. Such imperatives include maximizing the liberty of individual consumers to choose and access products that aid their health; maximizing public understanding of the relative harms and risks associated with commercial products; maximizing the efficacy of e-cigarettes as cessation aids; maximizing the safety of regulated products; maximizing complete substitutions (as opposed to dual use); minimizing the use of unregulated and illicit products; maximizing compliance with regulations; minimizing regulatory burdens, maximizing innovations that reduce or eliminate risks to the consumer; and minimizing the public costs of regulation. Like the first-order imperatives, grappling with these involves judgment, for different stakeholders will place premiums on different imperatives, and for different reasons. Take, for example, the (classical) liberal argument suggesting that consumers should have a fundamental right to access products that serve their own sense of satisfaction and health interests. This argument may be hugely important for a consumer who enjoys nicotine but is desperate to avoid the harms caused by smoking, but will matter little to parents worried about the use of e-cigarettes by their school-aged children. Similarly, for users of e-cigarettes the safety and efficacy of the products matter hugely, but these factors may be purely academic to those who are convinced (unjustifiably, on the basis of the available information) that prohibitions would deliver the greatest public value.

Some of these second-order imperatives may be mutually reinforcing: Minimizing regulatory burdens may incentivize innovations and reduce the opportunity for illicit markets to develop. At the same time, they may help increase compliance with regulations and minimize regulatory costs, maximizing public understanding of the relative harms and risks associated with commercial products may itself increase complete substitutions and disincentivize the use of unregulated and illicit products. Conversely, the second-order imperatives may trade off against one another: Maximizing regulatory compliance may be achieved through enforcement, but enforcement is expensive, increasing regulatory costs. Maximizing the safety of regulated products also requires public capital expenditure and some of those who are unwilling to comply with regulations, or pay the price for regulated products, will serve as suppliers and consumers of illicit products.

There is yet another level of complexity: the second-order imperatives also interact with the first-order imperatives; some antagonistically, others sympathetically. For example, minimizing the use of unregulated and illicit products (a second order imperative) may be achieved with policies that make regulated e-cigarettes sufficiently attractive to gain (or at least retain) market share from the illicit market. Doing so may increase e-cigarettes' appeal to adult smokers interested in quitting, complementing the initial first-order imperative; but it will also appeal to curious non-smokers.

Ultimately, the success of a given policy is not only contingent upon the details of the regulation and how those relate to the public good (however defined) but upon consumers' responses to that policy. Some of these responses are difficult to measure, being uncertain and perhaps temporally removed from the present. If that were not challenging enough, because consumer behavior responds to prevailing public sentiment, emerging research, industry innovations, and changes in the regulatory and legal landscape, the optimal policy approach cannot be assumed to be fixed over time or across all different populations. Ideally, policies would respond dynamically to accommodate behavioral changes using regular post-implementation assessments. But that process may be iterative to the point of impracticality. How to proceed? Theoretical and practical guidance for policy-making is provided in Sects. 5 through 9 below. But first, the literature evaluating the population-level health effects of e-cigarettes is reviewed as a baseline for evaluating policy.

4 Existing Models of the Risks and Benefits for the Population

The evidence that e-cigarettes help smokers quit and reduce smoking-related risk has led several scholars to develop models to project the population-level effects of e-cigarette use under a range of different scenarios in the future. There are a variety of methodologies to determine the overall impact on public health, but each typically starts with known smoking rates and then adopts transition probabilities to project rates forward. These projections can then be used to calculate risks and benefits, stated in terms of lives or life-years lost or gained or health costs incurred or forgone. Comparisons can be made between different scenarios, most commonly one in which e-cigarettes are not available and another in which they are. Each scenario can have alternative versions, incorporating different assumptions about consumption patterns, transitions between products, estimations of relative risk and benefit, and other parameters of the models.[33]

Most of the models, whether funded by the tobacco industry or independent, predict large reductions in mortality from e-cigarettes displacing smoking. In research studies conducted independently of the tobacco industry, Warner and Mendez[34] predict that in the U.S., e-cigarettes could save between 583,000 and 3.3 million life-years by 2070; Levy, Borland et al.[35] report that large-scale transitioning to e-cigarettes could result in between 1.6 and 6.6 million fewer deaths in the U.S. by the year 2100; and Levy, Tam et al.[36] find that under current patterns of e-cigarette use and substitution, there will be 1.8 million fewer premature deaths and 38.9 million life-years gained by 2060. These studies, and most similar ones, account for the novel risk brought about by the uptake of e-cigarettes by non-smokers and any gateway effect to smoking, along with the prolonged use of e-cigarettes by those who switch exclusively. Health harms from novel use of e-cigarettes have also been studied. Bachand et al.[37] (funded by R.J. Reynolds and Swedish Match) conclude that if just 2% of smokers in all age groups switched away from smoking to a reduced-risk tobacco product (with a risk multiple of 0.08 compared to smoking, as may be the case for Swedish snus), the population-level benefits would offset the health consequences of projected uptake by never-smokers, even if the initiation rate for the reduced-risk product was half as large as for cigarettes. Cherng et al.,[38] in an independent study, did not model health risk from using e-cigarettes but also concluded that e-cigarettes would likely lead to substantially greater decreases in smoking prevalence than increases in smoking initiation, since even small increases in cessation due to e-cigarettes would outweigh a potential gateway effect.[39] A similar conclusion, but directly in terms of health, was reached by Lee et al.[40] in a study stemming from industry-funded research, even when considering a near horizon (2040) and only the four main tobacco-related diseases. The facts that there are many current smokers and relatively few young people starting to smoke anymore drive these findings. A small increase in the likelihood of cessation has a significant effect on a large base, and any increase in the likelihood of initiation has only a minor effect on a small base.

Most studies fit their model to data from the U.S., but one focused on the U.K. In a study funded by BAT, Hill and Camacho[41] modeled a scenario with e-cigarettes and a counterfactual scenario without e-cigarettes in the U.K. from 2000 to 2050. The conservative approach adopted by the researchers assumes that dual use confers no risk reduction relative to smoking (similar to Bachand et al., reviewed above). Thus, any benefits from e-cigarettes for existing smokers would therefore be reliant on complete substitution. Even so, the estimated prevalence of adult smokers (including dual users) in 2050 was modeled to be 2.3 percentage points lower with e-cigarettes than in the no-e-cigarettes scenario (10.5% vs. 8.2%). That equates to a projected 1.8 million fewer smokers than would be expected in the absence of e-cigarettes.

One of two outliers among this body of research[42] is the study by Soneji et al.,[43] who projected that between 1.1 and 1.3 million life-years could be lost by introducing e-cigarettes in the U.S. Their model assumes that e-cigarettes hinder cessation and that the portion of e-cigarette users who subsequently transition to smoking is very high. For the former, the researchers used an indirect method predicated on the assumption that using e-cigarettes *lowers* the odds of quitting smoking by 14%[44] to arrive at assumed impacts of e-cigarette use on cessation from smoking. The resulting transition probabilities vary from lowering the chance of quitting by almost a percentage point for younger adults (those below 35 years old) to increasing the chance of quitting by no more than 1.26 percentage points for any older group, including essentially no impact on quit probabilities for anyone over 50 years of age.[45] These modeling choices contradict the evidence on the efficacy of e-cigarettes as a cessation aid reviewed in Volume II, Chapter 2, estimates from the U.S. showing that use of e-cigarettes is associated with a 3.5 percentage point increase in cessation,[46] and evidence from the U.K. that real-world use of e-cigarettes is more effective than using NRT to quit smoking.[47] As a result of their pessimistic assumptions, Soneji et al. compute that, for the U.S. cohort of smokers in 2014, only about 2,100 additional smokers would achieve cessation because of e-cigarettes and that (because there is a *decrease* in cessation among the youngest smokers) there is a *loss* of 3,000 life-years from changes in cessation. Warner and Mendez's modeling, based on the cessation statistics just mentioned,[46] instead predict that e-cigarettes would lead to millions of cessation-related life-years saved.

For the other main difference from other studies, Soneji et al.'s high assumed transition probability from vaping to smoking, the authors took results from observational studies comparing the likelihood of smoking initiation between young people who had ever used e-cigarettes and those who never had, and assumed that the findings represented a causal relationship leading from e-cigarette use to beginning to smoke. This approach tacitly assumes e-cigarette use preceded smoking, even though the survey evidence did not address temporal precedence. Crucially for their results, relying on observational findings assumes that *none* of the difference in smoking initiation rates between these two groups consists of individuals who would have begun smoking even in the absence of e-cigarette availability (i.e., that there is no selection bias based on unobservable factors). This is a highly suspect position as we discussed in Volume II, Chapter 1, Sect. 6.2, for it presumes that both the common liability and diversion hypotheses are completely false.[48] The position is also suspect because it simply does not accord with observed trends in youth smoking and vaping.[49] After assuming that e-cigarettes hurt chances for cessation and create many new smokers, it is no surprise that Soneji et al. conclude that even with 95% harm reduction, e-cigarettes result in 1.5 million lost life-years. If nothing else, their results demonstrate that, no matter how sophisticated the modeling efforts, the results depend crucially on the key assumptions concerning the gateway hypothesis and whether e-cigarettes help or hinder efforts to quit smoking.

Kalkhoran and Glantz[50] produced the other study with outlying conclusions. Although not a cohort-based system dynamics study, their widely cited study had the similar goal of estimating population-level impacts from e-cigarettes on health. The study embodies similarly pessimistic assumptions as Soneji et al., namely, that using e-cigarettes hinders cessation and that there is a very large gateway effect from e-cigarettes to smoking. Many scenarios are considered, some leading to overall health gains and others to losses. The authors consider the impact of varying risk multiples for using e-cigarettes vs. smoking, all the way up to a relative health risk of 50% (when most studies use 5% or 10%), which in the end allows them to conclude that there is a lot of potential for net harm. In contrast, at a relative risk of 5%, the most commonly used assumption, the only scenarios leading to harm in the U.S. case they analyze are two unrealistic cases. In the first, the only young people ever starting to use e-cigarettes never would have smoked otherwise (i.e., the gateway hypothesis is completely true and the diversionary hypothesis is completely false). In the other, e-cigarettes cause smoking to be "renormalized" (the great fear of many in the tobacco control community), with the result that interest in cessation drops by one-quarter among smokers and e-cigarettes do not become increasingly popular cessation aids (and, in any event, these authors assume that use of e-cigarettes hinder the success of cessation attempts).

A final study addresses the net benefits of e-cigarettes using quite different methodology. Allcott and Rafkin,[51] in a study already discussed in Volume II, Chapter 1, Sect. 5, lay out an economic model of consumer choices for cigarettes and e-cigarettes. The choices a consumer makes are not necessarily the best from the individual's own point of view because of present bias, incorrect beliefs about health effects of consumption, or a false sense of resistance to addiction. Against a backdrop of externalities created by consumption of the two goods and an assumed balanced-budget requirement for the government, the impact of taxes for cigarettes and e-cigarettes on the welfare of consumers are derived. With externalities and irrational or misinformed decision-making, taxes could improve welfare (even as determined by the consumers in their own estimation). Within this context, the authors use parameters for their model from U.S. data from a variety of sources and consider the impact of banning e-cigarettes, which is equivalent to setting an infinitely high tax rate for them.

Using a harm ratio of 5% for e-cigarettes vs. cigarettes, the results show that in all 17 scenarios considered, banning e-cigarettes lowers social welfare. However, at the alternative harm ratio of 37% (chosen as the mean from an expert elicitation survey, as discussed in Volume II, Chapter 1), a ban on e-cigarettes improves welfare only in scenarios in which the two products are perfect substitutes (instead of being nearly independent in the base case), the negative "internalities" (i.e., the differential between the perceived and actual marginal utility of consumption) of smoking and vaping are smaller than in the base case, or people overestimate the health risks from using e-cigarettes relative to smoking. The problems with this estimate for the harm ratio (37%) have already been discussed in Volume II, Chapter 1, suffice it for here to remind readers that the statistic is from an opinion survey. Additionally, one can note here that the evidence for substitution between cigarettes and e-cigarettes is robust elsewhere in the economic literature,[52,53,54,55,56,57,58,59,60,61,62,63] and thus the scenario with substitution between the products may represent reality better than the base case. Furthermore, the evidence for consumers overestimating the relative risks of e-cigarette use is quite strong.[64,65,66,67] In the U.S., for example, there exists a substantial amount of misinformation regarding e-cigarettes, leading to a significant overestimation of the relative risks associated with vaping and smoking. An increasing proportion of American adults, now more than half, believe that e-cigarettes are equally as harmful as cigarettes.[68] Approximately two-thirds of adults perceived that e-cigarettes are as harmful to health as smoking. Another one-quarter believe that vaping is more hazardous than smoking. Additionally, fewer than one in nine individuals believes that e-cigarettes exhibit any degree of reduced harm compared to conventional cigarettes.[69] Thus, even accepting the high harm ratio, Allcott and Rafkin's results indicate that under other plausible assumptions, banning e-cigarettes may still be worse for consumers than allowing them.

This review of the literature highlights a few useful facts and possibilities. First, how the impacts of e-cigarettes play out in the population is complicated, since they can affect so many transitions: non-smoking to smoking, smoking to former smoker, former smoker to relapse into smoking. The evolution of the health or welfare of the population is a complex dynamic system that is affected by e-cigarettes at many points, sometimes to the benefit and sometimes to the detriment of health. Second, given the large number of smokers, the reduced risk from e-cigarettes, and the much smaller group of never-smokers who begin to use e-cigarettes regularly, a relatively modest increase in cessation from the use of e-cigarettes would more than cover the consequences of projected uptake of e-cigarettes by never-smokers and a gateway effect. The population of adult smokers who stand to gain from quitting is much larger than the population of non-smokers using e-cigarettes. In the U.K., non-smokers have never represented more than 10% of all current adult e-cigarette users,[70] and as of 2022, only 1.7% of never-smokers aged 11–17 used e-cigarettes on an at least monthly basis, compared with 55.4% of smokers and 29.7% of former smokers in the same age range.[71] In the U.S. in 2020, 3.7% of U.S. adults (9.1 million people) used e-cigarettes,[72] but never-smokers account for fewer than one in five adult e-cigarette users.[73] And in 2021, only 4.2% of middle- and high-schoolers in the U.S. who never had smoked currently used e-cigarettes, compared to 34.5% of former smokers.[74] The population of adult e-cigarette users with a history of smoking still outweighs the population of e-cigarette users that are either never-smokers or school-aged. And the latter group is certainly not a subset of the former group: about half (47%) of e-cigarette users in middle- or high-school in the U.S. have a history of smoking, and across the world the average is almost as high.[75] Third, to arrive at a negative impact on public health, a model must employ exceedingly pessimistic assumptions—assumptions that are either not founded on causal estimates of the key parameters or are at odds with other available evidence—to conclude that e-cigarettes have negative overall impacts on population health.

Apart from the study of Allcott and Rafkin, the studies reviewed above generally have a single-minded focus on mortality risk and consider only the endpoints of excess deaths or lost life-years. While this approach is familiar to public health researchers, much is left out of these analyses. For one, externalities are generally not considered, under the justification that they pale in comparison to the direct health effects of smoking on the consumer (which is likely true). More broadly, the societal costs of tobacco control, enforcement, healthcare, environmental damage, and lost productivity associated with smoking[76] might also be reduced if vaping supplants smoking at the population level. Of course, e-cigarettes will bring about some costs in these categories too. Still, at least with regard to healthcare and lost productivity, the evidence that e-cigarettes are less harmful suggests that the vaping-specific costs will be less than those currently inflicted by smoking. Thus, the utility of e-cigarettes is not limited to those who currently smoke; instead, if e-cigarettes replace smoking, the advantages may be spread more widely throughout society.

Also left out of the modeling, again with the exception of Allcott and Rafkin's work, is any consideration of how either consumers or society value consumption of the products or changes in health risk. This topic will be taken up below, but for now note that a purely risk- or mortality-focused approach cannot be a complete guide to public policy, otherwise (to employ *reductio ad absurdum*) there would be no legal use of automobiles, skiing and other risky leisure activities would be banned, and no one would be allowed to leave their homes (or stay in them, due to the possibility of radon exposure or household accidents). Questions of risk are highly important but are not the only factor in the social calculus.

Finally, the public health models to date generally fail to consider scenarios in which nuanced public policy—policy, that is, apart from the false dichotomy of laissez-faire and a ban—affects the relevant transition probabilities. For example, as Allcott and Rafkin at least attempt to address, differential taxation can encourage the probability of switching from smoking to using e-cigarettes. And when a possibly policy-relevant scenario is modeled, such as a lower initiation rate of youth using e-cigarettes due to passage and enforcement of minimum age laws, the unintended consequences of such policy found in the empirical literature (encouragement of youth smoking, in this case)[77,78,79] is not modeled. Moving beyond the incomplete frameworks adopted by the public health literature is the task of the rest of this chapter.

5 Pursuing Optimal E-cigarette Regulation

Having set forth basic principles that should guide regulation of e-cigarettes and the inherent tradeoff between helping smokers quit and drawing youth into nicotine addiction, the discussion now turns to what optimal regulation might involve. This section is primarily theoretical, with specific applications of the theory discussed in Sect. 6. Section 5.1 of the present section makes the case for varying degrees of regulation for different products, in accord with their position along the risk continuum. A simple model of health harm is then offered to allow insight into the conditions under which regulation is likely to improve public health. The model will also serve as a touchstone for the policy discussion to follow. In Sect. 5.3, the discussion moves toward a cost–benefit analysis by discussing the pieces missing from a narrow view of public health gains: consumer responses to policy, the supply side of the market for tobacco products, and extra-welfarist considerations besides health gains. The concept of a social welfare function is introduced in Sect. 5.4, along with discussion of what that function should include for present purposes. The final part in this section offers concluding thoughts and useful lessons for good policy-making toward e-cigarettes.[80]

5.1 *Risk Proportionate Regulation: The Case for Regulatory Differentials*

Overt regulation of a market is commonly justified by claims of market failure. In the U.S., for example, Executive Department guidance for regulatory analysis instructs federal agencies to justify proposed regulation by explaining the "significant market failure" or "other compelling public need" that the new rules intend to address.[81] For tobacco products, the oft mentioned candidates for market failure are externalities and "internalities." The former are due to health harm from environmental smoke and excess burden placed on national health systems. Internalities in this case refer to the health costs that tobacco consumers place on themselves via their consumption decisions that are not in their own self-interest (as evaluated subjectively by the consumers themselves).[82] The most commonly cited phenomena giving rise to internalities involved with smoking and consumption of other tobacco products are time-inconsistent preferences (consumer myopia or present-bias), in which consumption today leads to regret tomorrow, and misperception of health harms.[83] Both externalities and internalities lead to a "behavioral wedge" between the price paid and the marginal benefit from consumption; in the present case, the internalities result in the marginal benefit being lower, perhaps much lower, than the price, leading to overconsumption.[84]

Consider the implication of these rationales for regulation when two related but distinct products, e.g., cigarettes and e-cigarettes, have very different levels of health harm associated with them. It follows that they should be regulated differently, with the less harmful product subject to less stringent regulations. Whether the argument for externalities is based on environmental smoke and vapor or the additional strain placed on publicly funded healthcare systems, the size of the externality created by the marginal unit of consumption would be much lower for e-cigarettes compared to smoking (see Volume II, Chapter 1). Similarly, since the size of the behavioral wedge depends on how much health harm individuals are not accounting for in their consumption decisions, vaping is associated with much lower internalities as well. This reasoning suggests that whichever regulations are applied to e-cigarettes, they must be less stringent, and likely substantially less stringent, than those applied to combustible cigarettes. Furthermore, the argument for differential regulation is strengthened further by recognizing that lighter regulation on e-cigarettes will encourage substitution away from smoking. That is, products that provide a benefit by reducing the costs otherwise inflicted by a substitute should face a further reduction in the stringency of the regulations to which they are subjected. While the modern economist's mind immediately jumps to Hicksian-style mathematical demonstrations of why differential regulation is better than a uniform set of rules, this insight goes back at least as far as Bentham, who stated (in the context of legal penalties) that "where two offenses come in competition, the punishment for the greater offense must be sufficient to induce a man to prefer the less."[85]

Thus far the logic for risk-proportionate regulation has been developed on purely economic grounds. However, the proportionality principle, which states that an intervention should be proportionate to the threat or harm that it seeks to prevent or mitigate, underlies much legal, military, and ethical thinking as well.[86] While the economic way of thinking, in general, need not lead to the same outcomes as suggested by the proportionality principle itself,[87] happily in the present context they coincide. In the face of the continued availability of cigarettes, bans on e-cigarette are disproportionate and should be avoided, though less restrictive interventions may still be acceptable if they are commensurate with the costs imposed by the use of a product.

In addition to creating additional incentives for smokers to substitute to a safer alternative, thereby encouraging smoking cessation, regulatory differentials may also allow regulators to signal the relative harms of the two products to the public. That is especially valuable, given the high proportion of current smokers who report that skepticism about the safety of e-cigarettes keeps them smoking.[88] Risk-proportionate regulation may also incentivize complete substitutions, protecting against long-term dual use. In Japan, for example, while recent sales data confirm a marked decline in demand for combustibles,[89] the prevalence of smoking is not declining as fast as that might suggest. Instead of substituting completely, thereby quitting smoking, many consumers continue to use cigarettes and heated tobacco products interchangeably.[90] While dual use may be desirable if it is accompanied by significant reductions in smoking, or if it makes subsequent cessation more likely, dual use may also carry specific risks, and certainly the fullest benefits of reduced smoking may only be seen if it leads to cessation.[91]

Risk-proportionate regulation might also empower medical professionals and others in a position to inform private consumer decisions about the value of switching for those who cannot otherwise quit. Risk-proportionate regulation has the additional advantage, forgone by prohibitions and risked by more stringent regulations that stimulate illicit markets, of keeping consumption with a set of products covered by safety standards (see Volume II, Chapter 2).

5.2 *A Model of Harm*

To formalize the argument and to be precise about which aspects of smoking and use of e-cigarettes regulatory differentials can target, the following simplified model for transition among states of nicotine use will be helpful. Break changes over time into periods, and consider how smoking behavior and use of e-cigarettes might evolve by the end of the period. The transition probabilities can pertain to an individual, a particular demographic group (e.g., a race × age × smoking history cohort), or the entire population, depending on the specificity of information one has available to estimate the transition probabilities. Similarly, the period length could be a year, a lifetime, or anything in between, again depending on the data available. The three initial states are never-smoker (N), current smoker (S), or former smoker (Q, for quitter). For presentation, it is assumed that initially there is no use of e-cigarettes, both to reduce the possibilities to consider and because many of the models discussed above began with assuming the no one was using e-cigarettes yet. These initial states will be denoted with superscripts in the notation to follow. The four terminal states at the period's conclusion are the various combinations of current smoking of cigarettes (yes or no, denoted $C =$ 1 or 0 in subscripts to variables) and current use of e-cigarettes (also dichotomous, denoted $V = 1$ or 0). Other products such as cigars or modified risk tobacco products other than e-cigarettes could be added to the modeling, but are not here for the sake of clarity of presentation.

The transition possibilities and probabilities are shown in the figure. The probabilities are shown to depend on a binary variable W reflecting the state of the world: $W = 0$ denotes that e-cigarettes are unavailable (i.e., were never invented, marketed, and used) and $W = 1$ denotes that e-cigarettes are available. Thus, for example, the probability $P^N_{V|C=1}(1)$ pertains to the probability that the individual (or group) uses e-cigarettes at the end of the period, conditional on also smoking then and for the case in which the person was a never-smoker initially and e-cigarettes are available. For the case $W = 0$ (no e-cigarettes) it is understood that there are only two terminal states; i.e., $P^i_{V|C=1}(0) = P^i_{V|C=0}(0) = 0$, for $i = N, S, Q$. The separate columns in the figure for the probabilities and outcomes for smoking and vaping are merely for analytical convenience and are not meant to indicate temporal precedence. The probabilities for using e-cigarettes are expressed as conditional on whether the individual also smokes in the terminal state, but nothing is assumed about which of the two activities began first within the period[92] (Fig. 1).

Following Lee et al.'s review of mortality models for the effects of e-cigarettes on population health, let the risk to health per period be normalized to 1 for smoking and 0 for not smoking. Using e-cigarettes alone creates expected health harm F and dually using them with cigarettes creates total harm G. If e-cigarettes are indeed a reduced-harm product (and vaping intensity is not greatly different than smoking intensity) then $F < 1$. If so, then if dual use takes the form of substituting some smoking for vaping (and not in a manner that greatly increases total nicotine consumption) then $G < 1$; if dual use takes the form of just adding vaping to pre-existing smoking habits then $G > 1$. In either event, it is expected that exclusive use of e-cigarettes is less risky than dual use: $F < G$. Note that each activity is binary—for simplicity, questions about how the intensity of smoking or vaping might transition are set aside, except in the case of dual use—and so the harm parameters are taken to represent averages over all intensities for the type of individual or group being modeled. With these parameters in place, the

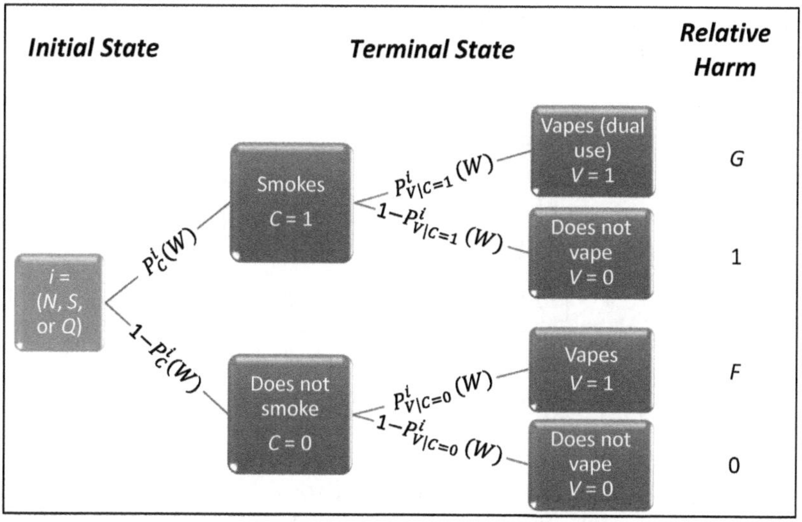

Fig. 1 Schematic presentation of the model for transition probabilities among smoking and vaping states

expected harm from the situation modeled above, when e-cigarettes are available and the initial state is i, is the probabilities of the four final states multiplied by the harms:

$$\begin{aligned} H^i(W=1) &= P_C^i(1)P_{V|C=1}^i(1) \times G + P_C^i(1)\left[1 - P_{V|C=1}^i(1)\right] \times 1 \\ &+\left[1 - P_C^i(1)\right]P_{V|C=0}^i(1) \times F \\ &+\left[1 - P_C^i(1)\right]\left[1 - P_{V|C=0}^i(1)\right] \times 0 \\ &= P_C^i(1)P_{V|C=1}^i(1)G + P_C^i(1)\left[1 - P_{V|C=1}^i(1)\right] \\ &+\left[1 - P_C^i(1)\right]P_{V|C=0}^i(1)F \end{aligned}$$

The expected harm for the same situation, except that e-cigarettes are not available, is:

$$H^i(W=0) = P_C^i(0) \times 1 + \left[1 - P_C^i(0)\right] \times 0 = P_C^i(0)$$

Thus, the change in harm due to e-cigarettes is the difference between these two expressions:

$$\Delta H^i = \underbrace{\Delta P_C^i}_{\substack{\text{harm from additional}\\ \text{smoking due}\\ \text{to e-cigarettes}}} + \underbrace{\left\{\left[1 - P_C^i(1)\right] P_{V|C=0}^i(1)\right\} F}_{\substack{\text{novel harm created}\\ \text{by e-cigarettes}}} + \underbrace{-\left[P_C^i(1) P_{V|C=0}^i(1)\right](1 - G)}_{\substack{\text{reduction in harm from}\\ \text{dual use instead of}\\ \text{single use of cigarettes}}} \tag{1}$$

where the change notation is understood to mean $\Delta X = X(W = 1) - X(W = 0)$ for any quantity X. The first term on the right side of Eq. (1) reflects how the availability of e-cigarettes changes participation in smoking. For never-smokers ($i = N$), this term is positive if e-cigarettes provide a causal gateway into smoking and negative if they divert otherwise-smoking initiators into using e-cigarettes instead. For smokers ($i = S$), the first term is negative if e-cigarettes aid cessation from smoking, but positive if they hinder cessation. For quitters ($i = Q$), the first term is positive if e-cigarettes encourage relapse into smoking and negative is they help smokers stay quit.

The second term on the right side of Eq. (1) is the new health harm caused by exclusive vaping. This harm exists only in scenario $W = 1$, of course. The size of this harm, which is positive as long as e-cigarettes are not completely risk free, is greater when either the probability of becoming an exclusive vaper or the harm from doing so increases. The final term in the equation is the reduction in harm from dual use instead of smoking only. Again, the magnitude of this component depends on the probability of ending up as a dual user and the differential between the harm of dual use G and the counterfactual single-use harm of smoking (which is 1). If $G < 1$, then this term indeed represents a reduction in the overall net change in harm.

To aggregate the change in harm from e-cigarette availability across the population, define M^N to be the number of individuals in the group who have never smoked at the start of the period, M^S to be the number of current smokers initially, and M^Q to be the number of former smokers initially. Then we can sum Eq. (1) across the initial states to yield total incremental harm, ΔH:

$$\Delta H = \underbrace{\sum_{i=N,S,Q} M^i \Delta P_C^i}_{①} + \underbrace{\left[\sum_{i=N,S,Q} M^i P_{V=1,C=0}^i(1)\right] F}_{②} \underbrace{- \left[\sum_{i=N,S,Q} M^i P_{V=1,C=1}^i(1)\right](1-G)}_{③} \tag{2}$$

(In the expression above, the joint probability of vaping without smoking and dual use are denoted $P_{V=1,C=0}^i$ and $P_{V=1,C=1}^i$, respectively.) In in the previous equation, term 1 is the harm from any additional (or continued) smoking due to e-cigarette availability, term 2 is the additional harm from single-use vaping, and term 3 is the reduction in additional harm from dual use versus smoking only.

Table 1 summarizes the elements of Eq. (2) and presents pessimistic and optimistic cases for each.

To illustrate the potential tradeoffs involved with introducing e-cigarettes (or making them less expensive, more accessible, or otherwise more attractive to consumers), some elements of Eq. (2) are reproduced here as a condition for the change in total harm to decrease. To simplify the long equation, impacts on former smokers are ignored since they are likely to be smaller than impacts on current smokers and (potentially) non-smoking youth. For further simplification, the possibility that a non-smokers jumps directly to dual use is left out and only a single period is considered. Then we have:

$$\Delta H < 0 \Leftrightarrow$$

$$M^N \Delta P_C^N + \left[M^N P_{V=1,C=0}^N(1) + M^S P_{V=1,C=0}^S(1)\right] F < -M^S \Delta P_C^S + \left[M^S P_{V=1,C=1}^S(1)\right](1-G) \tag{3}$$

Table 1 Possible elements of harm or harm reduction from e-cigarettes

Quantity	*Pessimistic case*	*Optimistic case*	*What the current evidence says*
Increase in the per-person average harm from starting smoking (which is also the change in probability of initiating cigarette use), e-cigarette scenario compared to non-e-cigarette scenario: ΔP_C^N	Gateway hypothesis: > 0. Lots of new smokers (youth and young adults). E-cigarettes are a mechanism to hook youth on vaping, whence they progress to smoking	Diversion hypothesis: < 0. Some young people who otherwise would have smoked single-use e-cigarettes instead	The current evidence is more compelling for the diversion hypothesis than for the gateway hypothesis at the population level. See Volume II, Chapter 1, Sect. 6.2
Increase in the per-person average harm from continuing smoking (which is also the change in probability of not quitting cigarette use and not transitioning to dual use [latter in scenario 1 only]), e-cigarette scenario compared to non-e-cigarette scenario: ΔP_C^S	Case 1) $= 0$. E-cigarettes are unattractive to smokers and are only used by non-smokers Case 2) > 0, because e-cigarette use in general (from which these individuals [exclusive smokers] are excluded) renormalizes/ destigmatizes smoking	< 0. E-cigarettes are attractive to smokers and encourage transition out of continued single-use smoking	The majority of e-cigarette users are current or past smokers. Moreover, e-cigarettes are often used specifically to avoid smoking and related harms. See Volume I, Chapter 3, Sect. 4.4. Data from many types of studies support the view that e-cigarettes are replacing smoking both at the individual level and at the population level. See Volume II, Chapter 2, particularly Sect. 3

Quantity	*Pessimistic case*	*Optimistic case*	*What the current evidence says*
Increase in the per-person average harm from relapsing back into smoking (which is also the change in probability of restarting cigarette use and not transitioning to dual use [latter in scenario 1 only]), e-cigarette scenario compared to non-e-cigarette scenario: ΔP_C^Q	Relapse hypothesis: > 0. E-cigarettes entice former smokers back into using nicotine, whence they recommence smoking. (This would require fully transitioning to smoking only before the end of the period if dual-using at the beginning)	Maintenance hypothesis: < 0. E-cigarettes help smokers to stay quit from smoking	Some e-cigarette users revert to smoking. However, the evidence suggests that, on aggregate, e-cigarette use (particularly frequent use) is associated with smoking cessation. See Volume II, Chapter 2, Sect. 3
Probability for initial never-smokers of ending up using e-cigarettes alone: $P_{V=1,C=0}^N(1)$	Large. E-cigarettes are designed to appeal to young people and many will get hooked on them	Small or immaterial. Either not that many young people will do more than use e-cigarettes occasionally or the number of regular users does not matter because harms F are so low	The majority of e-cigarette users are current or past smokers. See Volume I, Chapter 3, Sect. 4.4.[a]
Probability for initial smokers of ending up using e-cigarettes alone: $P_{V=1,C=0}^S(1)$	Small, because of the prolongation hypothesis. E-cigarettes delay or prevent cessation. Dual use becomes the endpoint instead of quitting smoking	Larger, because of the cessation hypothesis. E-cigarettes help smokers to quit	Between 25 and 33% of those who quit smoking in the U.S. in the past 5 years used e-cigarettes to achieve cessation, and in the U.K. e-cigarette prevalence is positively associated with the overall quit-rate. See Volume II, Chapter 2, Sect. 4

(continued)

Table 1 (continued)

Quantity	*Pessimistic case*	*Optimistic case*	*What the current evidence says*
Probability for initial former smokers of ending up using e-cigarettes alone: $P^{Q}_{V=1,C=0}(1)$	Indeterminate. Perhaps large because of the first stage of the relapse hypothesis; perhaps small if most former smokers have progressed into the second stage (relapse into smoking)	Indeterminate. Perhaps large if many former smokers used and continue to use e-cigarettes to quit or maintain cessation; perhaps small if former smokers quit all nicotine use	Good data on relapse and e-cigarettes is lacking. Cross-sectional data suggests that many e-cigarette users are also former smokers (see Volume I, Chapter 3, Sect. 4.3.1), but which type of use preceded the other is typically unknown. However, there is some evidence that the prevalence of current e-cigarette use has, over time, increased among former smokers[93]
Probability for initial never-smokers of ending up dual-using: $P^{N}_{V=1,C=1}(1)$	Large. E-cigarettes are designed to appeal to young people and many will get hooked on them + gateway hypothesis	Small. Not that many young people will do more than use e-cigarettes occasionally, and the gateway hypothesis is largely false	The majority of e-cigarette users are current or past smokers. See Volume I, Chapter 3, D. a. 2. Out of youth who ever try e-cigarettes, only one in 10 become daily vapers. Evidence for the gateway hypothesis is weak. See Volume II, Chapter 1, Sect. 6.2

Quantity	*Pessimistic case*	*Optimistic case*	*What the current evidence says*
Probability for initial smokers of ending up dual-using: $P^{S}_{V=1,C=1}$ (1)	Indeterminate. Large if dual using increases total harm and small if the opposite	Indeterminate. Small if dual using increases total harm and larger if the opposite. In the latter case, not too large because single-using e-cigarettes would be better	Many e-cigarette users continue to smoke for some period. The evidence on this topic is mixed. See Volume II, Chapter 2, Sect. 5
Probability for initial former smokers of ending up dual-using: $P^{Q}_{V=1,C=1}$ (1)	Large because of the relapse hypothesis. E-cigarettes entice former smokers back into using nicotine, whence they recommence smoking	Small because of the cessation hypothesis. E-cigarettes help former smokers maintain cessation	Good data on relapse and e-cigarettes is lacking. Cross-sectional data suggests that many e-cigarette users are also former smokers (see Volume I, Chapter 3, Sect. 4.3.1), but which type of use preceded the other is typically unknown. Limited longitudinal data suggests that long-quit former smokers who use e-cigarettes were significantly more likely than those who had never used e-cigarettes to relapse to current smoking.[94] However, it is possible that use of e-cigarettes by former smokers *and* relapse are due to common liabilities (selection bias)

(continued)

Table 1 (continued)

Quantity	*Pessimistic case*	*Optimistic case*	*What the current evidence says*
Relative harm of using e-cigarettes vs. smoking F	Large. E-cigarettes have many sizeable health risks, and are just a dangerous or more dangerous than smoking	Small. E-cigarettes have no more than 5% the health risk of smoking	A general (but not universal) consensus has emerged that, while not risk free, e-cigarettes carry only a fraction of the risk of smoking. The precise comparator in risk exposure between e-cigarettes and cigarettes is debated. See Volume II, Chapter 2
Relative harm of dual using vs. single-use smoking G	Higher than 1. Dual users just add e-cigarettes to pre-existing patterns of smoking, increasing total harm	Much less than 1. Dual users replace much of their smoking with vaping, and the harm of vaping (F) is low	Dual use covers a wide range of observed consumption patterns, and no causal studies have yet separated the observed data from the common liabilities problem (selection bias). The ultimate harms depend on for how long and with what intensity dual users smoke. The evidence on this topic is mixed. See Volume II, Chapter 2, Sect. 5

[a] In addition, *frequent* e-cigarette users are a small fraction of those who have ever-used e-cigarettes. Therefore, many people who start using e-cigarettes will not get the full "dose" of harm F. See Volume II Chapter 1, Sect. 6.1.

Notes Mathematical notation is with reference to Eq. (2). Cessation refers to quitting using cigarettes

Under the optimistic scenario, the first term on the left side of the inequality (additional smoking initiation) is small or, under the diversionary hypothesis, negative (fewer youth will initiate smoking because some will single-use e-cigarettes instead). The other term on the left side (direct harm from using e-cigarettes) is small (again, under optimistic assumptions) because the harm from vaping, *F*, is low. The first term on the right side, cessation from smoking, is positive and sizable if e-cigarettes promote cessation and the second term (harm-reduction from dual use versus smoking only) also makes the inequality easier to be satisfied if dual use indeed entails any harm reduction. Overall, if the left side is negative or a small positive number and the right side is a large positive number, overall harm will be reduced by e-cigarettes. In the pessimistic case, as outlined in Table 1, the left side would be larger, the right side smaller, and the inequality may not be satisfied, implying that e-cigarettes increase harm on net. In Volume II, Chapters 1 and 2, we discussed why a review of the evidence leads toward the optimistic position. Furthermore, policy in practice need not consist of choosing a single value along a single continuum. For example, there are very few countries in which the sole policy toward e-cigarettes consists of a tax rate. Once additional policy levers can be pulled, then inequality (3) for overall harm reduction becomes easier to satisfy. Stronger policies designed to keep cigarettes out of the hands of youth, for instance, can lower the size of the first term (if it is positive) or turn it negative without much affecting the other terms. Note that given the evidence that taxes or higher minimum purchase age restrictions for e-cigarettes cause increased rates of youth smoking,[95,96] these policies should not be expected to lower the first term in inequality (3).

The above is all for a single period. Models using this approach typically take a system dynamics approach, in which an initial distribution of the population is grouped by smoking status, age, gender, and (for quitters) time since cessation.[97] Then the number of people in each group evolves each period in accord with the transitions between groups shown in Fig. 1, other inflow from population growth due to births or immigration, and other outflow due to deaths or emigration. Transition probabilities can depend on the group and group history. For example, the relapse rate back into smoking can be treated as a function of time since cessation. In most such studies, harms are defined solely in terms of mortality risk, and the risk from smoking (but usually not relative risks *F* and *G*, due to lack of information) are allowed to depend on the group and group history.

For example, mortality risk of 60-year-old male smokers is allowed to be higher than the mortality risk of 60-year-old male former smokers who quit 20 years ago. (These mortality risks are taken either from life tables from national vital statistics or, where those are unavailable, from relevant published studies). Mortality is counted over the length of the study period and then compared between scenarios by summing Eq. (2) across all periods.[98] The studies reviewed in Sect. 4 above do not employ any discounting; a premature death averted 40 years from now receives as much weight as a death averted this year. This approach may be justified by appeal to intergenerational equity and is an extreme form of the "dual discounting" approach used in some instances of cost-effectiveness analysis, in which costs of a health intervention are discounted with one rate and health effects are discounted with a much lower rate.[99,100]

5.3 *Moving Toward Cost–Benefit Analysis*

The modeling in the previous section focuses solely on the direct health effects of the introduction of e-cigarettes or other tobacco policy. To move toward cost–benefit or social welfare analysis requires examining other impacts as well. Consumer and producer responses to regulation, as well as other extra-welfarist considerations besides changes in population health, should also be incorporated into the policy analysis.

5.3.1 *Consumer Responses to Regulation and the Role of Prices*

Any reasonably competent cost–benefit analysis of regulation (or other social welfare framework, to be explored in the next section) must account for the behavioral response of individuals. Regulators' intent regarding an intervention action matters far less than a realistic expectation of how the various affected parties in the economy, whether consumers, industry, or potential entrants, will respond. If the tools of microeconomic theory, perhaps as modified by behavioral economics, apply to smoking and use of e-cigarettes, then we have a path forward to form reasonable expectations about the responses of various agents in the economy. Before starting down that path, however, it is worth bringing readers who are not health economists up to speed on current economic thinking about consumer choice for these products. After all, one may wonder whether standard demand theory, which is based on the choice-making of a rational, informed consumer, has any relevance to consumption of an addictive good.

In fact, before the work of Nobel-prize winning economist Gary Becker and colleagues in the 1980's, smoking was largely seen as an exception to microeconomic demand theory.[101,102] One leading view held that consumers smoked because they did not understand that cigarettes were dangerous, while another assumed that after becoming addicted to nicotine consumers no longer had a choice whether to continue consumption of cigarettes. If the first view were correct, then informing people about the health risks from smoking would have been all that was needed to largely eradicate the practice. Hence the great publicity surrounding the U.S. Surgeon General's 1964 report on smoking,[103] the appearance of health warnings on cigarette packaging two years later and anti-smoking messages on broadcast media three years later, followed by the television and radio advertising ban seven years later, to correct misinformation and avoid its promulgation.[104] If the second view were correct, then stop-smoking campaigns based on persuasion would be entirely ineffective, smoking would best be treated as a mental illness or a disease, and NRT and other pharmacotherapies (along, perhaps, with psychotherapy) would be the only solutions. Furthermore, the focus on addiction also leads efforts toward preventing initiation, since treating addiction is difficult, expensive, and often prone to failure. Hence the introduction of school-based smoking prevention programs into U.S. schools in the 1980s. Importantly, if either view were strictly correct, then prices would play little to no role in either encouraging cessation or preventing initiation.

Becker's and others' work showed, instead, both that demand for tobacco *could* be explained entirely by rational choice theory[105] and that demand for tobacco in actual markets *does* obey the Law of Demand, which states that as the price of a good rises, less of it is demanded by consumers.[106,107,108] For present purposes, we need not get into the debate over Becker's "rational addiction" theory, or even whether standard microeconomic theory or the newer approach of behavioral economics is more appropriate to model demand for tobacco, for all predict that prices matter. Regardless which theory has the most explanatory power for the real world, the empirical fact that the Law of Demand pertains to demand for cigarettes and other tobacco products is incontrovertible. There is a huge literature taking various approaches to estimating the demand function for cigarettes, and nearly every study, regardless of methodology, finds that demand is sensitive to price.[109,110,111] As one set of authors noted, "numerous studies using a wide variety of data and statistical methods have found that tobacco use is no exception to the basic principles of economics."[112] Even tobacco control experts who are hostile to some aspects of the microeconomic approach to smoking (for example, to the notion that consumer welfare from consumption of cigarettes can or should be measured from prices and the demand curve; more on this below) have no problem with accepting the Law of Demand, because it implies that taxation will lead to lower consumption of tobacco. Thus, the first important behavioral response to policy is that consumers as a group will purchase fewer cigarettes and other tobacco products, including e-cigarettes, when the prices of these good rise.

The Law of Demand both points toward some policy options and raises cautions about others. If higher prices lower consumption, then tax policy becomes not only a revenue source for government but also a powerful tool for tobacco control. Furthermore, since one of the reasons for the law of demand is that consumers substitute toward alternative goods when the price of the focal good rises, tax differentials can encourage consumers toward less risky sources of nicotine. However, some substitutes, such as unregulated illicit or counterfeit tobacco products, may be even less salutary than (licit) cigarettes, which may introduce unintended consequences into tobacco excise tax policy. Furthermore, once prices are defined expansively to include all costs borne by consumers, including hassle costs or costs from violating place-of-use restrictions, then the Law of Demand also points toward policies such as workplace, restaurant, and other place-based restrictions on smoking. These considerations are discussed below.

So far, so good, for both predictive analysis and tobacco control efforts. If microeconomic theory and the Law of Demand provide useful models for analyzing consumer behavior toward tobacco products, however, then the question immediately rises of what to do with the self-perceived benefits of consumption. Such benefits typically play a large role in economic analyses of markets and regulatory interventions in markets other than for tobacco products.[113] However, one of the most obvious omissions in the mortality-based approach[114] of public health and industry researchers is any weight placed on the self-perceived satisfaction from consuming either e-cigarettes or traditional tobacco products. The value to the consumer from consumption, net of the price paid for the product, is known as consumer surplus and is a standard and large component of typical cost–benefit analyses. The notion of consumer surplus for tobacco products is the subject of much debate in the economic and regulatory literature, however. Consumer surplus, and its more refined cousins, equivalent variation and compensating variation, are all intended to put a dollar value on the subjective pleasure received from consumption.[115] If consumers are informed and rational, then anyone choosing to consume a harmful product does so, even if it is addictive, only because he or she believes the pleasure of consumption is worth the risk, and consumer surplus measures the net benefits to the consumer.[116]

The issue of consumer surplus is tied up with the notion of externalities in the discussion about the social impacts of tobacco regulation. Externalities are those effects on social welfare—health-related, in the case of smoking—not accounted for in consumers' private calculations. Set aside traditional externalities such as ill effects of second-hand smoke for the moment. The externalities most at issue in the economics of smoking are health costs borne by consumers but ignored in their decision-making. Behavioral economists call this type of externality an *internality*. Many analyses of tobacco regulation begin with the full monetized value of health improvements expected to result and then subtract consumer surplus to recognize the lost pleasure of consumption and any health costs that the consumer already internalized.[117] In the pure public health approach, whether founded on the misinformation or addiction assumptions, *all* health costs are assumed to be internalities. Furthermore, some adherents of this view deny that consumers gain any enjoyment or benefits from consumption of nicotine at all.[118,119] In this case, there is nothing to subtract from the monetized health benefits in the social calculus at all.

Most behavioral economists do not take such an extreme position, but are nevertheless quick to point out that consumer surplus is computed from revealed preferences (choices made by consumers in the marketplace) that are distorted by irrationality and misinformed beliefs. In the former case, consumers are assumed to have made decisions that their future selves will not have wished them to make by becoming addicted to a harmful substance and overly discounting future health harm. In the latter case, it is assumed that consumption occurs without accurate knowledge about health harms. Thus, in between the rational addiction model, implying that only consumer surplus matters, and the pure public health model, implying that only external (and they are all external) health benefits matter, there is much room for intermediate positions that depend on the assumed degree of irrationality or misinformation held by consumers.

Due to the debate over the role of consumer surplus in regulatory impact analyses for tobacco control measures, a wide variety of approaches are used. In an early World Bank study it was assumed that three-quarters of all health costs from smoking were internalities (i.e., that consumer surplus accounted for only one-quarter of health costs).[120,121] This would imply that the monetary value of the improvement in health from a price increase or regulation that reduced consumption of tobacco would be marked down by only 25% to represent the true change in consumer welfare (as opposed to 100% in the case of rational addiction). In 2010, the FDA marked the value of health improvements down by 50% in its preliminary regulatory impact analysis of graphical health warnings on packaging[122] to reflect consumer surplus and the partial internalization of health costs; a range of markdowns of about 10% to 50%[123] was used in its final analysis.[124]

These approaches essentially take consumer surplus at face value but assume that it is an incomplete measure of the individual's welfare, to be supplemented by costs borne but not fully accounted for by the consumer. As a matter of practice, federal regulatory agencies are generally not free to disregard consumer surplus entirely, since the official guidance for regulatory impact analyses explicitly mentions it.[125] In one influential article responding to the FDA's analysis, several economists (some of whom are heavily involved in tobacco control efforts) take a different stance. They call for counting only about one-quarter of consumer surplus in cost–benefit analysis.[126] The main argument behind this discounting is that the consumer surplus for smokers who initiated regular use of cigarettes before age 18 should be completely ignored under the assumption that "society has clearly decided that the decision to initiate smoking is an irrational decision." (This was also the logic behind the World Bank study mentioned above.) These disagreements highlight that assumptions about whether consumers make informed choices, weighing the psychic benefits from smoking and use of e-cigarettes against the health costs, and which consumers do so, can greatly affect the apparent social benefits of a regulatory intervention.

5.3.2 *Supply-Side Responses to Regulation*

The models from Sect. 4 above, by focusing solely on public health as measured in excess mortality or life-years, ignore the supply side of the market for tobacco products. A standard cost–benefit analysis would include—indeed, for federal agencies in the U.S., is ***mandated*** to include—economic impacts on suppliers as well as on consumers. However, even if one held the view that the profits of the tobacco industry should be assigned a weight of zero in the social calculus, it would be unwise to ignore the supply side when assessing potential regulatory changes. Economic agents on the supply side, whether manufacturers, distributors, or retailers, and whether they are already serving the market or would enter in response to opportunities opened by regulation, respond to incentives. When these incentives are not aligned with the goal of the regulation, supply-side responses can partially thwart the success of tobacco control efforts.

That firms would adjust their prices, output, or other variables under their control to maximize profit in the face of the changed tax or regulatory environment is expected for anyone familiar with the economic way of thinking, but nevertheless seems to catch some in the public health community off guard. Excise taxation provides a good example. Textbook microeconomic theory shows that in competitive markets the economic incidence of commodity taxation is generally shared between consumers and producers,[127] and slightly more advanced theory shows that pass-through rates of excise taxes can also be greater than 100% when the firms enjoy market power.[128] Nevertheless, it is hard to read much of the tobacco control literature on the tobacco industry's response to tax increases without gaining the impression that the authors are almost morally affronted that cigarette manufacturers do not pass tax increases through dollar for dollar. Industry is either condemned for "undershifting" tax increases through to prices, with the charge that firms are "undermining" the tax increases, or vilified for "overshifting" tax increases, resulting in "inordinate profitability."[129] Apart from choosing a tax pass-through, manufacturers also employ other responses to tax increases, including differential pass-through by product type (typically, overshifting taxes onto high-end products and undershifting taxes on low-end products), increasing brand segmentation (introducing relatively cheap low-end products), quantity- or price-related promotions as a form of second-degree price discrimination, shrinkflation (reducing package size to disguise increased unit costs), and other tactics.[130] Industry response to regulation, assuming that the profit motive will guide their actions, must be part of a realistic cost–benefit analysis.

Perhaps more difficult to predict but no less important in the medium to long run are the dynamic responses of suppliers and entrants. If regulation makes certain products less profitable to supply, then we may expect that incumbent manufacturers of tobacco products will shift their resources to introduce and produce other products that they expect to be more profitable. Just as differential taxation could be used to steer consumers toward reduced-harm products, it can also steer producers in that direction. In the longer run, we should also expect new entrants to arise, in both the legal and illicit markets, in response to openings created by regulatory action. As an example of legal innovation and market entry, there is no question that high taxes on cigarettes gave companies like Juul an opening into the nicotine market that otherwise would have been far smaller. A non-scientific poll in 2023 found that among adult Juul users in the U.S. who no longer smoked, the average monthly savings from switching from cigarettes to Juul was almost US$60.[131] Consider that today many states tax Juul pods, whereas when the product was introduced in 2015 only a handful of states did so; historically the potential savings for consumers substituting to Juul would have been even greater than it is today. If Juul faced a market in which there were no cigarette excise taxes, then cigarettes on average might have been almost $2.90 less expensive per pack,[132] which would have greatly reduced the appeal of the new product (and hence the incentive for the company to invest in the R&D and marketing necessary to bring the product to market). It is also known that illicit sales of tobacco, whether under the counter or on the street, are supported by the tax-induced high prices of legal retailers,[133,134] as discussed briefly in Sect. 3.2 of the previous chapter.

The upshot of this discussion is that suppliers cannot be viewed as passive recipients of regulation, dutifully acting exactly as regulators wish. The only safe assumption to make about incumbents and potential entrants is that they will seek to adapt to new regulation in the manner that maximizes their profit, whether in the short term by adjusting prices or in the long term by altering their products or product mix. A further complication is introduced once recognizing that regulation can influence the degree of market power wielded by firms, which in turn affects how they will respond to regulation. This question, along with other important issues such as how regulatory burdens or regulatory uncertainty affect the actions of firms, is addressed in Sect. 7 below.

5.3.3 *Extra-Welfarist Considerations*

Apart from population health effects, consumers' self-perceived welfare, and the profit of suppliers, there are many other elements, less germane to cost–benefit analysis, that could also play a role in policy evaluation. Society cares as much or more about liberty and equality, for example, then pure economic efficiency.

Individual liberty and personal autonomy are held to be important values in democratic countries. The freedom to choose what to consume, subject to the constraints of what the market is offering and money available in the budget, is part of the "pursuit of Happiness" that so closely follows the first mention of Liberty in the U.S. Declaration of Independence. An instrumental rationale for freedom of consumer choice goes back at least as far as Adam Smith in *The Wealth of Nations*, for it is part of the dynamic free market that leads to the most efficient and productive allocation of resources in the economy.[135] Honoring the human dignity that arises from individual autonomy also requires preservation of the freedom of consumers. Is this basic notion inapplicable, or at least in need of modification, for addictive or harmful goods? A libertarian position would say no, for if people want to harm themselves, so long as they do not harm others the state has no justification for intervening. John Stuart Mill argued in *On Liberty* that exercising the power of the state to restrict what we would now call lifestyle choices violates an individual's liberty and absolute right of independence.[136] This position leads toward allowing consumers freely to use e-cigarettes (or to smoke, for that matter), as long as consumption can be done so without creating negative externalities for others. This argument is weaker the larger the externalities, but recall the evidence discussed in Volume II, Chapter 1, that e-cigarettes do not harm bystanders, or do so to a far lesser extent than smoking. Thus, the libertarian critique is on firmer ground when employed against e-cigarette regulation than when directed against restrictions on smoking.

Liberal arguments are also invoked by some to call *for* tobacco control. Philosopher Kalle Grill describes several such arguments.[137,138] While interventions may impinge on individual freedom in the short term, in the long term tobacco restrictions could advance liberty for those same individuals, both because individual freedom and personal choice are served when individuals eliminate the costs (financial and health) of tobacco dependence, and because a longer, healthier life necessarily entails more freedoms than a shorter sicker one.[139] Furthermore, while individuals may have a right to choose to engage in risky behaviors, smoking is not always (or perhaps even often) clearly a freely made choice made with full information and, in the case of youth, in adherence to one's own values (or to values one will subsequently hold as an adult). The decision to initiate or continue smoking may be uninformed or irrational.[140] Finally, some portion of people who smoke, although not a majority of such, support banning cigarettes. Thus, some of those who have not chosen to quit smoking yet would support a policy essentially forcing them (and everyone else) to quit. If there are family or peer effects that raise the personal cost of cessation while one's friends and family continue to smoke, such support for removing everyone's freedom of choice may be entirely individually rational. For these individuals, restrictions could be seen to advance liberty. Grill argues that the availability of e-cigarettes as a less-risky substitute for combustibles strengthens the liberal case for tobacco control; the existence of the former makes restrictions on the latter more of a nudge and less of an absolute removal of choice. Thus, on moral grounds, the option to switch to e-cigarettes could support stricter tobacco controls aimed at combustibles.[141] Apart from this moral argument, there are practical reasons why e-cigarettes enable stricter tobacco control, which are discussed at the end of this chapter.

Another value of democratic society is equality. As is well known in economics, efficient distributions of economic output or benefits may be highly inequitable. In much of the traditional approach to economics, however, questions of efficiency have primacy and distributional questions are analyzed separately. The theoretical grounds for separating the two goals of efficiency and equity come from fundamental theorems of welfare economics. The first welfare theorem states that competitive markets (lacking externalities, problems with information, or market power by any agent) lead to efficient (Pareto optimal) outcomes.[142] The second fundamental welfare theorem states, informally, that if society does not like the outcome, any other desired Pareto optimal outcome can also be achieved instead by the market mechanism by reallocating the initial endowments of resources. Many economists working in this tradition therefore focus solely on efficiency and, implicitly or explicitly, leave redistribution to the political process, even though the lump-sum transfers required by the second welfare theorem are politically infeasible.[143,144]

As is also well known, people are generally willing to give up some degree of efficiency or total benefits to more fairly distribute benefits.[145] One way to do this without giving up a formal approach to optimization is to replace a utilitarian social welfare function (one in which the net benefits gained by each individual have equal weight) with another in which greater weight is given to the distributional outcomes of members of groups deemed to be disadvantaged or otherwise worthy of special attention. The latter approach moves us toward recent variants of normative social choice theory, to be discussed below. Particular implications of policy toward e-cigarettes regarding equity are discussed briefly in the next chapter.

5.4 *What Are We Trying to Maximize? The Social Welfare Function*

As set forth at the beginning of this chapter, to speak of optimal regulation implies the existence of an objective function. Before discussing what our objective should be, it may be useful to briefly discard a few things that it should not be. The goal of regulation to best further social welfare is not to drive tobacco companies out of business or even to shrink their profits. Those results may occur, but should be viewed as incidental to the improvement of public health and welfare rather than the objectives. The goal should also not be to stamp out all use of nicotine. Again, great steps may be made toward that end resulting from policies chosen. But since nicotine use per se is not proportional to health harms, given the great range in the harmfulness of a dose of nicotine depending on how it is consumed, maximizing public health gains or improvements in other components of social welfare will not necessarily be coincident with minimizing consumption of nicotine. Whether the goal should be to maximize health gains is a deeper question, to be addressed below.

To proceed toward optimal regulation, a social welfare function (SWF) must be specified. In the field of welfare economics, a SWF is a rule for ranking the outcomes for individuals in a society. It necessarily depends on having a measure of the well-being of the individuals.[146] To those unfamiliar with thinking about assessing distributional outcomes in society in such a formal manner, the notion of a social welfare function may appear artificial at best and anti-democratic or dehumanizing at worst. However, a SWF is nothing more than a tool used to describe how society ranks all possible social outcomes. That ranking depends on judgment, and that judgment may be supplied by autocratic or democratic means,[147] or anything in between. As long as one accepts that some social outcomes are better than others, that any given outcome can be compared with any other and the two can be ranked, and that the choices are sensible in the sense that they are not circular,[148] then a SWF will exist that describes those social preferences.[149] Thus, while we can discuss what might or might not appear in a SWF, and how much importance any given element should be given in it, this is not at heart a discussion about an artificial mathematical function but rather is about the social preferences giving rise to the formal expression.

There are three required elements in any SWF framework, the SWF itself to rank social outcomes, a choice of how to measure individual well-being (to feed into the SWF), and a way to deal with uncertain outcomes. Before further discussing options for the SWF or moving on to the treatment of uncertainty, note that above we have already discussed the compensation approach to expressing changes in the well-being of an individual with a monetary equivalent, typically consumer surplus, as is done in CBA. Alternatively, a quantity such as a life-year gained can be treated as a direct component of increased welfare, which is termed the "objective goods" approach.[150,151] Valuation of health improvements in the same manner for all individuals leads to cost-effectiveness analysis (CEA). CEA is often seen as an extra-welfarist (i.e., adding something other than the true subjectively perceived welfare of individuals to the SWF) approach. Other choices for measuring individual welfare include transforming wealth levels with a concave function (such as a logarithm) to reflect prioritarian concerns (discussed below).[152] Behavioral economists tweak the notion of the individual's welfare by assuming that due to cognitive biases or incomplete information, the individual misperceives their own true welfare. In this case, the "biased" welfare function can be replaced with an assumed "corrected" function with the claim that the new measure of well-being is the true one in light of the individual's own preferences sans irrationality or lack of information.

If the personal preferences of individuals, outcomes for public health, concern for inequality of outcomes, traditional cost–benefit analysis, and, perhaps, paternalistic attitudes toward youth and irrational consumers are all seen to be important elements of the social calculus that policy toward e-cigarettes must address, then normative welfare economics can provide an appropriate theoretical framework. Welfare economics is concerned with the evaluation and ranking of actual and possible states of the economy and how policy interventions can change welfare outcomes. While a history of welfare analysis in economics is beyond the scope and needs of the present discussion, it does not do too much violence to the facts to say that approaches in use today fall under two categories.

The first, which may be considered the traditional or most common approach, is known as the New Welfare Economics.[153,154,155] The fundamental notion is the *Pareto criterion*, which states that if one social state is better for at least one individual and no worse for any other individual than a second state, then social welfare is higher in the first state. Note that by relying only on the subjective assessments by the individuals themselves, no interpersonal comparisons of well-being are required, and no SWF is necessary. By the Pareto principle, a policy makes society better-off if it results in a such a Pareto improvement. Since the "win–win" (or at least, "win-not lose") possibilities required for a Pareto improvement may be scarce, the New Welfare Economics program introduces the additional concept of the *compensation principle*, under which a policy improves social welfare if there exists a set of ex-post side-payments that would yield a Pareto improvement compared to the pre-policy social state. In other words, policy changes that create winners and losers are accepted to be welfare-enhancing as long as the gains to the winners are large enough that they could "pay off" the losers. Importantly, the compensation principle does not require that such payments actually be made, only that they could be. The compensation principle, however, provides a way forward to think about policy in the real world, where the Pareto optimal social outcomes from the first welfare theorem are likely to be infeasible to attain, the lump sum transfers required by the second welfare theorem are politically or practically impossible to operationalize, an acceptable SWF may not be at hand, and even Pareto improvements may not be available or obvious. Any policy that satisfies the compensation principle improves aggregate welfare (if not every individual's welfare) and is a step toward Pareto optimality and efficiency. Cost–benefit analysis has a natural connection to the compensation principle, for any policy passing a cost–benefit test also satisfies the latter. Cost–benefit analysis can also be seen as a particular type of SWF where an individual's (or a group's) welfare is measured with monetary equivalents (consumer surplus, compensating variation, or equivalent variation as determined by the consumer's own subjective valuation) and the sum total of these across the economy are maximized.

The second main category of approaches to social choices involves additional elements not found in traditional welfare economics, and thus can be called *normative social choice theory* (NSCT).[156] Describing this methodology is more difficult because it encompasses a great variety of departures from the purely welfarist approach rooted in the assumed rationality of individuals. Such departures include explicit use of an arbitrary SWF, inclusion of extra-welfaristic considerations as discussed in the previous section, accommodation of social and economic constraints such as incomplete markets, irrational consumer behavior, and social value judgments concerning equity. The use of NSCT may be particularly apt for questions involving health because of informational problems, such as the likely cognitive biases among at least some consumers regarding current behavior and future health consequences.[157] Furthermore, in contrast to standard cost–benefit analysis, there may be a desire in society to protect the health of the most vulnerable members of society beyond their willingness to pay (WTP) for improvements in their own health, since a low monetary equivalent for health may merely result from low income.[158] In other words, for a desirable aspect of human existence like health there may be a weak relationship between WTP and the individual's self-perceived welfare.[159] Furthermore, since WTP for health may also be low among lower-income groups because their life expectancy is shorter to begin with (so that improvements in health are enjoyed for less time compared with the same health gain for a higher-income individual), using straight WTP for policy decisions would appear to compound existing inequalities.[160]

In practice, governmental health policy analysis appears to sidestep the problems with WTP by valuing a health improvement (e.g., a quality adjusted life-year, or QALY) with a single value regardless of who gained it. For example, the value assigned to a QALY may come from surveys or revealed preferences, but the evidence is aggregated across the sample or market studied to produce an average WTP for a QALY. This leads to one extreme form of extra-welfarist social choice theory, cost-effectiveness analysis (CEA), which focuses solely on maximizing health or health gains instead of any other component of welfare. The concept of CEA has been discussed already in Sect. 4, where the models of e-cigarettes' impact on population health were reviewed. In addition to the shortcomings of only looking at deaths averted or life-years gained discussed there, we can now also note that a strict CEA approach to policy analysis is willing to trade a life for a life in the social calculus (or, more accurately, a quality adjusted life-year for a quality adjusted life-year), even when one of those lives would otherwise be granted extra protection or consideration on the grounds of redressing social and healthcare-related disadvantages. Examples of such disadvantage could include disability (which in some cases pushes an individual down the priority list for medical care), chronic illness, low income, or minority status.[161] CEA thus completely ignores the distributional consequences of a policy.

Perhaps the simplest way to incorporate distributional concerns explicitly into the SWF to analyze health-related policy, however individual welfare is measured, is to assign non-identical distributional weights to the welfare of various groups in society.[162,163] In particular, higher weight can be given to health improvements or other gains in welfare that benefit relatively disadvantaged social strata. In one example of this approach,[164] applied to whether a drug should be added to a national health system's formulary of supported pharmaceuticals, distributional weights were determined by the ratio of an income group's marginal utility of income to the average marginal utility of income.[165] This procedure resulted in a larger value attached to lives saved (relative to other costs and benefits) by the policy in question, since the drug in question would disproportionately affect those with low income and poor health. Another way to address the distribution of outcomes in a SWF is to sum not the raw welfare gains of individuals but instead their values after transformation with a concave, increasing function. This procedure, a formalization of prioritarianism,[166,167] also results in greater social weight being given to improvements in well-being of worse-off individuals.[168] As a practical matter, however, it may be more feasible to decide upon a set of distributional weights for a finite number of income (or other) groups than to settle on a definite transformation function (since the latter are drawn from an infinite dimensional space).

Having discussed the first two elements of the SWF framework, measurement of individual well-being and how to rank outcomes with a particular SWF, the final element—the "uncertainty module"—may now be discussed.[169] To complete the framework, a procedure for handling uncertainty must be chosen. Without rehearsing the distinction between risk and Knightian uncertainty discussed in Volume II, Chapter 3, assume first that uncertainty takes the form of known probabilities attached to various possible outcomes. Then particular policies can themselves be seen as offering a set of possible outcomes, only to be resolved *ex post*. In this case, the most natural SWF would then be the expected sum of the individual measures of well-being (perhaps after weighting or transforming as discussed above).[170,171] That is, the SWF would be the average of the total social welfare expected to obtain in the various potential outcomes. In the case of Knightian uncertainty, if possible outcomes can be specified (even though no probabilities can be attached to them) then sensitivity analysis can give the policy-maker insight into the set of possible outcomes pertaining to a policy. These outcomes could then, in addition, be used in a min–max or satisficing decision rule.

5.5 *Concluding Thoughts*

What to take from the preceding discussion? At this point we could write down an explicit SWF, but the review of the population health studies in Sect. 4 above showed that even with the most straightforward and simplest approach to a SWF framework, CEA, so much is unknown about the transition probabilities among the various states of cigarette and e-cigarette use and relative harms that a variety of conclusions come out of the different models. Adding assumptions about the other choices involved in specifying aSWF would likely only add further confusion about what would be driving the policy conclusions. Instead, we distill a few useful lessons from the discussion in this section.

1. Notwithstanding concerns about misinformation or lack of fully rational decision-making on the part of consumers, policy analysis pertaining to e-cigarettes and other tobacco products can assume that consumers respond to price signals and other costs imposed by regulation. Policy-makers cannot assume that consumers will act in accordance with the intent of a policy if it is contrary to their preferences and incentives. There is therefore scope to use differential taxation to nudge people, smokers, and non-smokers alike, away from cigarettes and toward e-cigarettes and cessation. Furthermore, unintended consequences of regulation such as illicit markets should not be unexpected consequences (see Sects. 5.3.1 and 5.3.2).
2. Given the controversy and wide range of decisions over how to treat consumer surplus (or other measures of self-perceived welfare) from consumers of tobacco products, it is worth noting that any policy that encourages a smoker to switch to e-cigarettes, if it does so by making e-cigarettes more attractive instead of making cigarettes the opposite, must improve that individual's welfare. (This assumes that whatever degree of irrationality exists concerning the decision to smoke, it will not be of higher degree for using e-cigarettes. Given that many people appear to have a one-sided inaccurate impression of the harm from using e-cigarettes but not for smoking, this does not appear to be a stretch.)[172] This is not to say that a socially beneficial policy might not include raising the all-inclusive cost of smoking even higher. The point here is just that in that case the *a fortiori* argument from revealed preference that allows sidestepping

the question of how much consumer surplus should "count" does not apply (see Sect. 5.3.1).

3. Although there are disagreements over the value society should place on personal liberty and consumer autonomy when individuals may be misinformed or irrational, other things equal, policy structured to *encourage* better choices related to risky activities should be preferred over others intended to coerce behavior. A libertarian, free-market approach to e-cigarette regulation is essentially nowhere on the table, at least not in any country that is influenced by the WHO (which is to say, nearly all of them). So, setting that aside as practically irrelevant without further discussion, what remains is the choice along the spectrum between nudge and shove. Both the externalities-based and behavioral rationales for abrogating consumer sovereignty are weaker for e-cigarettes than cigarettes, and the availability of the former strengthens the moral case for restricting autonomy regarding the latter (see Sect. 5.3.3).
4. Look for Pareto improvements wherever possible. The advantage of the new welfare economics program is that it avoids any comparison of utility or well-being between individuals. If a policy leads to a Pareto improvement, then (subject to any opportunity costs it may have) it is a step in the right direction. An obvious example of a policy that Pareto improves over the status quo would be to promulgate accurate information about harms and relative harms of e-cigarette products. Misinformation or disinformation, whether on the part of manufacturers, public health campaigns, or governmental pronouncements serves only to distort people's choices.[173] On the other hand, effective communication that e-cigarettes are less risky than smoking has been shown to increase the accuracy of the public's perceptions regarding harm reduction[174] (see Sect. 5.4).
5. For such a vital part of human existence as health, explicit concern for distributional consequences seems to be warranted. CBA, in its textbook form based on individual's WTP, would appear to undervalue improvements to the health and lives of members of disadvantaged groups. Policies toward e-cigarettes that provide protection or extra benefits to such individuals may be attractive. Current smokers tend to have lower income and have lower socio-economic status than e-cigarette users; non-vaping smokers are more likely to be minorities and have lower income (see Fig. 2) and educational attainment (Fig. 3).[175] Therefore, concern for the distributional

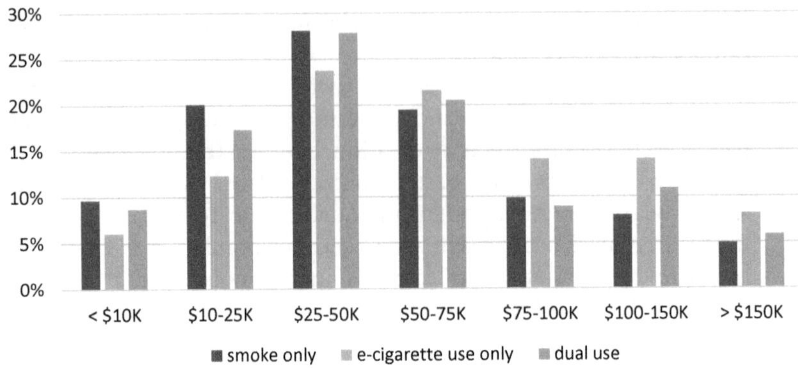

Fig. 2 Family income in the U.S. by smoking and use of e-cigarettes (adults) (*Notes* Estimates are for the population of age 18 or older, and are calculated by the authors using data from the CPS-TUS 2018–2019)

aspects of policy may provide additional reasons to focus on policy designed to help smokers switch to e-cigarettes to improve health without allowing fears about nicotine addiction from e-cigarette use to lead toward prohibitionist policies (see Sect. 5.4).

6. The previous two points notwithstanding, there is no need for distributional concern to cause an overreaction toward adopting

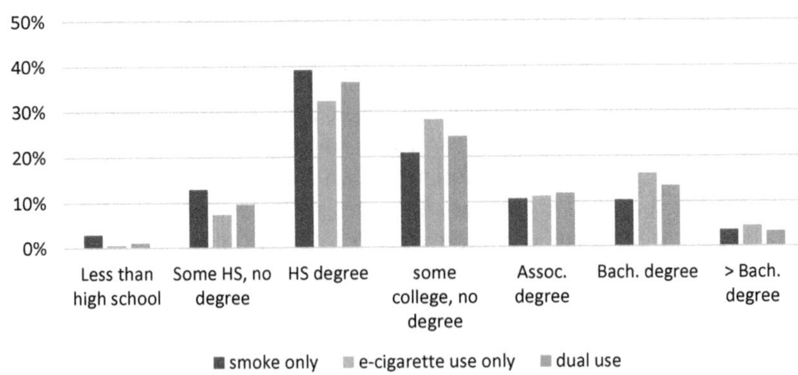

Fig. 3 Educational attainment in the U.S. by smoking and use of e-cigarettes (adults) (*Note* See notes to previous table)

pureCEA and jettisoning all other elements of social welfare analysis. Focusing solely on premature deaths averted or life-years gained ignores other aspects of life that people care about (consumption, income, autonomy, etc.). It also is a more indirect method to address concerns about inequality than explicitly using weights or transformation functions in the SWF (see Sect. 5.4).

7. Therefore, it is best to be explicit in the SWF about the treatment of inequality, if any. CEA and CBA make strong assumptions about the degree of social concern (or lack thereof) for the distributional consequences of policy, yet at the same time hide those assumptions. Explicitly specifying a SWF with weights (or other means) to address distributional effects brings the discussion into the light of the political process and democratic conversation. Lest this suggestion be considered too theoretical, note that in many areas governments already explicitly place greater value on the economic welfare of particular groups. For example, in developed and developing countries alike, government procurement policies often include explicit, numerically defined set-asides for minority-owned businesses.[176] Another example is the system of bidder credits extended to female- and minority-owned telecommunications companies in spectrum auctions run by the U.S. Federal Communications Commission.[177] Every dollar bid by these businesses was multiplied by 1.15 (or 1.25 if both female *and* minority owned) before comparing with bids by other firms to allocate spectrum.[178] While it is not clear (and the FCC did not explain) why women or minorities needed exactly that weight (or why intersectionality was worth more than nothing but less than the sum), making the preference for these groups explicit enables discussion, lobbying, public comment, and evaluation of results ex post—all important parts of the public's civic engagement with government.[179]
8. Behavioralist concerns about irrational decisions made by consumers of tobacco products will affect a policy analysis mainly through the extensive margin of the decision to use any addictive products at all, since the choice to become addicted (if indeed it is a conscious choice) is likely the most subject to cognitive biases and misinformation. Conditional on consumption of nicotine, such concerns would be greatest for the most harmful products (cigarettes) for which the cognitive biases would loom largest. A possible exception may be that if e-cigarettes are widely misperceived to be more harmful than

they actually are (e.g., as harmful as smoking), then a behavioralist concern about bias in the welfare function may call for policy to correct or overcome that misperception (see Sect. 5.4).

9. The mere fact that outcomes are uncertain does not justify use of a strict form of the precautionary principle that seeks to ban new products. In the first place, as discussed in Volume II, Chapter 3, a zero-risk standard for e-cigarettes makes no sense when the alternative is the known risk of cigarettes for many people. There are many less extreme available choices for dealing with risk and uncertainty in social welfare analysis (see Sect. 5.4). If the choice of the uncertainty module is itself in contention, then perhaps the safest route is to perform a sensitivity analysis with regard to various assumptions about uncertain outcomes, allowing the consumers of the analysis to form their own judgment about the overall desirability of a policy given their subjective assessment of the likelihood of the various outcomes.

6 The Devil is in the Details: Optimizing Differential Nicotine Regulation

What are the practical options to operationalize this theoretical approach at the policy level? Differential regulation of e-cigarettes and more harmful tobacco products can take many forms: taxes, restrictions on public use, health warnings, restrictions on advertising, minimum legal sales ages, nicotine limits, and restrictions on allowed flavors or other additives. While the focus here is on encouraging switching from smoking to using e-cigarettes, we note that a commitment to risk-proportionate regulation does not preclude measures to protect against youth experimentation or uptake of e-cigarettes by non-smokers. Those arguing against risk-proportionate regulation of e-cigarettes point out the potential that preferential treatment could make e-cigarettes attractive to non-smokers. However, there are numerous ways in which risk-proportionate regulations could be adapted to mitigate the risk of encouraging youth uptake, without sacrificing the broader incentives for adult smoking cessation. In terms of Eq. (2), the goal is to make term 1 a larger negative number for smokers (cessation), without increasing term 2 for non-smokers (initiation of vaping by non-smokers).

6.1 Differential Taxes

Taxation can be used to create a price differential to encourage substitutions toward less risky products.[180,181] This includes, but does not require, taxes that result in an absolute cost savings for vaping over smoking.[182] The two types of products are not perfect substitutes, and instead of fixating on making e-cigarettes cheaper than smoking, as if price were the sole differentiator in the minds of consumers, it is better to recognize that switching will likely be a smoothly decreasing function of the price differential ($p_{\text{e-cig}} - p_{\text{cig}}$), whether it is positive or negative. Crucially, however, differential taxation does not mean that e-cigarettes must be free from all taxes or surcharges.

There are many rationales for taxing tobacco products in general: to raise revenue, to correct for health externalities, to improve public health, and to correct for internalities caused by irrationality or misinformation. Regardless of the goal, however, the optimal tax rates to achieve the desired end involve taxing e-cigarettes less than cigarettes.[183] This result follows from three facts: compared to cigarettes, e-cigarettes have lesser health harms and higher elasticity of demand; and the two products are economic substitutes. Thus, if the goal is to raise revenue, then standard results from public finance theory apply, suggesting that taxes should be higher on more inelastic goods (here, cigarettes).[184] If the goal is to correct for externalities, then the lower health harms (second-hand aerosol versus second-hand smoke) again imply lower taxes for e-cigarettes. The lower direct health harms, coupled with the preponderance of overestimation of harm from vaping, imply that the behavioral rationale based on internalities also leads to lower taxes on e-cigarettes. One may object that the relative health harms from vaping and smoking are not pinned down yet. However, one of the present authors has shown elsewhere that the case for e-cigarettes to be taxed at a lower rate, justified by the internalities argument about direct health effects to users, holds as long as the marginal harm from cigarettes is at least 75% higher than that from e-cigarettes.[185] This appears to be highly likely to be true; recall that U.K. health officials tell smokers in England that cigarettes are around 1,900% riskier than e-cigarettes.[186]

Apart from using tax policy to encourage switching from smoking to vaping, there may also be a role for taxes to correct for environmental externalities.[187] For example, an environmental deposit system could be implemented to deter inappropriate disposal of e-cigarettes, similar to that used in the U.S. for certain beverage cans and bottles, automobile batteries, and automobile tires. Indeed, Altria already has experimented with such a program for some of its brands. Altria voluntarily enacted some limited forms of Extended Producer Responsibility-type buyback programs via subsidiaries: Green Smoke and MarkTen (though neither brands are sold any longer).[188] If coupled with a nonrefundable environmental surcharge, the proceeds could fund recycling programs to mitigate the environmental consequences of use, and these could be higher for disposables than reusable vaping systems. Note, however, that if environmental externalities are used to justify taxing e-cigarettes, then they should also be applied to cigarettes, which also create hazardous pollution through discarded butts (and for equivalent amounts of nicotine, there would be between 4 and 20 butts for every fully- or pod-disposable e-cigarette).[189] Note further that Pigouvian taxes to correct for environmental externalities would likely be very small on a per unit basis; while the aggregate harm to the environment from discarded cigarette butts may be significant, that is only because trillions of butts are discarded around the world each year; the harm from any single cigarette (or e-cigarette) must be quite low.

Advocates often propose imposing high taxes on e-cigarettes as a means to discourage youth vaping (term 2 for non-smokers in Eq. (2)). However, it is important to note that the factors mentioned in the previous paragraph regarding elasticity, health harm, and substitution, also apply to youth demand, and so the results regarding the best relative tax rates also still apply. There are also additional considerations, however. As previously discussed, taxing e-cigarettes fuels youth demand for traditional cigarettes, which is counterproductive for public health (see Volume III, Chapter 1, Sect. 3.2.2.1).[190] One study found that "the unintended effects of ENDS taxation [on youth] may considerably undercut or even outweigh any public health gains."[191] Furthermore, taxes are blunt instruments to discourage usage by youth, as most consumers of e-cigarettes are adults.[192] Implementing interventions that directly target youth, such as setting minimum legal sales ages (discussed below), are more likely to effectively reduce youth usage without diminishing the incentive for adult smokers to transition to e-cigarettes. Differential taxation based on age or smoking status is infeasible, at least in terms of official tax rates, but other policies that effectively subsidize e-cigarettes (to lower the net tax rate) for adult smokers but not youth are worth exploring. For example, government health systems or private insurance companies could incentivize switching to e-cigarettes the same way they do so for quitting smoking.[193] Lastly, due to disparities in income, the demand for e-cigarettes is likely to be more responsive to price changes among youths than adults. Therefore, even a modest tax levied on e-cigarettes could substantially reduce youth demand while still encouraging adult smokers to switch.

6.2 *Differential Restrictions on Public Use*

Smoke-free laws were justified on the basis that public-use bans would limit bystanders' exposure to harmful environmental tobacco smoke,[194] increase smokers' awareness of harms, and encourage quitting.[195] In 2016, the WHO recommended banning the use of e-cigarettes in areas already designated as smoke-free.[196] About 70 countries now prohibit vaping in enclosed public spaces such as bars, restaurants, and workplaces or other public places.[197] In the U.S., several states and hundreds of municipalities have outlawed vaping in smoke-free areas.[198] But compared with smoking, secondhand e-cigarette emissions appear to present a much lower risk (see Volume II, Chapter 1, Sect. 6),[199,200,201] and so the justification for that restriction is less forceful for vaping. On the basis of concerns for second-hand exposure, commensurate smoke-free laws violate the principle of proportionality in regulation.

Furthermore, forcing e-cigarette users into the same spaces as smokers puts the health of the e-cigarette users at risk by exposing them to environmental smoke. For e-cigarette users who are former smokers such treatment may increase their chances of relapse and for all users, commensurate public-use restrictions promote the false notion that smoking and vaping are of commensurate harms. As Public Health England stated in a guide to workplace policy-making,

> To help smokers to stop smoking and stay smokefree, a more enabling approach to vaping may be appropriate to make it an easier choice than smoking. In particular, vapers should not be required to use the same space as smokers, as this could undermine their ability to quit and stay smokefree.[202]

Accordingly, a recent U.S. study found that the inclusion of vaping in smoke-free worksite restrictions not only failed to reduce vaping among emerging adults but may have attenuated the policies' effect on current smoking.[203]

Still, banning vaping from public areas could plausibly help avoid the "normalization" of vaping, and thus could protect against uptake by non-smokers and youth. Some restrictions on public use may therefore be desired. Where feasible, a differential restriction may help satisfy both goals. Smokers could be subject to a more stringent restriction, requiring them to leave the premises entirely as per many current restrictions. Rather than allowing vaping in communal areas, or forcing e-cigarette users into the same spaces as smokers, designated rooms or outdoor areas could be reserved for e-cigarette use only. That might increase the appeal of vaping for smokers, who would no longer have to go outside to consume nicotine, and do so without normalizing e-cigarette use by modeling that behavior in general communal areas. In the U.K. in 2019, some NHS hospital trusts opened vape stores in hospital settings to encourage switching from smoking to vaping.[204] On the grounds of those hospitals, using e-cigarettes is allowed anywhere outside (away from doorways) while smoking is banned entirely and erstwhile smoking shelters have been converted to areas for using e-cigarettes. The government provides guidance to NHS trusts suggesting that e-cigarettes be exempt from smoke-free regulations.[205] And several NHS hospitals are offering free e-cigarette starter kits to smokers in a bid to encourage substitutions.[206]

6.3 Differential Health Warnings

Health warning labels have become commonplace on tobacco products. Often similar labels are applied to e-cigarettes. In the U.S., for example, e-cigarette packages have had to display textual warnings since 2016 stating, "This product contains nicotine. Nicotine is an addictive chemical"[207] and packaging in the EU has carried a similar warning ("This product contains nicotine which is a highly addictive substance") for about as long. Such advice appears to be unproblematic *prima facie,* since the information is objectively true. It is also the case that such warnings for e-cigarettes imply that differential regulation is already in place, since warnings for cigarettes make explicit mention to health harm (cancer, lung disease, etc.) and, in many countries, additionally display graphical (and graphic!) warnings.

However, more could be done to emphasize the relative risks of the two products. Referring to nicotine in a warning label, while factual, is highly likely to create confusion since many people believe that it is the nicotine itself in cigarettes that causes cancer.[208] In contrast, even cancer researchers who suspect nicotine might play some role in carcinogenesis admit that there is no conclusive evidence that nicotine is a complete carcinogen itself.[209] Thus, nicotine warnings on e-cigarette packaging without an explicit statement of harm potential relative to cigarettes may promote a false equivalency between the types of tobacco products.

Information on relative risk matters for consumer choice. A discrete choice experiment in the U.S. reported that e-cigarette warning labels that overstate e-cigarette risk relative to combustibles may discourage uptake by smokers, deterring cessation.[210] There are several possible avenues for differential labeling. In addition to the textual and graphic warning labels on combustible tobacco, cigarette packs could contain information advising smokers of the potential benefits of substituting to e-cigarettes, and that those products are highly likely to be a safer alternative. Such messages on cigarette packs would likely have little potential to sway the perceptions of non-smokers, because they will not be likely to see them (at least in any context of high salience), especially since cigarette ads (with accompanying warning messages) are illegal in many countries. Meanwhile, e-cigarette textual warnings could continue to inform consumers about the addictive potential from consuming nicotine.[211] That combination of messages has the advantage that e-cigarette harm-reduction messages could be specifically targeted to current smokers, while those not interacting with cigarettes would only be confronted with the messages currently in use facing the general public. That combination could encourage switching but not novel uptake of e-cigarettes by non-smokers.

6.4 *Differential Restrictions on Advertising*

To avoid attracting young non-smokers to any form of nicotine, e-cigarette marketing restrictions should ban advertisements targeted to youth. Legally defining what such targeting includes may be difficult, but restrictions could include prohibiting the use of underage models in ads and disallowing placement in locations or outlets where young people are a majority of the audience or readership. Further content restrictions, such as prohibiting ads from using cartoon characters,[212] lifestyle themes, or other indirect appeals—associations with wealth, prestige, social approval, individualistic behavior, or sexual attraction, as found in alcohol advertising[213]—may be considered but are more likely to suffer legal challenges in countries with strong protections for commercial freedom of speech. It may be easier to ban advertising altogether for a product, or to ban it by venue, than to engage in subjective content restrictions on the contents of the ads. Or, given experience in Canada in the 1980s, where a blanket ban on advertising of tobacco products was struck down by the Supreme Court for imposing "intolerable limits on free speech," it may not.[214]

Banning all e-cigarette marketing, however, forgoes the opportunity to encourage switching. While in many countries it has been deemed justifiable to ban all forms of advertising of combustibles, a somewhat more permissive approach to e-cigarette advertising could involve limiting the ads to adult (or at least non-youth oriented) audiences and emphasizing the idea of substitution. An even stronger differential could allow e-cigarette marketing only in age-gated venues such as bars, clubs, specialty tobacco shops, or other venues in which tobacco is sold (although point-of-sale advertising in general-access retail outlets that also sell tobacco re-introduces the issue of youth exposure to the ads). Irvine and Nguyen[215] suggest that cigarette manufacturers could be permitted to advertise lower-risk products on their cigarette packs. That approach has the benefit of targeting specifically individuals who already smoke, and (if ads are otherwise banned or severely restricted) could additionally be incentive compatible with corporate interests,[216] i.e., cigarette manufacturers could advertise their own e-cigarette brands. This approach could additionally spur industry transformation by incentivizing cigarette manufacturers to enter the vapor market. Disadvantages of this approach include the possibly deficient incentives for manufacturers to cannibalize their own demand for cigarettes by advertising e-cigarettes, and the advantage established cigarette manufacturers would have over entrants into the e-cigarette market (which would not be able to advertise on cigarette packs; see Sect. 7.2 below).

6.5 *Differential Minimum Age Restrictions for Legal Retail Sales*

Given the possibility that nicotine negatively affects brain development for youth, coupled with the fact that youth vaping is largely motivated by experimentation rather than smoking cessation,[217] it is appropriate to try to prevent minors from accessing either e-cigarettes or combustible tobacco products. Compared with some other policy areas, age restrictions provide a relatively straightforward means of distinguishing between combustibles and e-cigarettes on the basis of risk. For example, some authors point out that the optimal tax rate on e-cigarettes, whatever it is, is likely higher for youth than for older consumers.[218] However, age-based taxation is likely infeasible, both in practical terms and because of anti-discrimination laws pertaining to the age of the consumer in many countries. Still, given that prohibitions are, effectively, an infinite tax, age restrictions could serve as a tax targeted exclusively to minors. At what age, then, should access be restricted?

There are different opinions about where the legal age threshold for e-cigarettes should be set. On one hand, given that the relative harms of vaping are likely much less than those of smoking (see Volume II, Chapter 1), there is a case to be made to have a lower age limit for e-cigarettes than for combustibles, for example 18 for e-cigarettes and 21 for combustibles.[219,220] Some jurisdictions, including Brookline, Massachusetts, the U.K., and New Zealand have considered rolling age restrictions for tobacco products. Any government adopting a similar approach could design it with a lag for reduced-risk products, so that there is an age band that always has access to the latter even when unable to legally purchase cigarettes. That might help prevent demand from those who missed the cut-off by a couple of months or years from turning to the illicit market. The minimum age for e-cigarettes could even be fixed while the one from combustibles moves ahead on the rolling basis. That could help "capture" some of those who are under the age for legal purchase of cigarettes who already smoke and who might otherwise turn to illicit sources for combustible tobacco. In either scenario, establishing a higher age limit for combustibles may serve as a "nudge" mechanism, encouraging young adults who experiment with nicotine products to do so with less risky options which, over time, could help displace cigarettes. Setting an age restriction at 18 for e-cigarettes could also allow the majority of the world using that age as the minimum for cigarette sales to raise the age restriction to 21 with greater success at encouraging cessation and non-initiation. Again, this might help avoid young adults who interact with nicotine between the ages of 18 and 20 from becoming smokers."[221]

On the other hand, an age limit of 18 years may be problematic since those in their final years of secondary education have classmates who are still below that age. Setting the age limit for e-cigarette purchases at 19 instead of 18 would decrease access for school-aged children. Wherever the age limit is set, social distribution (receiving tobacco products from friends, which is the most common source of access to e-cigarette among U.S. youth[222]) and illicit markets undermine age-gating. Unscrupulous vendors violating the rules can also provide access for young people and a lack of enforcement capacity exacerbates the problem. If sales could be sufficiently well age-gated, this would reduce the perceived need for more "blunt" policy approaches such as flavor restrictions and nicotine limits, the use of which could undermine adult substitutions to e-cigarettes and thus perpetuate smoking.

So far, the discussion has dealt with the tradeoff between youth uptake of vaping and cessation for smokers. However, even if the health of youth is the only item of concern (which it should not be), age restrictions on access to e-cigarettes still involve large tradeoffs. Policy-makers need to be cognizant that, in addition to losing out on encouraging switching away from cigarettes for young adult smokers, setting age limits (high or low) for e-cigarettes will also create some new smokers among youth. This is an inescapable consequence of e-cigarettes and cigarettes being economic substitutes and is not merely a theoretical surmise. As already discussed in Volume III, Chapter 1 (Sect. 3.2.2.3), evidence from several high-quality quasi-experimental econometric studies, all using data from the U.S., have demonstrated that restricting access by minors to e-cigarettes is causally associated with increased smoking among youth. During the period studied, some states prohibiting sales under age 18, others under age 19, and other had no minimum legal sale age laws on e-cigarette purchases (e-MLSAs). One study found that the average e-MLSA in a state increased smoking among 12 to 17 year-olds by 0.9 percentage points, which is roughly 9% of the average smoking rate for this group during the years studied, 10.2%.[223] Two other studies found that for high school students, e-MLSAs increased the rate of regular cigarette use by 0.8 to 1.0 percentage points, again over a tenth of the overall smoking rate.[224] A third study found that e-MLSAs increased lifetime daily cigarette use and daily cigar use by 35%, a greater percentage change than the concomitant percentage reduction in lifetime e-cigarette use.[225] Another study found that e-MLSAs increased smoking during pregnancy by teen mothers rural areas, with especially high increases among black teenagers and those who already smoked before pregnancy.[226] Another study came to a contrary conclusion, but examined only high school seniors and any use of cigarettes during the past month instead of regular or daily smoking.[227]

Minimum age laws can send effective signals to youth and their parents that use of e-cigarettes entails risk to health (through the expressive value of the law).[228] Nevertheless, an e-MLSA may have the unintended consequences for some youth of putting e-cigarettes and cigarettes on a level playing field. Given the empirical results just discussed, it is worth asking why the application of age restrictions on one product increases consumption of another product to which an age restriction already applies. Do some young e-cigarette users actually prefer smoking, and figure, "if they are both illegal, why not smoke?" Are e-cigarette vendors more compliant with MLSA laws than those selling cigarettes? Both are possible, but neither would have to be the case to explain the response to the MLSAs. It is also possible that the ubiquity of cigarettes simply offers more opportunities for age-gate restrictions to be flouted, contributing to the shift in demand. The physical nature of the products may also be relevant: A pack of cigarettes obtained with one MLSA violation provides 20 cigarettes, which might then be distributed among a school-aged social group. In contrast, an e-cigarette purchase is not so easily sub-divided. Under-age users who are able to obtain e-cigarettes in violation of e-MLSAs may be less willing to part with that product entirely than they would be of one or two cigarettes from a pack. Perhaps this explains why, with MLSAs applied to both products, smoking increases. There is clearly room for additional research, perhaps from sociologists, exploring the hows and whys of the choice among youth to use cigarettes and e-cigarettes when both are unavailable *de jure*.[229]

The weight of the evidence shows that while e-MLSAs can reduce youth vaping, that success comes at high cost in terms of the health of young people as a group. The most recent of the studies above, which is also the one with the strongest study design, finds that e-MLSAs decreased the prevalence of ever-e-cigarette use by 2.2 percentage points but increased the prevalence of daily cigarette use by 0.5 percentage points.[230] As the "funnel of use" depicted in Volume II, Chapter 1, Sect. 6.3.1 showed, fewer than half of youth who have ever used e-cigarettes are current users, and only one in 10 are daily vapers. Gaining one additional *daily* cigarette smoker while losing four to five *ever* users of e-cigarettes implies (almost surely) a net decrease in the health of the young population affected. Such effects may be transitory, the outcome of only a short-term consumer response to the shock of the new restriction. Nonetheless, the evidence points out that e-MLSAs may be a bitter pill to swallow, at least at first, and raises the question of whether the e-MLSAs adopted in the U.S. did more harm than good. That is not to say that there should be no minimum age requirements for purchase of e-cigarettes, but regulators would do well to consider how to design and implement e-MLSAs to avoid this kind of response.[231]

6.6 *Differential Limits for Nicotine Content*

In the EU,[232] U.K.,[233] and Canada,[234] nicotine limits have been adopted for e-cigarettes, capping nicotine concentration to 20 mg/ml. In contrast, many popular U.S. e-cigarettes have nicotine concentrations two or three times higher, which has been cited as a reason for the high levels of youth experimentation and nicotine addiction in the U.S.[235] Critics suggest that nicotine limits undermine smoking cessation by reducing the degree to which e-cigarettes replicate the experience of smoking.[236] That concern is borne out by smokers citing dissatisfaction with e-cigarettes as a justification for returning to smoking. However, the evidence from Europe suggests that e-cigarettes can remain effective cessation aids even with lower levels of nicotine.[237] The question, no doubt, is one of degree. One study found that the same total nicotine delivered over five minutes alleviated cravings to smoke similar to delivery over one minute, but that delivery over ten minutes had no significant impact on cravings at all.[238] Evidently, for smokers at least, there is a limit beyond which low-nicotine e-cigarettes are no longer sufficient to satisfy nicotine dependence.

The behavioral response of consumers using cigarettes and e-cigarettes to coerced changes in nicotine concentration or other product characteristics must be considered. Consumers of nicotine cannot be viewed as trees, where watering every other week instead of weekly results in their roots taking in half as much water. This has long been known for smokers. The drive from the 1960s to the mid-1980s to bring "safer cigarettes" to market ended when regulators learned from public health researchers that users' compensatory smoking behavior largely undid any lessening of health risk that otherwise might have obtained. For example, adding filters to create a low-nicotine or "low tar" cigarette merely resulted in smokers inhaling more deeply and frequently and consuming a larger fraction of each cigarette.[239] Hence the prohibition on terms such as “low tar” in the marketing of cigarettes since that time in many countries. Similar behavior has been found for users of e-cigarettes regarding the nicotine concentration in the e-liquid: when given e-cigarettes with lower nicotine concentration, consumers simply “self-titrate” and use more e-liquid in an attempt to satisfy their pharmacological dependence on nicotine.[240] The displacement effect—higher nicotine concentration, less e-liquid consumed—is only partial; lower-nicotine e-liquids do result in less total nicotine consumed.[241] Nevertheless, given that e-cigarette emissions contain a number of chemicals of concern and to the extent that they are not risk-free, compensatory consumer behavior responding to nicotine limits could increase exposure to e-liquid constituents.

Supply-side technological adaptations that may partially undo the intent of nicotine limits should also be anticipated. Increasing the wick size or the power of atomizers could allow the user to vaporize a larger amount of e-liquid, again exposing the consumer to greater emissions.[242] That could allow the consumer to subvert the intended benefit of the nicotine limit, but there are potentially important health implications of these adaptations, too; higher operating temperatures and increased volume exposure to e-cigarette aerosol could increase health risks.[243]

If e-cigarette users do find lower nicotine products to be dissatisfying, they may be incentivized to opt for illicit, riskier analogs. They might also add their own unregulated nicotine to regulated products, which could also result in harm (not necessarily from the nicotine itself but from the other unknown chemicals or impurities that may be present in an unregulated product). One possible avenue for regulation would be to impose modest (yet not severe) restrictions on the nicotine content of commercially available e-cigarettes while allowing, and perhaps even encouraging, higher concentration in pharmaceutically approved e-cigarettes prescribed for purposes of cessation from smoking.

In June 2022, the FDA announced plans to reduce the levels of nicotine in combustible cigarettes to levels incapable of sustaining addiction[244] in an attempt to encourage smokers to quit and to discourage future uptake. Faced with the prospect of very low-nicotine cigarettes (VLNC), a surge in demand for illicit products contravening the limit should be anticipated. While it is uncertain exactly what form supply of illicit cigarettes would take in the U.S. if large differences in state taxes were no longer the driving force behind interstate trafficking, experience with Prohibition and the War on Drugs shows that the creativity of illicit suppliers in response to a large profit motive should not be discounted.

Recall also the "Iron Law of Prohibition" discussed in Volume II, Chapter 3, Sect. 1.1.2.1, which states that the potency of an illicit addictive substance will *rise* as efforts to eradicate it increase. However, maintaining the level of nicotine in regulated e-cigarettes could help mitigate this response, and increase smoking cessation in the process.[245] Protecting the availability and consumer-acceptability of e-cigarettes is likely to be a key component of the success of the VLNC rule.[246]

6.7 *Differential Restrictions on Flavors*

Many countries ban the use of characterizing flavors in combustible cigarettes. The availability of a broader range of flavors is therefore an important difference between e-cigarettes and combustibles. When considering flavor restrictions for e-cigarettes, it is crucial to recognize the inherent tradeoffs, similar to those encountered in other areas of tobacco regulation. The propensity for youth using e-cigarettes to choose flavored e-cigarettes has been cited as both a driver of the "epidemic" in youth vaping and proof that manufacturers are targeting children. Many jurisdictions have banned sales of flavored e-cigarettes entirely.[247,248] Others, for example a few cities in the U.S., and British Columbia in Canada have restricted the sale of flavored e-cigarettes to adult-only venues such as specialty tobacco retailers.

However, a range of flavors appeals to adult e-cigarette users as well as to youth.[249] Figure 4 shows a quartic regression for the probability that a current adult e-cigarette user usually chooses a flavored (i.e., a flavor other than tobacco) e-cigarette, as a function of age. While the propensity to use flavored e-cigarettes declines with age, it is more likely than not for all ages from 18 to 69. Compared with the use of tobacco-flavored e-cigarettes, the use of other flavors appears to increase the likelihood of successfully quitting smoking,[250,251] although at least one study (albeit without a study design that permits estimation of causal effects) finds no such association.[252] Friedman and Warner[253] point out the problem with such interventions: they leave combustibles easier to access than appealing reduced-harm options. Accordingly, increased smoking has been reported in response to flavor restrictions.[254]

If there was evidence that specific flavors were uniquely, or at least specifically, appealing to young consumers, that might provide a path forward. Some studies have reported that age is predictive of certain flavor preferences.[255] In particular, a preference for tobacco and mint/

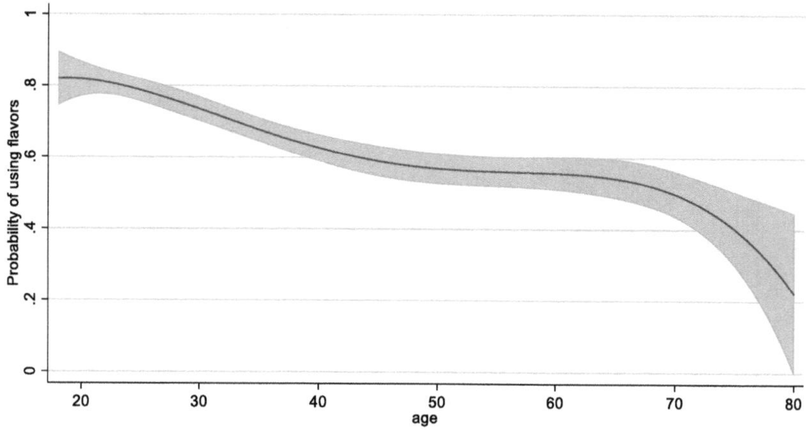

Fig. 4 How choice of using non-tobacco-flavored e-cigarettes varies with age among U.S. adults (*Notes* The plotted curve from the predicted values from a survey-weighted linear probability model in which a binary variable for usual usage of a flavored e-cigarette was regressed on a quartic specification of age. The estimates are for the subpopulation of some-day and every-day current e-cigarette users. The 95% confidence band accounts for the complex survey design. Estimation is by the authors; data are from the CPS-TUS 2018–2019)

menthol flavors appear to be less common among younger consumers: Data from the Population Assessment of Tobacco and Health (PATH) Study show that whereas 74% of adult e-cigarette users aged 25 and older used tobacco, menthol, or mint flavored e-cigarettes, only 42% of 18 to 24 year-olds and 36% of 12 to 17 year-olds did so.[256] Other studies have also reported a preference for mint/menthol and tobacco flavors among older e-cigarette users and dual users.[257,258,259,260] However, Fig. 5 (computed similarly to the previous figure) shows that the majority of adult users in the U.S. of all ages up to 71 also prefer e-cigarettes in flavors other than tobacco, mint, or menthol (including sweet and candy flavors). Whereas the PATH study just asked whether the individual had used a particular flavor in the past month, the relationship in Fig. 5, based on CPS-TUS data, is for the *usual* flavor of e-cigarettes consumed. Thus, even though many older adults say they used tobacco, menthol, or mint flavored e-cigarettes, at most ages they still usually prefer other flavors.

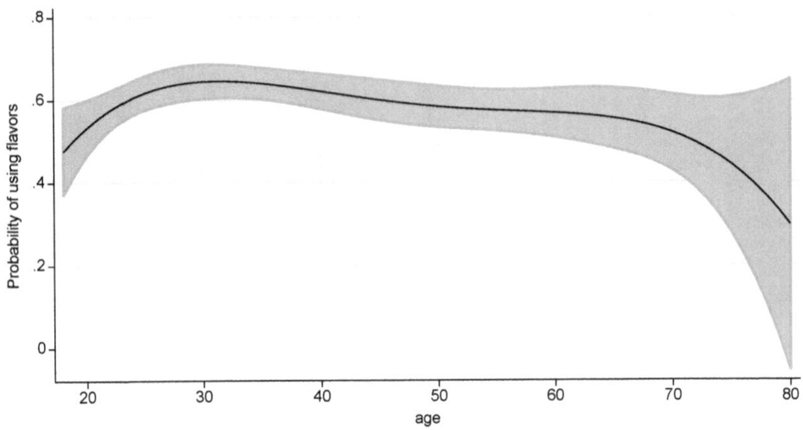

Fig. 5 How choice of using flavored e-cigarettes other than tobacco, menthol, or mint) varies with age among U.S. adults (*Notes* The plotted curve from the predicted values from a survey-weighted linear probability model in which a binary variable for usual usage of an e-cigarette that was clove, spice, herb, fruit, alcohol, candy, sweets, or chocolate flavored was regressed on a quartic specification of age. The estimates are for the subpopulation of some-day and every-day current e-cigarette users for which the non-tobacco flavor of usual e-cigarette is known. The 95% confidence band accounts for the complex survey design. Estimation is by the authors; data are from the CPS-TUS 2018–2019)

Former smokers and dual users may choose tobacco or menthol flavored e-cigarettes similar to the combustible cigarettes they have a history of using.[261] Since tobacco and menthol flavors are not typically as attractive to never-smokers as other flavors, it follows that at least these flavors should remain on the market. Challenging the suggestion that those flavors alone should remain available is the fact that both dual users and former smokers have been found to prefer fruit and other flavors to mint/menthol, tobacco and unflavored e-cigarettes.[262] (This is more specific than the evidence shown in Fig. 5, which is for all current users of e-cigarettes.) These results suggest that flavors drive interest in e-cigarettes by those seeking to quit smoking.[263] In fact, there is considerable overlap between the preferences of young e-cigarette users and older adults, especially regarding mint and fruit flavors.[264] Moreover, flavor migration has been reported among long-term e-cigarette users, and it appears to be common for e-cigarette users to begin with tobacco, menthol, or mint flavors but to shift to sweeter flavors over time.[265] If so, tobacco and menthol flavors might help newly quit ex-smokers approximate the experience of smoking cigarettes, but different flavors might be useful in preventing relapse.[266] Restricting access to non-tobacco e-cigarette flavors may discourage smokers from attempting to switch to e-cigarettes.[267]

As an alternative to a broad ban on flavored e-cigarettes, Friedman and Warner[268] suggest restricting the sale of all nicotine products to age-gated venues. If effective, that policy would prevent young people from legally accessing flavored e-cigarettes without sacrificing the usefulness of flavors for adults trying to quit or maintain abstinence from combustible cigarettes. Age restrictions should prevent youth from purchasing either cigarettes or e-cigarettes, but the ubiquity of product availability across a range of retail outlet types creates enforcement challenges undermining the efficacy of age restrictions. Friedman and Warner further suggest that limiting all sales to age-gated venues would facilitate enforcement. Point-of-entrance age-gating could even be automated. Still, the political viability of this proposal is, as the authors note, a likely obstacle. And commercial interests, including retail associations, distributors, and manufacturers, will likely lobby against it. However, if the alternative is the elimination of the flavors as a product category, such a proposal might be in their interests, too. Another proposal from the same authors suggests that any non-age-gated retailers could be required to stock all nicotine products out of sight. That could be coupled with a ban on marketing at point-of-sale to eliminate the environmental cues. Tobacco retailer license fees for open-access locations could also be set higher than those for non-age-gated venues, encouraging concentration of sales in the latter. That fee differential could also help the state recoup the costs of enforcement in open venues. That option, perhaps coupled with penalties for violations that are scaled in accordance with the retail outlet operating size, and increased for repeat offenders, could help prevent young people's access to e-cigarettes while reserving the features that make them appealing substitutes for older smokers.

Another possible variation on differential regulation is that retailers could be required to designate a proportion of shelf space to non-combustible alternatives as a condition of their tobacco-retail license. To the extent that environmental cues remain, those could be leveraged to encourage or at least make it easy to choose a less risky alternative.

7 Further Considerations for Optimizing E-cigarette Regulation

Apart from the tradeoffs and opportunities for regulatory differentials just discussed, there are several additional factors that policy-makers should consider as they craft regulation for e-cigarettes. Regulation can be more or less burdensome, depending on the form it takes. Regulation can result in a more concentrated market on the supply side, which has several negative consequences. Uncertainty involved with regulatory decisions can also adversely affect markets. Finally, enforcement issues must be considered.

7.1 Regulatory Burden

Regulation can create social benefits when prompted by, and well-designed to address, market failures. Nevertheless, even in such cases, regulation imposes costs on the regulated industry. The burden created for firms by the regulatory requirements are a choice variable for the regulator. Those costs must be considered against the benefits of regulation, whether the imperative comes from cost–benefit analysis, social welfare analysis, or government mandates to conduct regulatory impact analyses. In some cases, the current regulatory barriers are highly costly to overcome. PMI's regulatory application to be allowed to claim in the U.S. market that its iQOS heated tobacco product exposes users to reduced amounts of harmful chemicals (compared to smoking) provides a good example. The initial filing to the FDA involved many costly laboratory and clinical studies, promises to perform additional post-marketing studies, hundreds of documents, and thousands of pages. The FDA required several parts of the filing to be amended and resubmitted. The entire review process, not including the time spent by PMI preparing for the first submission, was over three and a half years.

Regulatory compliance creates fixed costs for product introduction and production. In addition to the direct costs of regulation for firms, regulatory delay itself creates an additional burden by diminishing the present value of future revenue. These regulatory costs of delay and other costly or complex aspects of regulation have been shown to reduce product innovation in several other industries such as telecommunications, finance, and pharmaceuticals.[269] Retarding innovation in reduced-harm tobacco products may have high costs in terms of health. The more innovative and appealing products there are aimed at the market of current smokers, the larger the first term for cessation on the right side of Eq. (3) and the likelihood that total health improves.

Regulation also can impose burdens on consumers. By raising product prices, either directly by increasing the variable costs of production or by increasing the market power of manufacturers or retailers (as discussed in the next section), regulation can have negative distributional effects. Several studies have shown that regulation increases prices for consumers, which disproportionately affects low-income individuals and increases inequality.[270] The importance of designing tobacco product regulations to avoid negative distributional consequences has already been discussed above in Sect. 5.5 (point 5). Placing heavy entry regulation on new tobacco products, if existing manufacturers remain free to introduce new brands of cigarettes with little oversight, appears to be especially perverse in this respect.

Perhaps it should not be surprising that regulators often have blind spots regarding the impact of the burden that regulation places on market participants. After all, many of the impacts are unseen, taking the form of beneficial outcomes that are prevented. While it is second nature for econometricians and other empirical social scientists to think about the impact of policy relative to the unseen, counterfactual state of the world that would have obtained in the absence of the policy, this is not a particularly natural way for government bureaucrats (much less the general public) to think. Annual regulatory reports do not list the products not created, the potential entrants that never materialized, or the lower product prices there might have been in the absence of the regulatory burden. Thus, as economist Russell Sobel has put it, regulation is often costlier than it at first appears.[271] This is particularly true when regulating a disruptive innovation such as e-cigarettes. When a new product falls within an agency's jurisdiction, but does not neatly fit into previously established pathways of regulation, then the innovation also creates regulatory disruption.[272] The resulting upheaval often results in additional regulation, as happened with at the FDA with the pre-market approval process set up for e-cigarette products. Almost humorously, the agency justified its new, lengthy, and burdensome rules for bringing new products to market and allowing existing products to stay on the market with the argument that in the absence of such "guidance" manufacturers would have an even more difficult time figuring out the existing regulatory pathway.[273] In other words, because the existing regulatory burden and uncertainty, more burden was needed to reduce the burden.[274] This sort of reasoning is endemic to bureaucracies. As William Niskanen and James Q. Wilson have pointed out, the tendency of all bureaus is to expand, because the incentive for bureaucrats is to maximize their budget.[275] One way to justify larger budgets is to present evidence to Congress of "measurable output" such as, in the present case, the number of pre-market clearance applications processed.

7.2 Avoid Concentrating Market Power

Despite any well-meaning intentions behind regulation, a common adverse consequence, viewed from society's perspective if not the regulator's, is the tendency for it to promote market concentration of the industry overseen. By raising the cost to bring a new product to market, or to bring an existing product to a new market, regulation creates entry barriers. These barriers benefit large incumbents at the expense of smaller firms and potential entrants.[276] The chain of logic, borne out by empirical evidence, is straightforward: regulatory compliance costs increase fixed costs (whether sunk costs of product introduction or ongoing fixed costs of production), which strengthens the magnitude of economies of scale, which results in larger firm sizes in equilibrium.[277] Whether this is the result of regulation motivated by the public interest or, less benignly, by the capture of the regulator by the regulated industry (as posited by the public choice literature), the result is the same. Large incumbents gain market power, and as a consequence, the prices they charge and their resulting profits may be expected to rise. Take cigarette and tobacco manufacturers in the U.S., for example. During a time of declining industry revenue, rising excise taxes, local and state product sales bans, and uncertainty regarding e-cigarette regulation, the industry's return on assets in 2019–2021 averaged 48.4% per annum, whereas from 2007 to 2018 the ROA averaged only 32.9%.[278] With higher prices and insulation from competition,[279] profit rates can rise even as revenue falls.

In contrast to many of the other industries studied by regulatory economists, tobacco products create negative externalities or health harms that short-sighted consumers do not fully price into their consumption decisions. Therefore, it may be tempting to conclude that if regulation helps consolidate industry supply into the hands of only a few firms, which will then charge oligopolistic prices, so much the better. The case for why externalities and internalities are likely to be much lower for e-cigarettes than for combustible tobacco has already been discussed. Regardless, there are other reasons why relying on market power is likely not the best—or even a good—remedy to reduce demand. Any target price desired by policy-makers could be achieved with a tax instead of through excess profits earned by tobacco companies, and the tax revenue could then be used to reduce public debt, lower distortionary income taxes, or fund tobacco control efforts. Furthermore, a concentrated industry will use its market power to pass taxes through to consumers in a manner it desires to maintain demand and profitability, not necessarily the manner in which the regulators hope for (refer to the discussion in Sect. 5.3.2). In contrast, at the other extreme of industrial organization, a fully competitive industry has no choice at all how to pass taxes through to consumers. Finally, taxes raise variable costs for all firms' sales, and therefore do not necessarily tip the market balance toward large firms.[280]

When supply is in the hands of a highly concentrated industry, and the market power of incumbents can be supported by regulation relatively favorable to them instead of entrants and smaller firms, public choice theory warns that socially inefficient rent-seeking will occur.[281] In this context, "rents" are excess returns paid to the owner of a resource, which is this case is membership in the oligopolists' club artificially supported by onerous regulation for small firms and would-be entrants.[282] Rent-seeking here can take the form of lobbying, but from a certain point of view the expense of jumping through regulatory hoops to be allowed to make reduced-harm claims for a product is also rent-seeking: nothing of intrinsic social value is produced, and the only reason the firms make the expenditure is to chase after oligopoly rents. Rent-seeking is a pure loss to economic welfare, however the latter is defined.

7.3 *Regulatory Uncertainty*

R&D, innovation, and commercializing a new product is expensive. As of 2023, PMI claims to have spent US$10.5 billion on smoke-free products since 2008 for R&D (including studies to support their regulatory filings for iQOS), capital costs for new production, and commercial development.[283] While it is not known who first uttered the phrase, "uncertainty kills investment," it is well known on Wall Street and in C-suites around the world. When the riskiness of the return available to an investment product or new product launch rises, the breakeven required expected return also rises. Much theoretical and empirical work in regulatory economics has shown that regulatory risk in general, and due to regulatory delay in particular, can lead to lower investment and fewer product introductions.[284]

As long as appropriate regulatory and legal protections are in place to hamper youth access to tobacco products, the considerations raised here and in the previous two sections call for steering away from regulatory frameworks that effectively raise high entry barriers for new products, whether from direct compliance costs, regulatory delay, or uncertainty. Pharmaceutical and medical device regulators such as the FDA are used to imposing costly pre-marketing requirement on firms wishing to gain approval for new products. After the fact, it is no surprise therefore that the agency applied a similar model to the tobacco products it is allowed to regulate. However, new drugs or medical devices make a poor analogy to reduced-harm tobacco products. It is important to remember that smokers are already consuming a highly dangerous product; for them, nearly any conceivable non-combustible product would present less risk upon switching. Thus, the mindset of a speed-safety tradeoff in regulatory approval time does not apply as it does for other new goods under the FDA's remit. For the potential market of current smokers, there is virtually no tradeoff at all. The faster a reduced-harm product can get to market, the sooner it can begin reducing health harm. Furthermore, even *if* the standard speed-safety tradeoff applies, researchers have shown that until legislators incentivized the FDA to speed up drug approvals, the agency was dragging its feet to the great detriments of health and economic surplus.[285] Furthermore, that example also revealed that the agency had no scientific guiding principles by which it determines the optimal amount of regulatory scrutiny and delay for new product introductions; simply put, "no product application would pass the FDA approval process with the quality and type of evidence that currently exists for evaluating the FDA policies themselves."[286]

8 Appropriate E-cigarette Regulations Complement Tobacco Control

As recounted in Volume II, Chapter 3, in some quarters the existence of e-cigarettes has been lamented as potentially undoing decades of progress in tobacco control.[287] In such arguments, the phrase "renormalization of smoking"—the great fear of many in the tobacco control community—occurs often. These fears prompt calls for prohibitions or at least strict regulation of e-cigarettes. However, as has been emphasized elsewhere in this book, tobacco control and the market for e-cigarettes are not two players in a zero-sum game. Appropriate regulation of e-cigarettes, by which we mean regulation that leaves the safer products available as attractive options for smokers to switch to while stemming youth access, can complement tobacco control aimed at traditional combustible products. As stated by Public Health England, e-cigarettes "have the potential to help drive down smoking rates, *de-normalize* smoking and improve public health" (emphasis added).[288] E-cigarettes may also increase the effectiveness of other cessation aids, foster compliance with smoke-free bans, convert public expenditure on expensive pharmacotherapies to relatively inexpensive private spending on e-cigarettes, and reduce certain unintended consequences of more stringent tobacco control.

Pharmaceutical aids to cessation from smoking are an important component of many smokers' efforts to quit. Regulation that promotes the use of e-cigarettes for cessation (as in England), or at least does not steer smokers away from using them to quit, can complement the efficacy of other cessation aids. As discussed in Volume II, Chapter 2, Sect. 6, combining e-cigarettes with traditional cessation therapies has been shown in a few studies to be particularly effective for smokers to achieve cessation.[289] E-cigarettes can satisfy the physiological craving for a nicotine hit and the behavioral desires for a hand-to-mouth experience and other sensory stimulation that other cessation aids do not provide.[290] However, more studies evaluating the effectiveness of e-cigarettes when used in combination with other cessation aids are needed.[291]

Another area in which e-cigarettes can complement tobacco control efforts concerns compliance. In some countries, compliance with smoke-free laws is generally high,[292] while in others (often lesser developed countries) it is abysmal.[293] As discussed in Sect. 6.2 above, more lenient public-use policies for e-cigarettes could increase compliance with bans on smoking in public places. While some public health researchers view use of e-cigarettes in public places as nothing more than "circumvention" of smoke-free laws and call for extending all public-use bans to vaping,[294] e-cigarettes can provide an outlet for individuals likely to flout smoking bans in areas with weak enforcement, and would create far fewer negative health externalities.

Given their appeal to a wide range of smokers and the potential to assist in smoking cessation, some smokers willingly pay for e-cigarettes even when subsidized or free alternative cessation aids are available. In the

U.K., where use of e-cigarettes are championed for smoking cessation, publicly funded expenditure on prescriptionNRT and other pharmacotherapies (varenicline and bupropion) in 2021/2022 was less than a quarter of the expenditure a decade earlier (in nominal terms).[295] Some but by no means all of this reduction is due to the declining prevalence of smoking, since the number of adult smokers declined by only about one-third during that time.[296] During 2020 to 2022, the quit rate for individuals attempting cessation was 55.7%, up over nine percentage points from a decade earlier. As mentioned in Volume III, Chapter 1, despite a recent pilot program offering free e-cigarette kits for purposes of cessation, smokers in the U.K. who use e-cigarettes to quit smoking have, to date, done so with money out of their own pockets. The public money saved in this regard, £50 million for England over the decade mentioned, can be reallocated to other public health needs or used to reduce the national debt.

Finally, the availability of affordable and regulated e-cigarettes can reduce unintended consequences of more stringent tobacco control. For example, e-cigarettes can help increase the efficacy of higher taxes on combustibles by providing a safety valve for demand that otherwise might go to illicit markets for cigarettes. Two econometric analyses of data from the EU and elsewhere suggests that the availability of e-cigarettes may attenuate smokers' tendency to respond to increased tobacco taxes by embracing illicit sources.[297] Reducing the price gap between e-cigarettes and combustibles is likely to reduce this desirable effect. The continued availability of e-cigarettes, at least in the near term, may also support the FDA's efforts to introduce a very low nicotine content rule for combustibles.[298] E-cigarettes can complement this and other regulatory interventions aimed at ending use of combustible tobacco.[299]

9 How Do We Get There from Here?

In Eugene Bardach's classic book on public policy analysis, he introduces the image of an eightfold path to organize efforts to solve social problems more effectively.[300] The first and second steps are to "define the problem" and "assemble some evidence." Volume I, Chapter 2 examined the nature and extent of smoking harms worldwide, concluding that despite the broad application of tobacco control policies and the widespread availability of behavioral therapy programs, pharmacotherapies andNRTs, smoking rates cannot be expected to reach "smoke-free" levels (sometimes defined as a prevalence below 5% in any given community) in this generation. Bardach's third step is to construct the alternatives. In Volume I, Chapter 3 we explored how e-cigarettes have disrupted the tobacco market, gaining market share on combustibles. By some estimates there are over 80 million users worldwide. But e-cigarettes' utility for smoking cessation is dictated by consumption patterns (who uses which products, how often, and why) which hinges on knowledge and beliefs about these products. These, in turn, are influenced by regulatory decisions. Volume II, Chapter 1 examined how, while e-cigarettes are not risk-free, they are significantly safer than their combustible substitutes. That chapter also explored concerns that e-cigarettes could also introduce novel risk elements. While this evidence does not generally constitute evidence that e-cigarettes are causing significant end-point harms in the real world, it should not be ignored out of hand. Volume II, Chapter 2 then explored the evidence regarding e-cigarettes' efficacy as a cessation aid, including for the many smokers who have been "left behind" by conventional approaches. Volume II, Chapter 3 explored how, beyond different interpretations of the available data, the debate over e-cigarettes has become polarized, misaligning the public's perceptions of e-cigarettes risks with the evidence, and ultimately influencing consumer behavior and regulatory decisions in ways that undermined their potential benefit to public health.

Bardach's next three steps are to "select the criteria by which a policy may be evaluated"; "project the outcomes," and "confront the trade-offs." Volume III attempts to address these topics, though we have not necessarily addressed these in the order presented by Bardach. Volume III, Chapter 1 reviewed the contemporary approaches to e-cigarettes and examined why these have not only failed to eliminate the demand for e-cigarettes but have resulted in unintended consequences. First, the free-market approach fails to curb experimental use leading to rapid uptake by young people and never-smokers, and fails to provide safeguards that protect the consumer; the absence of regulation leads to production and marketing practices that maximize the pursuit of profit, at the expense of public health, resulting in substandard products that unduly risk injury and illness. Prohibitions and bans also fail to eliminate use, driving demand, or at least some portion of it, underground to illicit markets where, again, the pursuit of profit leads to more dangerous products and marketing practices. And many young e-cigarette users living in jurisdictions that have introduced e-cigarette restrictions resembling tobacco control policies (age restrictions, flavor bans, and taxes for example) have responded by simply reverting to the most accessible (and dangerous) nicotine product—combustible cigarettes. E-cigarette bans also send a strong message to smokers that the use of combustibles is preferable to vaping. This directly contradicts the science, and reduces the incentive to use e-cigarettes to support smoking cessation, prompting a return to smoking on the part of those who have used e-cigarettes to quit along with, perhaps, a reduction in the rate of future substitutions, and greater demand for illicit products. Finally, regulations that place equal restrictions on e-cigarettes and combustible tobacco forgo an opportunity to encourage substitutions from more harmful cigarettes to less harmful e-cigarettes.

The resulting reduction in smoking cessation is not only a risk for adult smokers but also for the broader community. However, while the polarized debate about e-cigarettes often paints the regulatory options for e-cigarettes as a three-way choice between a regulatory free-for-all, stringent prohibitions, and the treat-as-tobacco model, there is a fourth option: risk-proportionate regulation. Volume III, Chapter 2, has explored how risk-proportionate regulation could maximize the benefits of alternative nicotine for adult smoking cessation, while also taking steps to minimize the costs associated with contemporary approaches. As implored by Bardach we have confronted tradeoffs and projected outcomes.

The final step in Bardach's path to effective policy-making is to "tell your story." This book, and the following pages in particular are dedicated to this endeavor. Many potentially beneficial policies are never adopted because those tasked with communicating the policy decision, and the data and analysis underpinning them, fail to secure "buy in" from key stakeholders, or fail to persuade their opponents that the data on which their decisions were made is even admissible to begin with. As discussed in Volume II, Chapter 3, advocates of THR frequently lament the emotional basis for many of the arguments made by skeptics against e-cigarettes and harm reduction and the fact that "ideology" forces the public in general (and regulators in particular) to overlook scientific evidence. But while such ideological, emotional, and rhetorical arguments are belied by the evidence (much of which has been presented in this book), emotion remains a powerful force, both for individual and collective behavior.

Regardless of the validity of the concerns about e-cigarettes, the perception that THR advocates are dismissive of, or condescending towards, skeptics' convictions is unlikely to help engender consensus.

The provision of more data, while often called for by skeptics, is also not necessarily conducive to resolution. Given that different participants in the discourse on e-cigarettes have different values and priorities, the articulation of ever-more compelling evidence is only going to change minds if it addresses the core concerns of the audience. This situation does not require that concessions be made when unsupported by evidence, nor does it suggest that more and better data would not be valuable. Nonetheless, a good measure of humility could help engender receptivity to the evidence. Advocating for harmed communities, THR recognizes the value in "meeting people where they are." THR advocates might do well to extend that maxim to their opponents; recognizing that they have different sentiments, concerns, and priorities: a more pronounced risk aversion; a stronger concern about nicotine dependence—even in the absence of the medical harms of combustion; and an expressed preference for protecting young people, even at the expense of a larger group of older adults. At the inter-personal level, it would likely be futile to challenge those partialities directly, and may even be counterproductive, engendering backlash.

However, that does not leave THR defenseless: We *should not* deny "risk" an important role in cost–benefit analyses, but risk should factor into both sides of the equation. Nicotine dependence *should not* necessarily be considered harmless, even in the absence of demonstrable medical risks; but whatever harms remain should be carefully articulated, and care must be taken not to equate addiction in the context of demonstrable smoking-harms to nicotine dependence decoupled from those risks. Recall also that total nicotine use appears to be declining even as the use of e-cigarettes increases. Finally, young people are an important group. With more future life-years in which to experience harms, there may even be some logic behind the intuition that young peoples' well-being matters more than those of older adults. But the evidence suggests that restrictions on e-cigarettes harm this group specifically by encouraging young experimenters back to combustibles and encouraging those initiating nicotine use to do so with more harmful cigarettes. Such restrictions also harm youth by perpetuating smoking in proximate adults, continuing a pattern by which smoking is modeled across generations, and exposing youth to second-hand smoke. Of course, there are numerous other reasons to (1.1 billion in fact—the number of smokers) to hope that e-cigarettes might have utility for the broader public. If advocates are serious about winning over skeptics, these are the "stories" that should be told.

Notes

1. Koop, C.E. Don't Forget the Smokers; *The Washington Post 03/08/1998.* Available at: https://www.washingtonpost.com/archive/opinions/1998/03/08/dont-forget-the-smokers/3560fbed-880a-45ff-8669-110fd8b63509/.
2. Buchanan, J.M., Tullock, G. *The Calculus of Consent: Logical Foundations of Constitutional Democracy* 1965 (Vol. 100). University of Michigan Press.
3. Eggertsson, T. *Imperfect Institutions: Possibilities and the Limits of Reform.* Ann Arbor, MI: University of Michigan Press, 2005.
4. Eichler, H.G., Bloechl-Daum, B., Brasseur, D., Breckenridge, A., Leufkens, H., Raine, J., Salmonson, T., Schneider, C.K., Rasi, G. The Risks of Risk Aversion in Drug Regulation. Nat Rev Drug Discov. 2013;12(12):907–916. https://doi.org/10.1038/nrd4129.
5. Choi, S.J., Pritchard, A.C. Behavioral Economics and the SEC. Stan L Rev. 2003:1–73.
6. Jolls, C., Sunstein, C.R., Thaler, R. A Behavioral Approach to Law and Economics. Stan L Rev. 1997;50:1471–1550. https://doi.org/10.2307/1229304
7. Le Grand, J. The Theory of Government Failure. Br J Polit Sci. 1991;21(4):423–442.
8. Schuck, P.H. *Why Government Fails so Often: And How It Can Do Better*. Princeton University Press, 2015.
9. Klein, D.E., Chaiton, M., Kundu, A., et al. A Literature Review on International E-cigarette Regulatory Policies. Curr Addict Rep. 2020;7:509–519. https://doi.org/10.1007/s40429-020-00332-w.
10. *Premarket Tobacco Product Applications and Recordkeeping Requirements*, 86 FR 55300.
11. Art. 13.1.b of the TPD prohibits any suggestion "that a particular tobacco product is less harmful than others or aims to reduce the effect of some harmful components of smoke." See

EU Directive 2014/40/EU (https://eur-lex.europa.eu/legal-content/EN/TXT/PDF/?uri=CELEX:32014L0040).

12. Food Standards Act 1999.
13. Title 21, U.S. Code of Federal Regulations, Part 110.110.
14. Klein, D.E., Chaiton, M., Kundu, A., et al. A Literature Review on International E-cigarette Regulatory Policies. Curr Addict Rep. 2020;7:509–519. https://doi.org/10.1007/s40429-020-00332-w.
15. Peltzman, S. The Effects of Automobile Safety Regulation. J Polit Econ. 1975;83:677–725. https://doi.org/10.1086/260352
16. The canonical example of the Peltzman effect is how mandating seatbelts in automobiles can lead to riskier driving, since drivers feel the expected costs of doing so has been decreased.
17. Here we gloss over the distinction that regulatory officials typically do not have the power to tax. In this section we use "regulator" as a shorthand for any policy-maker with authority (or potential authority) over e-cigarettes.
18. Klein, D.E., Chaiton, M., Kundu, A., et al. A Literature Review on International E-cigarette Regulatory Policies. Curr Addict Rep. 2020;7:509–519. https://doi.org/10.1007/s40429-020-00332-w.
19. World Health Organization. (2022). Font Style, Font Size and Colour of Health Warnings Are Mandated for Cigarette Packaging (Tobacco Control: Health Warnings). The Global Health Observatory, Indicators database. https://www.who.int/data/gho/data/indicators/indicator-details/GHO/gho-tobacco-control-warnings-cigarettes-w6-font-a.
20. Andrews, J.C., Netemeyer, R.G., Kees, J., Burton, S. How Graphic Visual Health Warnings Affect Young Smokers' Thoughts of Quitting. J Market Res. 2014;51(2):165–183. https://doi.org/10.1509/jmr.13.0092
21. Kees, J., Burton, S., Andrews, J.C., Kozup, J. Tests of Graphic Visuals and Cigarette Package Warning Combinations: Implications for the Framework Convention on Tobacco Control. J Public Policy & Market. 2006;25(2):212–223.
22. Netemeyer, R.G., Burton, S., Andrews, J.C., Kees, J. Graphic Health Warnings on Cigarette Packages: The Role of Emotions

in Affecting Adolescent Smoking Consideration and Secondhand Smoke Beliefs. J Public Policy & Market. 2016;35(1):124–143. https://doi.org/10.1509/jppm.15.008

23. However, any regulator operating under the requirement of evidence-based policy would likely have to change some of the warnings. For example, one of the warnings on packaging in the U.S. for decades states that "Smoking Causes Lung Cancer, Heart Disease, Emphysema, and May Complicate Pregnancy"; as discussed in Volume II, Chapter 1, the available evidence to date would not support such unqualified causal claims for e-cigarettes.

24. Sindelar, J.L. Regulating Vaping—Policies, Possibilities, and Perils. N Engl J Med. 2020 May 14;382(20):e54. https://doi.org/10.1056/NEJMp1917065.
25. Therapeutic Goods Administration. (December 21, 2020). TGA Confirms Nicotine E-cigarette Access Is by Prescription Only. Australian Government, Department of Health and Aged Care, Press release. https://www.tga.gov.au/news/media-releases/tga-confirms-nicotine-e-cigarette-access-prescription-only.
26. Aziani, A., Carbone, C., Favarin, S., Corradini, S. A Multi-Disciplinary Study into the Drivers of Smoking Cessation in Australia, 2020, available at: SSRN: https://ssrn.com/abstract=3813004
27. Mendelsohn, C. (April 15, 2019). Doctors Who Prescribe Nicotine. We Need YOU! *ATHRA*. https://www.athra.org.au/blog/2019/04/15/doctors-who-prescribe-nicotine-we-need-you.
28. White, S.L., Harper, T., DeMaio, S. (July 18, 2022). Failure to Enforce E-Cigarette Regulation Now Will Fail Us All. Insightplus. https://insightplus.mja.com.au/2022/27/failure-to-enforce-e-cigarette-regulation-now-will-fail-us-all/.
29. Yingying, Xu., Lanxin, Jiang., Shivaani, Prakash., Tengjiao, Chen. The Impact of Banning Electronic Nicotine Delivery Systems on Combustible Cigarette Sales: Evidence from US State-Level Policies. Value in Health. 2022;25(8):1352-1359. https://doi.org/10.1016/j.jval.2021.12.006.
30. U.S. Department of Health and Human Services. *The Health Consequences of Smoking—50 Years of Progress: A Report of the Surgeon General*. Atlanta: U.S. Department of Health and Human Services, Centers for Disease Control and Prevention,

National Center for Chronic Disease Prevention and Health Promotion, Office on Smoking and Health, 2014.
31. Cahill, K., Lindson-Hawley, N., Thomas, K.H., Fanshawe, T.R., Lancaster, T. Nicotine Receptor Partial Agonists for Smoking Cessation. Cochrane Database Syst Rev. 2016;5:Art. No.: CD006103. https://doi.org/10.1002/14651858.CD006103.pub7.
32. Sowell, T. *A Conflict of Visions: Ideological Origins of Political Struggles* (Revised ed.). Basic Books, 2007 [First published 1987].
33. Lee, P.N., Abrams, D., Bachand, A., Baker, G., Black, R., Camacho, O., Curtin, G., Djurdjevic, S., Hill, A., Mendez, D., Muhammad-Kah, R.S., Murillo, J.L., Niaura, R., Pithawalla, Y.B., Poland, B., Sulsky, S., Wei, L., Weitkunat, R. Estimating the Population Health Impact of Recently Introduced Modified Risk Tobacco Products: A Comparison of Different Approaches. Nicotine Tob Res. 2021 Feb 16;23(3):426–437. https://doi.org/10.1093/ntr/ntaa102.
34. Warner, K.E., Mendez, D. E-cigarettes: Comparing the Possible Risks of Increasing Smoking Initiation with the Potential Benefits of Increasing Smoking Cessation. Nicotine Tob Res. 2019 Jan 1;21(1):41–47. https://doi.org/10.1093/ntr/nty062.
35. Levy, D.T., Borland, R., Lindblom, E.N., et al. Potential Deaths Averted in USA by Replacing Cigarettes with E-cigarettes. Tob Control. 2018;27:18-25. https://doi.org/10.1136/tobaccocontrol-2017-053759
36. Levy, D.T., Tam, J., Sanchez-Romero, L.M., Li, Y., Yuan, Z., Jeon, J., Meza, R. Public Health Implications of Vaping in the USA: The Smoking and Vaping Simulation Model. Popul Health Metr. 2021;19:1–18. https://doi.org/10.1186/s12963-021-00250-7.
37. Bachand, A.M., Sulsky, S.I., Curtin, G.M. Assessing the Likelihood and Magnitude of a Population Health Benefit Following the Market Introduction of a Modified-Risk Tobacco Product: Enhancements to the Dynamic Population Modeler, DPM(+1). Risk Analysis. 2018;38(1):151–62. https://doi.org/10.1111/risa.12819.
38. Cherng, S.T., Tam, J., Christine, P.J., Meza, R. Modeling the Effects of E-cigarettes on Smoking Behavior: Implications

for Future Adult Smoking Prevalence. Epidemiology. 2016 Nov;27(6):819–26. https://doi.org/10.1097/EDE.0000000000000497.

39. This is not to say that in some of the extreme scenarios they consider, for example one in which e-cigarettes cause all cessation from smoking to cease and raise the smoking initiation rate by a factor of three (both of which are way out of line with the evidence), the opposite results can be generated.
40. Lee, P.N., Fry, J.S., Gilliland, S., Campbell, P., Joyce, A.R. Estimating the Reduction in US Mortality if Cigarettes Were Largely Replaced by E-cigarettes. Arch Toxicol. 2022 Jan;96(1):167-176. https://doi.org/10.1007/s00204-021-03180-3.
41. Hill, A., Camacho, O.M. A System Dynamics Modelling Approach to Assess the Impact of Launching a New Nicotine Product on Population Health Outcomes. Regulatory Toxicology and Pharmacology. 2017 Jun;86:265-278. https://doi.org/10.1016/j.yrtph.2017.03.012.
42. Soneji et al. is not a full system dynamics study in that it follows only the initial cohorts of smokers and non-smokers in the base year and follows them for their lives, instead of accounting for successive cohorts, population change, and migration over a fixed period of time.
43. Soneji, SS., Sung, H.Y., Primack, B.A., Pierce, J.P., Sargent, J.D. Quantifying Population-Level Health Benefits and Harms of E-cigarette Use in the United States. PLoS ONE. 2018 Mar 14;13(3):e0193328. https://doi.org/10.1371/journal.pone.0193328.
44. In particular, the study uses an odds ratio of 0.86 (e-cigarette users vs. others) for quitting smoking among smokers with an interest in quitting. This statistic was taken from a meta-study criticized elsewhere on various grounds, including selective inclusion of evidence, misrepresentation of studies covered, inclusion of studies subject to severe sample selection bias, and the fact that its conclusions are at odds with actual experience in the U.K., where the cessation rate rose as use of e-cigarettes increased (cite: West R, Bauld L, O'Connor R, Hajek P, McNeill A. Expert Reaction to Meta-analysis Looking at E-cigarette Use and Smoking

Cessation [Internet]. https://www.sciencemediacentre.org/expert-reaction-to-metaanalysis-looking-at-e-cigarette-use-and-smoking-cessation).

45. The figures mentioned are mean probabilities. In the authors' Monte Carlo methodology, other probabilities could be used in any one given of the simulation, but even the highest endpoint for the upper limit of the 95% confidence intervals for any age group is less than 5 percentage points increase in cessation from using e-cigarettes.
46. Zhu, S.H., Zhuang, Y.L., Wong, S., Cummins, S.E., Tedeschi, G.J. E-cigarette Use and Associated Changes in Population Smoking Cessation: Evidence from US Current Population Surveys. BMJ. 2017;358. https://doi.org/10.1136/bmj.j3262.
47. Brown, J., Beard, E., Kotz, D., Michie, S., West, R. Real-World Effectiveness of E-cigarettes When Used to Aid Smoking Cessation: A Cross-Sectional Population Study. Addiction. 2014;109(9):1531–1540. https://doi.org/10.1111/add.12623.
48. While the latter may not hold, the former almost certainly is true to some extent: there are clearly biological, genetic, cognitive, social, environmental, and preference factors in a young person's life other than the demographic variables and even the psychosocial and behavioral risk factors appearing in public health analyses that can predispose toward nicotine use, whether smoking, vaping, or both.
49. Levy, D.T., Warner, K.E., Cummings, K.M., et al. Examining the Relationship of Vaping to Smoking Initiation Among US Youth and Young Adults: A Reality Check. Tob Control. 2019;28:629–635. https://doi.org/10.1136/tobaccocontrol-2018-054446.
50. Kalkhoran, S., Glantz, S.A. Modeling the Health Effects of Expanding E-cigarette Sales in the United States and United Kingdom: A Monte Carlo Analysis. JAMA Intern Med. 2015 Oct 1;175(10):1671–1680. https://doi.org/10.1001/jamainternmed.2015.4209.
51. Allcott, H., Rafkin, C. Optimal Regulation of E-cigarettes: Theory and Evidence. Am Econ J Econ Policy. 2022;14(4):1–50. https://doi.org/10.1257/pol.20200805

52. Friedman, A.S. How Does Electronic Cigarette Access Affect Adolescent Smoking? J Health Econ. 2015;44:300–308. https://doi.org/10.1016/j.jhealeco.2015.10.003.
53. Pesko, M.F., Hughes, J.M., Faisal, F.S. The Influence of Electronic Cigarette Age Purchasing Restrictions on Adolescent Tobacco and Marijuana Use. Prev Med. 2016;87:207–212. https://doi.org/10.1016/j.ypmed.2016.02.001.
54. Cooper, M.T., Pesko, M.F. The Effect of E-cigarette Indoor Vaping Restrictions on Adult Prenatal Smoking and Birth Outcomes. J Health Econ. 2017;56:178–190. https://doi.org/10.1016/j.jhealeco.2017.10.002
55. Pesko, M.F., Warman, C. (2017). The Effect of Prices on Youth Cigarette and E-cigarette Use: Economic Substitutes or Complements? https://dx.doi.org/10.2139/ssrn.3077468.
56. Saffer, H., Dench, D., Dave, D., Grossman, M. E-cigarettes and Adult Smoking. NBER Working Paper No. 24212. 2018. https://dx.doi.org/10.3386/w24212.
57. Saffer, H., Grossman, M., Dave, D. E-cigarettes and Adult Smoking: Evidence from Minnesota. NBER Working Paper No. 26589. 2019. https://dx.doi.org/10.3386/w26589.
58. Abouk, R., Feng, B., Maclean, J.C., Pesko, M.F. The Effect of E-cigarette Taxes on Pre-Pregnancy and Prenatal Smoking, and Birth Outcomes. NBER Working Paper No. 26126. 2019. https://dx.doi.org/10.3386/w26126.
59. Cantrell, J., Huang, J., Greenberg, M.S., Xiao, H., Hair, E.C., Vallone, D. Impact of E-cigarette and Cigarette Prices on Youth and Young Adult E-cigarette and Cigarette Behaviour: Evidence from a National Longitudinal Cohort. Tob Control. 2020 Jul;29(4):374-380. https://dx.doi.org/10.1136/tobaccocontrol-2018-054764.
60. Dave, D., Feng, B., Pesko, M.F. The Effects of E-cigarette Minimum Legal Sale Age Laws on Youth Substance Use. Health Econ. 2019;28(3):419–436. https://dx.doi.org/10.1002/hec.3854.

61. Pesko, M.F., Currie, J.M. E-cigarette Minimum Legal Sale Age Laws and Traditional Cigarette Use Among Rural Pregnant Teenagers. J Health Econ. 2019;66:71–90. https://dx.doi.org/10.1016/j.jhealeco.2019.05.003
62. Cotti, C.D., Courtmanche, C.J., MacLean, J.C., Nesson, E., Pesko, M., Tefft, N. The Effects of E-cigarette Taxes on E-cigarette Prices and Tobacco Product Sales: Evidence from Retail Panel Data. NBER Working Paper No. 26724. 2022. https://dx.doi.org/10.3386/w26724.
63. Pesko, M.F., Courtemanche, C.J., Maclean, J.C. "The Effects of Traditional Cigarette and E-Cigarette Taxes on Adult Tobacco Product Use," J Risk Uncertain. 2020 Jun;60(3):229-258. https://dx.doi.org/10.1007/s11166-020-09330-9.
64. Viscusi, W.K. Electronic Cigarette Risk Beliefs and Usage After the Vaping Illness Outbreak. J Risk Uncertain. 2020;60:259–279. https://doi.org/10.1007/s11166-020-09328-3.
65. Viscusi, W.K. Risk Beliefs and Preferences for E-cigarettes. Am J Health Econ. 2016;2(2):213–240.
66. Elton-Marshall, T., Driezen, P., Fong, G.T., Cummings, K.M., Persoskie, A., Wackowski, O., Choi, K., Kaufman, A., Strong, D., Gravely, S., Taylor, K., Kwan, J., Bansal-Travers, M., Travers, M., Hyland, A. Adult Perceptions of the Relative Harm of Tobacco Prod- ucts and Subsequent Tobacco Product Use: Longitudinal Findings from Waves 1 and 2 of the Population Assessment of Tobacco and Health (PATH) Study. Addict Behav. 2020;106(106337):1–7.
67. McNeill, A., Brose, L.S., Calder, R., Bauld, L., Robson, D. (2018). "Evidence Review of E-cigarettes and Heated Tobacco Products 2018." Technical Report, Public Health England.
68. Huang, J., Feng, B., Weaver, S.R., Pechacek, T.F., Slovic, P., Eriksen, M.P. Changing Perceptions of Harm of E-cigarette vs Cigarette Use Among Adults in 2 US National Surveys from 2012 to 2017. Jama Network Open. 2019;2(3):e191047. https://doi.org/10.1001/jamanetworkopen.2019.1047.

69. NIH, *Health Information National Trends Survey*. https://hints.cancer.gov/view-questions-topics/question-details.aspx?red=1&qid=1282&PK_Cycle=13.
70. Action on Smoking and Health. Use of E-cigarettes (Vapes) Among Adults in Great Britain, 2022, available at: https://ash.org.uk/uploads/Use-of-e-cigarettes-vapes-among-adults-in-Great-Britain-2022.pdf?v=1661865959.
71. Action on Smoking and Health. Use of E-cigarettes (Vapes) Among Young People in Great Britain, 2022, available at: https://ash.org.uk/uploads/Use-of-e-cigarettes-among-young-people-in-Great-Britain-2022.pdf.
72. Cornelius, M.E., Loretan, C.G., Wang, T.W., Jamal, A., Homa, D.M. Tobacco Product Use Among Adults—United States, 2020. MMWR Morb Mortal Wkly Rep 2022;71:397–405. http://dx.doi.org/10.15585/mmwr.mm7111a1external icon.
73. Cornelius, M.E., Wang, T.W., Jamal, A., Loretan, C., Neff, L. Tobacco Product Use Among Adults—United States, 2019. Morbidity and Mortality Weekly Report. 2020;69(46):1736–1742. http://dx.doi.org/10.15585/mmwr.mm6946a4.
74. Estimates are from the 2021 NYTS data, analyzed by the authors.
75. For the U.S. statistic, see Note 74. Internationally, the proportion of youth who currently used e-cigarettes in the 75 countries of the WHO's Global Youth Tobacco Survey during 2014 to 2019 who also were current smokers is 42% (computed from the statistics in Table 2 of Sreeramareddy et al. (cite: Sreeramareddy CT, Acharya K, Manoharan A. Electronic Cigarettes Use and "Dual Use" Among the Youth in 75 Countries: Estimates from Global Youth Tobacco Surveys (2014–2019). Scientific Reports. 2022;12(1):20967).
76. Goodchild, M., Nargis, N., Tursan d'Espaignet, E. E-global Economic Cost of Smoking-Attributable Diseases. Tob Control. 2018;27:58–64. http://dx.doi.org/10.1136/tobaccocontrol-2016-053305.

Vulovic, V. *Economic Costs of Tobacco Use. A Tobacconomics Policy Brief*. Chicago, IL: Tobacconomics, Health Policy Center, Institute for Health Research and Policy, University of Illinois at Chicago, 2019. www.tobacconomics.org.

77. Friedman, A.S. How Does Electronic Cigarette Access Affect Adolescent Smoking? J Health Econ. 2015;44:300–308. http://dx.doi.org/10.1016/j.jhealeco.2015.10.003
78. Abouk, R., Courtemanche, C., Dave, D., Feng, B., Friedman, A.S., Maclean, J.C., Safford, S., et al. Intended and Unintended Effects of E-cigarette Taxes on Youth Tobacco Use. J Health Econ. 2023;87:102720. http://dx.doi.org/10.1016/j.jhealeco.2022.102720.
79. Pesko, M.F. Effects of E-cigarette Minimum Legal Sales Ages on Youth Tobacco Use in the United States. J Risk and Uncertain. 2023. 66, 261–277 (2023). https://doi.org/10.1007/s11166-022-09402-y.
80. Parts 2 through 4 of this section may be daunting for non-economists, at least compared to the rest of this book. Anyone so desiring may, after reading the non-technical presentation in part 1, skip directly to part 5.
81. Office of Management and Budget, Executive Office of the President. (September 17, 2003). OMB Circular A-4, Regulatory Analysis. https://obamawhitehouse.archives.gov/omb/circulars_a004_a-4/.
82. Gruber, J. Smoking's 'Internalities.' Regulation. 2002;25(4):52.
83. Prieger, J.E. (2021). Smoke or Vapor? Regulation of Tobacco and Vaping. In Hoffer A, Nesbit T (Eds.), *Regulation and Economic Opportunity: Blueprints for Reform*. The Center for Growth and Opportunity, Utah State University.
84. Farhi, E., Gabaix, X. Optimal Taxation with Behavioral Agents. Am Econ Rev. 2020;110(1):298–336. https://doi.org/10.1257/aer.20151079
85. Bentham, J. (1907). *An Introduction to the Principles of Morals and Legislation*. Clarendon Press (Original work published in 1789; reprint of 1823 edition).
86. Von Hirsch, A. Proportionality in the Philosophy of Punishment. Crime and Justice. 1992;16:55–98.

Engle E. The General Principle of Proportionality and Aristotle. In Huppes-Cluysenaer L, Coelho N. (Eds.), *Aristotle and the Philosophy of Law: Theory, Practice and Justice*. Springer, 2013

Cohen, A., Zlotogorski, D. *Proportionality in International Humanitarian Law: Consequences, Precautions, and Procedures*. Oxford University Press, 2021.

87. The example of penal utilitarianism makes the point. If harsh punishment of a few innocent individuals would deter much crime, a purely incentives-based calculus might conclude such injustice is justified, while the proportionality principle would not.
88. "False Fears Preventing Smokers from Using E-Cigarettes to Quit." GOV.UK. https://www.gov.uk/government/news/false-fears-preventing-smokers-from-using-e-cigarettes-to-quit. Accessed 10 May 2023.
89. Cummings, K.M., Nahhas, G.J., Sweanor, D.T. What Is Accounting for the Rapid Decline in Cigarette Sales in Japan? Int J Environ Res Public Health. 2020 May 20;17(10):3570. https://doi.org/10.3390/ijerph17103570.
90. Sutanto, E., Miller, C., Smith, D.M., Borland, R., Hyland, A., Cummings, K.M., Quah, A.C., Xu, S.S., Fong, G.T., Ouimet, J., et al. Concurrent Daily and Non-Daily Use of Heated Tobacco Products with Combustible Cigarettes: Findings from the 2018 ITC Japan Survey. Int J Environ Res Public Health. 2020;17:2098. https://doi.org/10.3390/ijerph17062098.
91. Begh, R., Lindson-Hawley, N., Aveyard, P. Does Reduced Smoking if You Can't Stop Make Any Difference? BMC Med. 2015 Oct 12;13:257. https://doi.org/10.1186/s12916-015-0505-2.
92. Thus, the probability discussed above is the sum of the probabilities for the cases in which vaping preceded smoking, vice versa, or initiation was simultaneous.
93. Owusu, D., Huang, J., Weaver, S.R., Pechacek, T.F., Ashley, D.L., Nayak, P., Eriksen, M.P. Patterns and Trends of Dual Use of E-Cigarettes and Cigarettes Among U.S. Adults, 2015–2018. Prev Med Rep. 2019 Oct 25;16:101009. https://doi.org/10.1016/j.pmedr.2019.101009.
94. Barufaldi, L.A., Guerra, R.L., de Albuquerque, R.C.R., Nascimento, A., Chança, R.D., de Souza, M.C., de Almeida, L.M.. Risk of Smoking Relapse with the Use of Electronic Cigarettes: A Systematic Review with Meta-Analysis of Longitudinal Studies. Tob Prev Cessat. 2021 Apr 27;29:29. https://doi.org/10.18332/tpc/132964.

95. Pesko, M.F., Warman, C. Re-exploring the Early Relationship Between Teenage Cigarette and E-cigarette Use Using Price and Tax Changes. Health Econ. 2022;31(1):137-153. https://doi.org/10.1002/hec.4439.

Pesko, M.F., Hughes, J.M., Faisal, F.S. The Influence of Electronic Cigarette Age Purchasing Restrictions on Adolescent Tobacco and Marijuana Use. Prev Med. 2016;87:207-212. https://doi.org/10.1016/j.ypmed.2016.02.001.

96. Dave, D., Feng, B., Pesko, M.F. The Effects of E-cigarette Minimum Legal Sale Age Laws on Youth Substance Use. Health Econ. 2019;28(3):419–436. DOI: 10.1002/hec.3854

Friedman, A.S. How Does Electronic Cigarette Access Affect Adolescent Smoking? J Health Econ. 2015;44:300–308. https://doi.org/10.1016/j.jhealeco.2015.10.003

97. Hill, A., Camacho, O.M. A System Dynamics Modelling Approach to Assess the Impact of Launching a New Nicotine Product on Population Health Outcomes. Regul Toxicol Pharmacol. 2017 Jun;86:265-278. https://doi.org/10.1016/j.yrtph.2017.03.012

98. Of course, there are many nuances in the literature beyond the simple description in the model presented here. For example, Hill and Camacho allow the current number of smokers to affect initiation rates (P_C^{NS}) through a "smoking normality effect" (Hill & Camacho). See Lee et al. for a summary of various cohort/system dynamics studies. The models also exclude changes in mortality due to reduced exposure to second-hand smoke, mainly because such risk is small compared with the direct health effects of smoking. For example, the estimated relative risk of lung cancer from environmental tobacco smoke (ETS) is in the range of 1.2 to 1.5 (see: Zhong L, Goldberg MS, Parent MÉ, Hanley JA. Exposure to Environmental Tobacco Smoke and the Risk of Lung Cancer: A Meta-Analysis. Lung cancer. 2000;27(1):3–18), whereas for smokers the relative risk is about 9 to 10 for smokers with under 15 pack-years (i.e., equivalent to a pack a day for 15 years) of consumption and rises from there up to over

60 for those with more than 60 pack-years of smoking history (see: Prescott E, Osier M, Rein HO, Borch-Johnsen K, Lange P, Schnohr P, Vestbo J. Gender and Smoking-Related Risk of Lung Cancer. Epidemiology. 1998;9(1):79–83). Thus the ratio of excess risk between exposure to ETS and actually smoking ranges from about (0.2 ÷ 59 =) 0.3% to only (.5 ÷ 59 =) 0.8%. To put it another way, the excess lung cancer risk from being exposed to ETS is less than 1% of the same excess risk from smoking.

See: Lee, P.N., Abrams, D., Bachand, A., Baker, G., Black, R., Camacho, O., Curtin, G., Djurdjevic, S., Hill, A., Mendez, D., Muhammad-Kah, R.S., Murillo, J.L., Niaura, R., Pithawalla, Y.B., Poland, B., Sulsky, S., Wei, L., Weitkunat, R. Estimating the Population Health Impact of Recently Introduced Modified Risk Tobacco Products: A Comparison of Different Approaches. Nicotine Tob Res. 2021 Feb 16;23(3):426–437. https://doi.org/10.1093/ntr/ntaa102. Hill, A., Camacho, O.M. A System Dynamics Modelling Approach to Assess the Impact of Launching a New Nicotine Product on Population Health Outcomes. Regul Toxicol Pharmacol. 2017, Jun;86:265-278. https://doi.org/10.1016/j.yrtph.2017.03.012.

99. For example, from 1996 to 2004, guidance from the U.K. Department of Health instructed that costs were to be discounted at a real annual rate of 6% while health effects were to be discounted at only 1.5%. See: Claxton, K., Paulden, M., Gravelle, H., Brouwer, W., Culyer, A.J. Discounting and Decision Making in the Economic Evaluation of Health-Care Technologies. Health Econ. 2011;20(1):2–15. https://doi.org/10.1002/hec.1612.
100. Claxton, K., Paulden, M., Gravelle, H., Brouwer, W., Culyer, A.J. Discounting and Decision Making in the Economic Evaluation of Health-Care Technologies. Health Econ. 2011;20(1):2–15. https://doi.org/10.1002/hec.1612.
101. Reubi, D. (2017). Rational Sin. *Limn*, 9. https://limn.it/articles/rational-sin/.
102. Chaloupka, F.J., Warner, K.E. The economics of smoking, In Anthony J. Culyer, Joseph P. Newhouse (Eds.), *Handbook of Health Economics* (Chapter 29, Volume 1, Part B, Pages 1539–1627). Elsevier, 2020.

103. US Department of Health E, and Welfare. (1964). Smoking and Health: Report of the Advisory Committee to the Surgeon General of the Public Health Service. Washington, D.C.
104. Lewit, E.M., Coate, D., Grossman, M. The Effects of Government Regulation on Teenage Smoking. J L & Econ. 1981;24(3):545–569.
105. Becker, G.S., Murphy, K.M. A Theory of Rational Addiction. J Polit Econ.1988;96(4):675–700.
106. Lewit, E.M., Coate, D. The Potential for Using Excise Taxes to Reduce Smoking. J Health Econ. 1982;1(2):121–145. https://doi.org/10.1016/0167-6296(82)90011-x.
107. Lewit, E.M., Coate, D., Grossman, M. The Effects of Government Regulation on Teenage Smoking. J L & Econ. 1981;24(3):545–569.
108. Baltagi, B.H., Levin, D. Estimating Dynamic Demand for Cigarettes Using Panel Data: The Effects of Bootlegging, Taxation and Advertising Reconsidered. Rev Econ and Stat. 1986;68(1):148–155. https://doi.org/10.2307/1924938.
109. Chaloupka, F.J., Warner, K.E. The economics of smoking, In Anthony J. Culyer, Joseph P. Newhouse (Eds.), *Handbook of Health Economics* (Chapter 29, Volume 1, Part B, Pages 1539–1627). Elsevier, 2000.
110. Andrews, R.L., Franke, G.R. The Determinants of Cigarette Consumption: A Meta-Analysis. J Public Policy & Market. 1991;10(1):81–100. https://doi.org/10.1177/074391569101000107.
111. Gallet, C.A., List, J.A. Cigarette Demand: A Meta-Analysis of Elasticities. Health Econ. 2003;12(10):821–835. https://doi.org/10.1002/hec.765.
112. Chaloupka, F.J., Wakefield, M., Czart, C. Taxing Tobacco: The Impact of Tobacco Taxes on Cigarette Smoking and Other Tobacco Use. Regul Tob. 2001:39–71.
113. In fact, consumer welfare plays an even larger role in certain policy analyses than is called for by economic theory. While consumer benefits contribute to aggregate social welfare, so do the profits of firms (which, after all, are ultimately owned by people), and every student of introductory microeconomics learns that total surplus in a market is the sum of consumer surplus and producer surplus. However, for decades antitrust

law in the U.S. has been guided by a standard of consumer welfare, not total welfare, although that appears to be changing at the Federal Trade Commission in recent years (see: Ashton F. Why the Consumer Welfare Standard Is the Backbone of Antitrust Policy, American Action Forum Insight. https://www.americanactionforum.org/insight/why-the-consumer-welfare-standard-is-the-backbone-of-antitrust-policy) The FDA, in contrast, considers the impacts of its proposed regulations on both consumers and producers, as required for federal agencies when performing regulatory analysis.

114. Lee, P.N., Fry, J.S., Gilliland, S., Campbell, P., Joyce, A.R. Estimating the Reduction in US Mortality if Cigarettes Were Largely Replaced by E-cigarettes. Archiv Toxicol. 2022: Jan;96(1):167-176. https://doi.org/10.1007/s00204-021-03180-3.
115. Consider the example of a price change for e-cigarettes due to a tax increase. The equivalent variation is the maximum amount a consumer would pay *ex ante* to avoid the price increase. The compensating variation is the minimum amount a consumer would need to be paid *ex post* to return him to his previous level of satisfaction. If there are no income effects in demand, these two measures coincide. Otherwise, the consumer surplus is an approximate measure that falls between the other two.
116. The rational addiction model of Gary Becker and Kevin Murphy represents the extreme form of this thinking. Becker, G.S., Murphy, K.M. A Theory of Rational Addiction. J Polit Econ. 1988;96(4):675–700.
117. Food and Drug Administration. (June 22, 2011). "Required Warnings for Cigarette Packages and Advertisements; Final Rule," 36714.
118. Chaloupka, F.J., Gruber, J., Warner, K.E. Accounting for 'Lost Pleasure' in a Cost–Benefit Analysis of Government Regulation: The Case of the Food and Drug Administration's Proposed Cigarette Labeling Regulation. Ann Intern Med. 2015;162(1):64–65. https://doi.org/10.7326/M14-1910.
119. Sullum, J. (1994). The Costs and Benefits of Smoking. Reason.com. https://reason.com/1994/10/03/the-costs-and-benefits-of-smok/.
120. Barnum, H. The Economic Burden of the Global Trade in Tobacco. Tob Control. 1994;3:358–361.

Barnum, H. (1993). "Initial Analysis of the Economic Costs and Benefits of Investing in Tobacco." World Bank, Human Development Department, unpublished.

121. Lemieux, P. (2019). Consumer Surplus in the FDA's Tobacco Regulations with Applications to Nicotine Reduction and E-cigarette Flavors. Reason Foundation. https://reason.org/wp-content/uploads/consumer-surplus-in-fda-tobacco-regulations.pdf.
122. Food and Drug Administration. Required Warnings for Cigarette Packages and Advertisements, Proposed Rule. Fed Reg. 2010;75:69524–69565.
123. The agency's assumptions for the various cases it considered were stated in terms of the ratio of net (of consumer surplus losses) health benefits to gross health benefits. Stated that way, a ratio of 0% implies that internal and external benefits were equal (hence a 50% markdown of total health benefits); a ratio of 100% implies that all health costs are internalities (100% markdown of total health benefits). These ratios ranged from 7% to 90%, which implies the approximate markdown range mentioned in the text.
124. Food and Drug Administration. (June 22, 2011). "Required Warnings for Cigarette Packages and Advertisements; Final Rule," 36714.
125. The Office of Management and Budget's (OMB's) Circular A-4, which contains guidance to U.S. federal agencies for regulatory analysis, states, for example, that part of the opportunity cost of banning a product is the forgone consumer and producer surplus it would have created.
126. Chaloupka, F.J., Warner, K.E., Acemoğlu, D., Gruber, J., Laux, F., Max, W., Newhouse, J., Schelling, T., Sindelar, J. An Evaluation of the FDA's Analysis of the Costs and Benefits of the Graphic Warning Label Regulation. Tob Control. 2015;24(2):112–112. https://doi.org/10.1136/tobaccocontrol-2014-052022.
127. Kotlikoff, L.J., Summers, L.H. Tax Incidence. In *Handbook of Public Economics* (Vol. 2, pp. 1043–1092). Elsevier, 1987.
128. Delipalla, S., Keen, M. The Comparison Between Ad Valorem and Specific Taxation Under Imperfect Competition. Journal of Public Economics. 1992;49(3):351–367.

Stern, N. The Effects of Taxation, Price Control and Government Contracts in Oligopoly and Monopolistic Competition. J Public Econ. 1987;32(2):133–158.

129. Sheikh, et al. review the many studies by tobacco control experts, public health researchers, and economists examining or commenting on the tobacco industry's response to excise taxes (see: Sheikh, Z.D., Branston, J.R., Gilmore, A.B. Tobacco Industry Pricing Strategies in Response to Excise Tax Policies: A Systematic Review. Tob Control. 2023;32(2):239–250). https://doi.org/10.1136/tobaccocontrol-2021-056630
130. Sheikh, Z.D., Branston, J.R., Gilmore, A.B. Tobacco Industry Pricing Strategies in Response to Excise Tax Policies: A Systematic Review. Tob Control. 2023;32(2):239–250. https://doi.org/10.1136/tobaccocontrol-2021-056630
131. Brown, M. (April 5, 2023) The Cost of JUUL: Is It Saving Smokers Money? LendEDU.com. https://lendedu.com/blog/financial-cost-of-juul.
132. This surmise combines the average state and federal excise tax of $2.61 (see: Prieger, J.E. (2021). Smoke or Vapor? Regulation of Tobacco and Vaping. In A. Hoffer & T. Nesbit (Eds.), *Regulation and Economic Opportunity: Blueprints for Reform.* The Center for Growth and Opportunity, Utah State University) with the common empirical finding that excise taxes on cigarettes have a pass-through to prices greater than 1 (e.g., 1.1 in the classic study of Keeler et al.) (see: Keeler, T., Hu, T.W, Barnett, P., et al. Do Cigarette Producers Price Discriminate by State? An Empirical Analysis of Local Cigarette Pricing and Taxation. J Health Econ. 1996;15:499–512).
133. von Lampe, K., Kurti, M., Johnson, J., Rengifo, A.F. "I Wouldn't Take My Chances on the Street" Navigating Illegal Cigarette Purchases in the South Bronx. J Res Crime Delinq. 2016;53(5):654–680. https://doi.org/10.1177/002242781663788.
134. Prieger, J.E., Kulick, J. Cigarette Taxes and Illicit Trade in Europe. Econ Inquiry. 2018;56:1706–1723. https://doi.org/10.1111/ecin.12564.
135. Of course, the modern economist would hasten to add a long list of qualifying conditions before accepting the conclusion,

including the absence of externalities, information problems, irrationality of the part of economic agents, etc.

136. Mill, J.S. On Liberty. London, UK: J.W. Parker and Son, 1859.
137. Grill, K., Voigt, K. The Case for Banning Cigarettes. J Med Ethics. 2016;42(5):293–301. https://doi.org/10.1136/medethics-2015-102682.
138. Halliday, D. The Ethics of a Smoking License. J Med Ethics. 2016;42(5):278–284. https://doi.org/10.1136/medethics-2013-101347.
139. Schmidt, A.T. Is There a Human Right to Tobacco Control. In Gispen ME, Toebes B (Eds.), Human Rights and Tobacco Control: International, Regional, and Domestic Legal Perspectives. In press.
140. Goodin, R.E. No Smoking: The Ethical Issues. Chicago, IL: University of Chicago Press, 1989.
141. Grill, K. E-cigarettes: The Long-Term Liberal Perspective. Nicotine Tob Res. 2021 Jan;23(1):9–13. https://doi.org/10.1093/ntr/ntaa085.
142. A Pareto optimal outcome is a distribution of output and consumption that is efficient in the sense that no economic agent can be made better-off (in its own estimation) without making at least other agent worse-off.
143. Blaug, M. The Fundamental Theorems of Modern Welfare Economics, Historically Contemplated. History Polit Econ. 2007;39(2):185–207. https://doi.org/10.1215/00182702-2007-001.
144. Hurley, J. An Overview of the Normative Economics of the Health Sector. In Culyer AJ, Newhouse JP (Eds.), *Handbook of Health Economics* (Vol. 1A, pp. 55–118). North-Holland, 2000
145. Social attitudes toward the tradeoff between equality and efficiency have been explored empirically by economists, philosopher, psychologists, political scientists, and others. See:

    Amiel, Y., Cowell, F.A. *Thinking About Inequality*. Cambridge University Press, 1999.

    Devooght, K. Measuring Inequality By Counting 'Complaints': Theory and Empirics. Econ Philos. 2003;19(2):241–263. https://doi.org/10.1017/S0266267103001147.

    Mitchell, G., Tetlock, P.E., Mellers, B.A., Ordonez, L.D. Judgments of Social Justice: Compromises Between Equality and

Efficiency. J Pers Soc Psychol. 1993;65(4):629. https://doi.org/10.1037/0022-3514.65.4.629.

Scott, J.T., Matland, R.E., Michelbach, P.A., Bornstein, B.H. Just Deserts: An Experimental Study of Distributive Justice Norms. Am J Polit Sci. 2001:749–767. https://doi.org/10.2307/2669322.

Steinberger, F., Minder, T., Trutnevyte, E. Efficiency Versus Equity in Spatial Siting of Electricity Generation: Citizen Preferences in a Serious Board Game in Switzerland. Energies. 2020;13(18):4961. https://doi.org/10.3390/en13184961.

146. Adler, M.D. The Social Welfare Function: A New Tool for Regulatory Policy Analysis. In Grundmann S, Hacker P (Eds.), *Theories of Choice: The Social Science and the Law of Decision Making*. Oxford University Press, 2021. https://doi.org/10.1093/oso/9780198863175.003.0009.
147. By "democratic means," we mean that weights or priorities can be determined by voting or other forms of political representation and participation. That is, the parameters of a SWF themselves can be determined by voting. However, it is well known that there can be severe difficulties in moving from individual preferences to social choices in a voting system. Arrow's Impossibility Theorem states that no electoral system that ranks social outcomes (i.e., determines a SWF) exists that satisfies all four of the following criteria for fairness: universality (the SWF ranks all possible choices and does so the same way every time), non-dictatorial preferences (the SWF does not merely express the preferences of a single individual), Pareto efficiency (if every individual would vote for one outcome over another, then the SWF must also rank the first outcome higher), and independence of irrelevant alternatives (if every individual's ranking of two outcomes remains unchanged when preferences for some other comparison changes, the social ranking of those two outcomes does not change) (see: Arrow, K.J. A Difficulty in the Concept of Social Welfare. Journal of Political Economy. 1950;58(4):328–346. Arrow, K.J (2012). *Social Choice and Individual Values* (3rd ed.). Cowles Foundation for Research in Economics monograph 12. Yale University Press).
148. By "not circular," we mean transitive: if outcome A is better than outcome B, and outcome C is better than B, then C cannot be worse than A.

149. Formally, the existence of a continuous, complete, and transitive binary preference relation over a set of possible social outcomes that are represented by a suitably well-behaved topological space X (such as Euclidean N-space), implies the existence of a real-valued continuous utility function that represents the preferences (see: Debreu, G. Representation of a Preference Ordering by a Numerical Function. Decision Processes. 1954;3:159–165). There is also a large literature on such utility representation theorems that relax various of these assumptions (see, e.g., Nishimura and Ok (2016) and the research cited therein) (see: Nishimura, H., Ok, E.A. Utility Representation of an Incomplete and Nontransitive Preference Relation. J Econ Theory. 2016;166:164–185).
150. Adler, M. *Well-Being and Fair Distribution: Beyond Cost–Benefit Analysis*. Oxford University Press, 2011.
151. Hurka, T. Objective goods. In. In Adler MD, Fleurbaey M. (Eds.), *The Oxford handbook of wellbeing and public policy*. Oxford University Press, 2016.
152. Adler, M.D. The Social Welfare Function: A New Tool for Regulatory Policy Analysis. In Grundmann S, Hacker P (Eds.), *Theories of Choice: The Social Science and the Law of Decision Making*. Oxford University Press, 2021.
153. The name is intended to distinguish this approach from an older utilitarian way of thinking that assumed that the well-being of two individuals could be quantified and compared directly. It is traditional both in the sense that the New Welfare Economics predates all but the original utilitarian thinking in economics and that textbooks or coursework that touch only lightly on welfare economics often treat only the former approach.
154. Blaug, M. The Fundamental Theorems of Modern Welfare Economics, Historically Contemplated. Hist Polit Econ. 2007;39(2):185–207. https://doi.org/10.1215/00182702-2007-001.

    Hicks, J.R. The Foundation of Welfare Economics. Econ J. 49. 1939; 196:696–712. https://doi.org/10.2307/2225023.
155. Kaldor, N. Welfare Propositions of Economics and Interpersonal Comparisons of Utility. Econ J. 49. 1939;195:549–552. https://doi.org/10.2307/2224835

156. Clarke, M. Economic Growth and Social Welfare: Operationalising Normative Social Choice Theory (Clarke M, Islam SMN, Eds.). Elsevier Science, 2004.
157. Islam, S.M.N., Mak, C.S.Y. Normative Health Economics: A New Pragmatic Approach to Cost Benefit Analysis, Mathematical Models and Applications. Palgrave Macmillan, 2007.
158. The link between income and WTP is the marginal utility of income, which is typically assumed (with empirical support) to be declining as income rises. Thus, other things equal, high-income individuals are likely to be willing to give up more income (i.e., have a higher WTP) for a health improvement than low-income individuals (see: Gyrd-Hansen, D. Willingness to Pay for a QALY: Theoretical and Methodological Issues. Pharmacoeconomics. 2005;23, 423–432). https://doi.org/10.2165/00019053-200523050-00002.
159. Sunstein, C.R. Willingness to Pay vs. Welfare. Harv. L. & Pol'y Rev. 2007;1:303.
160. There are some income-related effects that may work in the opposite direction, however. If an individual is in such poor health that he or she gains little enjoyment from consumption, the marginal utility of income will be low and therefore the WTP for health improvement will be high. Given the connection between income and health, there might be more low-income individuals in the poor-health group with high WTP (see to: Gyrd-Hansen (2005), in Note 158).
161. Ubel, P.A., Nord, E., Gold, M., Menzel, P., Prades, J.L.P., Richardson, J. Improving Value Measurement in Cost-Effectiveness Analysis. Medical Care. 2000;892–901. https://doi.org/10.1097/00005650-200009000-00003.
162. Hurley, J. An Overview of the Normative Economics of the Health Sector. In Culyer, A.J., Newhouse, J.P. (Eds.), *Handbook of Health Economics* (Vol. 1A, pp. 55–118). North-Holland, 2000.
163. Culyer, A.J. The Normative Economics of Health Care Finance and Provision. Oxf Rev Econ Policy. 1989;5(1): 34–58. https://doi.org/10.1093/oxrep/5.1.34.
164. Islam, S.M.N., Mak, C.S.Y. *Normative Health Economics: A New Pragmatic Approach to Cost Benefit Analysis, Mathematical Models and Applications*. Palgrave Macmillan, 2007.

165. Little, I.M.D., Mirlees, J.A. *Project Appraisal and Planning for Developing Countries*. Economic Analysis of Projects. London: Heinemann Educational Books. Squires L, van der Tak HG. Baltimore: John Hopkins University Press, 1975. Note that the marginal utility of income, which is the extra satisfaction or happiness gained from an additional dollar of income, is typically measured to decline as income increases. Thus, weighting groups' utility by the marginal utility of income assigns higher weights to lower-income groups.
166. Parfit, D. Equality and Priority 1. In *The Notion of Equality* (pp. 427–446). Routledge, 2018.
167. Adler, M.D. *Measuring Social Welfare: An Introduction*. USA: Oxford University Press, 2019.
168. This occurs because transformation with a concave function implies that a unit increase in individual welfare (however measured) increases the change in transformed welfare less and less as the original level of welfare rises. See Fig. 8.1 and related discussion in Adler (2021) (see: Adler, M.D. (2021). The Social Welfare Function: A New Tool for Regulatory Policy Analysis. In Grundmann, S., Hacker, P. (Eds.), *Theories of Choice: The Social Science and the Law of Decision Making*. Oxford University Press. https://doi.org/10.1093/oso/9780198863175.003.0009).
169. Adler, M.D. The Social Welfare Function: A New Tool for Regulatory Policy Analysis. In Grundmann, S., Hacker, P. (Eds.), *Theories of Choice: The Social Science and the Law of Decision Making*. Oxford University Press, 2021. https://doi.org/10.1093/oso/9780198863175.003.0009.
170. Adler, M.D. (2017). terms taking the expected sum of the individual measures of well-being as *utilitarianism-under-uncertainty* and taking the expected sum of the transformed measures as *ex post prioritarianism*. If it is desired to account for individuals' risk aversion, then one can also take the sum of the transformed expected individual well-being measures (*ex ante prioritarianism*) (See: Adler, M.D. (2017). A Better Calculus for Regulators: From Cost–Benefit Analysis to the Social Welfare Function. *Duke Law School Public Law & Legal Theory Series*, 2017–2019).
171. Harsanyi, J.C. Nonlinear Social Welfare Functions. Theory Decis. 1975;6(3):311–332.

172. Some studies find that the public *overestimates* the risks of smoking (see: Viscusi, W.K. The New Cigarette Paternalism. Regulation. 2002;25(4):58–64) while others find that the public underestimates those risks (see: Krosnick, J.A., Malhotra, N., Mo, C.H., Bruera, E.F., Chang, L., et al. Correction: Perceptions of Health Risks of Cigarette Smoking: A New Measure Reveals Widespread Misunderstanding. PLoS ONE. 2019;14(2):e0212705. https://doi.org/10.1371/journal.pone.0212705). In contrast, the evidence is nearly unanimous that most people today believe that e-cigarettes are just as harmful or more harmful than cigarettes (see to: Huang, J., Feng, B., Weaver, S.R., Pechacek, T.F., Slovic, P., Eriksen, M.P. Changing Perceptions of Harm of E-cigarette vs Cigarette Use Among Adults in 2 US National Surveys from 2012 to 2017. Jama Network Open. 2019;2(3):e191047. https://doi.org/10.1001/jamanetworkopen.2019.1047. McNeill, A., Brose, L., Calder, R., Bauld, L., Robson, D. (2020). Vaping in England: An evidence update including mental health and pregnancy, March 2020: A Report Commissioned by Public Health England. London: Public Health England).
173. Kozlowski, L.T., Edwards, B.Q. "Not Safe" Is Not Enough: Smokers Have a Right to Know More Than There Is No Safe Tobacco Product. Tob Control. 2005;14(suppl 2):ii3–ii7. https://doi.org/10.1136/tc.2004.008334.
174. Viscusi, W.K. The Perceived Risks of E-cigarettes to Others and During Pregnancy. J Public Health. 2023;45(1):202–205. https://doi.org/10.1093/pubmed/fdab352.
175. While 23% of adult non-smoking e-cigarette users in the U.S. and 24% of dual users are minorities (not White alone race or of Hispanic ethnicity), 31% of smokers who do not also use e-cigarettes are minorities. Figure 1 shows that lower-income categories are overrepresented for smokers compared to e-cigarette users and dual users. In particular, the distribution of income among e-cigarette users first-order stochastically dominate the distribution for smokers. Figure 2 shows a similar result for educational attainment. For similar evidence from the U.K., see Kock, et al. (2019) (see: Kock, L., Shahab, L., West, R.,

Brown, J. E-cigarette Use in England 2014–17 as a Function of Socio-Economic Profile. Addiction (Abingdon, England). 2019;114(2):294–303. https://doi.org/10.1111/add.14446.

176. McCrudden, C. (November 2004). Using Public Procurement to Achieve Social Outcomes. In *Natural Resources Forum* (Vol. 28, No. 4, pp. 257–267). Oxford, UK: Blackwell Publishing Ltd. https://doi.org/10.1111/j.1477-8947.2004.00099.
177. McAfee, R.P., McMillan, J., Wilkie, S. The Greatest Auction in History. In Siegfried JJ (Ed.), *Better Living Through Economics* (pp. 168–184). Harvard University Press, 2010.
178. Federal Communications Commission (June 29, 1994). *Fifth Report and Order in the Matter of Implementation of Section 309(j) of the Communications Act—Competitive Bidding.* FCC 94–178. https://tinyurl.com/4vtjvbwf.
179. In fact, the bidding credits mentioned are for the original PCS spectrum auction. The credits were modified many times over the years (see: Salmon, T.C. (2004). Spectrum auctions by the United States Federal Communications Commission. In Janssen, M.C.W. (Ed.), *Auctioning Public Assets: Analysis and Alternatives* (pp. 147–176). Cambridge University. Press), perhaps in response to the public's input.
180. Early suggestions in published scholarly literature to use differential taxation for lower and higher risk tobacco products include Harris (1980) and Kozlowski (1989) (the former is not publicly available and is cited in the latter). Cite:

    Harris, J.E. (1980). Public Policy Issues in the Promotion of Less Hazardous Cigarettes. In Gori, G.B., Bock, F.G. (Eds.), *A Safe Cigarette? Banbury Report 3* (pp. 333–340). Cold Spring Harbor Laboratory.

    Kozlowski, L.T. Reduction of Tobacco Health Hazards in Continuing Users: Individual Behavioral and Public Health Approaches. Journal of Substance Abuse. 1989;1(3):345–357.
181. Chaloupka, F.J., Sweanor, D., Warner, K.E. Differential Taxes for Differential Risks—Toward Reduced Harm from Nicotine-Yielding Products. N Engl J Med. 2015;373(7):594–597. https://doi.org/10.1056/NEJMp1505710.
182. Sindelar, J.L. Regulating Vaping—Policies, Possibilities, and Perils. N Engl J Med. 2020 May 14;382(20):e54. https://doi.org/10.1056/NEJMp1917065.

183. Prieger, J.E. Optimal Taxation of Cigarettes and E-cigarettes: Principles for Taxing Reduced-Harm Tobacco Products. 2023;26(2):41–64. https://doi.org/10.1515/fhep-2022-0025.
184. See Prieger (2023), cited in previous note, for a thorough review of elasticity estimates for both products.
185. Prieger, J.E. Optimal Taxation of Cigarettes and E-cigarettes: Principles for Taxing Reduced-Harm Tobacco Products. 2023;26(2):41–64. https://doi.org/10.1515/fhep-2022-0025.
186. Of course, they do not state it that way. Instead, officials there communicate relative risk with the statement that e-cigarettes are around 95% less harmful than cigarettes.
187. See Volume III, Chapter 3, Sect. 6 for discussion of the environmental effects of e-cigarette production and waste.
188. Hendlin YH. Alert: Public Health Implications of Electronic Cigarette Waste. Am J Public Health. 2018 Nov;108(11):1489–1490. https://doi.org/10.2105/AJPH.2018.304699. 30303735.
189. As discussed in Volume I, Chapter 3, Sect. 4.7.1, smokers might inhale about 1.1 mg to 1.8 mg per cigarette. There is no more than 40 mg of nicotine in a disposable compliant with European rules (20 mg/mL concentration × 2 mL tank volume). Estimates of nicotine transfer efficiency for e-cigarettes vary widely by study and device; available figures include the range of 14–58% for early-generation cig-a-likes and 68% for Juul. Assume this same range for modern disposables (although the estimate for Juul is likely to be more accurate) yields a nicotine equivalency of one disposable to 4–19 cigarettes (where the midpoint of 1.45 mg for nicotine inhalation from a cigarette is used in the computation). Several other studies find that (in terms of nicotine delivered) a Juul pod is roughly comparable to a pack of 20 cigarettes (see: Prochaska, J.J., Vogel, E.A., Benowitz, N. Nicotine Delivery and Cigarette Equivalents from Vaping a JUULpod. Tob Control. 2022;31(e1):e88–e93. Pagano T, DiFrancesco AG, Smith SB, George J, Wink G, Rahman I, Robinson RJ. Determination of Nicotine Content and Delivery in Disposable Electronic Cigarettes Available in the United States by Gas Chromatography-Mass Spectrometry. Nicotine Tob Res. 2016;18(5):700–707).

190. Abouk, R., Courtemanche, C., Dave, D., Feng, B., Friedman, A.S., Maclean, J.C., Safford, S., et al. Intended and Unintended Effects of E-cigarette Taxes on Youth Tobacco Use. J Health Econ. 2023;87:102720. https://doi.org/10.1016/j.jhealeco.2022.102720.

Pesko, M.F., Hughes, J.M., Faisal, F.S. The Influence of Electronic Cigarette Age Purchasing Restrictions on Adolescent Tobacco and Marijuana Use. Prev Med. 2016;87:207–212. https://doi.org/10.1016/j.ypmed.2016.02.001.

191. Abouk, R., Courtemanche, C., Dave, D., Feng, B., Friedman, A.S., Maclean, J.C., Safford, S., et al. Intended and Unintended Effects of E-cigarette Taxes on Youth Tobacco Use. J Health Econ. 2023;87:102720. https://doi.org/10.1016/j.jhealeco.2022.102720.

192. In 2021 there were only 513,925 daily e-cigarette users in middle school and high school, per the NYTS. In contrast, data from the 2018–2019 TUS imply that there were 2,694,234 daily e-cigarette users 18 years old or above (calculations by the authors).

193. For example, in the U.S. some private companies offer their employees financial incentives to quit smoking or health insurance surcharges for continued smoking (cite: Sammer J. (October 29, 2018). Employer incentives encourage employees to quit smoking. *SHRM HR News*, November/December 2018. https://www.shrm.org/hr-today/news/hr-magazine/1118/pages/employer-incentives-encourage-employees-to-quit-smoking.aspx).

194. Kim, K.H., Kabir, E., Jahan, S.A. Review of Electronic Cigarettes as Tobacco Cigarette Substitutes: Their Potential Human Health Impact. J Environ Sci Health, Part C. 2016;34(4):262–275. https://doi.org/10.1080/10590501.2016.1236604.

195. Institute of Medicine (US) Committee on Secondhand Smoke Exposure and Acute Coronary Events. Secondhand Smoke Exposure and Cardiovascular Effects: Making Sense of the Evidence. Washington, D.C.: National Academies Press, 2010, 5, The Background of Smoking Bans. Available at: https://www.ncbi.nlm.nih.gov/books/NBK219563/.

196. Electronic Nicotine Delivery Systems and Electronic Non-Nicotine Delivery Systems (ENDS/ENNDS). Geneva: World

Health Organization, 2016, available at: http://www.who.int/fctc/cop/cop7/FCTC_COP_7_11_EN.pdf?ua=1.
197. Institute for Global Tobacco Control. (n.d.). Country Laws Regulating E-cigaretts: Vape-Free Public Places. GlobalTobaccoControl.org. https://www.globaltobaccocontrol.org/en/policy-scan/e-cigarettes/vape-free-public-places, visited 25 May 2023.
198. Bhalerao, A., Sivandzade, F., Archie, S.R., Cucullo, L. Public Health Policies on E-cigarettes. Curr Cardiol Rep. 2019;21(10):111. https://doi.org/10.1007/s11886-019-1204-y.
199. McNeill, A., Brose, L.S., Calder, R., Bauld, L. Robson, D. Evidence Review of Ecigarettes and Heated Tobacco Products 2018. A Report Commissioned by Public Health England. London: Public Health England, 2018, available at: https://assets.publishing.service.gov.uk/government/uploads/system/uploads/attachment_data/file/684963/Evidence_review_of_e-cigarettes_and_heated_tobacco_products_2018.pdf.
200. McNeill, A., Etter, J.F., Farsalinos, K., Hajek, P., le Houezec, J., McRobbie, H. A Critique of an E-cigarette Review. Addiction. 2014;109:2128–2134. https://doi.org/10.1111/add.12730.
201. National Academies of Sciences, Engineering, and Medicine; Health and Medicine Division; Board on Population Health and Public Health Practice; Committee on the Review of the Health Effects of Electronic Nicotine Delivery Systems; Eaton, D.L., Kwan, L.Y., Stratton, K., eds. (January 23, 2018). *Public Health Consequences of E-cigarettes*. Washington, D.C.: National Academies Press, 5, Toxicology of E-Cigarette Constituents. Available at: https://www.ncbi.nlm.nih.gov/books/NBK507184/?report=classic.
202. Public Health England. (2016). E-cigarettes in Public Places and Workplaces: A 5-Point Guide to Policy Making. Gov.uk. https://www.gov.uk/government/publications/use-of-e-cigarettes-in-public-places-and-workplaces/e-cigarettes-in-public-places-and-workplaces-a-5-point-guide-to-policy-making.
203. Friedman, A.S., Oliver, J.F., Busch, S.H. Adding Vaping Restrictions to Smoke-Free Air Laws: Associations with Conventional and Electronic Cigarette Use. Addiction. 2021 Aug;116(8):2198-2206. https://doi.org/10.1111/add.15434.

204. Press Association. (July 10, 2019). "Vape Shops Open in Two UK Hospitals to Help Smokers Kick the Habit," *The Guardian*. https://www.theguardian.com/society/2019/jul/10/vape-shops-hospital-smokers-kick-habit-west-midlands.
205. Public Health England, "Using Electronic Cigarettes in NHS Mental Health Organisations" (Public Health England, 2020). https://www.gov.uk/government/publications/e-cigarettes-use-by-patients-in-nhs-mental-health-organisations/using-electronic-cigarettes-in-nhs-mental-health-organisations.
206. Caruana, D. (May 19, 2021). "Some UK Hospitals Will Give Free Vapes to Smokers Attending Emergency Depts." *Vaping Post*. https://www.vapingpost.com/2021/05/19/some-uk-hospitals-will-give-free-vapes-to-smokers-attending-emergency-depts/.
207. Deeming Tobacco Products to Be Subject to the Federal Food, Drug, and Cosmetic Act, as Amended by the Family Smoking Prevention and Tobacco Control Act; Restrictions on the Sale and Distribution of Tobacco Products and Required Warning Statements for Tobacco Products. Final Rule. Food and Drug Administration, HHS. Fed Regist. 2016 May 10;81(90):28973–29106.
208. National Cancer Institute. (October 2018). Beliefs About Nicotine and Low Nicotine Cigarettes Among US Adults. *HINTS Briefs*, 37. https://hints.cancer.gov/docs/Briefs/HINTS_Brief_37.pdf.
209. Sanner, T., Grimsrud, T.K. Nicotine: Carcinogenicity and Effects on Response to Cancer Treatment—A Review. Frontiers in Oncology. 2015;5:196. https://doi.org/10.3389/fonc.2015.00196.
210. Kenkel, D.S., Peng, S., Pesko, M.F., Wang, H. Mostly Harmless Regulation? Electronic Cigarettes, Public Policy, and Consumer Welfare. Health Econ. 2020;29:1364–1377. https://doi.org/10.1002/hec.4136.
211. In that regard, the EU's wording that nicotine is a "highly addictive substance" is better than the US version, which both omits the adverbial intensifier and needlessly uses the scare word "chemical" instead of the equally correct but more neutral "substance." Any reader doubting that many people have irrational fears

of chemicals should peruse the Wikipedia page for dihydrogen monoxide.

212. Kelly, K.J., Slater, M.D., Karan, D., Hunn, L. The Use of Human Models and Cartoon Characters in Magazine Advertisements for Cigarettes, Beer, and Nonalcoholic Beverages. Journal of Public Policy & Marketing. 2000;19(2):189–200. https://doi.org/10.1509/jppm.19.2.189.17135

    Trudeau G. (July 19, 1989). *Doonesbury* (introduction of Mr. Butts). https://www.gocomics.com/doonesbury/2017/07/19.

213. Breed, W., De Foe, J.R. Themes in Magazine Alcohol Advertisements: A Critique. Journal of Drug Issues. 1979;9(4):511–522. https://doi.org/10.1177/002204267900900404.
214. Fulton, E.K., Chisholm, P., Fisher, L., Caragata, W. (2007). Tobacco Advertising Ban Unconsititional. *The Canadian Encyclopedia.* https://www.thecanadianencyclopedia.ca/en/article/tobacco-advertising-ban-unconstitutional.
215. Irvine, I., Nguyen, H. "Shock and Awe or Incentive Compatible Harm Reduction? Graphic Health Warnings on Tobacco Packages?" Harm Reduct J. 2021;18:Article No. 43. Available at: https://harmreductionjournal.biomedcentral.com/articles/10.1186/s12954-021-00487-3.
216. Note, however, that manufacturers that produce both cigarettes and e-cigarettes may have greater incentive to promote dual use than complete switching to e-cigarettes, depending on the degree of substitution between the products and the profit margins on each. Furthermore, if this were the only form of advertising for e-cigarettes that were allowed, manufacturers of e-cigarettes that do not also produce cigarettes may have a legal claim of discrimination, or, perversely, have incentive to enter the combustible market to be allowed to advertise their (main) e-cigarette products.
217. Only 5.8% of middle-school and high-school students in the U.S. who currently use e-cigarettes say that they began using them to try to quit another tobacco product (calculation by the authors using data from 2021 NYTS).
218. DeSimone, J., Grossman, D., Ziebarth, N. (2022). Regression Discontinuity Evidence on the Effectiveness of the Minimum Legal E-Cigarette Purchasing Age. Am J Health Econ, forthcoming. https://doi.org/10.1086/723401.

219. Dave, D., Feng, B., Pesko, M.F. The Effects of E-cigarette Minimum Legal Sale Age Laws on Youth Substance Use. Health Econo. 2019;28(3):419–436. https://doi.org/10.1002/hec.3854.
220. Pesko, M.F. Combustible Tobacco Age-of-Sale Laws: An Opportunity? Addiction (Abingdon, England). 2022;117(3):514-516. https://doi.org/10.1111/add.15685.
221. Dave, D., Feng, B., Pesko, M.F. The Effects of E-cigarette Minimum Legal Sale Age Laws on Youth Substance Use. Health Econo. 2019;28(3):419–436. https://doi.org/10.1002/hec.3854.
222. Abouk, R., Courtemanche, C., Dave, D., Feng, B., Friedman, A.S., Maclean, J.C., Safford, S., et al. Intended and Unintended Effects of E-cigarette Taxes on Youth Tobacco Use. J Health Econ. 2023;87:102720. https://doi.org/10.1016/j.jhealeco.2022.102720.
223. Friedman, A.S. How Does Electronic Cigarette Access Affect Adolescent Smoking? J Health Econ. 2015;44:300–308. https://doi.org/10.1016/j.jhealeco.2015.10.003.
224. Pesko, M.F., Hughes, J.M., Faisal, F.S. The Influence of Electronic Cigarette Age Purchasing Restrictions on Adolescent Tobacco and Marijuana Use. Prev Med. 2016;87:207–212. https://doi.org/10.1016/j.ypmed.2016.02.001.

Dave, D., Feng, B., Pesko, M.F. The Effects of E-cigarette Minimum Legal Sale Age Laws on Youth Substance Use. Health Econ. 2019;28(3):419–436. https://doi.org/10.1002/hec.3854.
225. Pesko, M.F. Effects of E-cigarette Minimum Legal Sales Ages on Youth Tobacco Use in the United States. J Risk Uncertain. 2023: 66, 261–277. https://doi.org/10.1007/s11166-022-09402-y.
226. Pesko, M.F., Currie, J.M. E-cigarette Minimum Legal Sale Age Laws and Traditional Cigarette Use Among Rural Pregnant Teenagers. J Health Econ. 2019;66:71–90. https://doi.org/10.1016/j.jhealeco.2019.05.003.
227. Abouk, R., Adams, S. Bans on Electronic Cigarette Sales to Minors and Smoking Among High School Students. J Health Econ. 2017;54:17–24. https://doi.org/10.1016/j.jhealeco.2017.03.003.

228. Sunstein, C.R. On the Expressive Function of Law. U Pa L Rev. 1996;144(5):2021–2053.
229. Antin, T.M., Hunt, G., Kaner, E., Lipperman-Kreda, S. Youth Perspectives on Concurrent Smoking and Vaping: Implications for Tobacco Control. International J Drug Policy. 2019;66:57–63. https://doi.org/10.1016/j.drugpo.2019.01.018.
230. Pesko, M.F. Effects of E-cigarette Minimum Legal Sales Ages on Youth Tobacco Use in the United States. J Risk Uncertain. 2023: 66, 261–277 (2023). https://doi.org/10.1007/s11166-022-09402-y.
231. The issue of enforcement of MLSAs also arises. Policy-makers certainly should not expect all retailers to comply with the law in the absence of enforcement. One study of retailers in Massachusetts found that one-third of underage cigarette purchase attempts were successful, and the odds of success did not depend on whether merchants participated in *It's the Law* programs (tobacco industry-supported efforts including distribution of educational materials and window stickers to retailers). See: DiFranza JR, Savageau JA, Aisquith BF. Youth Access to Tobacco: The Effects of Age, Gender, Vending Machine Locks, and "It's the Law" Programs. Am JPublic Health. 1996;86(2):221–224.
232. European Parliament, "Revision of the Tobacco Products Directive," 2014/40/EU § (2016). https://eur-lex.europa.eu/legal-content/EN/TXT/PDF/?uri=CELEX:32014L0040.
233. "Tobacco and Related Products Regulations 2016," Pub. L. No. 2016, 507 (n.d.). https://www.legislation.gov.uk/uksi/2016/507/contents.
234. Ministry of Health Government of Canada in Council, "Nicotine Concentration in Vaping Products Regulations," SOR/2021–123 § (2021). https://laws-lois.justice.gc.ca/eng/regulations/SOR-2021-123/page-1.html.
235. Hammond, D., Reid, J.L., Burkhalter, R., O'Connor, R.J., Goniewicz, M.L., Wackowski, O.A., Thrasher, J.F., Hitchman, S.C. Trends in E-cigarette Brands, Devices and the Nicotine Profile of Products Used by Youth in England, Canada and the USA: 2017-2019. Tobacco Control. 2021 Jun 7:tobaccocontrol-2020-056371. https://doi.org/10.1136/tobaccocontrol-2020-056371.

236. Farsalinos, K.E., Spyrou, A., Tsimopoulou, K., Stefopoulos, C., Romagna, G., Voudris, V. Nicotine Absorption from Electronic Cigarette Use: Comparison Between First and New-Generation Devices. Sci Rep. 2014;4(1):4133. https://doi.org/10.1038/srep04133.
237. Lillard, D.R. The Economics of Nicotine Consumption. In *Handbook of Labor, Human Resources and Population Economics* (pp. 1-31). Springer, 2020.
238. Jensen, K.P., Valentine, G., Gueorguieva, R., Sofuoglu, M. Differential Effects of Nicotine Delivery Rate on Subjective Drug Effects, Urges to Smoke, Heart Rate and Blood Pressure in Tobacco Smokers. Psychopharmacology. 2020;237:1359–1369. https://doi.org/10.1007/s00213-020-05463-6.
239. Fairchild, A., Colgrove, J. Out of the Ashes: The Life, Death, and Rebirth of the "Safer" Cigarette in the United States. Am J Public Health. 2004;94(2):192–204. https://doi.org/10.2105/ajph.94.2.192.
240. Dawkins, L.E., Kimber, C.F., Doig, M., Feyerabend, C., Corcoran, O. Self-titration by Experienced E-cigarette Users: Blood Nicotine Delivery and Subjective Effects. Psychopharmacology. 2016;233:2933–2941. https://doi.org/10.1007/s00213-016-4338-2.

Soar, K., Kimber, C., McRobbie, H., Dawkins, L.E. Nicotine Absorption from E-cigarettes Over 12 Months. Addict Behav. 2019;91:102–105. https://doi.org/10.1016/j.addbeh.2018.07.019.
241. Farsalinos, K., Poulas, K., Voudris, V. Changes in Puffing Topography and Nicotine Consumption Depending on the Power Setting of Electronic Cigarettes. Nicotine Tob Res. 2018;20(8):993–997. https://doi.org/10.1093/ntr/ntx219.

Dawkins, L.E., Kimber, C.F., Doig, M., Feyerabend, C., Corcoran, O. Self-Titration by Experienced E-cigarette Users: Blood Nicotine Delivery and Subjective Effects. Psychopharmacology. 2016;233(15–16), 2933–2941. https://doi.org/10.1007/s00213-016-4338-2.
242. Irvine, I. "Concentration of Nicotine in Vaping Products Regulations: A Commentary from an Economics Perspective," SSRN Scholarly Paper (Rochester, NY: Social Science Research

Network, March 1, 2021). https://doi.org/10.2139/ssrn.3798634.

243. In fact, some of the early studies purporting to find hazardous chemicals in e-cigarette emissions, e.g., aldehydes, have been criticized as relying on high battery power levels to produce unrealistically high operating temperatures to drive the results (see: Farsalinos KE, Voudris V, Poulas K. E-cigarettes Generate High Levels of Aldehydes only in "Dry Puff" Conditions. Addiction. 2015;110(8):1352–1356).
244. https://www.fda.gov/news-events/press-announcements/fda-announces-plans-proposed-rule-reduce-addictiveness-cigarettes-and-other-combusted-tobacco.
245. Balfour, D.J.K., Benowitz, N.L., Colby, S.M., Hatsukami, D.K., Lando, H.A., Leischow, S.J., Lerman, C., Mermelstein, R.J., Niaura, R., Perkins, K.A., Pomerleau, O.F., Rigotti, N.A., Swan, G.E., Warner, K.E., West, R. Balancing Consideration of the Risks and Benefits of E-Cigarettes. Am J Public Health. 2021 Sep;111(9):1661-1672. https://doi.org/10.2105/AJPH.2021.306416.
246. Benowitz, N.L., Donny, E.C., and Hatsukami, D.K. Reduced Nicotine Content Cigarettes, E-cigarettes and the Cigarette End Game. Addiction. 2017;112:6–7. https://doi.org/10.1111/add.13534.
247. McDonald, J. (2023, April 23). Vape Bans: E-cigarette Restrictions in the U.S. and Worldwide. Vaping360.com. https://vaping360.com/learn/countries-where-vaping-is-banned-illegal/.
248. Campaign for Tobacco-Free Kids (2023, March 17 [from PDF document date of creation]). States & localities that have restricted the sale of flavored tobacco products. https://www.tobaccofreekids.org/assets/factsheets/0398.pdf.
249. Friedman, A.S., Warner, K.E. The E-Cigarette Flavor Debate—Promoting Adolescent and Adult Welfare. N Engl J Med. 2022 Apr 28;386(17):1581–1583. https://doi.org/10.1056/NEJMp2119107.
250. Chen, J.C. Flavored E-cigarette Use and Cigarette Smoking Reduction and Cessation—A Large National Study Among Young Adult Smokers. Substance Use & Misuse. 2018;53(12):2017–2031.

251. Friedman, A.S., Xu, S. Associations of flavored e-cigarette uptake with subsequent smoking initiation and cessation. JAMA Netw Open. 2020;3(6):e203826. https://doi.org/10.1001/jamanetworkopen.2020.3826.
252. Zavala-Arciniega, L., Hirschtick, J.L., Meza, R., Fleischer, N.L. E-cigarette Characteristics and Cigarette Smoking Cessation Behaviors Among US Adult Dual Users of Cigarettes and E-cigarettes. Prev Med Rep. 2022;26:101748.
253. Friedman, A.S., Warner, K.E. The E-cigarette Flavor Debate—Promoting Adolescent and Adult Welfare. N Engl J Med. 2022 Apr 28;386(17):1581–1583. https://doi.org/10.1056/NEJMp2119107.
254. Siegel, M., Katchmar, A. Effect of Flavored E-cigarette Bans in the United States: What Does the Evidence Show? Prev Med. 2022:107063. https://doi.org/10.1016/j.ypmed.2022.107063.
255. Cotti, C.D., Courtmanche, C.J., MacLean, J.C., Nesson, E., Pesko, M., Tefft, N. (2022). The Effects of E-cigarette Taxes on E-cigarette Prices and Tobacco Product Sales: Evidence from Retail Panel Data. NBER Working Paper No. 26724. https://www.doi.org/10.3386/w26724.
256. Soneji, S.S., Knutzen, K.E., Villanti, A.C. Use of Flavored E-cigarettes Among Adolescents, Young Adults, and Older Adults: Findings from the Population Assessment for Tobacco and Health Study. Public Health Reports. 2019;134(3):282–292. https://doi.org/10.1177/0033354919830967.
257. Schneller, L.M., Bansal-Travers, M., Goniewicz, M.L. Use of Flavored E-cigarettes and the Type of E-cigarette Devices Used among Adults and Youth in the US-Results from Wave 3 of the Population Assessment of Tobacco and Health Study (2015–2016). Int J Environ Res and Public Health. 2019;16(16): 2991. https://doi.org/10.3390/ijerph16162991.
258. Meghan, E. Morean, et al. Preferring More E-cigarette Flavors Is Associated with E-cigarette Use Frequency Among Adolescents but Not Adults, PLoS ONE. 2018 Jan 413(1):e0189015. https://doi.org/10.1371/journal.pone.0189015.
259. Soneji, S.S., Knutzen, K.E., Villanti, A.C. Use of Flavored E-cigarettes Among Adolescents, Young Adults, and Older Adults: Findings from the Population Assessment for Tobacco and Health

Study. Public Health Reports. 2019;134(3):282–292. https://doi.org/10.1177/0033354919830967.

260. Schneller, L.M., Bansal-Travers, M, Goniewicz, M.L. Use of Flavored E-cigarettes and the Type of E-cigarette Devices Used among Adults and Youth in the US-Results from Wave 3 of the Population Assessment of Tobacco and Health Study (2015–2016). Int J Environ Res and Public Health. 2019;16(16): 2991. https://www.doi.org/10.3390/ijerph16162991.
261. Rostron, B.L., Chang, J.T., Chang, C.M., et al. ENDS Flavor Preference by Menthol Cigarette Smoking Status Among US Adults, 2018–2019. Int J Environ Res and Public Health. 2020;18(1):240. https://doi.org/10.3390/ijerph18010240.
262. Rostron, B.L., Chang, J.T., Chang, C.M., et al. ENDS Flavor Preference by Menthol Cigarette Smoking Status among US Adults, 2018–2019. Int J Environ Res and Public Health. 2020;18(1):240. https://doi.org/10.3390/ijerph18010240.
263. Schneller, L.M., Bansal-Travers, M., Goniewicz, M.L. Use of Flavored E-cigarettes and the Type of E-cigarette Devices Used among Adults and Youth in the US-Results from Wave 3 of the Population Assessment of Tobacco and Health Study (2015–2016). Int J Environ Res and Public Health. 2019;16(16): 2991. https://www.doi.org/10.1001/jama.2019.18387.

Harrell, M.B., Weaver, S.R., Loukas, A., et al. Flavored E-cigarette Use: Characterizing Youth, Young Adult, and Adult Users. Prev Med Rep. 2016;5:33–40. https://www.doi.org/10.1016/j.pmedr.2016.11.001.

Romijnders, K.A., Krüsemann, E.J., Boesveldt, S., et al. E-liquid Flavor Preferences and Individual Factors Related to Vaping: A Survey among Dutch Never-Users, Smokers, Dual Users, and Exclusive Vapers. Int J Environ Res and Public Health. 2019;16(23):4661. https://www.doi.org/10.3390/ijerph16234661.

Schneller, L.M., Bansal-Travers, M., Goniewicz, M.L. Use of Flavored E-cigarettes and the Type of E-cigarette Devices Used among Adults and Youth in the US-Results from Wave 3 of the Population Assessment of Tobacco and Health Study (2015–2016). Int J Environ Res and Public Health. 2019;16(16): 2991. https://www.doi.org/10.3390/ijerph16162991.

264. Rostron, B.L., Chang, J.T., Chang, C.M., et al. ENDS Flavor Preference by Menthol Cigarette Smoking Status Among US Adults, 2018–2019. Int J Environ Res and Public Health. 2020;18(1):240. https://doi.org/10.3390/ijerph18010240.

Du, P., Bascom, R., Fan, T., et al. Changes in Flavor Preference in a Cohort of Long-Term Electronic Cigarette Users. Ann Am Thorac Soc. 2020;17(5):573–581. https://doi.org/10.1513/AnnalsATS.201906-472OC.

Soneji, S.S., Knutzen, K.E., Villanti, A.C. Use of Flavored E-cigarettes Among Adolescents, Young Adults, and Older Adults: Findings from the Population Assessment for Tobacco and Health Study. Public Health Reports. 2019;134(3):282–292. https://doi.org/10.1177/0033354919830967.

265. Du, P., Bascom, R., Fan, T., Sinharoy, A., Yingst, J., Mondal, P., Foulds, J. Changes in Flavor Preference in a Cohort of Long-Term Electronic Cigarette Users. Ann Am Thorac Soc. 2020 May;17(5):573–581. https://doi.org/10.1513/AnnalsATS.201906-472OC.

266. Russell, C., McKeganey, N., Dickson, T., et al. Changing Patterns of First E-cigarette Flavor Used and Current Flavors Used by 20,836 Adult Frequent E-cigarette Users in the USA. Harm Reduct J. 2018;15(33). https://doi.org/10.1186/s12954-018-0238-6.

267. Russell, C., McKeganey, N., Dickson, T., et al. Changing Patterns of First E-cigarette Flavor Used and Current Flavors Used by 20,836 Adult Frequent E-cigarette Users in the USA. Harm Reduct J. 2018;15(33). https://doi.org/10.1186/s12954-018-0238-6.

268. Friedman, A.S., Warner, K.E. The E-cigarette Flavor Debate—Promoting Adolescent and Adult Welfare. N Engl J Med. 2022 Apr 28;386(17):1581–1583. https://doi.org/10.1056/NEJMp2119107.

269. Prieger, J.E. Regulation, Innovation, and the Introduction of New Telecommunications Services. Rev Econ Stat. 2002;84(4):704–715. https://doi.org/10.1162/003465302760556512.

Prieger, J.E. Regulatory Delay and the Timing of Product Innovation. Int J Ind Organ. 2007;25(2):219–236. https://doi.org/10.1016/j.ijindorg.2006.05.001.

Thomas, L.G. Regulation and FIrm Size: FDA Impacts on Innovation. Rand J Econ. 1990;21(4):497–517. https://doi.org/10.2307/2555465.

Onur, I., Söderberg, M. The Impact of Regulatory Review Time on Incremental and Radical Innovation: Evidence from the High-Risk Medical Device Market. J Regul Econ. 2020;57(4):134–158. https://doi.org/10.1007/s11149-020-09401-4.

Bentzen, E., Freij, Å., Varnes, C.J. The Role of Flexibility and Complexity in Response to Regulatory Change: A Case Study of Innovation in a Major Danish Financial Institution. Int J Entrep Innov. 2021;22(4):229–239. https://doi.org/10.1177/1465750320987929.

Laubach, G.D. Federal Regulation and Pharmaceutical Innovation. Proceedings of the Academy of Political Science. 1980;33(4):60–80.

Stern, A.D. Innovation Under Regulatory Uncertainty: Evidence from Medical Technology. J Public Econ. 2017;145:181–200. https://doi.org/10.1016/j.jpubeco.2016.11.010.

Peltzman, S., 1974. *Regulation of Pharmaceutical Innovation: the 1962 Amendments*. American Enterprise Institute. https://policycommons.net/artifacts/1296024/regulation-of-pharmaceutical-innovation/1899266.

270. Chambers, D., McLaughlin, P.A., Stanley, L. Regulation and Poverty: An Empirical Examination of the Relationship Between the Incidence of Federal Regulation and the Occurrence of Poverty Across the US States. Public Choice. 2019;180:131–144. https://doi.org/10.1007/s11127-018-0603-8.

Chambers, D., O'Reilly, C. Regulation and Income Inequality in the United States. Eur J Political Econ. 2022;72:102101. https://doi.org/10.1016/j.ejpoleco.2021.102101.

Chambers, D., Collins, C.A., Krause, A. How Do Federal Regulations Affect Consumer Prices? An Analysis of the Regressive Effects of Regulation. Public Choice. 2019;180:57–90. https://doi.org/10.1007/s11127-017-0479-z

Thomas, D.W. A Process Perspective on Regulation: Who Bears the Dispersed Costs of Regulation? The Review of

Austrian Economics. 2018;31(4):395–402. https://doi.org/10.1007/s11138-018-0426-3

271. Sobel, R. (2023). Regulation and Entrepreneurship: Theory, Impacts, and Implications. In Hoffer A, Nesbit T (Eds.), *Regulation and Economic Opportunity: Blueprints for Reform*. The Center for Growth and Opportunity.
272. Cortez, N. Regulating Disruptive Innovation. Berkeley Tech. LJ. 2014;29:175.
273. U.S. Food and Drug Administration (2019). Premarket tobacco product applications and recordkeeping requirements: Final regulatory impact analysis; final regulatory flexibility analysis; unfunded mandates reform act analysis. Department of Health and Human Services. https://www.fda.gov/media/152622/download.
274. To the agency's credit, however, it did list this reasoning under the heading of "government failure" in the regulatory impact analysis. See citation Note 273.
275. Niskanen, W.A. *Bureaucracy and Representative Government*. Transaction Publishers, 1971.

     Wilson, J.Q. The Rise of the Bureaucratic State. Public Interest. 1975;41:77–103.
276. Bailey, J.B., Thomas, D.W. Regulating Away Competition: The Effect of Regulation on Entrepreneurship and Employment. J Regul Econ. 2017;52:237–254. https://doi.org/10.1007/s11149-017-9343-9.
277. Calcagno, P.T., Sobel, R.S. Regulatory Costs on Entrepreneurship and Establishment Employment Size. Small Business Economics. 2013;41(1):541–240. https://doi.org/10.1007/s11187-013-9493-9.
278. Jozkowski, E. (February 2023). US industry (NAICS) Report 31222: Cigarette & Tobacco Manufacturing in the US. IBISWorld database.
279. In 1997, the four largest tobacco product manufacturers had 89.0% of the value of shipments. By 2017 this was virtually unchanged at 91.1%. (Data from the Economic Census, 1997 and 2017).
280. In fact, raising average variable costs by a fixed amount (as with a specific tax) will decrease the minimum efficient scale (i.e., the minimum of the average cost curve), which will reduce firm

sizes in the industry in equilibrium. However, this effect may be empirically small, depending on the shape of the cost function.

281. Tullock, G. The Welfare Costs of Tariffs, Monopolies, and Theft. Econ Inquiry. 1967;5(3):224–232. https://doi.org/10.1111/j.1465-7295.1967.tb01923.x.
282. Of course, the economies of scale inherent in manufacturing imply that large firms would likely play an important role in the market for new tobacco products even in the absence of regulation. However, the likelihood of a come-from-nowhere entrant such as Juul would be much lower under entry regulation.
283. Philip Morris International. (n.d.). Our Science. PMI.com. https://www.pmi.com/our-science, last visited 29 May 2023.

    Philip Morris International. (March 15, 2021). PMI Aims to Become a Majority Smoke-Free Business by 2025. PMI.com. https://www.pmi.com/our-transformation/pmi-aims-to-become-a-majority-smoke-free-business-by-2025.
284. Teisberg, E.O. Capital Investment Strategies Under Uncertain Regulation. The RAND Journal of Economics. 1993;591–604. https://doi.org/10.2307/2555747.

    Braeutigam, R.R. The Effect of Uncertainty in Regulatory Delay on the Rate of Innovation. Law & Contemp. Probs. 1979;43:98.

    Prieger, J.E. Regulatory Delay and the Timing of Product Innovation. Int J Indust Organ. 2007;25(2):219–236. https://doi.org/10.1016/j.ijindorg.2006.05.001.
285. Philipson, T., Berndt, E.R., Gottschalk, A.H., Sun, E. Cost–Benefit Analysis of the FDA: The Case of the Prescription Drug User Fee Acts. J Public Econ. 2008;92(5–6):1306–1325. https://doi.org/10.1016/j.jpubeco.2007.09.010.
286. Philipson, T., Berndt, E.R., Gottschalk, A.H., Sun, E. Cost–Benefit Analysis of the FDA: The Case of the Prescription Drug User Fee Acts. J Public Econ. 2008;92(5–6):1306–1325. https://doi.org/10.1016/j.jpubeco.2007.09.010.
287. Fairchild, A.L., Bayer, R., Colgrove, J. The Renormalization of Smoking? E-cigarettes and the Tobacco "Endgame". N Engl J Med. 2014;370(4):293–295. https://doi.org/10.1056/NEJMp1313940.

    Mascarelli, A.L. The Dangerous Rise of Electronic Cigarettes. Science News for Students. 2014;5:14–22.

Voigt, K. Smoking Norms and the Regulation of E-cigarettes. Am J Public Health. 2015;105:1967–1972. https://doi.org/10.2105/AJPH.2015.302764.

288. Public Health England. (2016). E-cigarettes in Public Places and Workplaces: A 5-Point Guide to Policy Making. Gov.uk. https://www.gov.uk/government/publications/use-of-e-cigarettes-in-public-places-and-workplaces/e-cigarettes-in-public-places-and-workplaces-a-5-point-guide-to-policy-making.
289. Eisenberg, M.J., Hébert-Losier, A., Windle, S.B., et al. Effect of E-Cigarettes Plus Counseling vs Counseling Alone on Smoking Cessation: A Randomized Clinical Trial. JAMA. 2020;324(18):1844–1854. https://doi.org/10.1001/jama.2020.18889.

Hajek, P., Phillips-Waller, A., Przulj, D., Pesola, F., Myers Smith, K., Bisal, N., Li, J., Parrott, S., Sasieni, P., Dawkins, L., Ross, L., Goniewicz, M., Wu, Q., McRobbie, H.J. A Randomized Trial of E-cigarettes Versus Nicotine-Replacement Therapy. N Engl J Med. 2019 Feb 14;380(7):629–637. https://doi.org/10.1056/NEJMoa1808779.

290. Farsalinos, K.E., Romagna, G., Tsiapras, D., Kyrzopoulos, S., Voudris, V. Evaluating Nicotine Levels Selection and Patterns of Electronic Cigarette Use in a Group of "Vapers" Who Had Achieved Complete Substitution of Smoking. Substance Abuse. 2013;7:139–146. https://doi.org/10.4137/SART.S12756.
291. Rigotti, N.A. Randomized Trials of E-cigarettes for Smoking Cessation. JAMA. 2020;324(18):1835–1837. https://doi.org/10.1001/jama.2020.18967.
292. Borland, R., Yong, H.H., Siahpush, M., Hyland, A., Campbell, S., Hastings, G., … & Fong, G.T. Support for and reported compliance with smoke-free restaurants and bars by smokers in four countries: findings from the International Tobacco Control (ITC) Four Country Survey. Tobacco control, 2006;15(suppl 3):iii34-iii41. https://doi.org/10.1136/tc.2004.008748.
293. Barnoya, J., Monzon, J.C., Briz, P., Navas-Acien, A. Compliance to the Smoke-Free Law in Guatemala 5-Years After Implementation. BMC Public Health. 2016; 16, 318. https://doi.org/10.1186/s12889-016-2960-x.

Chowdhury, S.R., Sunna, T.C., Das, D.C., Chowdhury, M.R., Mahmud, H.M., Hossain, A. Compliance with Smoke-Free Legislation in Public Places: An Observational Study in a Northeast City of Bangladesh. PLoS ONE. 2023;18(4), e0283650. https://doi.org/10.1371/journal.pone.0283650.

Zasimova, L. Analysis of Non-compliance with Smoke-Free Legislation in Russia. Int J Public Health. 2019;64:413–422. https://doi.org/10.1007/s00038-018-1198-z.

294. Barnoya, J., Monzon, J.C., Briz, P., Navas-Acien, A. Compliance to the Smoke-Free Law in Guatemala 5-Years After Implementation. BMC Public Health. 16, 318 (2016). https://doi.org/10.1186/s12889-016-2960-x.
295. National Health Service. (November 24, 2022). Statistics on NHS Stop Smoking Services in England—April 2021 to March 2022: Part 3—Prescriptions and Pharmacotherapy. NHS.uk. https://tinyurl.com/e5ajtbm6.
296. Office of National Statistics. (December 6, 2022). Adult Smoking Habits in the UK: 2021. ONS website, statistical bulletin. https://tinyurl.com/2j6knbd9.
297. Prieger, J.E., Kleiman, M., Kulick, J., Aziani, A., Levi, M., Hampsher, S., Manning, C., Hahn, R. (June 15, 2019). The Impact of E-cigarette Regulation on the Illicit Trade in Tobacco Products in the European Union. Available at SSRN: https://ssrn.com/abstract=3435177 or http://dx.doi.org/10.2139/ssrn.3435177.

    Prieger, J.E. Hampsher, S. (November 2022). Mitigating Unintended Consequences from Banning Menthol Cigarettes. Available at SSRN: https://papers.ssrn.com/sol3/papers.cfm?abstract_id=4554393.
298. Food and Drug Administration. Tobacco Product Standard for Nicotine Level of Combusted Cigarettes. Department of Health and Human Services. Federal Register, 2018 Mar 16:11818.
299. Benowitz, N.L., Donny, E.C., Hatsukami, D.K. Reduced Nicotine Content Cigarettes, E-cigarettes and the Cigarette End Game. Addiction (Abingdon, England). 2017;112(1):6-7. https://doi.org/10.1111/add.13534.

300. Bardach, E. *A Practical Guide for Policy Analysis—The Eightfold Path to More Effective Problem Solving* (4th ed.). Los Angeles: Sage. 2012.

CHAPTER 3

Remaining Questions

Everyone is entitled to their opinion, but not their own facts.
—U.S. Senator Daniel Patrick Moynihan.[1]

1 What Are the Remaining Knowledge Gaps, and How Can These Be Filled?

As these volumes have hopefully demonstrated, there is a wealth of data on e-cigarettes, smoking, and the impact of regulation of these products that is more than sufficient to inform decisions about e-cigarettes and how they should be regulated. Nonetheless, important gaps in our knowledge remain. Some important factors have no well-supported answers yet: How many smokers who quit with e-cigarettes would have quit unaided, and in what timeframe? How many young e-cigarette users would have been smokers in the absence of e-cigarettes? Answers to these questions would help inform our understanding of the risks and benefits associated with vaping. These counterfactuals cannot be measured in a lab or an RCT but are potentially addressable with quasi-experimental methods from econometrics. In addition to the fruitful application of difference-in-differences methods to questions regarding the impact on smoking or vaping from various policies, perhaps one day other methods can be brought to bear on issues involving selection effects. For example, a small but growing set of Mendelian randomization studies uses genetic markers for predisposition for smoking (found from genome-wide association studies) as

S. C. Hampsher-Monk et al., *Tobacco Regulation, Economics, and Public Health, Volume III*, https://doi.org/10.1007/978-3-031-47096-7_3

instrumental variables to deal with the endogeneity inherent in individuals' choices to smoke.[2,3] To date, this approach has been used mainly to assess the role of smoking in various health outcomes, but perhaps such information could shed light on, for example, the question of how many adolescent vapers likely would have smoked otherwise.

Other research goals may be more readily addressed. Toxicologists will continue to refine their methodologies for assessing the harm potential of e-cigarette emissions in their aerosolized form, investigating any entourage effects (by which combinations of different chemical constituents could have different harm potentials than the sum of those from their constituents) and isolating the effect of specific device components on the toxicity of aerosols. This may help support the development of lists of approved or banned ingredients and stipulations concerning the technical and physical properties of e-cigarettes that could decrease further the risk of using regulated e-cigarettes. Economic research will continue to develop our understanding of the price elasticity of demand for e-cigarettes and, particularly, the degree to which e-cigarettes substitute for combustible tobacco products. There is a wide range of estimates of cross-price elasticity of demand for cigarettes and e-cigarettes, and even if these quantities were estimated with high accuracy today (which they are not),[4] changes in the market, preferences, and regulation will all cause the relationship between the two products to continue to evolve. Further research is also needed to learn under what conditions and in which groups substitution from smoking to e-cigarettes is most likely, helping provide a foundation of evidence useful for regulators to design tax structures to encourage substitutions and discourage uptake among non-smokers and young people.

As different jurisdictions experiment with different regulatory strategies, policy analysts will be able to evaluate the intended and unintended consequences of those strategies, building further the evidence base with which to inform future regulations. For example, California's recently passed Proposition 31 bans the sale of all flavored tobacco products, including e-cigarettes. Will this intervention reduce uptake among youth as intended? How much demand will shift to cross-border purchases or illicit in-state sales, including of unregulated products, eliminating an opportunity to age-gate sales, harming the well-being of the very group the ban intended to benefit? Randomized controlled trials will continue to isolate the conditions under which specific e-cigarettes out-perform "cold-turkey" quit attempts and those supported by conventional NRTs, pharmacotherapies, or behavioral therapy. Meanwhile, survey questions can be updated to elicit more information on past and contemporary consumption patterns, which would help researchers better understand how factors such as duration of e-cigarette use, age of initiation, consumption modalities, and dual or poly use (and which came first, smoking or vaping) affect health outcomes including, ultimately, cessation. Finally, longitudinal studies of e-cigarette users might allow epidemiologists to isolate the long-term health consequences of e-cigarette use by controlling for smoking history (particularly if combined with genetic instruments for usage, as described above), providing the robust statistical information that is currently absent regarding the ultimate effects of e-cigarettes on various medical conditions.

Given that some adverse health outcomes may take decades to present, such studies will likely remain unavailable in the near term. When they do become available, longitudinal data may finally resolve some of the open questions about which there is so much disagreement. In the interim, the available evidence must still inform the discourse on e-cigarettes. A historical lack of generalizability and inconsistency in the nomenclature relating to e-cigarettes has limited the utility of much of the available data. However, researchers in the U.K. have recently begun to develop E-CigO, an e-cigarette ontology, to define explicitly terms for various entities (e.g., an "e-cigarette," which is not a "cannabis vaporizing device") and to their relationships among each other.[5] Such an ontology would enhance clarity of thinking, research, and communication of research findings. Perhaps this and other contributions will help organize and contextualize the available evidence, and help overcome some of the generalizability concerns that impede the generation of evidence-based e-cigarette policies.

2 If Smoking Rates Are Declining, Why Do We Need E-cigarettes?

These volumes have made the case that e-cigarettes, appropriately regulated, can be beneficial for public health. While e-cigarettes are not free from risk, careful and considered regulation can mitigate many of those risks and maximize the benefits. But, even if e-cigarettes can be a tool with which to reduce smoking harms, are they necessary? In the context of declining smoking, why do we need e-cigarettes? The answer is simple: Because smoking rates are not falling fast enough. Even in jurisdictions where there is a long history of robust tobacco control policies, along with free access to behavioral therapies and a range of pharmacotherapies, cessation rates are still disappointing: Smoking rates typically remain above 10% for adults. A significant portion of smokers have demonstrated that they are unable or unwilling to quit using the methods that helped others do so. It is unrealistic to expect the cessation-resistant population to quit with nothing more than the tools that have failed them thus far. Tightening the screws by using additional taxation and removing desirable features from combustible tobacco will bring about additional harms by nudging consumers toward unregulated products and illicit markets, which undermine the benefits of tobacco control by exposing consumers to cheap unregulated products, not to mention other economic and social harms resulting from the criminalization of consumer choice. Not acting is also unconscionable: a failure to do so would resign the population of current smokers to a shorter, sicker lifetime.

Fortunately, this unpalatable choice is a false binary. The uptake of snus in Sweden provides a recent analog. Here, snus has largely replaced combustible cigarettes, and as a result, Sweden has some of the lowest rates of daily smoking and tobacco-related mortality in Europe. As discussed in Volume II, Chapter 3, there is good evidence that the risks associated with using snus are considerably lower than those with cigarette smoking.[6] Alternative nicotine, when appropriately regulated, can and does help smokers who would not otherwise be able to quit do so without imposing commensurate harms on non-smokers. This book has focused on e-cigarettes, but the same logic applies to other non-combustible nicotine products including modern oral nicotine and heated tobacco products. These products occupy different positions on the risk continuum, and (especially for heated tobacco) exactly where is still being determined. However, if these products are acceptable substitutes for smokers, if they really are significantly less risky, and if they help smokers quit and reduce the harms that smoking exposes them to, then the regulation of those products should be designed in proportion to their risk and potential benefits.

3 Why Should We Allow Tobacco Companies to Profit from the Sale of E-cigarettes?

Of course, even those who are convinced by the need for alternative nicotine products might reasonably be skeptical of the need for those products to be available on a commercial basis and sold by companies still selling combustible tobacco. Given the historic harm that has been willfully and knowingly unleashed by traditional tobacco companies (TTCs) in the pursuit of profit, and the decades of denials and outright lies with which the major firms in the industry undermined public understanding about how harmful cigarettes are, such questions are not unreasonable. However, the first e-cigarettes were not invented by the tobacco industry but instead by people committed to reducing the harm for smokers who had thus far not quit. Advocating e-cigarette-led tobacco harm reduction does not necessarily imply on the part of the advocate any goodwill toward the tobacco industry. To the contrary, disdain for TTCs may motivate the desire to disrupt the cigarette industry. Nonetheless, the tobacco industry today has a considerable stake in the e-cigarette market. Even before Altria purchased their 35% stake in Juul in 2018, destroying what remained of a distinction between e-cigarettes and "big tobacco" in the public eye, all of the leading international cigarette manufacturers had acquired or were producing e-cigarettes or heated tobacco products (predominantly e-cigarettes). Today, the largest e-cigarette brands by market share (outside China) are owned in whole or part by companies that also sell combustible cigarettes.[7] What do these companies want with e-cigarettes?

What any company wants with any business decision, of course, is to make profit. Product switching among manufacturers is the hallmark in a dynamic economy, not the exception. Given that one-half of U.S. manufacturing firms alter the product classes they produce in every five years,[8] if anything the question should be what took tobacco manufacturers so long. One interpretation is that, just as the advent of digital photography posed an existential threat to Kodak, the potential for e-cigarettes to disrupt their business model with a superior product forced manufacturers of cigarettes to adapt or die.[9] Selling cigarettes is a dying market—literally—and innovation (or acquisition of innovating firms) is a time-honored tradition to escape decline. So is investing and innovating in response to new or increased competition in the manufacturing sector.[10] The industrial organization literature in economics shows that dominant firms often have incentive to innovate or diversify their product mix to stave off competition from potential entrants,[11,12,13] but those results do not seem to apply here. Entry from a multitude of competitors, most of which have only a small e-cigarette market share, had already occurred before the TTCs got involved.[14] Rather than deterring entry, the moves appear to be defensive. Or maybe, setting aside any strategic considerations, after year upon year of unit sales declines of their traditional products, the chance to enter one of the rare growing segments of the tobacco product market just made sense to cigarette manufacturers.

Cigarettes are not the only industry that faces disruption by e-cigarettes. In some countries at least, prescriptions for NRTs have declined as e-cigarettes rose in popularity.[15] On the other hand, in the U.S. there is some evidence that e-cigarettes may be economic complements with some NRTs.[16] In either scenario the pharmaceutical industry may be affected by changes in demand for e-cigarettes. However, the pharmaceutical companies such as GlaxoSmithKline that make NRTs have been reluctant to enter the e-cigarette market, perhaps viewing these products as too controversial.[17] In any event, the diversification of the pharmaceutical industry's product portfolio insulates them from the disruption that e-cigarettes posed to their NRT products. On the other hand, for cigarette manufacturers, the disruption risk posed by staying out of the market for alternative nicotine, along with the potential lifeline entering that market offered, surely was more compelling.

Still, despite declining smoking prevalence, cigarette production continues to be phenomenally profitable. In 2018, the six largest tobacco companies made US$55 billion before taxes, more than the combined profits of Coca-Cola, Pepsico, Nestle, Mondelez, Fedex, General Mills, Starbucks, Heineken, and Carlsberg.[18] And as discussed in Volume III, Chapter 2 (Sect. 7.2), the return on assets for U.S. tobacco manufacturers was actually much higher in recent years than 5 to 15 years ago. These profits were not created by entering the e-cigarette market; by 2022 Altria had lost 95% of the value of its investment in Juul,[19] and BAT's "new products" category (which includes e-cigarettes) did not achieve profitability until 2023, and then only because of an oral nicotine product.[20] So is the TTCs' transformation really motivated by a newly-found concern for the well-being of their consumers, as they claim, or is it all about profit (which has not yet materialized)? These questions are debatable, but they are of secondary importance for those most interested in public health rather than in punishing tobacco firms. The more important questions are, "Is tobacco industry transformation genuine?" and "What is be gained or lost from the tobacco industry's involvement in the e-cigarette market?"

3.1 Is the Tobacco Industry Transformation Genuine?

The tobacco companies certainly want their investors and the general public to believe that they are changing. Their websites are awash with references to "transformation," "moving beyond smoking," "challenging ourselves to do better" and harm reduction. Altria claims it will "Responsibly lead the transition of adult smokers to a non-combustible future."[21] According to British American Tobacco (BAT), the firm is on a mission "To build A Better Tomorrow by reducing the health impact of our business."[22] Likewise, Imperial Brands highlights its efforts to develop its portfolio of "Next Generation Product" and make a "Meaningful contribution to harm reduction."[23] Philip Morris International (PMI) goes as far as to advocate for its vision of a "Smoke-free future,"[24] followed by: "Because it's the right thing to do."[25]

Even in the glossy marketing copy produced by TTCs, words are cheap. Tobacco control advocates have argued that the transformation is less about an altruistic departure from the companies' traditional (lethal) business model, and more about the adoption of a new product category in pursuit of commercial interests.[26] If the goal is to improve public health or social welfare more broadly defined, the *motives* of these companies is irrelevant—it is only the consequences that matter. The profit motive will be addressed further in the next section.

Words may be cheap, but bringing smoke-free alternatives to market is anything but. Since 2008, PMI has invested more than US$9 billion in R&D on smoke-free products. Between 2020 and 2021, PMI increased R&D expenditure on smoke-free products by 14%, and in 2021 alone BAT and PMI invested a combined $1.15 billion in combustion-free alternatives.[27] Several tobacco manufacturers have also set ambitious targets for their smoke-free segments. PMI announced in 2021 that its aims to be a majority smoke-free business by 2025,[28] and BAT announced plans to have 50 million customers for its non-consumables by 2030. In 2017, non-combustibles accounted for just 4% of BAT's revenue, but by 2021 it was 12%, and in some national markets it was close to 40%.[29] The fact that reduced-risk products represent a growing portion of at least some companies' revenue also suggests that those companies are indeed changing: between 2020 and 2022, PMI increased its volume share of reduced-risk products from 8 to 13%, BAT increased its share from 7 to 10%, and Altria increased its share from 25 to 26%.[30] Nevertheless, if there is a transformation it is still in its early stages. For example, for every one e-cigarette pod or unit that it sold in 2022, BAT still sold about 50 packs of cigarettes.[31]

It is evident that, however "transformation" is defined, some companies out-perform others. The Foundation for a Smoke-free World, has developed *The Tobacco Transformation Index* (TTI), ranking the world's 15 largest tobacco companies on their progress toward harm reduction. The various metrics used to compute the TTI include strategy and management, product sales, capital allocation and expenditure, product mix, marketing policy and compliance (e.g. preventing youth access to tobacco products), and lobbying and advocacy. In the 2022 report (covering 2019–2021)[32] the TTI shows that progress toward transformation among tobacco companies has been inconsistent, and that industry transformation overall is immature. Reduced-risk tobacco products accounted for only 5% of the indexed companies' revenue for 2021, and only Swedish Match had sales of reduced-risk products comprising more than 50% if its revenue (in the company's last full year before it was acquired by PMI).[33] However, there are distinct differences among the largest tobacco companies. Swedish Match, PMI, Altria and BAT are credited with having demonstrated "strategic commitment to tobacco harm reduction" with consistent execution. Imperial, JT and KT&G have "recognized harm reduction" but are not as consistent in execution. Others, including ITC, CNTC, Djarum have little or no strategic commitment to or progress toward tobacco harm reduction.

Just as the notion of industry transformation has come under fire for masking the fact that tobacco companies continue to sell combustible tobacco products, the TTI has, itself, faced criticism for adopting the industry's emphasis on new product generation and de-emphasizing the phasing out of combustibles.[34] While the progress of industry-wide transformation may be disappointing, spending on non-combustible alternatives lends credibility to the notion that at least some tobacco companies' commitment to transformation is genuine.[35] If so, attempts to discourage such may have unintended consequences.[36]

3.2 *What Can Be Gained or Lost from the Tobacco Industry's Involvement in the E-cigarette Market?*

As the global e-cigarette market continues to develop, industry players will continue to jockey for position as they leverage manufacturing capacity, financial capital, and product innovation for commercial gain. In this area, the pursuit of profit is not antithetical to the public good. Policy decisions may either help or hinder this process. By distinguishing among products based on risk, regulators can create an environment that accelerates a shift in demand toward less harmful products, encouraging tobacco industry transformation by rewarding the fastest and most radical transformers with market share and brand recognition. Conversely, regulatory standards could also easily impede this process.

Denying the evidence that non-combustible products are safer, regulating them on parity with traditional cigarettes, and denying that the industry is (or is even capable of) changing ultimately helps insulate those tobacco firms who remain focused on traditional cigarettes. By undermining consumer demand for non-combustible products, regulators ultimately keep nicotine dependence aligned with smoking; and by creating barriers to entry, they prevent competitors from introducing safer alternatives that would erode demand for combustible products. As exemplified by the compliance burdens manifest by the FDA's PMTA process, stringent regulatory requirements result in high compliance costs for industry participants. These compliance costs serve as barriers to entry, which are difficult or impossible for smaller, independent firms to accommodate.

On the other hand, larger firms with sufficient capital to cover the costs of compliance may be rewarded with regulatory authorization, allowing them to operate in a market insulated from competition from smaller rivals. The dangers of excessive concentration in the market have already been discussed in Volume III, Chapter 2 (Sect. 7.2); suffice it to say here that it is better to gain any perceived improvement in public health from higher prices by means of taxing tobacco products than by allowing a small group of dominant firms to raise prices to reap high profits. Furthermore, if production of e-cigarettes are concentrated among firms that also manufacture cigarettes, then they will have less incentive to entice smokers to switch to vaping (whether through price or other means), since they would be cannibalizing their own demand. A smaller price differential may be expected to reduce substitutions and, by extension, reduce smoking cessation.

As a practical matter, regulators in any industry typically prefer a smaller number of firms producing a stable set of products. This makes regulatory oversight easier and encourages investment in the flow of information and relationship-specific capital on both sides. However, the social goal of regulation is not to make life easy for the regulators but to protect consumers. As long as all firms and products are held to the same standards, it is not at all clear why a smaller number of producers is to be preferred. Any economic argument based on duplication of entry or other fixed costs is almost surely outweighed by the benefits of additional product diversity to convince smokers to switch the e-cigarettes via innovation and competition.

Apart from capacity to overcome the regulatory burden, there are two other potential advantages of allowing or even encouraging tobacco industry transformation. The first is that tobacco companies are provided with an exit strategy from their traditional business model—the one which leads to the premature death of every second consumer. If tobacco control advocates truly believe that public health would be well-served if all tobacco companies were to abandon the manufacture of cigarettes, then would not encouraging transformation at least qualify as partial progress toward that goal? The second advantage is that TTCs may have unique knowledge of their customers' preferences, marketing capacity, and distribution networks to encourage substitution from smoking to e-cigarettes. If we are committed to the use of e-cigarettes for the purposes of smoking cessation, well-capitalized firms with a century of experience producing and marketing nicotine products, a large store of institutional knowledge regarding their consumers' preferences and consumption habits, and control over the marketing channels and distribution networks by which smokers obtain their products would seem like an important ally.

One oft-heard objection to the involvement of cigarette manufacturers in harm reduction is the claim that if these firms were serious about the effort then they would stop selling cigarettes.[37] According to the Federal Trade Commission, in 2019 the four major U.S. tobacco companies spent US$7.62 billion marketing conventional cigarettes in the U.S. alone.[38] If TTCs were really committed to transformation, would they not withdraw combustibles immediately?[39] There are logical and economic reasons why this would not be so. First, there is a collective action problem to consider: faced with the declining demand for combustibles, it might be in all tobacco companies' interest to transform, moving away from combustibles. But any first mover abandoning the market for cigarettes would pay a large penalty of the pioneer. They would raise their rivals' revenue in the combustibles market (after all, just because supply would be reduced does not mean that demand for cigarettes would be), deepening those competitors' capacity to fund R&D and product innovation in the new market segment. First movers are further penalized with the costs of complying with regulators "moving the goal posts" as they figure out how the new products should be regulated. They would also bear the brunt of public criticism regarding their motivations for transformation. In addition, for-profit companies have a fiduciary obligation to maximize value for their shareholders, making it practically impossible for any of the major tobacco companies—which are all publicly held—to abandon their primary market overnight. If they did, their shareholders would launch an class lawsuit for damages, and the executive leadership would be removed and replaced by those willing to walk back the transformation.

Another possible objection to allowing TTCs to transform is the sense that doing so somehow absolves, or at least fails to make TTCs pay, for their historic transgressions. Clearly, this is not an economic argument; the purpose of sanctions against companies for misbehavior is not to address the sunk cost of past actions but to deter future similar conduct. The massive settlement against TTCs in the U.S. served that goal. However, even on the grounds of justice (or even pique), this objection does not stand. While the history of industry-led deception is inexcusable, restricting smokers' access to e-cigarettes because they are made by companies with a reputation for causing harm would be akin to telling the passengers of the Titanic not to board the lifeboats because they, too, were manufactured by the White Star Line. Of course, the industry itself has itself to blame for this situation. The mistrust that was fostered by industry disinformation now perpetuates harm by fostering antipathy to safer alternatives and regulations that would promote switching among those who are unable or unwilling to do so unassisted.

For-profit companies are inevitably going to seek opportunities to maximize value to their shareholders, and shareholder value will never be perfectly aligned with the interests of the public. That is why shareholder capitalism and the firms operating under it are subject to liability law and regulation in modern economies. But seeking profit is in itself not intrinsically antithetical to the interests of public health. The challenge for regulators then, is to use policy to best align the profit motive with the social good. Tobacco harm reduction provides one such opportunity.

If tobacco industry transformation is to be encouraged, there are carrots to consider as well as sticks. The profits from brand recognition and market share for non-combustibles serve as incentives (carrots) in themselves. But regulators could further entice TTCs toward these benefits by abandoning nomenclature that undermines the distinction between cigarettes and non-combustible alternatives and by ceasing to assert that all TTCs have the same malevolent intent. Furthermore, as David Sweanor has articulated,[40] the tobacco industry should not be considered to be a monolithic entity but instead a collection of heterogeneous organizations with different priorities and strategies. Within that milieux, those strategies that are more closely aligned with the public interest should be recognized and not unduly discouraged. When TTCs' actions are misaligned with the public interest, disincentives (sticks) are called for. E-cigarettes may help here, too. As discussed in the previous chapter (see Sect. 8 there), providing e-cigarettes and other non-combustible nicotine products as a viable alternative to combustible tobacco increases the viability of more stringent restrictions on combustibles. Thus, the stringency of regulations applied to combustibles may be ramped up while maintaining considerably less stringent regulations for e-cigarettes. Doing so would further encourage consumer substitutions to safer alternatives, rewarding those tobacco companies most committed to transformation and eroding the profitability of the remainder.

4 Should We Ignore All Research on Tobacco and Nicotine Conducted by Industry?

If we are, perhaps reluctantly, willing to let TTCs play an important role in the e-cigarette industry, does that mean we should accept the results of their research on tobacco and nicotine? How valuable would such research be, given the taint of its authorship and the firms' incentives to arrive at certain results and to avoid others? It depends. There are certainly important questions related to e-cigarettes that remain unanswered, and utilizing industry resources could help fill these knowledge gaps. In many sectors, including telecommunications, pharmaceuticals, food products, medical devices, energy, and transportation, industry funding pays for important contributions to research, even though it is widely recognized that firms are likely financially invested in the results and there is debate over bias.[41] As one researcher asked in the context of another FDA-regulated product area, "Who do you think pays for the process of moving a rough idea into an approved product? With rare exceptions, it is neither academic institutions nor the government."[42] It is industry. However, as a legacy of the research-related fraud committed by the tobacco industry in the past, the public is justifiably skeptical of anything produced by the tobacco industry and those funded by it. As discussed in Volume II, Chapter 3, "industry" researchers are frequently barred from academic conferences and publishing in many journals. This applies to alternative nicotine products as it does to tobacco, meaning that many potentially important contributions to the evidence base are ignored as inadmissible.

While understandable, this skepticism may actually be thwarting the exact end that non-affiliated researchers seek to support, namely impartial research. Given that one of the concerns about e-cigarettes is a lack of evidence, it is somewhat ironic to deny, *prima facie*, contributions from any circle. This is especially so considering that the deep pockets and consumer information possessed by industry allows some forms of research that would be difficult or impossible to fund or perform by other parties. Further, in its original enunciation, the precautionary principle placed the onus of responsibility for demonstrating a sufficient standard of safety on the advocates of the potentially risky innovation. So, it is inconsistent that proponents of the precautionary principle would now bar the industry from contributing to the production of the evidence base. More so, since many of the organizations producing research that *is* deemed admissible are themselves not free from potential biases including financial motives. Many vocal opponents of e-cigarettes are funded by philanthropies with their own agendas, and whose only accountability mechanism is the loosest legal requirement to be seen to be serving public benefit. "Non-profit" does not imply disinterest in the financial viability of the NGO.

No research, regardless of its authorship, should be taken at face value. Scientific evidence must be judged on the rigor of the analytical methods used and its ability to produce replicable results and test hypotheses. Either research qualifies as admissible by this standard, in which case the background of the author is irrelevant, or it fails, in which case the evidence should not be admissible anyway. Authorship affiliations and funding alone should therefore be neither necessary nor sufficient to determine the admissibility of evidence. If those in a position to determine the admissibility of the data were confident in their ability to judge contributions impartially, without reference to the authorship, then any contributions that did not meet the described standards could be rejected on their own merits without appealing to a fallacious and inconsistently applied *ad hominem* standard. Meanwhile, any contributions from the industry (or any other source for that matter) could be interrogated on its merits. This is especially important in cases where industry data, if not analysis, could provide important contributions to the discourse. For example, information on consumer behavior and preferences could help shed light on how consumption patterns evolve over time, including in response to regulatory decisions. When industry research is intended to influence public discourse and policy, the underlying data should not be hidden behind claims of its proprietary nature; the data, methodology should be made available for scrutiny, replication, and evaluation by independent analysts, including those in government employment. Of course, by the same token, tobacco-related datasets created by governments and NGOs should follow the same rules. Not all currently do so.[43]

5 Is More Nicotine Use a Price Worth Paying for Less Smoking?

If we make e-cigarettes available, appealing, affordable and attractive, their uptake will increase. That is likely to have two effects: Smoking-related harms will decrease as smokers switch to less harmful alternatives; and nicotine use, and dependence, will continue. Paradoxically, the relative risk-reduction offered by e-cigarettes may reduce the public concerns about nicotine use, protracting use and dependence.[44] "Dependence," especially among those who may not have used nicotine in the absence of e-cigarettes, is a central concern for many who are opposed to e-cigarettes.

An idiomatic understanding of "addiction," informed by the context of alcohol abuse, illicit drug use, and smoking (all of which are associated with harmful comorbidities), often leads observers to mischaracterize the effects of "dependence" in the context of combustion-free nicotine, implying that it is more harmful than the evidence suggests. Given the different risk profiles of cigarettes and e-cigarettes, dependence in either context must be differentiated from the other. Granted, the ultimate health consequences of long-term e-cigarette use are unknown, so it is unclear that dependence in the context of e-cigarette use will not also result in some future medical harm. But it is also increasingly clear from the available data, reviewed in Volume II, Chapter 1, that e-cigarettes are much less harmful than combustible tobacco. The concept of dependence is therefore more nuanced than is often acknowledged in the literature.

That, however, does not mean that dependence, even in the context of non-combustible nicotine, should be disregarded. Besides any attendant medical risks, dependence per se may result in other categories of harm, including social harm and negative economic consequences for the consumer. Such harms are not inherently trivial, but they are also categorically distinct from the medical harms associated with smoking and illicit drug use. These differences should be made explicit by those appealing to dependence to inform public decision-making regarding e-cigarettes.

One way in which dependence on combustion-free nicotine could be harmful in the absence of attendant medical risks relates to liberty: Dependence might be said to deny the consumer of their personal agency or autonomy.[45] This and similar arguments have already been covered in Volume III, Chapter 2 (Sect. 5.3.3). The harm reduction perspective counters with the observation that if dependence results in economic and social harms (including stigma), those are largely results of the social and political responses to the behavior. Moreover, harm reduction advocates value e-cigarettes precisely because they are freely chosen by the individual as a safer alternative to smoking, ideally enabling smoking cessation. The substitution to a safer alternative also allows the consumer to avoid, at least partially, the effects of coercive interventions which, after a point, exacerbate those harms, with consequences for, again, individual liberty.

However, grant for the sake of argument that there will be some e-cigarette users whose liberty will be harmed by subsequent "dependence," and others for whom their liberty is advanced by the availability of e-cigarettes. Given that both groups exist, appeals to liberty are not *prima facie* sufficient to justify restrictions. To adjudicate between these competing claims on liberty it becomes necessary to determine how many individuals' liberty is, respectively, harmed or hindered by nicotine use. That brings us back to the cost–benefit analysis. That analysis should be informed by several observations: The overwhelming majority of e-cigarette users were already using nicotine when they started using e-cigarettes[46]; many of those who were not could reasonably have been expected to go on to do so[47]; and the majority of e-cigarette use by never-smokers is experimental and transient, and therefore not indicative of "dependence."[48] This suggests that the pool of consumers whose liberty is violated by the presence of e-cigarettes is significantly smaller than the group whose liberty is advanced by e-cigarettes.

As a final moral consideration, the distribution of nicotine dependence is also relevant. As a principle of social justice, to the extent that nicotine dependence is harmful, for any given total amount of harm it may be preferable for that harm to be spread over the general population, rather than being concentrated among specific groups.[49] This may be especially true if, as is often the case, the harms of smoking have historically been concentrated among groups facing structural disadvantages. Grill argues that "the same aggregate loss of (quality-adjusted) life-years may weigh less heavily, morally speaking, if it is shared among a larger number of future vapers than if it is shared among a smaller number of current smokers."[50] While a more equitable distribution of risk may be desirable in itself, it is also worth reiterating that the aggregate costs of nicotine use with e-cigarettes as an option are likely to be far lower than those in a scenario without e-cigarettes.[51] Thus, while the absolute number of nicotine users may increase with e-cigarettes, this should be a primary concern on neither moral nor public health grounds.

Viral epidemiology provides an analogy that may help frame this discussion. Viruses that are highly transmissible but less virulent are a nuisance but are not typically a public health priority. Rhinoviruses, for example, which cause the common cold, infect lots of people but kill few. Instead, priority is given to more virulent viruses (such as coronaviruses), especially viruses that are both virulent and highly transmissible (such as Ebola). It is, therefore, not the transmissibility that is cause for concern in isolation, but the severity of the resulting infection. Similarly, once decoupled from combustion, nicotine addiction should also be less of a concern than it would be in the context of smoking, even if it is more persistent or widespread.

6 What Are the Environmental Impacts of E-cigarettes, and Can These Be Mitigated?

The literature on harms from e-cigarette focuses largely on medical risks. However, these are not the only harms that warrant consideration. E-cigarette waste introduces plastics, heavy metals and chemicals into the environment, contaminating the soil and polluting waterways.[52] In many cases the material constituents of e-cigarettes will remain in the environment for many years. In addition to material waste, the mining of materials (lithium, copper etc.), manufacture, transportation, and packaging also cause environmental harm through emissions, energy usage and waste production.[52] The problem is most severe for disposable e-cigarettes, which have increased in popularity in many national markets. Whereas non-disposables have a service life extending to months or even years, the materials in disposable are discarded after a short period of use. Refillable pod technology and tank systems (see Volume I, Chapter 3) therefore produce significantly less waste relative to disposables (on a unit of nicotine basis). Rechargeable devices also use much smaller batteries than disposables, and because the latter larger devices must be disposed of after "a single use" (approximately 400–600 puffs in the case of U.K. e-cigarettes) disposable devices have become a special point of focus for those concerned with e-cigarette's environmental harms. According to the U.K. Charity Material Focus, 1.3 million disposable vapes are discarded each week in the U.K., introducing to the environment 10 tons of lithium per year; the equivalent of the batteries of 1,200 electric vehicles.[53] According to the CDC Foundation more than 200 million new e-cigarette devices were sold in U.S. alone in 2020, resulting in vast quantities of plastic, aluminum, lithium ion batteries, and packaging ending up in landfill as a result."[54] The environmental harms resulting from the improper disposal of e-cigarettes have been cited in support of restrictions on vapes in Scotland[55] and Ireland.[56]

E-cigarettes are a form of hazardous e-waste[57] and should not be disposed of in the conventional waste stream. Damaged and improperly disposed lithium-ion batteries can cause fires and need to be disposed of via designated waste streams[58] in which the hard plastics, lithium-ion batteries, and electronic circuit boards can be disassembled, sorted, recycled, and disposed of.[52] In this regard, however, e-cigarettes are no different than many other forms of hazardous waste from household electronic products. However, according to a Truth Initiative survey[54] only 15% of young e-cigarette users (15–24) dispose of e-cigarettes via electronic recycling centers. More than half of users report throwing them into the regular trash and one in ten reports littering. More than 70% of consumers surveyed reported being aware that it was improper to discard e-cigarette waste in the trash, but almost 60% of respondents found it inconvenient to dispose of e-cigarettes responsibly and almost half reported that manufacturers did not provide information on appropriate disposal.

To some extent, the environmental consequences of disposable e-cigarettes may be seen as an unintended consequence of certain regulatory decisions. In the U.S., federal restrictions on flavors applied to pod-type e-cigarettes but not disposables, precipitating a significant increase in the demand for disposable devices. In the U.K., flavored pods continue to be permitted, but disposables have nonetheless increased as a share of the market. ASH U.K. report that disposables were the main type of devices used by only 15% of e-cigarette users in 2022,[59] but among 18–34-year-old e-cigarette users, 48% did so, up from just 2.8% in 2021.[60] U.K. regulations cap e-cigarette reservoir volumes at 2 ml, meaning that disposables there are smaller than in many other markets. This feature was designed to reduce the appeal of e-cigarettes, but as an unintended consequence the environmental footprint of e-cigarettes on a unit of nicotine basis has increased. In Canada, where there are currently no regulations limiting the tank size of disposables, devices with 14 ml tanks are common. Larger devices offer a longer service life, reducing the amount of material disposed of compared to a consumer using the same volume of e-liquid via U.K.-compliant disposables. Of course, the fact that larger disposables produce less waste on a unit of nicotine basis does not necessarily justify the availability of those larger devices, nor does it suggest that volume limits should be abandoned. Although the environmental costs of e-cigarette consumer behavior are just one factor to consider when designing e-cigarette regulations, they are a factor that *should* be considered.

As with other topics of e-cigarette regulation, e-cigarette environmental risks must be framed in relation to the environmental risks of the economic substitute: combustible cigarettes. As discussed in Volume I, Chapter 1, combustibles have their own environmental harms. The WHO estimates that 6.25 trillion plastic cellulose acetate cigarette butts are littered annually.[61] In addition to disposal, the production, cultivation, curing, manufacture, transportation, and use of tobacco also produce environmental harms including emission of greenhouse gasses, habitat destruction, pollution, waste, and degradation of natural resources including soil, waterways and air.[62] According to the CDC, the estimated annual emissions produced by the manufacturing of tobacco alone are equal to the emissions of roughly 3 million transatlantic flights. Any calculation of e-cigarettes' net environmental harm must be reduced by the forgone environmental harms resulting from the displacement of combustible cigarettes by e-cigarette alternatives. Comparing the environmental impact of a discarded cigarette pack and 20 butts with a disposable e-cigarette delivering a roughly comparable volume of nicotine, the comparatively greater environmental impact of the e-cigarette may seem obvious. However, the salient comparison is also affected by production methods, transportation, and disposal among numerous other factors. Local production, reusability, materials selection, and the inclusion of disposal instructions all provide opportuntites to reduce e-cigarettes' environmental impact. The wide degree of variation in these parameters complicates the Environmental Impact Assessment of the supply chain for each product necessary for cross product comparisons.

If the environmental impact of e-cigarettes does exceed that of smoking, the resulting harms trade off against the health benefits of smoking cessation (where delivered). Direct comparison of these risks and benefits is difficult, but consideration of other waste streams (medical waste for example) supports the view that some excess environmental costs may be justified on the basis of securing public health benefit. Though, of course, this does not mean that steps should not also be taken to mitigate environmental harms where possible. At a minimum, producers should be required to provide information to consumers on appropriate disposal. But product prices and other aspects of regulation relating to products' accessibility and appeal could also be leveraged to steer consumer demand toward rechargeable devices with a smaller environmental footprint, in lieu of disposable ones. Some commenters have noted that since e-cigarette waste contains both electronic and hazardous waste, it is currently impossible to legally recycle disposable e-cigarettes in the U.S.[63] However, that status quo is neither universal nor inevitable. Waste disposal fees could be used to fund recycling programs and public awareness campaigns to inform consumers about the importance of correct disposal and direct users toward existing facilities. User fees could be made to be refundable to disincentivize inappropriate disposal. Regulators could also standardize the protocol for recycling of e-cigarette devices and might require manufacturers to offer take-back programs, or even mandate cradle-to-cradle production as a precondition for marketing approval. Manufactures producing other forms of e-waste (cellphones, for example) have long since operated extended producer responsibility (EPR) programs[64] From the perspective of the producer, that need not be an entirely altruistic endeavor: diverting e-waste allows producers to recapture materials that could be reused, repurposed, or recycled potentially reducing production costs. Similarly, production costs could be reduced by limiting the materials used in manufacture with the additional benefit of reducing e-waste. Such programs with monetary incentives have been largely absent from the e-cigarette recycling ecosystem. However, Altria voluntarily enacted some limited forms of EPR-type buyback programs via subsidiaries: Green Smoke and MarkTen (though neither brands are sold any longer).[52] In January 2023, the U.K.'s Vaping Industry Association (UKVIA) announced that it was working with DEFRA and the Office for Product Safety and Standards to find a waste management solution that minimizes the impact of vapes on the environment without sacrificing the utility of the broader e-cigarette category for the purposes of smoking cessation. UKVIA also called on the industry to innovate products to facilitate recycling.[65]

Industry EPR programs could also extend to production including the use of renewable energy sources.[66] Regulation could incentivize less environmentally harmful commercial practices as part of gaining marketing authorization. For example, the FDA requires PMTA applicants to submit Environmental Impact Assessment or a Finding of No Significant Impact. More comprehensive and widespread adoption of EPRs in the e-cigarette industry may have been disincentivized by the derision with which analogous campaigns to reduce the environmental impact of combustible tobacco products have been received. Such efforts have been dismissed as "greenwashing": hypocritical PR stunts designed to misdirect public attention away from the harm of their business model.[54] Industry-led efforts to reduce their environmental footprint may be flawed and motivated by profit maximization but if criticism disincentivize those efforts, environmental harms may be perpetuated. Instead, as with broader industry transformation, critical analysis of industry-led ERP initiatives should encourage the adoption of more comprehensive alternatives.

7 Do E-cigarettes Help or Hinder Smoking-Related Disparities?

As we saw in Volume I, Chapter 2, a relatively common feature of societies in which the prevalence of smoking has declined is that the harms from remaining smoking have become concentrated in lower socio-economic status (SES) groups and other disadvantaged communities.[67] There is a moral imperative to redress this disparity, which has been acknowledged by many national governments including in the U.K.[68] Among national regulators, the U.K. government has adopted an unusually enthusiastic stance toward e-cigarettes, which has been credited with increasing the proportion of quitting attempts and the success of those attempts in the U.K.[69] However, it is unclear whether these benefits are evenly distributed between different subnational communities, thus the effect of e-cigarette uptake on smoking-disparities remains unclear.

Given the common liability toward risky behaviors, e-cigarette use may, initially at least, be concentrated among the same communities where smoking rates are highest and the harms are greatest. That may be viewed with concern; to the extent that vaping among non-smokers confers risk, if the uptake of e-cigarettes by non-smokers was greater among disadvantaged communities relative to background rates, e-cigarettes could introduce a novel health-disparity. On the other hand, to the extent that vaping by smokers increases the likelihood of successfully quitting smoking, or reduces smoking-related harms, a greater uptake of vaping among the communities where smoking is already concentrated may be desirable. Provided that the effect of e-cigarette use on smoking cessation is similar between communities where smoking rates are concentrated and the general population, a relatively higher frequency of vaping among disadvantaged communities may be accompanied by relatively higher rates of smoking cessation, thereby alleviating some of the existing smoking-related disparities. However, the theory underlying consumer adoption of new technology suggests that disadvantaged communities will actually be slower to adopt e-cigarettes relative to wealthier communities.[70] In this scenario, the introduction of e-cigarettes may perpetuate or even exacerbate existing smoking-related disparities, at least for a time, by concentrating the benefits of smoking cessation in less-disadvantaged groups. In accord with this conjecture, there is evidence (for the U.S. at least) that smokers tend to have lower socio-economic status than e-cigarette users in Vol. III, Chapter 2, Section 5.5.[71]

A lack of granular data on both smoking and vaping, disaggregated by income and locality, makes investigating these possibilities difficult. Both due to confidentiality restrictions and lack of sufficient observations, most survey datasets on smoking and vaping do not allow examination of harms at the neighborhood or even town level. However, researchers have begun to explore the possible effects of e-cigarettes on disparities. Green et al.[72] report that in the U.K. lower SES status was associated with vaping among young never-smokers, and adult ex-smokers, but not adult never-smokers or adult current smokers. On the other hand, the positive association between having quit among ever smokers and being from a lower SES group was moderately weaker among those who used e-cigarettes. The authors conclude that the inequalities in vaping could exacerbate health disparities by concentrating the harms of vaping by non- and ex-smokers among lower SES groups and reduce disparities by helping lower SES smokers quit.

Using longitudinal data from England's Smoking Toolkit Study for 2014–2017, Koch et al.[73] find that higher SES smokers were more likely to use e-cigarettes than lower SES smokers, though the disparity reduced over time. While these groups were similar in their use of e-cigarettes during a quitting attempt, use of e-cigarettes by ex-smokers increased over time in all groups and was concentrated among those with lower SES. The latter concentration may be interpreted in different ways. Perhaps e-cigarette use among ex-smokers reduces the chance of relapse to smoking, in which case e-cigarettes could reduce pre-existing smoking-related disparities. Alternatively, if those individuals would otherwise have remained abstinent from smoking anyway, the concentration of e-cigarette use among ex-smokers in disadvantaged communities could represent a novel disparity.

Reporting on NHIS surveys of individuals in the 25–54 age group in the U.S., 2014–2016, Friedman and Horn[74] find that, in contrast to the strong negative gradients between SES and smoking, the comparable gradients for e-cigarette use are small and not statistically significant. This can be compared with evidence from another study using the CPS-TUS, 2018–2019, which also finds a smaller (but statistically significant) income gradient for using e-cigarettes than for smoking.[75] Friedman and Horn also show that among ever-smokers, transitioning to e-cigarettes is more common among more educated groups. The authors conclude that the apparent differential may exacerbate socioeconomic disparities in smoking-related morbidity and mortality, but nonetheless lower the total burden of tobacco-related disease.

Lucherini and colleagues'[76] metanalysis summarizes the heterogeneity in the evidence on this topic between different contexts. The authors conclude that, as a relatively recent innovation, the diffusion of e-cigarettes through society is still immature. As diffusion continues throughout society, it is possible that uptake of e-cigarettes for the purposes of cessation will become more uniform across the smoking population. If so, and if quitting rates resulting from e-cigarette use are also uniform, that could, in time, reduce the harms experienced by lower SES groups from smoking being more common in these communities. It remains to be seen if, and over what timeframe, this occurs. Further research will also be needed to uncover whether dual use and the efficacy of e-cigarette-supported smoking cessation differ among socioeconomic groups. For example, it may be the case that lower SES groups are just as likely to take up e-cigarettes as less-disadvantaged communities, but that having done so those groups remain less likely to quit or more likely to continue patterns of dual use. The effect of e-cigarette use on smoking-related disparities remains an important area of research. As with smoking, evidence of e-cigarette-related disparities suggests that interventions, policy communication, and service provision should be tailored to specific communities.

8 Are E-cigarettes an Appropriate Solution for Smoking in All Contexts?

Part of the reason why e-cigarettes appeal to smokers as a reduced-risk alternative is that traditional tobacco control has succeeded in educating the public about the dangers of smoking and the benefits of quitting. It is no coincidence that the largest markets for e-cigarettes occur in countries with a long history of tobacco control. That history is not shared by all countries. In populations where public awareness of smoking risks is limited, the availability of e-cigarettes cannot be expected to lead to as much cessation. Furthermore, economic realities facing consumers also come to bear. In jurisdictions with high taxes resulting in high prices for combustible tobacco, e-cigarettes may (regulation permitting) be a significantly less expensive way of consuming nicotine. Conversely, where cigarettes and other tobacco products are inexpensive, a higher relative cost of e-cigarettes (again, perhaps as a result of regulation) would reduce their appeal relative to combustibles.

Where traditional forms of tobacco control have been absent, or improperly implemented, those shortcomings should be corrected, to educate and incentivize cessation. Where taxes give improper signals of relative harm to nicotine consumers, those should also be modified. However, given that the traditional approaches have proved imperfect, these should not be the only approaches moving forward. The evidence suggests that a significant portion of smokers will be failed by the traditional approach, and a considerable subset of that tranche may succeed with the assistance of e-cigarettes. To insist on the former and deny the latter would resemble suggesting today that telecommunications companies install dial-up before deploying broadband in an area unserved with internet access. E-cigarettes do not preclude broader tobacco control regulation, but neither does the need for tobacco control preclude the availability of e-cigarettes. Indeed, as discussed in Volume III, Chapter 2 (see Sect. 8), the availability of e-cigarettes may reduce the unintended consequences associated with traditional interventions and increase the efficacy (thereby reducing the cost) of traditional treatment. So, while we cannot expect consumers in all contexts to respond exactly as those in countries such as the U.K. have to date, this does not suggest that we should not make e-cigarettes available to smokers in any context in which they could help to eliminate smoking harms.

9 Can We Export "Lessons Learned" from One Geographical Context to Another?

Policy sharing has, for decades, been a cornerstone of tobacco control. In contexts where aspects of e-cigarette and tobacco regulation are devolved, regional or even local governments may experiment with regulatory approaches that they perceive to be in the interests of their constituents. Given the context-specific nature of the effects of regulation, devolution of regulatory authority may allow for the needs of regional or local communities to be better met than if regulatory decisions were the sole responsibility of a centralized authority. A plurality of regulatory authorities creates more opportunities for these policy experiments than is possible in contexts where authority is centralized. For these reasons Canadian provinces, American states, and European countries serve as policy laboratories enacting regulations that diverge to some extent from those of the federal or, in the case of the EU, the transnational government. This develops the evidence base, helping inform decision-makers elsewhere. Policy sharing, facilitated by the adoption of the FCTC and encouraged by supranational governance structures such as the EU and international organizations like the WHO, has accelerated the adoption of ostensibly similar interventions. The achievements of policy pioneers can thus be replicated in other jurisdictions, but so too can their mistakes. Excessive policy sharing—regulatory herding—may be one reason current policies toward e-cigarettes are not serving the public interest, as discussed in Volume III, Chapter 2 (Sect. 4.5).

Smoking behaviors are complex and are influenced by a range of economic, social, political, psychological, and cultural realities. Unless these specific contexts are accounted for, there can be no guarantee that consumers in one context will respond in a similar manner as consumers in another. Using the language of empirical social science, a policy's results for one place, group, or social stratum may lack external validity. Policies from one location may provide regulators in another with inspiration, but they must still undertake their own cost–benefit analysis tailored to the local context to evaluate the full range of available strategies, determine which option is best suited to the unique needs of their stakeholders, and project whether the intended benefits of the seemingly best policy will outweigh any unintended consequences. Again, the experience of the first mover can help provide empirical data with which to inform this process, but it does not obviate the need for that work. These volumes have, by design, drawn on evidence from many countries. However, studies from Western Europe and North America feature heavily in the literature simply because those geographies are producing a disproportionately higher volume of e-cigarette research. The same caveats apply here: our discussion helps illuminate the tradeoffs that regulators must contend with when designing optimal e-cigarette policies, but context specifics will dictate the precise point at which benefits and risks balance. This point will be different for different communities. Thus, while our approach provides broad brushstrokes, the heavy lifting of local policy analysis is still needed to provide fine-tuning.

10 How Should Regulation Respond to Shifting Consumption Patterns?

Just as the precise details of optimal e-cigarette policy will vary between localities, changes in consumer behavior in response to the constantly shifting sands of regulation, public attitudes, and commercial innovation will mean that, even in a single context, regulation that is optimal now may not remain so. This does not concede to the argument that contemporary regulation should require the most stringent regulations to prevent the mere possibility of future risks. Present decisions should respond to what is known (and knowable) at the present time. However, because consumer behaviors are not fixed, e-cigarette policies would benefit from the ability to respond dynamically to those changes. Built-in sunset clauses and evaluation criteria could help mitigate the risk of harm brought about when sub-optimal policies prevail by requiring that the effectiveness of interventions be regularly assessed. In contrast, one-and-done policies may be popular or expedient in the short term but pay few dividends in the long run, and many result in unintended consequences after the brief window of public scrutiny has passed. Continuing review of policy certainly creates work for the tobacco control community. Researchers and officials will need to constantly collect new data, re-examine hypotheses, analyze policies and programs, and update them where appropriate. But this work should not be dissimilar, at least in nature, to that already undertaken for regulation of combustible tobacco products.

The benefits of such an approach are considerable. Designing policies with the ability to course-correct may help mitigate the harms of any future unintended consequences that may not be foreseen, or adequately considered by ex-ante cost–benefit analysis. The dynamic response may also help maximize regulatory capital by fostering greater public trust in the regulator, their process and their decisions. Further, by reserving the ability to change as needed, dynamic regulations may provide greater opportunity for stakeholder engagement, increasing the opportunities for those affected by decisions to raise their concerns, especially when evidence vindicating those concerns comes to light. Thus, dynamism can advance the principles of inclusion and social justice.[77]

11 Should Physicians Recommend E-cigarettes to Smokers?

Physicians' advice to patients who smoke may be a powerful means of providing health-information. Among past-year quitters in the U.S., 75% of those who had seen a medical doctor in the 12 months before cessation say the physician advised them to stop smoking.[78] Kozlowski and Edwards argue[79] that while the value of harm reduction strategies are supported by science-based data on comparative risks, the right to health information exists independently, and "should be respected whether or not harm reduction policies are judged advisable." Physicians, however, are often wary about the long-term health effects of vaping, even in the absence of evidence for any, which makes them reluctant to endorse e-cigarettes as a less harmful alternative to smoking.[80] The possibility of physicians' cognitive bias against iatrogenic harms, as discussed in Volume III, Chapter 1 also comes into play here.[81] A recent survey explored communication between U.S. physicians and patients to explore the advice given to older intensive smokers with multiple failed quitting attempts and first-time smoking quitters with light cigarette consumption.[82] Around 70% of physicians reported that they had been asked about e-cigarettes but only 22% had recommended them to patients. Sixty percent of physicians stated that they perceived all tobacco products, including e-cigarettes and combustible cigarettes, to be equally harmful, displaying a concerning ignorance of the scientific literature. (Attitudes toward the relative harm of smoking and using e-cigarettes appears to vary greatly from survey to survey, however, and several studies find majority support for the belief that e-cigarettes are less harmful).[83] Factors that increased the likelihood of physicians recommending e-cigarettes for quitting smoking were being a specialist in cardiology or pulmonology, routinely implementing public health guidelines, endorsing tobacco harm reduction, being asked specifically about cigarettes, and if the patient were an older, intensive smoker. While studies of physicians' perceptions outside the U.S. are not widespread, some in other countries also suggest low rates of recommendation toward harm reduction.[84,85,86]

The reluctance of physicians to advise smokers to consider e-cigarettes as part of a cessation attempt may be unsurprising given the attitudes of the broader public health community to e-cigarettes. Public health interventions are typically evaluated on the basis of safety and efficacy. However, as Michie, Van Stralen, and West have argued, interventions should also be evaluated on other dimensions including practicality, acceptability, affordability and equity.[87] Recognizing that the safety and efficacy of an intervention is irrelevant if no one wants to use that product or service, West invites physicians to consider which kinds of advice most likely to prompt a quitting attempt, yield the surest chances of its success, and result in the greatest health benefit.[88] West considers four types of advice that could be offered to those considering e-cigarettes to quit smoking: endorsement, encouragement to use after failure of alternatives, admonition to use something other than e-cigarettes, and providing no advice at all. Based on available evidence of transition probabilities, West argues that advising smokers to switch immediately results in a greatest probability of a patient quitting.

There are no empirical data on the quitting outcomes of patients exposed to various kinds of advice in in-patient settings yet.[88] However, in the U.K., the National Institute for Health and Care Excellence (NICE) guidelines call for smokers to be told that many people have found e-cigarettes to be helpful smoking cessation aids and that the evidence shows that, although not risk-free, e-cigarettes are substantially less harmful to health than smoking.[89] Similarly, NHS guidelines advise smokers to switch to e-cigarettes (without qualification to try other methods first).[90] Despite this, many doctors in the U.K. are still reluctant to offer that advice.[91] Moreover, and unsurprisingly, in countries where the prevailing attitudes to e-cigarettes are more hostile, physicians are even less likely to advise smokers switch.[92] Still, as West describes, there is a rational approach that physicians can follow to decide what advice to give patents regarding e-cigarettes.[88] Even the limited data available are more than sufficient to warrant public health agencies and medical practitioners to advise smokers to switch. That advice should come with context: the long-term risks are yet imperfectly understood; there are other (likely less) effective methods of supporting smoking cessation including NRTs, behavioral therapy and pharmacotherapy; and those other methods are better understood. There is no reason why physicians should not counsel other options alongside e-cigarettes. But it would be inconsistent for medical advice to emphasize that many people taking up e-cigarettes do not stop smoking, when the evidence shows that the large majority of quit attempts—regardless of aid employed in the attempt—fail.[93] Thus, e-cigarettes should form part of a broad set of tools that the healthcare community educates smokers about.

Messaging from physicians needs to be carefully constructed. "Vape, don't smoke," is, in isolation, neither informative enough nor specific enough to educate the patient. Since medical advice is intended toward a desired health outcome, advice regarding e-cigarettes should provide smokers with accurate information with at least some detail. Physicians might advise smokers about the frequency with which they should vape and what characteristics they should look for in e-cigarettes conducive to supporting cessation. They might advise users what other products could be used and that NRTs and behavioral therapies might also be appropriate, alternatively or in conjunction with e-cigarettes. Certainly, there will be smokers who are uninterested in those options, and for those the messaging from public health agencies should at least be honest that switching to reduced-harm alternatives is a significant improvement on continuing to smoke. Medical advice surrounding e-cigarettes should also educate the public about the benefits of complete substitutions, the risks from partial substitutions, and how e-cigarette users should respond in the case of relapse to smoking. Physicians could also advise their patients on how, having completely switched, former smokers could also be helped to quit vaping, so long as doing so does not put them at risk of relapse to smoking.

12 Wouldn't It Be Better to Provide E-cigarettes as a Medical Product?

The topic of medical advice raises another important question in the e-cigarette debate: If substituting from combustible tobacco to e-cigarettes improves health outcomes, should not they be regulated as medicine-delivery devices and produced by companies under the standards for testing medical devices and pharmaceuticals? This is referred to as "medicalization" of e-cigarettes. As with so many areas of e-cigarette regulation, there are both pros and cons to consider. To start with, it helps to clarify what the alternative would be.

In the case of replacing a prohibition with an exclusively medicalized market, providing people who smoke with access to a regulated e-cigarette where there was previously none would have some benefits. Allowing access, even if severely restricted, would appear to be a Pareto improvement over prohibition. People who smoke would benefit by having a larger set of choices of cessation supports. Youth and non-smoking adults would not be harmed via the availability of medicalized e-cigarettes, since in both cases prescribing guidelines would presumably deny access. Under this scenario, illicit markets for e-cigarettes would likely not disappear entirely, but they would lose some market share, to the benefit of society at large. Manufacturers and retailers of e-cigarettes (at least those operating in a legal manner) would obviously gain. Perhaps manufacturers and retailers of cigarettes would lose from such a policy change, if e-cigarettes indeed increase the pace of cessation among smokers. If so, the claim of Pareto improvement would be lost (but likely such a policy would still satisfy the compensation principle for a welfare-improving change; see Volume III, Chapter 2, Sec. 5.4). On the other hand, under a medicalization regime it is likely that only deep pocketed firms such as TTCs could afford to gain approval for their e-cigarette devices and e-liquids, and so perhaps there would be little or no loss, or even a net gain, to the profits of these firms as well.

Some of the specific benefits of medicalization might include the following. It would likely help dispel false beliefs about e-cigarettes' safety and efficacy. These false beliefs, encouraged by regulators around the world, lead smokers to continue with a riskier habit—smoking. Medicalization could allow manufacturers to advertise verified medical claims of their products' therapeutic benefits, an option that is illegal even if true under prohibition, the FDA's current approach to regulation of e-cigarettes (so far).[94] Medicalization would also create opportunities for advice at point of sale that could help increase the efficacy of e-cigarettes as cessation aids. Under medicalization, e-cigarettes would be tightly regulated, providing more robust safeguards against the use of untested and potentially dangerous chemicals. Along with the gatekeeping function of keeping youth and non-smokers away from e-cigarettes, these are significant benefits, especially compared with a counterfactual in which e-cigarettes are so tightly restricted that potential switchers simply smoke instead or use unregulated products.

However, medicalization also has some large drawbacks. Many e-cigarette users vape not because of the promise of improved health, but simply because it is a less expensive, more acceptable, and more enjoyable way of using nicotine. Different consumers value different product features including different types of e-cigarettes, different flavors, different nicotine contents, etc. The process of gaining medical approval would likely inhibit the wide variation of characteristics available in a commercial market. The experience of the NRT market illustrates this: after approval of initial "low and slow" dose products, innovation in the product category virtually ceased, with little subsequent attempt to increase the appeal to smokers. Compared with a diverse commercial market, a tightly controlled medical market with only a small number of approved products would likely reduce the acceptability of the product category for some current and future users. That might deter experimental use, but it could also risk sacrificing an opportunity for smoking cessation or, worse, nudge consumers toward either unregulated e-vapor products or back to combustible tobacco. Recall from the modeling in Volume III, Chapter 2, that this is likely to be a poor trade, since there are far more smokers who could benefit from e-cigarettes for cessation than there are non-smokers who use e-cigarettes.

Because of the high bar set for gaining medical approval, the resulting regulatory burden would almost certainly result in an oligopoly. That would make products more expensive than they would be in a more competitive market, further reducing the appeal relative to combustibles (and, perhaps, causing additional burden to national health insurance systems). Finally, medicalization would prevent smokers from accessing some products they might wish to try but which lack authorization. Some such would-be consumers should be expected to turn to more harmful alternatives, including combustible tobacco products and unregulated e-vapor products. Finally, there is the potential problem (as seen when states in Australia medicalized e-cigarettes) that physicians may still be loath to prescribe e-cigarettes for cessation, at least if they are not educated on the scientific base of evidence.[95]

Perhaps the best option would be a hybrid system, combining regulated commercial products with a parallel medicalized market. Some pharmaceutical classes of products (e.g., pain relievers), and (in some jurisdictions) cannabis provide examples, albeit imperfect ones, which suggest that it might be possible for both a medical and a commercial market for ostensibly similar products to coexist. This dual approach may also create opportunities for differential regulation. For example, some product features such as higher nicotine concentrations and claims of reduced-risk could be limited to the medical market. These possibilities warrant further investigation, not least because it remains to be seen whether the medical market would be an economically viable option for manufacturers, particularly if over-the-counter alternative products are simultaneously available.

13 Should We Encourage Young Smokers to Switch to E-cigarettes Too?

Throughout this book, the argument has been made that use of e-cigarettes is not appropriate for minors. But if we acknowledge that e-cigarettes can be an appropriate cessation tool for recalcitrant adult smokers, it may seem inconsistent to deny the same products to youth who already smoke, purely on the basis of their age. However, youth and adults are distinct in two important areas. First, as we saw in Volume II, Chapter 1, nicotine appears to affect young people and adults differently: While contested, there are suggestions that nicotine may harm the developing brain.[96] That suggests that nicotine is problematic for youth, whereas, in the adult population, risks are largely limited to the products of combustion. That disparity justifies greater caution about e-cigarette use by young people than by adults. Second, there is evidence that among youth, social and psychological factors play a unique role in nicotine product use, especially among initiation and prior to the onset of regular use.[97] Since e-cigarettes reduce the risks associated with the combustion of tobacco but do not eliminate nicotine dependence, this implies that e-cigarettes have more potential for harm reduction among nicotine dependent adults than for youngsters. That age-dependent context also implies that behavioral interventions that may fail many older adults with pharmacological nicotine addiction might be more effective among young people.

Superficially at least, there is another difference between young people and many adults: many adult smokers have spent years trying and failing to quit smoking using conventional means. In this group, that failure is sufficient (if not necessary) to justify the use of e-cigarettes. The same is less likely to apply to young smokers who, by nature of their age, are, on average, less likely to have exhausted all of the cessation support options available to them. For this reason, the emphasis for smoking youth should be placed on other cessation supports. Robust measures to prevent youth access are warranted, subject to the concerns about appropriately differential regulation and encouraging smoking discussed in Volume III, Chapter 2, (Sect. 6.5), so long as the benefits of cessation for the wider population are not sacrificed.

None of this suggests that young people should be provided with anything less than honest information about the relative risk-reduction afforded by e-cigarettes. That admonition may be a tough sell to NGOs with a history of producing youth-oriented anti-vaping campaigns appealing to emotion and anti-tobacco sentiment to encourage abstinence, sometimes at the expense of logic and frequently overlooking salient empirical evidence. Educators and parents should be equipped to guide those under their supervision, as these children will inevitably encounter tobacco and nicotine products at some point in their lives. Their guidance should include the information that neither type of product is safe, but also that their risks are not equivalent.

That leaves a question mark over any younger smokers who *have* tried traditional cessation supports to no avail. That is likely a very small group, but the presence of such individuals lends weight to the calls for a medical e-cigarette. In the U.K., NRTs are available to children over 12. While, for the reasons discussed, commercial e-cigarettes are not appropriate for minors, perhaps a medically regulated e-cigarette, prescribed via consultation with and used under supervision of a physician, could be an intermediate option for some younger people if traditional smoking cessation therapies have proven unsuccessful.

14 Should Public Resources Be Used to Support Vaping Cessation?

Tobacco control in general and cessation treatments in particular are often justified on the basis of externalities.[98] Smoking-related externalities have already been discussed in Volume III, Chapter 2, as have the reasons to believe that the externalities of vaping are less severe than those of smoking. To the extent that e-cigarettes contribute to smoking cessation, the net reduction in externalities would justify funding public health messaging encouraging substitutions from smoking to e-cigarettes. Widespread use of e-cigarettes for smoking cessation may also ease the public cost burden of stop-smoking services by both easing demand and increasing the efficacy of those programs.

As a consumer-funded intervention, e-cigarettes may also shift some of the costs of tobacco control from the public to the private purse. If so, some financial resources earmarked for tobacco control could be reallocated toward other interventions such as enforcement of youth access controls and programs for communities where smoking harms are concentrated. Should national, state, and local governments provide and fund e-cigarette cessation programs, too? If current or future e-cigarette users do decide that they want to quit vaping, and if vaping does generate some public health costs, then there may be a public health argument (if not much of a traditional economic argument based on externalities) for using public resources to help them quit. Such efforts would need to focus on cessation from vaping, however, not blanket discouragement of use that might deter smokers from switching. For those who do wish to stop vaping, behavioral therapy, medical NRTs and pharmacotherapies provide options. And while these options have failed to help many smokers quit, that does not *necessarily* mean they will not help users abstain from e-cigarettes. Non-nicotine e-cigarettes are another option. Unfortunately, the literature on e-cigarette cessation is surprisingly sparse, and there is a dearth of randomized clinical trials exploring discontinuation of vaping.[99] There is some evidence to suggest that e-cigarette users are less nicotine dependent than smokers,[100] which may suggest that, as a group, e-cigarette users may find it easier to abstain from those products than smokers from cigarettes. A majority of e-cigarette users express an interest in eventually quitting. However, former smokers using e-cigarettes may be more inclined to quit vaping than never-smoking e-cigarette users and current dual users,[101] in the latter case perhaps because dual users rightly prioritize smoking cessation over quitting e-cigarettes. Perhaps, having finally quit smoking, former smokers using e-cigarettes have greater self-efficacy regarding their ability to quit vaping than current dual users and those smoking exclusively.

15 Could E-cigarettes Allow Us to Eventually Ban Smoking?

Prohibitions fail to eliminate demand and bring about unintended consequences that offset—and potentially overwhelm—the intended benefits. Prohibition of smoking is not likely to differ much from the historical bans on alcohol and drugs, which created thriving and violent illicit markets and imposed enormous social, economic, and health costs on individuals and communities.[102] Whether e-cigarettes could allow the prohibition of smoking is the wrong question. A better question is whether e-cigarettes and other safer nicotine products can take us to a place where a ban on smoking is unnecessary. E-cigarettes and safer nicotine products are not a panacea, but with thoughtful and considered regulation, they could be an important part of the solution. Presenting an appealing, affordable, and accessible alternative could persuade millions of current smokers to switch. Moreover, because e-cigarettes are substitutes for combustible tobacco, e-cigarettes interrupt the tendency for smokers to respond to more stringent regulations by embracing illicit market analogs. Under the right regulatory conditions (i.e., risk-proportionate regulation), the availability of e-cigarettes could therefore allow for restrictions on combustibles that were previously made impractical by the potential illicit-market response. Such interventions include higher taxes, comprehensive flavor bans and very-low-nicotine product standards. The combination of those interventions coupled with safer nicotine products is likely to be the best strategy to maximize smoking cessation.

16 Can We Agree to Disagree About Optimal E-cigarette Regulation?

Of course, there are aspects of the debate about e-cigarettes that are valid territory for different opinions. Different groups of stakeholders will always have different priorities, different goals, and advocate for different strategies. Evidence can always be interpreted in different ways and held to imply various courses of action. A healthy discourse includes disagreement, which, when honestly and clearly articulated, allows participants to test their assumptions and confront evidence that might correct biases and lead to better-informed decisions at both the individual and policy level. Skepticism toward the evidence produced by those advocating a different hypothesis is central to the scientific method. The problem with the debate about e-cigarettes is that, too often, those seeking to make "evidence-based" claims about safer nicotine products and how they should be regulated fall back on unexamined philosophical and moral tenets. That is not to say that there is no role for philosophical debate here. Many questions pertinent to the debate—how should we handle uncertainty? what counts as harm? what weight should personal choice and the pursuit of pleasure have in public decision-making?—*are* moral questions. However, unless we explicitly examine, and validate to others, the philosophical judgments underpinning our interpretations of the empirical data then the discourse moves from one grounded in empiricism to one floating around in a sea of subjective sentiment. That is not science; it is ideology. And ideology is no basis from which to generate health policy.

Notes

1. Moynihan, D.P. More Than Social Security Was at Stake by Daniel P. Moynihan. *The Washington Post*, January 18, 1983. Quote Page A17, Column 5, Washington, D.C. (ProQuest).
2. Wehby, G.L., Murray, J.C., Wilcox, A., Lie, R.T. Smoking and Body Weight: Evidence Using Genetic Instruments. Econ Hum Biol. 2012;10(2):113–126.
3. Larsson, S.C., Burgess, S. Appraising the Causal Role of Smoking in Multiple Diseases: A Systematic Review and Meta-Analysis of Mendelian Randomization Studies. EBioMedicine. 2022;82:104154. https://doi.org/10.1016/j.ebiom.2022.104154.
4. Prieger, J.E. Optimal Taxation of Cigarettes and E-cigarettes: Principles for Taxing Reduced-Harm Tobacco Products. 2023;26(2):41–64. https://doi.org/10.1515/fhep-2022-0025.
5. Cox, S., Hastings, J., West, R., Notley, C. The Case for Development of an E-cigarette Ontology (E-CigO) to Improve Quality,

Efficiency and Clarity in the Conduct and Interpretation of Research. Qeios, 2020. https://doi.org/10.32388/5YYRPJ.
6. Clarke, E., Thompson, K., Weaver, S. et al. Snus: A Compelling Harm Reduction Alternative to Cigarettes. Harm Reduct J. 2019;16:62. https://doi.org/10.1186/s12954-019-0335-1.
7. Worldwide and in the U.S., the top two e-cigarettes by revenue share are Juul and British American Tobacco's Vuse (per data from Euromonitor International). The only other brands with more than 2% worldwide market share in 2021 were Blu by Imperial Brands (the world's fourth largest tobacco company) and a Chinese brand (RELX) sold by a manufacturer dedicated solely to e-cigarettes.
8. Bernard, A.B., Redding, S.J., Schott, P.K. Multiple-Product Firms and Product Switching. Am Econ Rev. 2010;100(1):70–97. https://doi.org/10.1257/aer.100.1.70
9. *The Economist*.. Kodak Moment: As Regulators Wrestle with E-smokes, The Tobacco Industry Is Changing Fast. *The Economist*, 2013, available at: https://www.economist.com/business/2013/09/28/kodak-moment.
10. Gutiérrez, G., Philippon, T. Declining Competition and Investment in the US (No. w23583). National Bureau of Economic Research, 2017.
11. Gilbert, R.J., Newbery, D.M. Preemptive Patenting and the Persistence of Monopoly. Am Econ Rev. 1982;72(3):514–526. https://www.jstor.org/stable/1831552
12. Lane, W.J. Product Differentiation in a Market with Endogenous Sequential Entry. Bell J Econ. 1980;11(1):237–260. https://doi.org/10.2307/3003410
13. Eaton, B.C., Lipsey, R.G. Product Differentiation. Handb Ind Organ. 1989;1:723–768. North-Holland.
14. The market for e-cigarettes today appears to be bipartite, with an oligopoly (the traditional tobacco giants) facing a monopolistically competitive fringe (the independent firms), depending on how one counts Juul. Altria no longer has a stake in JUUL.
15. Beard, E., West, R., Michie, S., Brown, J. Association Between Electronic Cigarette Use and Changes in Quit Attempts, Success of Quit Attempts, Use of Smoking Cessation Pharmacotherapy,

and Use of Stop Smoking Services in England: Time Series Analysis of Population Trends. BMJ. 2016;354:i4645. https://doi.org/10.1136/bmj.i4645.
16. Huang, J., Wang, Y., Duan, Z., Kim, Y., Emery, S.L., Chaloupka, F.J. Do E-cigarette Sales Reduce the Demand for Nicotine Replacement Therapy (NRT) Products in the US? Evidence from the Retail Sales Data. Prev Med. 2021;145:106376. https://doi.org/10.1016/j.ypmed.2020.106376.
17. Kelland, K. (January 16, 2015). GSK's Nicotine Patches and Gum Feel the Heat from E-cigarettes (online). Reuters. http://uk.reuters.com/article/2015/01/16/gsk-ceo-ecigarettesidUKL6N0UU3TU20150116.
18. Branston, J.R. Industry Profits Continue to Drive the Tobacco Epidemic: A New Endgame for Tobacco Control? Tobacco Prevention & Cessation. 2021 June;7:45. https://doi.org/10.18332/tpc/138232.
19. Associated Press. (July 28, 2022). Altria's $13B Investment in Juul E-cigarettes Vaporizes. USNews.com. https://www.usnews.com/news/business/articles/2022-07-28/altrias-13b-juul-investment-has-lost-95-of-its-value.
20. Di Lorenzo, A. (February 9, 2024). BAT's New Categories Perform Well, with Its Velo Nicotine Pouches Growing Rapidly. TobaccoIntelligence. https://tobaccointelligence.com/bats-new-categories-perform-well-with-its-velo-nicotine-pouches-growing-rapidly. Profitability in 2023 for the new products category was ahead of schedule; see earlier prediction of profitability only in 2024: British American Tobacco. (2023). *Delivering Transformation: Combined Annual and ESG Report: Annual Report and form 20-F 2022.* https://www.bat.com/group/sites/UK__9D9KCY.nsf/vwPagesWebLive/DOAWWGJT/$file/BAT_Annual_Report_Form_20-F_2022.pdf.
21. Altria. Our 10-Year Vision: Altria, 2021, available at: https://www.altria.com/en/about-altria/our-10-year-vision.
22. British American Tobacco. "Building the Enterprise of the Future" Performance Summary 2020. London: British American Tobacco, 2021.
23. Imperial Brands. *Our Strategy*. London: Imperial Brands, 2021, available at: https://www.imperialbrandsplc.com/about-us/Our-strategy.html.

24. Philip Morris International. *Our Transformation*. Geneva: Philip Morris international, 2020, available at: https://www.pmi.com/our-transformation.
25. Philip Morris International. *Our Transformation*. Geneva: Philip Morris international, 2020, available at: https://www.pmi.com/our-transformation.
26. Edwards, R., Hoek, J., Karreman, N., et al. Evaluating Tobacco Industry 'Transformation': A Proposed Rubric and Analysis. Tob Control. 2022;31:313-321.
27. VaporVoice. BAT and PMI Combine to Invest $1.15 Billion on R&D in 2021. VaporVoice, 2022, available at: https://vaporvoice.net/2022/07/31/bat-and-pmi-combine-to-spend-over-9-6-billion-on-rd/#:~:text=Two%20of%20the%20largest%20tobacco,combustible%20cigarettes%20combined%20in%202021.
28. Philip Morris International. PMI Aims to Become a Majority Smoke-Free Business by 2025, Press release, 2021, available at: https://www.pmi.com/our-transformation/pmi-aims-to-become-a-majority-smoke-free-business-by-2025.
29. Rss Print. BAT/Altria on Track to Meet Targets. Tobacco Asia, 2022, available at: https://www.tobaccoasia.com/news/bat-altria-on-track-to-meet-targets/.
30. Tobacco Transformation Index. Analytical Overview. Tobacco Transformation Index, 2022, available at: https://tobaccotransformationindex.org/analytical-overview.
31. British American Tobacco. (2023). *Delivering Transformation: Combined Annual and ESG Report: Annual Report and form 20-F 2022*. https://www.bat.com/group/sites/UK__9D9KCY.nsf/vwPagesWebLive/DOAWWGJT/$file/BAT_Annual_Report_Form_20-F_2022.pdf.
32. Foundation for a Smoke-Free World. Tobacco Transformation Index: Key Findings and Insights, video, 2022, available at: https://www.smokefreeworld.org/videos/2022-tobacco-transformation-index-key-findings-and-insights/.
33. Tobacco Transformation Index. Analytical Overview. Tobacco Transformation Index, 2022, available at: https://tobaccotransformationindex.org/analytical-overview.
34. Edwards, R., Hoek, J., Karreman, N., et al. Evaluating Tobacco Industry 'Transformation': A Proposed Rubric and Analysis.

Tob Control. 2022;31:313-321. https://www.10.1136/tobaccocontrol-2021-056687.

35. Cummings, K.M., Ballin, S., Sweanor, D. The Past Is Not the Future in Tobacco Control. Prev Med. 2020;140:106183. ISSN 0091-7435. https://doi.org/10.1016/j.ypmed.2020.106183.
36. Abrams, D.B., Bates, C.B., Niaura, R.S. World Health Organization Must Stop Its Baseless and Irresponsible Attack on Tobacco Harm Reduction (Letter to Tedros Adhanom Ghebreyesus, Director-General World Health Organization), 2021, available at: https://www.clivebates.com/documents/WNTDLetterMay2021.pdf.
37. Campaign for Tobacco-Free Kids. (September 13, 2017). If Philip Morris Is Serious About a "Smoke-Free World," It Should Stop Marketing Cigarettes, Fighting Efforts to Reduce Smoking, Press release. https://www.tobaccofreekids.org/press-releases/2017_09_13_pmi.
38. U.S. Federal Trade Commission (FTC). (2021). *Cigarette Report for 2019*. Washington: Federal Trade Commission.
39. Edwards, R., Hoek, J., Karreman, N., et al.: Evaluating Tobacco Industry 'Transformation': a Proposed Rubric and Analysis. Tob Control. 2022;31:313-321. https://doi.org/10.1136/tobaccocontrol-2021-056687.
40. Cummings, K.M., Ballin, S., Sweanor, D. The Past Is Not the Future in Tobacco Control. Prev Med. 2020 Nov;140:106183. https://doi.org/10.1016/j.ypmed.2020.106183.
41. Rao, A. Industry-Funded Research and Bias in Food Science. Quantitative Marketing and Economics. 2022;20(1):39–67. https://doi.org/10.1007/s11129-021-09244-z
42. Sessler, D.I., Alman, B.A., Treggiari, M.M., Mont, M.A. Pro-Con Debate: Interdisciplinary Perspectives on Industry-Sponsored Research. JOA J. 2023;38(6):986–991. https://doi.org/10.1016/j.arth.2023.02.018.
43. Some major datasets used to study behavior regarding use of tobacco products, such as the Smoking Toolkit Study in the U.K., are unavailable to researchers affiliated with industry.
44. Grill, K. E-cigarettes: The Long-Term Liberal Perspective. Nicotine Tob Res. 2021 Jan;23(1):9–13. https://doi.org/10.1093/ntr/ntaa085.

45. Summers, J.S. What Is Wrong with Addiction. Philos Psychiatry Psychol. 2015;22(1):25–40. https://doi.org/10.1353/ppp.2015.0011
46. McNeill, A., Brose, L.S., Calder, R., Bauld, L., Robson, D. Evidence Review of E-cigarettes and Heated Tobacco Products 2018. A Report Commissioned by Public Health England. London, England: Public Health England, 2018.
47. Levy, D.T., Warner, K.E., Cummings, K.M., et al. Examining the Relationship of Vaping to Smoking Initiation Among US Youth and Young Adults: A Reality Check. Tob Control. 2018:tobaccocontrol-2018-054446. https://doi.org/10.1136/tobaccocontrol-2018-054446.
48. Jackson, S.E., Brown, J., Jarvis, M.J. Dependence on Nicotine in US High School Students in the Context of Changing Patterns of Tobacco Product Use. Addiction. 2021;116(7):1859–1870. https://doi.org/10.1111/add.15403.
49. Temkin, L.S. *Rethinking the Good: Moral Ideals and the Nature of Practical Reasoning*. New York, NY: Oxford University Press, 2012.
50. Grill, K. E-cigarettes: The Long-Term Liberal Perspective. Nicotine Tob Res. 2021 Jan;23(1):9–13. https://doi.org/10.1093/ntr/ntaa085.
51. Levy, D.T., Borland, R., Lindblom, E.N., et al. Potential Deaths Averted in USA by Replacing Cigarettes with E-cigarettes. Tob Control. 2018;27:18-25. https://doi.org/10.1136/tobaccocontrol-2017-053759
52. Hendlin, Y.H. Alert: Public Health Implications of Electronic Cigarette Waste. Am J Public Health. 2018 Nov;108(11):1489–1490. https://doi.org/10.2105/AJPH.2018.304699.
53. Hambly, E. Should Disposable Vapes Be Banned? BBC News, 2022, available at: https://www.bbc.com/news/science-environment-63037553.
54. Truth Initiative. A Toxic, Plastic Problem: E-cigarette Waste and the Environment. Truth Iniative, 2022, available at: https://truthinitiative.org/sites/default/files/media/files/2021/04/E-Cigarette-Waste-Report-FINAL-042821.pdf.

55. Pooran, N. (January 19, 2023). Vaping Ban Scotland: Ministers to Consider Banning Disposable Vapes. *The Scotsman*. https://www.scotsman.com/news/environment/vaping-ban-scotland-ministers-to-consider-banning-disposable-vapes-3993413.
56. Collins, S. Government Looking to Ban Disposable Vapes in Ireland Due to Littering. *Irish Mirror*, 2022, available at: https://www.irishmirror.ie/news/irish-news/government-looking-ban-disposable-vapes-28230048.
57. Krause, M.J., Townsend, T.G. Hazardous waste Status of Discarded Electronic Cigarettes. Waste Manag. 2015;39:57–62. https://doi.org/10.1016/j.wasman.2015.02.005.
58. Hambly, E. Should Disposable Vapes Be Banned? BBC News, 2022, available at: https://www.bbc.com/news/science-environment-63037553.
59. ASH. Use of E-cigarettes (Vapes) Among Adults in Great Britain, Action on Smoking and Health UK, 2021, available at: https://ash.org.uk/uploads/Use-of-e-cigarettes-vapes-among-adults-in-Great-Britain-2021.pdf.
60. ASH. Use of E-cigarettes (vapes) Among Young People in Great Britain, Action on Smoking and Health UK, 2022, available at: https://ash.org.uk/uploads/Use-of-e-cigarettes-among-young-people-in-Great-Britain-2022.pdf?v=1661866458.
61. World Health Organization. Tobacco and Its Environmental Impact: An Overview, 2017, available at: http://www.who.int/tobacco/publications/environmental-impact-overview/en.
62. Tobacco and Its Environmental Impact: An Overview. Geneva: World Health Organization, 2017, available at: https://apps.who.int/iris/bitstream/handle/10665/255574/9789241512497-eng.pdf.
63. Pourchez, J., Mercier, C., Forest, V. From Smoking to Vaping: A New Environmental Threat? Lancet Respir Med. 2022 Jul;10(7):e63-e64. https://doi.org/10.1016/S2213-2600(22)00187-4.
64. Leclerc, S.H., Badami, M.G. Extended Producer Responsibility for E-Waste Management: Policy Drivers and Challenges. J Clean Prod. 2020;251:119657. https://doi.org/10.1016/j.jclepro.2019.119657.

65. UKVIA. (n.d.). Pressure Mounts to Ban Single Use Disposable Devices. UK Vaping Industria Association. Available at: https://www.ukvia.co.uk/pressure-mounts-to-ban-single-use-disposable-devices/.
66. Zafeiridou, M., Hopkinson, N., Voulvoulis, N. Environ Sci Technol. 2018;52:15, https://doi.org/10.1021/acs.est.8b01533.
67. Franks, P., Jerant, A.F., Leigh, J.P., Lee, D., Chiem, A., Lewis, I., Lee, S. Cigarette Prices, Smoking, and the Poor: Implications of Recent Trends. Am J Public Health. 2007;97(10):1873–1877. https://doi.org/10.2105/AJPH.2006.090134.
68. UK Dept Health. (2017). Towards a Smokefree Generation: A Tobacco Control Plan for England. https://assets.publishing.service.gov.uk/government/uploads/system/uploads/attachment_data/file/630217/Towards_a_Smoke_free_Generation_-_A_Tobacco_Control_Plan_for_England_2017-2022__2_.pdf.
69. Beard, E., West, R., Michie, S., Brown, J. Association of Prevalence of Electronic Cigarette Use with Smoking Cessation and Cigarette Consumption in England: A Time–Series Analysis Between 2006 and 2017. Addiction. 2017;115:961–974. https://doi.org/10.1111/add.14851.
70. Rogers, E.M. *Diffusion of Innovations*, 4th edn. New York: The Free Press, 1995.
71. See Volume III, Chapter 2, Sect. 3.5, point 5.
72. Green, M.J., Gray, L., Sweeting, H. et al. Socioeconomic Patterning of Vaping by Smoking Status Among UK Adults and Youth. BMC Public Health. 2020;20:183. https://doi.org/10.1186/s12889-020-8270-3.
73. Kock, L., Shahab, L., West, R., Brown, J. E-cigarette Use in England 2014–17 as a Function of Socio-Economic Profile. Addiction. 2019;114:294–303. https://doi.org/10.1111/add.14446.
74. Friedman, A.S., Horn, S.J.L., Socioeconomic Disparities in Electronic Cigarette Use and Transitions from Smoking, Nicotine Tob Res. 2019 Oct;21(10):1363–1370. https://doi.org/10.1093/ntr/nty120.

75. Prieger, J.E. (2022). Optimal Taxation of Cigarettes and E-cigarettes: Principles for Taxing Reduced-Harm Tobacco Products. 2023;26(2):41–64. https://doi.org/10.1515/fhep-2022-0025.
76. Lucherini, M., Hill, S., Smith, K. Potential for Non-Combustible Nicotine Products to Reduce Socioeconomic Inequalities in Smoking: A Systematic Review and Synthesis of Best Available Evidence. BMC Public Health. 2019;19:1469. https://doi.org/10.1186/s12889-019-7836-4.
77. Such dynamism should not degenerate into mere policy uncertainty, however, due to the latter's chilling effect on firm's investment (see Volume III, Chapter 2, Sect. 7.3). A clear set of principles should be enunciated, so that all industry participants know *how* regulatory details would change in response to *which* pieces of new information.
78. Data from the CPS-TUS 2018–2019, analyzed by the authors. The estimate is 75.5%, with a 95% confidence interval of 71.7% to 79.0%.
79. Kozlowski, L.T., Edwards, B.Q. "Not Safe" Is Not Enough: Smokers Have a Right to Know More Than There Is No Safe Tobacco Product. Tob Control. 2005 Aug;14 Suppl 2(Suppl 2):ii3-7. https://doi.org/10.1136/tc.2004.008334.
80. Hurst, S., Conway, M. Exploring Physician Attitudes Regarding Electronic Documentation of E-cigarette Use: A Qualitative Study. Tob Use Insights. 2018 Jan 1;11:1179173X1878287.
81. The study discussed in Volume III, Chapter 1 (Sect. 4.1) found the average physician required a minimum of between four and five additional lives to be saved by a new treatment for each iatrogenic death.
82. Delnevo, C.D., Jeong, M., Teotia, A., Manderski, M.M.B., Singh, B., Hrywna, M., Steinberg, M.B., et al. Communication Between US Physicians and Patients Regarding Electronic Cigarette Use. JAMA Network Open. 2022;5(4):e226692–e226692. https://doi.org/10.1001/jamanetworkopen.2022.6692.
83. Selamoglu, M., Erbas, B., Kasiviswanathan, K., Barton, C. General Practitioners' Knowledge, Attitudes, Beliefs and Practices Surrounding the Prescription of E-Cigarettes for Smoking Cessation: a Mixed-Methods Systematic Review. BMC Public

Health. 2022 Dec 23;22(1):2415. https://doi.org/10.1186/s12889-022-14696-3.

84. Zgliczyński, W.S., Jankowski, M., Rostkowska, O., Gujski, M., Wierzba, W., Pinkas, J. Knowledge and Beliefs of E-Cigarettes Among Physicians in Poland. Med Sci Monit. 2019 Aug 23;25:6322–6330. https://doi.org/10.12659/MSM.916920.
85. Tanriover, O., Hidiroglu, S., Ay, P., Cook, R.L. Do Family Physicians Perceive Electronic Cigarette Use as a Harm Reduction Strategy for Smokers? A Survey from Istanbul. Prim Health Care Res Dev. 2022;23:e15. https://doi.org/10.1017/S1463423622000056.
86. Shin, D.W., Kim, Y.I., Kim, S.J., Kim, J.S., Chong, S., Park, Y.S., et al. Lung Cancer Specialist Physicians' Attitudes Towards E-cigarettes: A Nationwide Survey. Garattini S, editor. PLoS ONE. 2017 Feb 24;12(2):e0172568. https://doi.org/10.1371/journal.pone.0172568.
87. Michie, S., van Stralen, M.M., West, R. The Behaviour Change Wheel: A New Method for Characterising and Designing Behaviour Change Interventions. Implementation Sci. 2011;6:42. https://doi.org/10.1186/1748-5908-6-42.
88. West, R. Should Health Professionals Recommend Smokers to Switch to E-cigarettes? *Society for Research in Nicotine and Tobacco* [video]. Oslo, 2019, available at: https://vimeo.com/361160577.
89. National Institute for Health and Clinical Excellence. Stop Smoking Interventions and Services NICE Guideline NG92 2018. https://www.nice.org.uk/guidance/ng92.
90. NHS. (n.d.). Vaping to Quit Smoking, UK National Health Society. Available at: https://www.nhs.uk/better-health/quit-smoking/vaping-to-quit-smoking/.
91. Corkill, J., Faber, S., Irshad, F., et al. S53 UK doctors [sic] Current Perceptions of E-cigarettes (Vaping) Thorax 2018;73:A32.
92. Drouin, O., McMillen, R.C., Klein, J.D., Winickoff, J.P. E-Cigarette Advice to Patients From Physicians and Dentists in the United States. Am J Health Promotion. 2018;32(5):1228-1233. https://doi.org/10.1177/0890117117710876.

93. As Ian Irvine writes, "Opponents of a switching policy claim (correctly), that cigarette-quit success rates, following a switch to vaping, are low. Researchers favoring the use of e-cigarettes point to the fact that successful quit rates are low for all devices, and that e-cigarette-based smoking quits are generally higher than, say, patch-based smoking quits" (see: Irvine I. [December 4, 2019]. The Vilification of Vaping. CDHowe.org. https://www.cdhowe.org/intelligence-memos/ian-irvine-%E2%80%93-vilification-vaping). On the estimated average number of quit attempts necessary to stop smoking, which ranges from 6 to 142 depending on methodology used, see: Chaiton, M., Diemert, L., Cohen, J.E., Bondy, S.J., Selby, P., Philipneri, A., & Schwartz, R. Estimating the Number of Quit Attempts It Takes to Quit Smoking Successfully in a Longitudinal Cohort of Smokers. BMJ Open. 2016;6(6):e011045. https://doi.org/10.1136/bmjopen-2016-011045.
94. As of mid-2023, the FDA has not granted any e-cigarette the permission to be advertised as a lower-risk product. The only products granted such permission through the agency's modified risk tobacco product gateway are smokeless tobacco products (snuff and snus). See https://www.fda.gov/tobacco-products/advertising-and-promotion/modified-risk-granted-orders.
95. Mendelsohn, C. (April 15, 2019). Doctors Who Prescribe Nicotine. We Need YOU! *ATHRA*. https://www.athra.org.au/blog/2019/04/15/doctors-who-prescribe-nicotine-we-need-you.
96. Leslie, F.M. Unique, Long-Term Effects of Nicotine on Adolescent Brain. Pharmacol Biochem Behav. 2020;197:173010. https://doi.org/10.1016/j.pbb.2020.173010.
97. National Center for Chronic Disease Prevention and Health Promotion (US) Office on Smoking and Health. Preventing Tobacco Use Among Youth and Young Adults: A Report of the Surgeon General. Atlanta (GA): Centers for Disease Control and Prevention (US); 2012. 4, Social, Environmental, Cognitive, and Genetic Influences on the Use of Tobacco Among Youth. Available at: https://www.ncbi.nlm.nih.gov/books/NBK99236/.

98. Ekpu, V.U., Brown, A.K. The Economic Impact of Smoking and of Reducing Smoking Prevalence: Review of Evidence. Tob Use Insights. 2015 Jul 14;8:1–35. https://doi.org/10.4137/TUI.S15628.
99. Palmer, A.M., Smith, T.T., Nahhas, G.J., et al. Interest in Quitting E-cigarettes Among Adult E-cigarette Users With and Without Cigarette Smoking History. JAMA Netw Open. 2021;4(4):e214146. https://doi.org/10.1001/jamanetworkopen.2021.4146.
100. Shiffman, S., Sembower, M.A. Dependence on E-cigarettes and Cigarettes in a Cross-Sectional Study of US Adults. Addiction. 2020 Oct;115(10):1924–1931. https://doi.org/10.1111/add.15060.
101. Palmer, A.M., Smith, T.T., Nahhas, G.J., et al. Interest in Quitting E-cigarettes Among Adult E-cigarette Users with and Without Cigarette Smoking History. JAMA Netw Open. 2021;4(4):e214146. https://doi.org/10.1001/jamanetworkopen.2021.4146.
102. Refer to the discussion in Volume II, Chapter 3, Sect. 1.1.2.1.

CHAPTER 4

Conclusions

> The government must embrace the promotion of vaping as an effective tool to help people to quit smoking tobacco. We know vapes are not a 'silver bullet' nor are they totally risk-free, but the alternative is far worse.
> —Javed Khan, *Making Smoking Obsolete.*[1]

In 1998, former Surgeon General C. Everett Koop warned, "We must not focus our efforts so narrowly on preventing tobacco use by youth that we send smokers the message that we have abandoned them—that their addiction is their own fault and that we don't care about them."[2] This, Koop argued, would play directly into the hands of cigarette companies by discouraging disenfranchised smokers from attempting to quit. As an alternative, Koop emphasized that prevention initiatives could be combined with efforts to support cessation. In the years since the Surgeon General penned those words, the prevalence of current smoking among U.S. adults has declined from more than 24% (47.2 million people)[3] to less than 12% (28.3 million people) in 2021.[4] Today, smoking is almost invisible throughout much of America. As Balfour et al. note, "the more privileged members of society … do not smoke. Their friends and colleagues do not smoke. There is no smoking in their workplaces, nor in the restaurants and bars they frequent."[5] But the lack of visible smoking in the higher echelons of society masks the reality. Almost one in seven adults still smokes in the U.S., and combustible cigarettes claim 480,000 American lives each year.[6] Worldwide, close to one in four adults smokes,[7] and 15% of all deaths are premature due to smoking.[8]

S. C. Hampsher-Monk et al., *Tobacco Regulation, Economics, and Public Health, Volume III*, https://doi.org/10.1007/978-3-031-47096-7_4

The mission to end smoking is now often recast as an imperative for social and global justice. Smoking has become increasingly concentrated in lower- and middle-income countries.[9] In wealthier nations, smoking and its attendant harms are concentrated among the economically disadvantaged, those with lower educational attainment,[10] racial and ethnic minorities,[11] the LGBTQ+ community,[12] the mentally ill,[13] substance abusers,[14] prisoners,[15] and those experiencing isolation[16] and homelessness.[17,18] Smoking contributes much to the life-expectancy gap between these communities and the rest of society.[19,20]

Despite the reduction in prevalence, the persistence of smoking and the health disparities it creates and perpetuates mean that the need to support smoking cessation is as much of a moral imperative today as it was in 1998. Since then, however, the ecosystem of treatment options has changed, most radically with the introduction of e-cigarettes. An increasingly robust evidence base, including randomized controlled trials[21] and population studies,[22,23,24,25] corroborates the claim that e-cigarettes can play an important role in facilitating cessation. As a popular and less risky[26] alternative to smoking, e-cigarettes have provided many smokers with an effective "off-ramp" from smoking.[27] The prospect that e-cigarettes could stimulate "accidental quitting" among those previously uninterested in quitting[28] and that they might help garner greater cessation among the disadvantaged communities in which smoking is concentrated[29,30,31] is particularly encouraging.

However, e-cigarettes' utility as a cessation aid depends as much on the prevailing regulatory environment as it does on the products' intrinsic features. Regulations that afford e-cigarettes competitive advantages over combustibles in relation to affordability, accessibility, acceptability, and appeal could facilitate smokers' move away from the most lethal tobacco products. Policy communications that highlight e-cigarettes' relatively lower risk may also stimulate substitution. Meanwhile regulated product standards, requirements for content disclosures, pre-market notification systems and post-market surveillance, and enforcing age restrictions also mitigate risks.

These benefits of appropriate regulation are sacrificed by bans and prohibitions, but even where bans have been enacted, e-cigarette use is not eliminated. Despite Thailand's ban, almost one in 25 7th graders use e-cigarettes[32] and the Australian restrictions did not stop an estimated one-third of 11–17-year-olds using e-cigarettes in the past month in 2018.[33] But unintentional creation of an illicit market forfeits the opportunity to test products, monitor sales, and age-gate access. Relatedly, regulating e-cigarettes on par with combustible tobacco products surrenders an opportunity to encourage a demonstrably effective pathway to cessation, thereby keeping more consumers using products that are more likely to sicken and kill them.

Balfour et al. conclude that the societal benefits of e-cigarette-led smoking cessation "could be much larger if the public health community paid serious attention to vaping's potential to help adult smokers, smokers received accurate information about the relative risks of vaping and smoking, and policies were designed with the potential effects on smokers in mind."[34] Ideological skepticism toward the enterprise of tobacco harm reduction, the idealization of abstinence, hostility toward the manufacturers under the guise of the FCTC Clause 5.3,[35] and above all the concern for the well-being of young people are prompting strident calls for restrictions, product-type bans, and prohibitions on e-cigarettes. Thus, while the available cessation treatment options have changed since Dr. Koop's plea not to abandon smokers, the tension between prevention and treatment remains. And once again, we are forgetting those who smoke.

We have already cited Mitch Zeller, former director of the FDA's Center for Tobacco Products, on his desire to synthesize the seemingly antithetical perspectives on e-cigarettes.[36] In these volumes, we have attempted to describe how the balance between the unintended consequences of liberalization on the one hand and the restrictive approach on the other might be operationalized at the policy level. We propose that e-cigarette regulations may be optimized (or at least moved in the correct direction), not with bans and prohibitions, nor with a laissez faire approach, but by using policy differentials, informed by the available data on benefits and risks to inform consumer decisions, incentivizing substitutions down the risk continuum. There are, of course, tradeoffs to consider, since some features of e-cigarettes are appealing to both adults who smoke and youth who do not. But, given the large number of current smokers, greater improvement in public health is generated by encouraging substitutions toward e-cigarettes than by discouraging demand. Blunt demand-reduction approaches not only sacrifice the benefits of substitutions that support smoking cessation, but also result in unintended consequences. Such ill effects include increased demand for combustibles and illicit products, which are more dangerous than those subject to regulatory oversight.

However, the goals of nudging smokers' toward less risky choices and reducing uptake by non-smokers are not mutually exclusive. As discussed in Volume III, Chapter 2, nuanced regulation, policy communication, and enforcement strategies can facilitate smoking cessation while still taking steps to protect against uptake by non-smokers. To tobacco control advocates, skeptical of the products of the despised tobacco industry, that might seem like a capitulation. It is not. If appropriately regulated, e-cigarettes complement the goals of tobacco control by reducing the smoker's tendency to enter the illicit market in response to other restrictions on combustibles (including, not least, taxes). E-cigarettes thus would be made more politically viable, more equitable and, likely, more effective for cessation. E-cigarettes may also internalize the costs of publicly provided Stop Smoking Services, freeing fiscal resources for other tobacco control activities such as enforcement of age-restrictions. And by providing quitters with an apparently more palatable alternative to NRTs, e-cigarettes may increase the efficacy of other cessation interventions, too. The utility of e-cigarettes does not negate the value of traditional tobacco control strategies. Indeed, the fact that e-cigarettes are as popular as they are attests to the achievements of tobacco control in educating the public about the harms of smoking and the benefits of quitting. Moving forward, the availability of a less risky cessation aid may complement many of these efforts.

The continued availability of e-cigarettes under regulation that makes them more attractive than smoking may seem unsatisfying to those who prioritize prevention of youth uptake above all else. But however they are regulated, or even if they are made illegal, e-cigarettes will remain part of the ecosystem of nicotine products. No regulatory choice will eliminate youth experimentation—with nicotine or anything else. Restrictions lead to illicit markets in which there is no incentive for sellers not to serve minors. Heavy-handed demand-reduction strategies for e-cigarettes may also lead young experimenters to initiate nicotine use instead with combustible tobacco. If, on the other hand, e-cigarettes are more broadly embraced as a harm reduction alternative to smoking, smoking will likely become further denormalized, and young people will be less likely to have smoking modeled to them. Perhaps, subsequently, they will be less likely to initiate smoking themselves.

Meanwhile, the landscape of e-cigarette regulation continues to evolve. For advocates of harm reduction, there is some cause for optimism, at least in some jurisdictions. The increasingly robust body of evidence on e-cigarettes has prompted the FDA to grant at least a few such products permission to be marketed, indicating that the agency is satisfied by the proffered evidence demonstrating that those products are appropriate for the protection of public health (while stopping short of allowing overt claims of reduced harm from use).[37] The U.K. has, more than any other country, embraced tobacco harm reduction, using tax and regulatory differentials (the absence of flavor restrictions for e-cigarettes) and policy communication to encourage smokers to switch. The U.K.'s Swap to Stop campaign announced in 2023 goes further, offering free e-cigarette starter kits to almost one in five smokers, and offering financial incentives to encourage smoking cessation.[38] These carrots offered to smokers are balanced with strict advertising restrictions and a cap on nicotine concentration. By some estimates more than 80 million consumers worldwide now use e-cigarettes.[39] Nations with large markets for regulated e-cigarettes have seen smoking rates fall faster than predicted by trends established prior to the introduction of e-cigarettes.[40]

Conversely, those skeptical of e-cigarettes' utility may take solace in the various bans adopted by many countries, including Brazil, Mexico, Argentina, Japan, India, and Australia. The regulatory strategies adopted by much of the rest of the world lie somewhere between these extremes, permitting e-cigarettes in some form but often with increasingly stringent restrictions. In Canada, for example, federal and provincial taxation, a federal nicotine limit, and provincial flavor bans have eroded at least some of the former regulatory differential between e-cigarettes and combustibles. In the U.S., only a handful of manufacturers have been granted authorization to market e-cigarettes. In fact, the FDA has denied well over 99% of applications to market e-cigarettes.[41] The approvals that were granted came only after great expense by the companies and long delays by the regulator. Many of the FDA's rulings, especially those dependent on the application of the controversial "deeming rule," have already faced judicial scrutiny, with lower-circuit courts finding both in favor of and against the FDA's decisions. The division among lower-circuit rulings regarding such cases raises the possibility of a Supreme Court ruling which could have significant implications for the U.S. e-cigarette market. The FDA's rulings mark an especially divisive period in the U.S. history of e-cigarette regulation, as evidenced by the FDA's decision to deny marketing approval to Juul in June 2022. The American Lung Association praised the FDA "for following the science and denying Juul the ability to sell its products that are clearly marketed to addict a new generation of youth to tobacco."[42] Meanwhile a professor of public health sciences described Juul as a lifesaving escape route from smoking and wrote that banning it because some potentially harmful chemicals might leach from some pods is a bit like locking the door to the fire escape because the steps may be slippery.[43] Litigation has challenged regulators' decisions, and will continue to do so and to attract the media and the broader public's attention, both critical and otherwise. The environmental harms of disposable e-cigarettes, flavor bans, and proactive harm-reduction approaches, including the U.K.'s Swap to Stop campaign,[44] will likely be flashpoints in the discourse.

The diversity of approaches to e-cigarette regulation evident among various jurisdictions provides researchers with opportunities to examine the consequences of each approach. As Thomas Kuhn wrote in *The Structure of Scientific Revolutions*,[45] "Truth emerges more readily from error than confusion." After all, the quasi-experimental studies reviewed in Volume III, Chapters 1 (Sect. 3.2.2) and 2 (Sect. 6) showing that taxes and other restrictions on e-cigarettes lead to higher rates of smoking for youth, adults, and expectant mothers would not have been possible without some misguided policy choices. The experience of different jurisdictions' approaches to e-cigarette regulation provides empirical evidence for the manner in which consumers (on the demand side) and the industry (on the supply side) respond. As has been argued in this book, the current evidence is sufficient to develop a framework by which regulators can consider more fully the complexities of e-cigarette regulation, leading to improved outcomes. However, such a framework need not lead to identical regulation in all jurisdictions. Further evidence gleaned from divergent regulatory approaches may corroborate these conclusions. Furthermore, with due care to contextual specifics, policy sharing may allow successful interventions to be replicated and unsuccessful ones to be avoided.

As the e-cigarette market matures, regulations evolve, and consumption patterns shift, various stakeholders will have differing roles to play. Public health agencies, regulators, health professionals, academic researchers, and harm-reduction advocates will each take a hand in shaping the future of the market and its regulation.

To supplement the toxicological, clinical, and epidemiological evidence on e-cigarettes, public health agencies will continue to have a vital role by collecting and communicating evidence on behavioral responses to economic and regulatory changes influencing e-cigarette use and, subsequently, smoking. These agencies should continue to monitor the characteristics of the retail market, which will continue to evolve with further innovations in response to consumer demand that is, in turn, shaped by policy decisions. Understanding these feedback loops requires an interdisciplinary approach, with contributions from economics and social sciences alongside the medical and natural science disciplines central to the field of public health.

In addition to transcending disciplinary boundaries, it is imperative that health agencies also transcend geographic and cultural boundaries as they conduct epidemiological research and evaluate the efficacy of interventions, by incorporating into their analysis evidence from outside their jurisdictions. Again, that is an interdisciplinary endeavor. Contextual differences between jurisdictions (including economic, social, legal, and cultural specifics) influence the degree to which evidence from one locale can inform predictions regarding another. However, accounting for this context via interdisciplinary investigative methods can provide public health agencies with a much broader knowledge base with which to better understand their own populations.

Regulators have an obligation to report the data on e-cigarette risks and benefits accurately, comprehensively, and impartially and, moreover, to use that information to develop regulations that are proportionate to the risks. To the extent that e-cigarettes and combustible tobacco are substitutes, regulators must avoid considering the regulation of either product in isolation. Regulators have the responsibility to use all admissible evidence in their cost–benefit analyses and to ensure that they consider all the available interventions, including inaction. Unlike specific stakeholder groups and individuals, who are free to favor the interests of one sub-section of the population, regulators must adjudicate impartially between apparently conflicting interests in the benefit of the whole public. And although regulatory agencies may have a statutory obligation to perform traditional cost–benefit analysis, they should broaden their viewpoint to include the other aspects of social welfare discussed in Volume III, Chapter 2.

Health professionals may be instrumental in educating the public about e-cigarettes, particularly for youth and young adults.[46] Educators and social workers may also be especially well positioned to inform those in their care who smoke about the full range of resources available to support cessation. If e-cigarettes are, in the future, regulated as medicinal products, pharmacists may be added to that list. These professionals must be equipped with data and empowered to provide honest information regarding the potential for alternative nicotine products to help support cessation.

Other stakeholder groups must also be provided with information on the conditions under which e-cigarettes help or hinder individual health. As with other aspects of human behavior, behaviors regarding nicotine are nuanced: Different groups and indeed individuals make different choices based on a unique milieu of knowledge, beliefs, and attitudes informed by social influences, environmental and economic considerations, media reporting, and regulatory conditions. The academy can help regulators evaluate options with which to elicit positive behavioral change by illuminating the real-world choices that consumers have available to them, characterizing the propensity of different groups of consumers to switch between products under different scenarios, and studying the health consequences of various consumption patterns over time. Clarity on these points will help resolve disputes and disagreements about e-cigarettes' utility in the broader population. Certainly, disagreements will persist regarding how the available evidence should be interpreted, but those disagreements can be much more productive if they are based in empiricism rather than (only) on opinion or sentiment. As Robert West has summarized, we are not going to get the kind of clarity we need regarding the risks and benefits of e-cigarettes if each polarized interpreter continues merely by accumulating and reporting only the data supporting their preconceived views, then overstating their results in public forums, which the media then distort further, fueling public outrage and alarm among policy-makers.[47]

Given the broad and vehement hostility toward nicotine, tobacco harm reduction advocates have their work cut out for them. The arguments against e-cigarettes, particularly those based on the unassailable sentiment that the welfare of minors must be protected, carry at least as much rhetorical weight as evidence suggesting that e-cigarettes help smokers quit. For both e-cigarette skeptics and enthusiasts, there is much to be gained from winning public confidence, and in this regard, beliefs matter at least as much as knowledge. Appeals to the utility of e-cigarettes as a cessation aid for adult smokers may be dismissed as irrelevant by those whose primary (or only) concern is to prevent youth from beginning to use any nicotine product. As detailed in Volume II, Chapter 1, the "epidemic in youth-vaping" has often been overstated. Regardless, the reality does not undermine the legitimacy of the original concern, which is, for most people, emotional rather than rational. The provision of empirical data may do little to assuage deeply held fears. Rhetoric not with standing, we need not concede to positions that are unsupported by the evidence. However, there remains a practical argument for taking seriously concerns about e-cigarette use by young people, even when those arguments are grounded more in sentiment than in science. Taking these concerns seriously, and *being seen* to take them seriously, may produce a discourse that is more receptive to the evidence that prohibitionist policies ultimately cause more harm—even for the narrow group of young non-smokers that the public values most. Resolving some of the polarization in the debate about e-cigarettes may help improve policy analyses and, ultimately, both public and private decision-making regarding e-cigarettes.

E-cigarettes are variously welcomed or vilified as a disruptive innovation. Most obviously, e-cigarettes disrupt the market for cigarettes, one of the most widely used and lethal consumer products in history. But e-cigarettes may also be seen to disrupt the orthodoxy of tobacco control in several ways. E-cigarettes, and tobacco harm reduction more generally, challenge many of the formerly unassailable presumptions which have defined tobacco control and shaped public thinking on tobacco for decades. In a tobacco market overwhelmingly dominated by combustibles, the conclusion that the products of the tobacco industry are always harmful for public health is compelling. However, in a market with a range of products and risk profiles, it becomes possible to benefit public health by encouraging substitutions from more- to less-harmful options. So long as the only commercially available nicotine comes in the form of combustible tobacco products, the logic that nicotine is harmful is intuitive; but once nicotine is decoupled from combustion, nicotine becomes detached from much, if not all, of the harm it was formerly associated with. While the industry's sales consist overwhelmingly of combustible cigarettes, the firms' profit motive remains antithetical to public health; but once these firms sell reduced-risk products, the profit motive may, with appropriate guardrails, be leveraged to reduce harms. Consider also that, in the absence of significantly safer licit alternatives, the primacy of abstinence may be sensible (setting aside concerns about paternalism and regressivity). The availability of safer alternatives means not only that abstinence from nicotine is no longer a precondition of avoiding smoking-related harms but, further, that other concerns may be better addressed, including those relating to social justice and health equity.

Importantly, however, while e-cigarettes challenge many of these still common assumptions, there is evidence that e-cigarettes and harm reduction in general can complement traditional tobacco control efforts to reduce smoking in important ways (as discussed above and in Volume III, Chapter 2, Sect. 8).

Nevertheless, promotion of e-cigarettes for cessation may still be *perceived* as an attempt to challenge the goals of tobacco control. There is little question that harm reduction diverges from the established orthodoxy concerning *how* to achieve tobacco control goals. As such, continued hostility toward e-cigarettes should not be surprising. The practice of science is often inherently conservative.[48,49] Scientific dogma (widely accepted scientific beliefs, theories, and frameworks) can become entrenched, meaning that those familiar with the established dogma and invested in the established view may be resistant to change, even in the face of new evidence or alternative hypotheses. Both individually and collectively, scientists may exhibit a tendency to become too attached to a particular theory or assumption, and so ignore or reject evidence that contradicts it. Confirmation bias may perpetuate theories even in the fact of contrary evidence. The susceptibility to groupthink (spurred on by the funding dynamics in public health that enforce orthodoxy) of important figureheads and organizations may further undermine the establishment's willingness to entertain contrarian thinking. Thus, dissent may be stifled while the production of research that conforms only to preconceived standards is encouraged, further reinforcing and perpetuating the prevailing perspectives. The history of scientific progress is riddled with examples of what happens to those who challenge the established orthodoxy: Galileo and Semmelweis serve as examples. Even Einstein faced derision from the scientific establishment of the day over his theory of relativity.[50] The latter's retort to his detractors was to point out that to disprove relativity does not need the words of a hundred scientists; it needs just one fact.[51]

Is tobacco harm reduction actually revolutionary? In his 1962 book *The Structure of Scientific Revolutions*, Thomas Kuhn popularized the notion of the paradigms that guide "normal science" and the disruptive paradigm shifts that lead to fundamental changes in the way science is performed. In the decades since the publication of Kuhn's magnum opus, it has become fashionable to refer to any innovation of seeming importance as a "paradigm shift." But a paradigm shift is not simply a change in theories or ideas but instead a fundamental reorganization of the way scientists approach and understand the world.[52] By that standard, e-cigarettes and harm reduction do not represent a paradigm shift. For one, tobacco control is not a paradigm, for tobacco control is of not science itself but rather a set of policies and goals based in part on scientific output. The paradigm is the fundamental investigative methods on which tobacco control is based—the "normal science" of epidemiology, public health, economics, and other fields. Tobacco Harm Reduction does not alter those. The necessity of and methods for characterizing and quantifying risk remain unchanged. The promise of harm reduction is not a fundamental overhauling of tobacco control science, but a simple pragmatic recognition that providing people with alternatives and the knowledge to choose between them benefits their well-being. This is, perhaps, a challenge to the assumptions of tobacco control, but not the science underlying the efforts to improve public health.

The conclusion that regulation can encourage adult smokers to quit while protecting against uptake by non-smokers and experimentation by youth is grounded in both pragmatism and dispassionate analysis of the available data. And yet, given that the patterns of e-cigarette use continue to change, it is worth considering how the emergence of new information could undermine this conclusion. To be blunt, what if we are wrong? What if new evidence emerges detailing a novel and specific harm resulting from vaping and if, in response to the proposed regulations, enough non-smokers initiate e-cigarette use that the calculation about public harms shifts? Unequivocally, that would require that the cost–benefit analysis incorporate the novel data, which might result in a different policy mix becoming optimal; no less is demanded by the scientific method, which applies to regulatory science as other areas of empirical study. The possibility of future evidence that would require a course correction underscores the importance for policy-makers to safeguard their ability to respond dynamically to shifting patterns of consumer behavior. There must be constant surveillance to monitor those patterns and to detect correction-triggering events as early as possible. However, the possibility of future harms manifesting does not change the fundamental approach to assessing costs and benefits in a dispassionate, rational manner. By the same standard, based on the available evidence, it is clear that many of the contemporary e-cigarette regulations must be replaced. Taxing e-cigarettes on par with cigarettes is an obvious example where the results are demonstrably harmful and the purported benefits are dubious. Hopefully this book has provided both greater perspective and a higher resolution focus on the pathways by which public policy toward e-cigarettes may be improved.

Finally, distinct from the products with which it is concerned, the e-cigarette debate itself has an important, albeit indirect, implication for broader public health. In October 2019, Dr. Robert West described how the way in which regulatory science is undertaken and communicated transcends the importance of those products. Just weeks before the world became aware of COVID-19, West, who is Professor Emeritus of Health Psychology at University College London and Editor-in-Chief of the journal Addiction, said:

> It's not a question of whether there will be a flu pandemic that will kill large numbers of people, but when.... to be ready for that... we need public health expertise to be trusted by the public... In e-cigarettes and in other areas of public health, we've got to deserve that trust: We've got to apply our acknowledged methods of science in a way that is dispassionate, and cautious; and we've got to be prepared to change our view if the evidence changes. So, when the public health community comes out and says something like 'there's a flu pandemic on the way, this is what you've got to do to protect your health' people get on board and take notice.[53]

Even with the worst of the COVID-19 pandemic behind us, the prescience of West's words remains compelling. It may be impossible to quantify what portion of global COVID-19 harms ultimately resulted from decisions based more on ideology and sentiment than a willingness to trust the available evidence—incomplete as it inevitably was. What is clear from comparing infection rates of vaccinated and unvaccinated populations, however, is that skepticism about evidence is not without costs.

Meanwhile, a longer-running epidemic continues.[54] However they are regulated, e-cigarettes are not a panacea. They will not save all tobacco users, or even most of them. For many who smoke, tobacco harm reduction will be too little and too late. But those who use e-cigarettes to help them quit smoking are markedly more likely to succeed. A doubling or tripling of the efficacy of quitting attempts[55] is an enormous victory. The total effect on cessation is multiplied by the much greater popularity of e-cigarettes than other cessation aids, which is all the more remarkable considering that the global tobacco control community persistently denounced them. As with vaccine skepticism in the context of

COVID-19, skepticism toward e-cigarettes based on an ideological opposition to nicotine use or the companies producing these products may be extremely costly, ultimately perpetuating the very behavior that tobacco control professionals work to prevent: smoking. The exhortation to eschew tobacco harm reduction, with precautionary appeals to "first do no harm" may be well-intended. But the tacit implication is that the status quo is in some sense tolerable and the traditional approaches to tobacco control are somehow sufficient. Given the current burden of smoking-related disease, neither premise can be true. Instead, what might happen if regulatory decisions incorporated the available evidence both for and against e-cigarettes and balanced the risks accordingly? If policy-makers are seen to do so, then public trust in the institutions of public health would increase. This increased confidence would prompt more smokers to give up smoking more quickly, ultimately saving lives.

Notes

1. Khan, J. *The Khan Review: Making Smoking Obsolete: Independent Review into SMOKEFREE 2030 policies*. GOV.UK, 2022. https://assets.publishing.service.gov.uk/government/uploads/system/uploads/attachment_data/file/1081366/khan-review-making-smoking-obsolete.pdf.
2. Koop, C.E. (March 8, 1998). Don't Forget the Smokers. *WP*. Available at: https://www.washingtonpost.com/archive/opinions/1998/03/08/dont-forget-the-smokers/3560fbed-880a-45ff-8669-110fd8b63509.
3. CDC. Cigarette Smoking Among Adults—United States, 1998 Centers for Disease Control and Prevention, 2000, available at: https://www.cdc.gov/mmwr/preview/mmwrhtml/mm4939a1.htm#tab1
4. Cornelius, M.E., Loretan, C.G., Wang, T.W., Jamal, A., Homa, D.M. Tobacco Product Use Among Adults—United States, 2020. MMWR Morb Mortal Wkly Rep. 2022;71:397–405.
5. Balfour, D.J.K., Benowitz, N.L., Colby, S.M., Hatsukami, D.K., Lando, H.A., Leischow, S.J., Lerman, C., Mermelstein, R.J., Niaura, R., Perkins, K.A., Pomerleau, O.F., Rigotti, N.A., Swan, G.E., Warner, K.E., West, R. Balancing Consideration of the Risks and Benefits of E-Cigarettes. Am J Public Health.

2021 Sep;111(9):1661–1672. https://doi.org/10.2105/AJPH.2021.306416.

6. CDC. (n.d.). Adult Cigarette Smoking Data, Centers for Disease Control and Prevention. Available at: https://www.cdc.gov/tobacco/data_statistics/fact_sheets/adult_data/cig_smoking/index.htm.
7. World Health Organization and the World Bank. (n.d.). Smoking, Our World in Data. Available at: https://ourworldindata.org/smoking.
8. IHME, Global Burden of Disease. Our World in Data, 2019, available at: https://ourworldindata.org/smoking.
9. WHO. Tobacco Control Can Save Billions of Dollars and Millions Of Lives. World Health Organization, 2017, available at: https://www.who.int/news/item/10-01-2017-tobacco-control-can-save-billions-of-dollars-and-millions-of-lives.
10. Drope, J., Liber, A.C., Cahn, Z., Stoklosa, M., Kennedy, R., Douglas, C.E., Henson, R., Drope, J. Who's Still Smoking? Disparities in Adult Cigarette Smoking Prevalence in the United States. CA: A Cancer Journal for Clinicians. 2018;68:106–115. https://doi.org/10.3322/caac.21444.
11. Tam, J., Levy, D.T., Feuer, E.J., Jeon, J., Holford, T.R., Meza, R. Using the Past to Understand the Future of U.S. and Global Smoking Disparities: A Birth Cohort Perspective. Am J Prev Med. 2023 Apr;64(4 Suppl 1):S1–S10. https://doi.org/10.1016/j.amepre.2022.12.003.
12. CDC. (n.d.). Tips from Former Smokers: Lesbian, Gay, Bisexual, Transgender, and Queer (LGBTQ+) People. Centers for Disease Control. Available at: https://www.cdc.gov/tobacco/campaign/tips/groups/lgbt.html#:~:text=Smoking%20among%20lesbian%2C%20gay%2C%20and,than%20among%20heterosexual%2Fstraight%20adults.&text=Smoking%20increases%20your%20risk%20for,and%20other%20smoking%2Drelated%20diseases.
13. Caponnetto, P., DiPiazza, J., Kim, J., Maglia, M., Polosa, R. A Single-arm, Open-label, Pilot, and Feasibility Study of a High Nicotine Strength E-cigarette Intervention for Smoking Cessation or Reduction for People with Schizophrenia Spectrum Disorders Who Smoke Cigarettes. Nicotine Tob Res. 2021;23(7):1113–1122. https://doi.org/10.1093/ntr/ntab005.

14. Centers for Disease Control and Prevention (May 4, 2023). Burden of Cigarette use in the US: Current Cigarette Smoking Among US Adults Aged 18 Years and Older. Available at: https://www.cdc.gov/tobacco/campaign/tips/resources/data/cigarette-smoking-in-united-states.html.
15. Spaulding, A.C., Eldridge, G.D., Chico, C.E., et al. Smoking in Correctional Settings Worldwide: Prevalence, Bans, and Interventions. Epidemiol Rev. 2018;40:82–95. https://doi.org/10.1093/epirev/mxy005
16. Dyal, S.R., Valente, T.W. A Systematic Review of Loneliness and Smoking: Small Effects, Big Implications. Subst Use Misuse. 2015;50(13):1697–1716. https://doi.org/10.3109/10826084.2015.1027933.
17. Baggett, T.P., Lebrun-Harris, L.A., Rigotti, N.A. Homelessness, Cigarette Smoking and Desire to Quit: Results from a US National Study. Addiction. 2013;108(11):2009–2018. https://doi.org/10.1111/add.12292.
18. Beard, E., Brown, J., Jackson, S.E., West, R., Kock, L., Boniface, S., Shahab, L. Independent Associations Between Different Measures of Socioeconomic Position and Smoking Status: A Cross-Sectional Study of Adults in England. Nicotine Tob Res. 2021 Jan;23(1):107–114. https://doi.org/10.1093/ntr/ntaa030
19. Chetty, R., Stepner, M., Abraham, S., et al. The Association Between Income and Life Expectancy in the United States, 2001–2014 [erratum in JAMA. 2017;317(1):90]. JAMA. 2016;315(16):1750–1766. https://doi.org/10.1001/jama.2016.4226.
20. Tam, J., Warner, K.E., Meza, R. Smoking and the Reduced Life Expectancy of Individuals with Serious Mental Illness. Am J Prev Med. 2016;51(6):958–966. https://doi.org/10.1016/j.amepre.2016.06.007.
21. Hartmann-Boyce, J., McRobbie, H., Lindson, N., et al. Electronic Cigarettes for Smoking Cessation. Cochrane Database Syst Rev. 2020;10(10):CD010216. https://doi.org/10.1002/14651858.CD010216.pub4.
22. West, R., Shahab, L., Brown, J. Estimating the Population Impact of E-cigarettes on Smoking Cessation in England. Addiction. 2016;111(6):1118–1119. https://doi.org/10.1111/add.13343.

23. Beard, E., West, R., Michie, S., Brown, J. Association Between Electronic Cigarette Use and Changes in Quit Attempts, success of Quit Attempts, Use of Smoking Cessation Pharmacotherapy, and Use of Stop Smoking Services in England: Time Series Analysis of Population Trends. BMJ. 2016;354:i4645. https://doi.org/10.1136/bmj.i4645
24. Beard, E., West, R., Michie, S., Brown, J. Association of Prevalence of Electronic Cigarette Use with Smoking Cessation and Cigarette Consumption in England: A Time–Series Analysis Between 2006 and 2017. Addiction. 2020;115(5):961–974. https://doi.org/10.1111/add.14851.
25. Zhu, S.H., Zhuang, Y.L., Wong, S., Cummins, S.E., Tedeschi, G.J. E-cigarette Use And Associated Changes in Population Smoking Cessation: Evidence From us Current Population Surveys. BMJ. 2017;358:j3262. https://doi.org/10.1136/bmj.j3262.
26. McNeill, A., Brose, L.S., Calder, R., Hitchman, S.C., Hajek, P., McRobbie, H. E-cigarettes: An Evidence Update A Report Commissioned by PHE, 2015, available at: https://assets.publishing.service.gov.uk/government/uploads/system/uploads/attachment_data/file/733022/Ecigarettes_an_evidence_update_A_report_commissioned_by_Public_Health_England_FINAL.pdf.
27. Balfour, D.J.K., Benowitz, N.L., Colby, S.M., Hatsukami, D.K., Lando, H.A., Leischow, S.J., Lerman, C., Mermelstein, R.J., Niaura, R., Perkins, K.A., Pomerleau, O.F., Rigotti, N.A., Swan, G.E., Warner, K.E., West, R. Balancing Consideration of the Risks and Benefits of E-Cigarettes. Am J Public Health. 2021 Sep;111(9):1661–1672. https://doi.org/10.2105/AJPH.2021.306416.
28. Kasza, K.A., Edwards, K.C., Kimmel, H.L., et al. Association of E-cigarette Use with Discontinuation of Cigarette Smoking Among Adult Smokers Who Were Initially Never Planning to Quit. JAMA Netw Open. 2021;4(12):e2140880. https://doi.org/10.1001/jamanetworkopen.2021.40880.
29. Caponnetto, P., DiPiazza, J., Kim, J., Maglia, M., Polosa, R. A Single-arm, Open-label, Pilot, and Feasibility Study of a High Nicotine Strength E-cigarette Intervention for Smoking Cessation or Reduction for People with Schizophrenia Spectrum Disorders Who Smoke Cigarettes. Nicotine Tob Res. 2021;23(7):1113–1122. https://doi.org/10.1093/ntr/ntab005.

30. Giovenco, D.P. Different Smokes for Different Folks? E-cigarettes and Tobacco Disparities. Am J Public Health. 2019;109(9):1162–1163. https://doi.org/10.2105/AJPH.2019.305250.
31. Pulvers, K., Nollen, N.L., Rice, M., et al. Effect of Pod E-cigarettes vs Cigarettes on Carcinogen Exposure Among African American and Latinx smokers: A Randomized Clinical Trial. JAMA Netw Open. 2020;3(11):e2026324. https://doi.org/10.1001/jamanetworkopen.2020.26324.
32. Patanavanich, R., Aekplakorn, W., Glantz, S.A., Kalayasiri, R. Use of E-Cigarettes and Associated Factors among Youth in Thailand. Asian Pac J Cancer Prev. 2021 Jul 1;22(7):2199–2207. https://doi.org/10.31557/APJCP.2021.22.7.2199.
33. Guerin, N., White, V. ASSAD 2017 Statistics & Trends: Australian Secondary Students' Use of Tobacco, Alcohol, Over-the-Counter Drugs, and Illicit Substances. Centre for Behavioural Research in Cancer: Cancer Council Victoria; 2018.
34. Balfour, D.J.K., Benowitz, N.L., Colby, S.M., Hatsukami, D.K., Lando, H.A., Leischow, S.J., Lerman, C., Mermelstein, R.J., Niaura, R., Perkins, K.A., Pomerleau, O.F., Rigotti, N.A., Swan, G.E., Warner, K.E., West, R. Balancing Consideration of the Risks and Benefits of E-Cigarettes. Am J Public Health. 2021 Sep;111(9):1661–1672. https://doi.org/10.2105/AJPH.2021.306416.
35. WHO. (n.d.). Guidelines for Implementation of Article 5.3 of the FCTC. WHO. Available at: https://fctc.who.int/publications/m/item/guidelines-for-implementation-of-article-5.3.
36. See the opening to Volume II, Chapter 3.
37. FDA. Premarket Tobacco Product Marketing Granted Orders, US Food and Drug Administration, 2023, available at: https://www.fda.gov/tobacco-products/premarket-tobacco-productapplications/premarket-tobacco-product-marketing-granted-orders..
38. UK Department of Health and Social Care. (April 11, 2023). Smokers Urged to Swap Cigarettes FOR Vapes IN World First Scheme, Press release. Available at: https://www.gov.uk/government/news/smokers-urged-to-swap-cigarettes-for-vapes-in-world-first-scheme.

39. Jerzyński, T., Stimson, G.V. (2023). Estimation of the Global Number of Vapers: 82 Million Worldwide in 2021. Drugs, Habits and Social Policy, ahead-of-print. https://doi.org/10.1108/DHS-07-2022-0028
40. Levy, D.T., Warner, K.E., Cummings, K.M., Hammond, D., Kuo, C., Fong, G.T., Thrasher, J.F., Goniewicz, M.L., Borland, R., 2019 Nov;28(6):629-635. https://doi.org/10.1136/tobaccocontrol-2018-054446.
41. Food and Drug Administration. (March 24, 2022). FDA Issues Decisions on Additional E-cigarette Products, Press release. https://www.fda.gov/news-events/press-announcements/fda-issues-decisions-additional-e-cigarette-products.
42. Cunningham, D. (June 23, 2022). FDA Bans All Juul E-cigarettes in U.S.; Lung Association Hails Decision. UPI. https://www.upi.com/Health_News/2022/06/23/FDA-ban-Juul-e-cigarettes/5021655989222/.
43. Lund, K. "Closing the life-saving escape route that smokers can have in snus and e-cigarettes is a bit like closing the door to the fire escape because the steps may be slippery." Twitter.com, 2021, available at: https://twitter.com/JonathanFoulds/status/1450236626291003394.
44. UK Department of Health and Social Care. (April 11, 2023). Smokers Urged to Swap Cigarettes for Vapes in World First Scheme, Press release. Available at: https://www.gov.uk/government/news/smokers-urged-to-swap-cigarettes-for-vapes-in-world-first-scheme.
45. Kuhn, T.S. *The Structure of Scientific Revolutions*. Chicago: University of Chicago Press, 1962.
46. National Academies of Sciences, Engineering, and Medicine; Health and Medicine Division; Board on Population Health and Public Health Practice; Committee on the Review of the Health Effects of Electronic Nicotine Delivery Systems; Eaton DL, Kwan LY, Stratton K, eds. *Public Health Consequences of E-cigarettes*. Washington, D.C.: National Academies Press, Toxicology of E-cigarette Constituents, 2018, available at: https://www.ncbi.nlm.nih.gov/books/NBK507184/?report=classic.

47. West, R. Should Health Professionals Recommend Smokers to Switch to E-cigarettes?, Society for Research in Nicotine and Tobacco, 2020, available at: https://vimeo.com/361160577.
48. Luukkonen, T. Conservatism and Risk-Taking in Peer Review: Emerging ERC Practices. Research Evaluation. 2012;21(1):48–60. https://doi.org/10.1093/reseval/rvs001
49. Stanford, P.K. Unconceived Alternatives and Conservatism in Science: The Impact of Professionalization, Peer-Review, and Big Science. Synthese. 2019;196:3915–3932. https://doi.org/10.1007/s11229-015-0856-4
50. Israel, H., Ruckhaber, H., Weinmann, R., eds. (1931). *Hundert Autoren gegen Einstein*. Leipzig: Voigtländer. Galileo was prosecuted for challenging the Aristotelian conception of astronomy, while Semmelweis was ridiculed for research and teaching on the salutary effect of hand-washing for medical hygiene.
51. Brittanica. (n.d.). Albert Einstein and Nazi backlash and coming to America. Brittanica Encyclopedia. Available at: https://www.britannica.com/biography/Albert-Einstein/Nazi-backlash-and-coming-to-America.
52. Kuhn, T.S. *The Structure of Scientific Revolutions*. Chicago: University of Chicago Press, 1962.
53. West, R. Should Health Professionals Recommend Smokers to Switch to E-cigarettes?, Society for Research in Nicotine and Tobacco, 2020, available at: https://vimeo.com/361160577.
54. GBD 2019 Tobacco Collaborators. Spatial, Temporal, and Demographic Patterns in Prevalence of Smoking Tobacco Use and Attributable Disease Burden in 204 Countries and Territories, 1990–2019: a Systematic Analysis from the Global Burden of Disease Study 2019. Lancet. 2021;397(10292):2337–2360. https://doi.org/10.1016/S0140-6736(21)01169-7.
55. Compared to behavioral support only or no support. See Volume II, Chapter 2, Sect. 3.1, especially Fig. 3 there.

Correction to: Tobacco Regulation, Economics, and Public Health, Volume III

Correction to:
S. C. Hampsher-Monk et al., *Tobacco Regulation, Economics, and Public Health, Volume III*, https://doi.org/10.1007/978-3-031-47096-7

The original version of this book was inadvertently published with incorrect figures in Chapters 1 and 2 which have now been corrected. The book and the chapters have been updated with the changes.

The updated version of this book can be found at
https://doi.org/10.1007/978-3-031-47096-7

S. C. Hampsher-Monk et al., *Tobacco Regulation, Economics, and Public Health, Volume III*, https://doi.org/10.1007/978-3-031-47096-7_5

Chapter 1

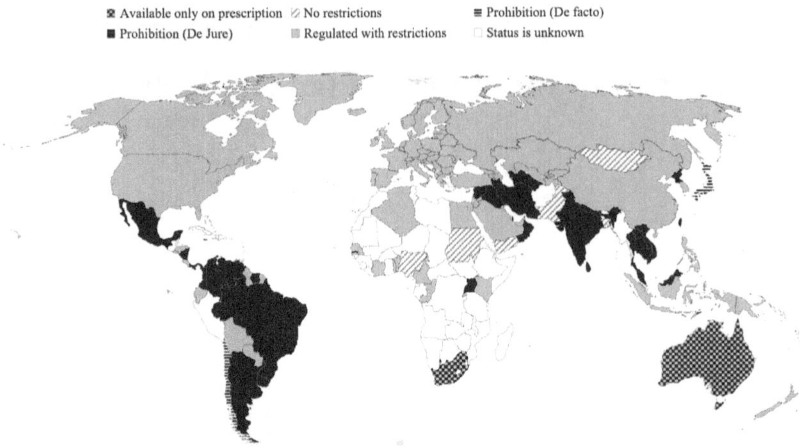

Fig. 1 Legal status of nicotine e-cigarettes around the world (*Note* The countries shaded green in the figure above include nations categorizing e-cigarettes as tobacco products, ENDSs, or commercial products. Such countries include a wide variety of regulations including but not limited to taxes, flavor and content restrictions, age limits, marketing restrictions, warning-label requirements, and child-proof packaging mandates. *Source* Author's interpretation of data provided by Johns Hopkins Institute for Global Tobacco Control https://globaltobaccocontrol.org/en/policy-scan/e-cigarettes/countries?country=263)

Chapter 2

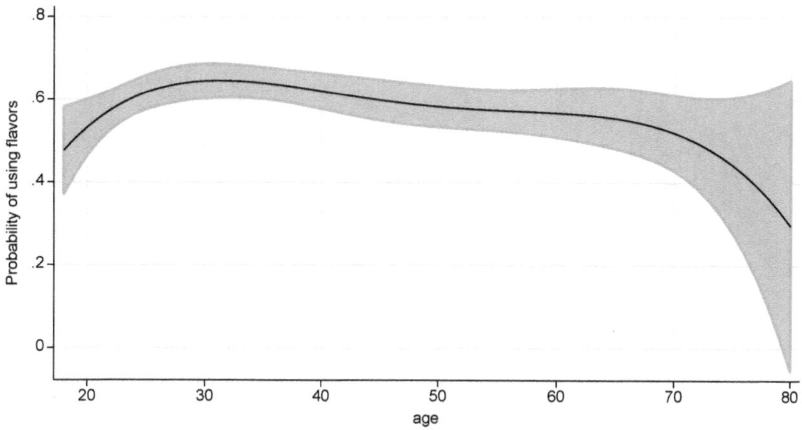

Fig. 5 How choice of using flavored e-cigarettes other than tobacco, menthol, or mint) varies with age among U.S. adults (*Notes* The plotted curve from the predicted values from a survey-weighted linear probability model in which a binary variable for usual usage of an e-cigarette that was clove, spice, herb, fruit, alcohol, candy, sweets, or chocolate flavored was regressed on a quartic specification of age. The estimates are for the subpopulation of some-day and every-day current e-cigarette users for which the non-tobacco flavor of usual e-cigarette is known. The 95% confidence band accounts for the complex survey design. Estimation is by the authors; data are from the CPS-TUS 2018–2019)

Index

S. C. Hampsher-Monk et al., *Tobacco Regulation, Economics, and Public Health, Volume III*, https://doi.org/10.1007/978-3-031-47096-7